Presentation Conferencing

The brand-new Presentation Conference... lets you deliver a presentation to many participants across a network.

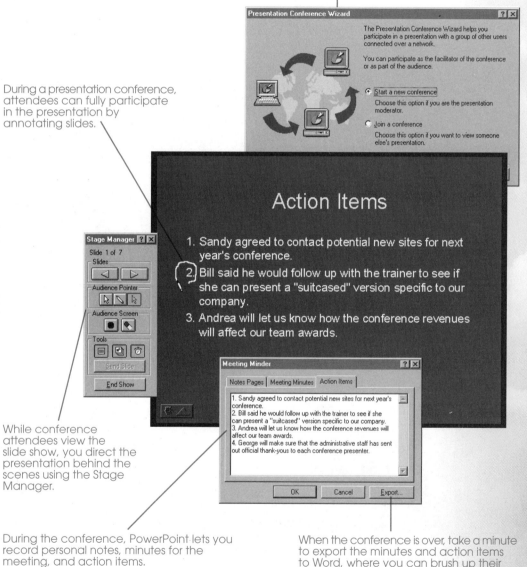

During a presentation conference, attendees can fully participate in the presentation by annotating slides.

While conference attendees view the slide show, you direct the presentation behind the scenes using the Stage Manager.

During the conference, PowerPoint lets you record personal notes, minutes for the meeting, and action items.

When the conference is over, take a minute to export the minutes and action items to Word, where you can brush up their appearance before mailing them off to the attendees.

Steve Sagman

Steve Sagman is the author of more than a dozen computer books, including *Traveling The Microsoft Network,* also published by Microsoft Press. His books have sold more than half a million copies in English, and they have been translated into eight languages.

When he's not writing books, Sagman runs a business called The Water Mill Group, which provides user documentation, software training, interface design, and, for The Microsoft Network, online publishing services.

And when he's not writing or running his business, Sagman plays jazz piano and toils in the fertile loam of his garden.

Sagman welcomes comments and suggestions about this book at one of the following addresses:

The Microsoft Network: SteveS
The Internet: steves@msn.com
CompuServe: 72456,3325
Mailing Address: 570 Mecox Road,
    Water Mill, NY 11976

In-Depth Reference

and Inside Tips from

the Software Experts

RUNNING

Microsoft®

POWERPOINT®

for Windows® 95

S T E P H E N   W .   S A G M A N

PUBLISHED BY
Microsoft Press
A Division of Microsoft Corporation
One Microsoft Way
Redmond, Washington 98052-6399

Library of Congress Cataloging-in-Publication Data
Sagman, Stephen W.
    Running Microsoft PowerPoint for Windows 95 / Stephen W. Sagman.
       p.   cm.
    Includes index.
    ISBN 1-55615-852-1
    1. Computer graphics.   2. Microsoft PowerPoint for Windows.
    I. Title.
    T385.S2356   1995
    006.6'869--dc20   95-35264
                                                          CIP

Printed and bound in the United States of America.

1 2 3 4 5 6 7 8 9   QFQF   0 9 8 7 6 5

Distributed to the book trade in Canada by Macmillan of Canada, a division of Canada Publishing Corporation.

A CIP catalogue record for this book is available from the British Library.

Microsoft Press books are available through booksellers and distributors worldwide. For further information about international editions, contact your local Microsoft Corporation office. Or contact Microsoft Press International directly at fax (206) 936-7329.

Macintosh and TrueType are registered trademarks of Apple Computer, Inc. AutoCAD is a registered trademark of Autodesk, Inc. CompuServe is a registered trademark of Compuserve, Inc. CorelDRAW is a registered trademark of Corel Systems Corporation. Kodak is a registered trademark of Eastman Kodak Company. Genigraphics is a registered trademark and GraphicsLink is a trademark of Genigraphics Corporation. Hewlett-Packard is a registered trademark of Hewlett-Packard Company. 1-2-3 and Lotus are registered trademarks of Lotus Development Corporation. Micrografx Designer and Micrografx Draw Plus are trademarks of Micrografx, Inc. Microsoft, PowerPoint, and Windows are registered trademarks of Microsoft Corporation. DrawPerfect is a registered trademark of Novell, Inc. PANTONE is a registered trademark of Pantone, Inc. PC Paintbrush is a registered trademark of Wordstar Atlanta Technology Center.

Acquisitions Editor: Lucinda Rowley
Project Editor: Ina Chang
Manuscript Editing and Technical Review: Online Press Inc.

Chapters at a Glance

Table of Contents

Acknowledgments

The author wishes to gratefully thank Mary Deaton and Lynn Van Deventer, who revised the original *Running Microsoft PowerPoint 4 for Windows* for this edition. He also wishes to thank Polly Fox Urban, Deb Fenwick, Christina Dudley, and Ken Sanchez at Online Press for their superb editing skills, and Bill Teel for polishing the pages. At Microsoft Press, Ina Chang, Peggy McCauley, and Lucinda Rowley provided important editorial support, and at Microsoft, Susan Grabau and John Tafoya generously offered important information about PowerPoint.

Introduction

Since its introduction in 1987, Microsoft PowerPoint has pioneered new ways of working with presentation graphics. PowerPoint introduced the concept of a presentation as a single entity rather than discrete slides, and it has introduced innovations with each new release.

Microsoft PowerPoint 7 for Windows 95 carries on the tradition, adding dozens of features designed to make creating presentations even easier and more intuitive. At the same time, it has become more like its colleagues in the Microsoft Office 95 suite of Windows-based applications, sharing on-screen controls like menus and dialog boxes, and techniques like drag and drop. PowerPoint has even mastered the common language of communication that is shared by the Office applications, so you can now effortlessly pass text, numbers, and graphics among the applications using drag and drop.

What's New in PowerPoint 7

Whether you're a new user or a veteran, you'll appreciate PowerPoint's many new features. And if you're already familiar with other Microsoft Office applications, such as Microsoft Word or Microsoft Excel, you'll recognize many of these innovations. Here is a partial list of the new features in PowerPoint 7:

- Dozens of enhancements that make PowerPoint easier to use. Many of these enhancements are built into the new Windows 95 operating system, including the ability to use long filenames so that you can more accurately describe your documents; true multitasking so that you can simultaneously work in PowerPoint, Word, and Excel, for example, while sending electronic mail; and a direct link to Microsoft Exchange, so that you can move your documents across a network or to The Microsoft Network.

- Complete integration with the full Microsoft Office 95 suite, including a shared list of commonly misspelled words that PowerPoint can automatically correct as you type, and the ability to add a PowerPoint slide to a binder of other Office documents.

- An expanded and improved AutoContent Wizard, which lets you select a presentation on the basis of both design and content. The wizard also contains more templates so that you have more presentation designs to choose from, and it offers additional autolayouts so that you have more flexibility when you create individual slides.

- AutoClipArt, which allows PowerPoint to suggest an appropriate drawing for a slide.

- Slide Meter and Meeting Minder, which let you track your time, take meeting notes, and schedule action items, all while your audience watches the presentation. When the presentation is over, PowerPoint can automatically move the minutes or notes to Word, where you can clean them up and send them as electronic mail.

- Presentation Conferencing, which lets you show your presentation to others on your company network, either for review or in place of holding a meeting.

- Presentation Conference controls, which let you use your laptop or a second computer to access your notes, the slide meter, a remote control device, and the slide navigator while you give a PowerPoint presentation.

- Fast Find, which enables you to locate a document file based on such information as a phrase within the document or part of its filename. Fast Find then presents a preview of the document file's first page so that you can confirm whether it is the file you want.

- Slide show improvements, which include more and better transitions between slides, more build effects, and greater multimedia support so that your slide shows can really dazzle an audience with animation, sound, and movies.

- The Pack and Go Wizard, which lets you assemble all of the documents you need for a presentation and put them on a disk. The wizard automatically includes any files that you have linked to your slide show, such as Word or Excel files.

About This Book

The object of this book is to give you the broadest possible understanding of PowerPoint in the shortest possible time. It serves as a tutorial as you're learning PowerPoint and as a reference for looking up topics. This book assumes that you have a working knowledge of Windows 95.

The parts and chapters of this book are organized in the order that you're likely to need information as you create presentations in PowerPoint. Part 1, which includes Chapters 1 and 2, introduces PowerPoint. You learn the basics of the PowerPoint environment, and you get off on the right footing by learning the essential steps to follow whenever you create a presentation.

Part 2, which includes Chapters 3 through 8, provides guidelines for creating the basic elements of a presentation. You learn how to start a presentation and how to work in Outline view and Slide view to enter and organize the text and add graphs, organization charts, and tables.

Part 3, which consists of Chapters 9 through 11, offers important information on adapting the basic presentation to your specific needs. You learn how to change the overall presentation design, format the graphs you've created, and use Slide Sorter view to view presentation-wide alterations.

Part 4, which includes Chapters 12 through 14, shows you how to embellish a presentation with text annotations, drawings, clip art, and bit-mapped images.

Part 5, which consists of Chapters 15, 16, and 17, gives you the information you need to produce the fruits of your labor: printed pages, audience handouts, and 35-mm slides. You also learn how to prepare and deliver electronic on-screen presentations called slide shows—complete with transitions, builds, video, sound, and music—both to a "live" audience and over a network as an online conference.

Part 6, which includes Chapters 18 and 19, covers advanced topics such as using PowerPoint with other Windows-based applications and customizing PowerPoint to suit the way you like to work.

Using This Book

In this book, when you see a key combination with a plus sign, like this:

Ctrl+Z

it means "Hold down the first key and then press the second key." For example, Ctrl+Z means "Hold down the Ctrl key and then press the Z key."

Tips that contain helpful suggestions for getting more out of PowerPoint or for enhancing the visual appeal of your presentations are identified with this icon:

 Finally, wherever you encounter the "See Also" icon, you'll find references to other sections in the book that provide additional, related information.

Part 1

SELECT EDITION

Introducing PowerPoint

Chapter 1

Setting the PowerPoint Stage

A word processor prepares the text in your everyday life. A spreadsheet calculates the numbers you need. And a database stores the text and numeric information you've compiled. But to communicate your knowledge and achievements, and to persuade the world at large, you need a powerful presentation processor.

What Is PowerPoint?

PowerPoint is a presentation processor that takes the text and numbers you've collected and hands back graphs and slides with the professional polish that today's sophisticated audiences demand.

PowerPoint follows the premise that you've never used presentation graphics software. That's probably helpful even if you've used such programs before. Unlike a word processor or spreadsheet that you might use daily, a presentation graphics program gets pulled off the electronic shelf only occasionally, so it must always seem familiar and easy to use.

PowerPoint 7 for Windows 95 is the newest version of Microsoft's presentation graphics software. You can buy it separately or as part of the Microsoft Office 95 bundle of Windows-based applications. In many large organizations, PowerPoint is the standard-issue presentation graphics software.

PowerPoint takes you by the hand at the very first screen and gently guides you through the process of creating a presentation. It asks for the text and numbers it needs—you can type them in or import them from other applications—and it asks you to select from a palette of designs for the presentation. Then PowerPoint produces the kind of vivid graphics and dazzling images you'd expect from a professional artist.

Once the presentation is complete, you can print pages to hand out at a meeting, add speaker's notes, or create transparencies to project with a standard overhead projector. You can even produce bright, crisp, 35-mm photographic slides (if you have slide-making equipment or are willing to hand the presentation to a slide-making company). And that's not all. You can also leave the images in a PowerPoint file, add special effects, and display them right on your computer screen—or, with a computer projector, on a large audience-sized screen. Electronic presentations like these are the hottest thing today, and PowerPoint's capabilities for creating and controlling electronic presentations are state-of-the-art.

Best of all, to create professional-quality visuals in PowerPoint, you don't have to be an artist. The program's built-in design templates take care of the presentation's appearance. And you don't have to be a computer expert to use all of PowerPoint's features. There's always an on-screen prompt to lead you to the next task, and often, when you have choices to make, one of PowerPoint's "wizards" appears to guide you through the preliminary decisions. About the only thing PowerPoint cannot do is help you enunciate while speaking, but the professional quality of the visuals will help give you the confidence to be at your very best.

PowerPoint's special presentation-making features can make your work easier no matter what your presentation needs:

You need quick and easy, high-impact visuals to accompany a talk.
PowerPoint's AutoContent Wizard and templates not only help you design a presentation, but they can give you a basic presentation outline to follow. You simply select a theme and design, and watch as PowerPoint generates eye-catching slides that are organized, consistent, and professional.

You need a fact-filled presentation with plenty of graphs and charts.
PowerPoint's Graph, Organization Chart, and Table modules can help you create elaborate visuals that depict numeric information, detail the structure of an organization, and make comparisons among ideas.

You need a sophisticated electronic presentation with lots of razzle-dazzle. Between slides, which can include animated graphs, sound, music, and even embedded video, PowerPoint's slide shows can serve up sophisticated video-inspired transitions. Slide shows can also be interactive—you can branch to a subtopic or call up hidden detail to support a supposition or respond to a viewer's question.

You need team-spirit presentations that display your group's logo and colors. Easily customizable slide masters and color schemes are all part of PowerPoint's repertoire. By editing the slide master, you can place a logo on the background of every slide or select special colors to match your corporation's colors.

You need to assemble existing text and graphics from other Microsoft Office applications. PowerPoint can easily integrate text, graphs, numbers, and diagrams from other Microsoft Office applications (such as Microsoft Word and Microsoft Excel) into presentation materials. With the built-in OLE software, you can even edit an object within PowerPoint that you created in another application. And while you are editing, you have access to all the editing tools provided by the other application.

You need to manage your presentations, whether you are in a board-room or in your office. PowerPoint gives you a Pack and Go Wizard to help you create a disk for taking on the road. With Presentation Conferencing, you can share your presentation across a company network and have colleagues review it with you. And with Meeting Minder and the Slide Meter, you can take notes, read your script, and keep track of time while PowerPoint presents your slide show to an audience.

See Also For more information about OLE, see Chapter 18, "Using PowerPoint with Other Applications," page 433.

PowerPoint Basics (Read This!)

Although PowerPoint is extremely friendly and easy to use, you've got to know a few basics before you can master the program. The rest of this chapter covers the little bit of groundwork you need. But don't worry; you'll soon start creating an actual presentation.

PowerPoint's Views

Unlike early presentation programs, which forced you to create and then save a single slide at a time, PowerPoint creates entire presentations of slides, all similar in appearance and all stored in a single file on your system.

> **NOTE** PowerPoint uses the word *slide* to refer to each page of visuals in a presentation even though you may print the presentation on paper or transparencies rather than create 35-mm slides.

The early presentation programs created only one slide per file, and thus only one view was necessary. Because PowerPoint can create an entire presentation's worth of slides per file, it must provide more than one way to view the slides. So instead of offering just Slide view, in which you work on a single slide, PowerPoint also offers Outline, Slide Sorter, Notes Pages, and Slide Show views. Each view lets you work on a different aspect of the presentation, and the changes you make in one view show up in all the other views as well.

Slide View

In Slide view, you can refine and embellish an individual slide in your presentation. You can enter and edit text, and you can add a graph, chart, or table to a slide. You can also dress up a slide with drawings, pictures, and text annotations. Figure 1-1 shows a slide in Slide view.

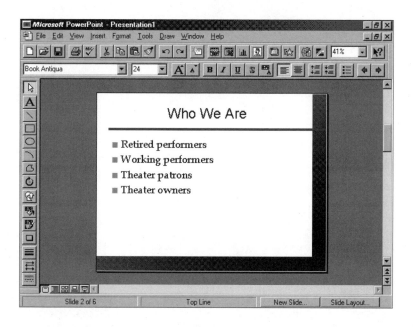

FIGURE 1-1
Slide view.

See Also   For more information about Slide view, see Chapter 5, "Working with Text in Slide View," page 91.

Outline View

In Outline view, PowerPoint displays only the text of the presentation, allowing you to enter additional text or edit existing text without the distractions you might find in Slide view. Figure 1-2 on the next page shows a sample presentation in Outline view. Because you work only with text in Outline view, you can concentrate on the words of the presentation and the flow of ideas through the slides. Outline view provides an excellent environment for organizing your thoughts and materials before you switch to a different view, where you might work on the design elements of the presentation.

For more information about Outline view, see Chapter 4, "Working with Text in Outline View," page 55.

See Also For more information about Outline view, see Chapter 4, "Working with Text in Outline View," page 55.

FIGURE 1-2

Outline view.

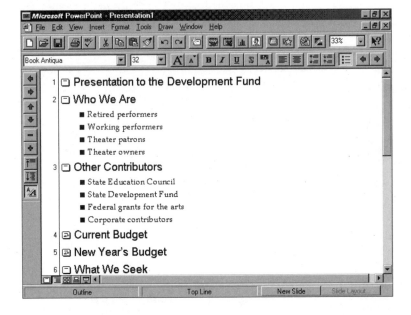

Slide Sorter View

In Slide Sorter view, you see the slides of the presentation laid out in neat rows and columns, as in Figure 1-3. Here you can see the results of sweeping changes to the appearance of the entire presentation, such as a change of the template that supplies the background design and color scheme. You cannot make changes to the content of individual slides in Slide Sorter view, but you can cut extraneous slides, duplicate slides, and shuffle the order of slides just as if you had laid out real 35-mm slides on a tabletop.

By using Slide Sorter view before you print a presentation or generate slides, you can check for inconsistencies among slides and gross errors such as a graph that is positioned on the wrong part of a page. You can also give your presentation a design overhaul by switching to a different template. When you change templates, virtually everything about your presentation's appearance changes too. As a result, a lively, colorful presentation for the sales force can become a stately, elegant presentation for the board of directors. Slide

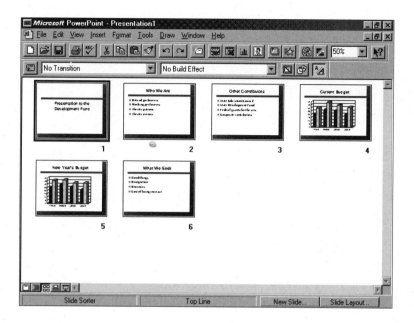

FIGURE 1-3
Slide Sorter view.

Sorter view is also the place to add and edit the transition effects used between slides during a slide show.

See Also For more information about Slide Sorter view, see Chapter 11, "Using Slide Sorter View," page 305.

Notes Pages View

The fourth PowerPoint view is dedicated to creating speaker's notes that the presenter can use at the podium. Notes Pages view produces a smaller version of the slide on the top half of a page and leaves the bottom half free for notes that the speaker can use during the presentation. While in Notes Pages view, you can view a reduced version of each slide and type in the accompanying text notes. Figure 1-4 on the next page shows a slide in Notes Pages view.

See Also For more information about Notes Pages view, see "Adding Speaker's Notes," page 328.

FIGURE 1-4

Notes Pages view.

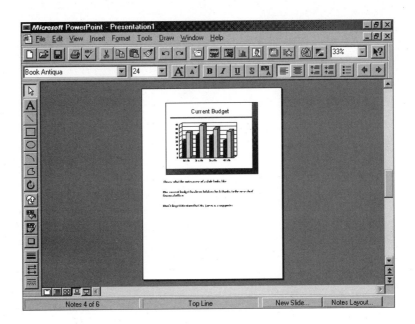

Slide Show View

The fifth PowerPoint view, Slide Show view, does not display a single, static image. Instead, it shows the presentation progressing from slide to slide just like a real slide show using projected 35-mm slides. However, unlike a real slide show, which at best can only fade out of one slide before fading into the next, a PowerPoint slide show can use eye-popping special effects to make the transition from slide to slide. As one slide dissolves off the screen, for example, the next slide can reveal itself gradually from top to bottom, and its bulleted lines of text can glide in one by one from the side. Figure 1-5 shows a slide as a new slide sweeps onto the screen from the lower right in Slide Show view.

See Also For more information about Slide Show view, see Chapter 16, "Creating Slide Shows," page 389.

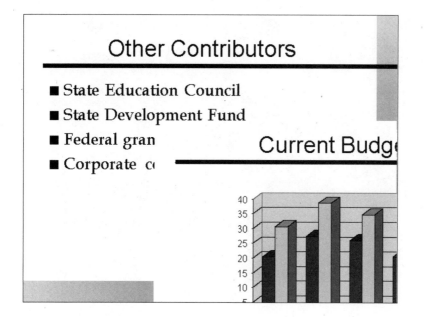

FIGURE 1-5
Slide Show view
showing the next
slide moving into
view from the
lower right corner.

Starting PowerPoint

Before you can see how easy it is to switch from one view to another, you must get PowerPoint up and running. After PowerPoint is installed, its name is added to the Programs menu. To begin using PowerPoint, click the Start button at the left end of the Taskbar, point to display a menu of the programs on your system (at this point, your screen should be similar to that shown in Figure 1-6 on the next page), and then click Microsoft PowerPoint. You can also put a copy of the PowerPoint icon directly on the Windows 95 desktop so that it is within easy reach. First double-click the My Computer icon on the desktop, and double-click the Hard Drive icon in the My Computer window. Then double-click the MSOffice folder, point to the Microsoft PowerPoint icon in the MSOffice window, hold down the Ctrl key, hold down the left mouse button, and drag the icon onto the desktop. (You can position the icon anywhere on the desktop by dragging it with the mouse.) Then double-click the Microsoft PowerPoint icon to start the program. (See the tip on page 12 for information about removing program icons from the desktop.) To close the open windows, click the Close button—the button with the "X"—in the upper right corner of each window.

FIGURE 1-6

Opening
PowerPoint from
the Start button on
the Windows 95
Taskbar.

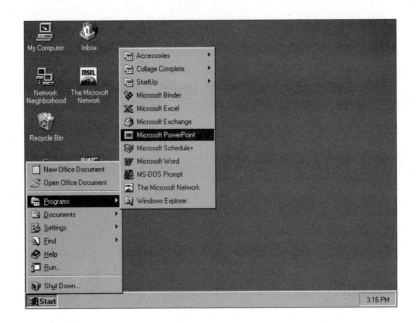

TIP To remove the Microsoft PowerPoint icon from the Windows 95 desktop (or to remove any program icon that you have added to the desktop), point to the icon, hold down the left mouse button, and drag the icon to the Recycle Bin. Next double-click the Recycle Bin icon on the desktop, click Microsoft PowerPoint in the Recycle Bin dialog box, choose Delete from the File menu, and click Yes when the Confirm File Delete message box appears.

When you start PowerPoint for the first time, you're invited to see a Quick Preview of the software. If you want to skip the preview, simply click the Cancel button. (You can always check what's new later by double-clicking What's New on the Contents tab of the Help Topics window.) After the preview ends or you click the Cancel button, the PowerPoint window appears, displaying the Tip of the Day. Read the enlightening tip, and then press Enter to display the PowerPoint dialog box shown in Figure 1-7. You use this dialog box to select a method for creating a new presentation.

TIP You can add a Microsoft PowerPoint button to the Office Shortcut Bar, which is located in the upper right corner of the Windows 95 desktop. Then, to start Power-Point, you can simply click its button. To add a PowerPoint button to the Shortcut Bar, first click the Office button—the button with interlocking puzzle pieces—at the left end of the Shortcut Bar, and choose Customize from the menu that appears. Then click the Buttons tab of the Customize dialog box, select Microsoft PowerPoint (you may have to scroll it into view), and click OK. To remove a button from the Shortcut Bar, follow the steps described above, and then deselect the button on the Buttons tab of the Custom-ize dialog box.

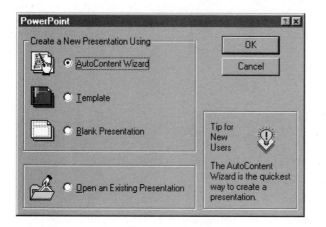

FIGURE 1-7
The PowerPoint dialog box.

TIP If you get tired of seeing a new Tip of the Day every time you load PowerPoint, deselect the Show Tips at Startup option in the lower left corner of the Tip of the Day dialog box, and then click OK.

To follow along with the rest of this chapter, select the Blank Presentation option and then click OK, or simply double-click the option. As shown in Figure 1-8, the next dialog box to appear is labeled New Slide. You use this dialog box to select a slide layout for your presentation. PowerPoint offers 24 layouts, called *autolayouts*, from which to choose. For now, click OK to create the first slide with the default Title Slide autolayout, which is the appropriate slide for the opening of a presentation.

FIGURE 1-8
The New Slide
dialog box.

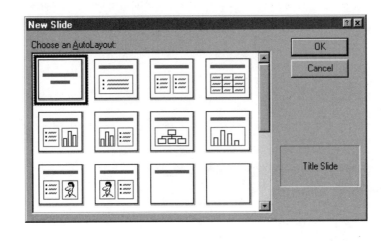

 See Also For more information about the PowerPoint dialog box and auto-layouts, see Chapter 2, "The Essential Steps," page 27.

Switching Views

If you have successfully started a blank presentation and selected the Title Slide autolayout, you are now in Slide view, looking at the first slide. Getting to a different view is simply a matter of clicking one of the five buttons in the lower left corner of the presentation window.

Go ahead and click the first four buttons one by one. When you click the fifth button, the blank first slide of the presentation appears full-screen in Slide Show view. No, your system hasn't crashed. You just haven't created any slides to present in Slide Show view yet. Simply press the Esc key to return to the previous view.

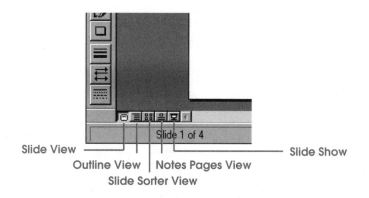

Slide View ———————— Slide Show

Outline View │ Notes Pages View

Slide Sorter View

Another way to switch between views is to use the View menu. To open the View menu, click the word *View* on the menu bar, or hold down the Alt key and then press the underlined letter in the menu name, in this case *V.*

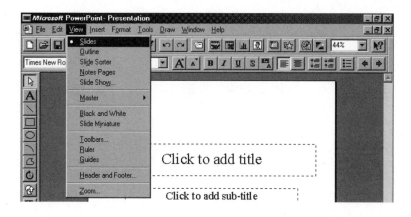

The first four entries on the View menu lead you to the first four views. The fifth entry, Slide Show, leads you to the Slide Show dialog box, from which you can run the slide show.

NOTE If a command on a menu is dimmed, the command is currently unavailable. If a command is followed by an ellipsis, a dialog box appears when you choose the command. If a command is preceded by a dot, it is one of a group of mutually exclusive commands. If a command is preceded by a check mark, the command is currently active and can be toggled on and off. If a command is followed by an arrowhead, choosing the command displays a submenu of additional commands.

Controlling the PowerPoint Window

Like all windows in Microsoft Windows 95, the PowerPoint window has Minimize, Maximize, and Close buttons in its upper right corner. Clicking the Minimize button shrinks the PowerPoint window to an icon, and clicking the Maximize button expands the window to fill the screen. Clicking the Close button closes PowerPoint. Clicking the Control button in the upper left corner displays a menu with additional commands for restoring the PowerPoint window to its previous size, for moving and sizing the window, and for closing PowerPoint.

> **NOTE** When the PowerPoint window is maximized, the Maximize button becomes the Restore button. If you click this button, the window is restored to its previous size. To return the window to full size, click the Maximize button or choose Maximize from the Control menu.

 **TIP**   When the PowerPoint window is not maximized, you can use the mouse to move and resize the window. For example, click and drag the window's title bar to move the window to a new location. To change the window's size, position the mouse pointer on one side of the window's frame, and when the pointer changes to a double-headed arrow, hold down the left mouse button and drag the frame in the desired direction.

Manipulating the Presentation Window

When you create a new presentation in PowerPoint or edit an existing one, the presentation window occupies most of the PowerPoint window. To change the presentation window's location or size, you can use its buttons and Control menu commands just like you use the PowerPoint window's buttons and commands.

You can have more than one presentation open at a time so that you can compare presentations or copy graphics or text from one presentation to another. To open more than one presentation, choose Open from the File menu, and when the File Open dialog box appears, locate the presentation you want to open, and click the Open button. The new presentation window covers any windows that are open, but you can use the commands on the Window menu to rearrange the windows. For example, the Arrange All command places the open windows side by side, as shown in Figure 1-9.

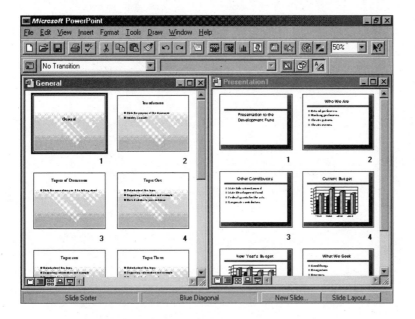

FIGURE 1-9

Two presentations arranged side by side using the Window menu's Arrange All command.

The Cascade command on the Window menu arranges open presentation windows in sequence so that you can see all their title bars. You can then click any title bar to bring that presentation window to the front. The Fit To Page command sizes the currently selected window so that it neatly fits the presentation slide.

> **NOTE** After you use any of the commands on the Window menu, you can still manipulate each window individually by using the window's buttons and Control menu commands.

Using the Toolbars

Every command in PowerPoint resides on one of PowerPoint's menus. This fact isn't very comforting, however, when you're in a rush and you'd rather not have to rummage through PowerPoint's menus. Fortunately, to make life a little easier, PowerPoint features several toolbars that contain buttons for the commands you use most often. These toolbars are conveniently displayed in the PowerPoint window so that you can access a command simply by clicking the corresponding toolbar button. As shown in Figure 1-10, the default Power-Point window displays three toolbars: the Standard, Formatting, and Drawing toolbars. In addition to these toolbars, PowerPoint provides the Drawing+, Microsoft, AutoShapes, and Animation Effects toolbars.

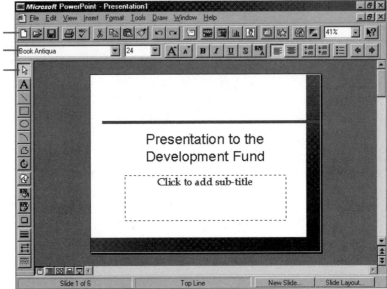

FIGURE 1-10
The Standard, Formatting, and Drawing toolbars.

Displaying Toolbars

To display a toolbar that does not appear by default, choose the Toolbars command from the View menu; when the Toolbars dialog box appears, as shown in Figure 1-11, click the check boxes for the toolbars you want. Check boxes like these act as toggles—you click once to turn on the option (add the check), and you click again to turn off the option (remove the check).

Try turning on an additional toolbar now by clicking the check box to the left of AutoShapes in the Toolbars dialog box. When you click OK, the AutoShapes toolbar appears in the PowerPoint window, just below the For-matting toolbar. The AutoShapes toolbar contains buttons that you can use to

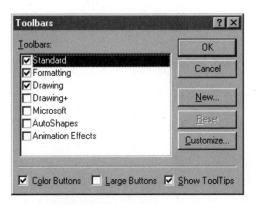

FIGURE 1-11
The Toolbars
dialog box.

add various shapes, such as stars and arrows, to slides. To remove the AutoShapes toolbar, return to the Toolbars dialog box and clear the AutoShapes check box by clicking it again.

All of PowerPoint's toolbars can be customized to include only the buttons you want. You can also move buttons from one toolbar to another. And you can make the toolbar buttons large or small and display them with or without color.

**See
Also** For more information about customizing toolbars, see "Customizing Toolbars," page 458.

Positioning Toolbars

By default, PowerPoint arranges its toolbars where they fit best on the screen, but you can change this arrangement to create a workspace that you find more comfortable. A toolbar can be located along one of the four sides of the PowerPoint window, or it can be free-floating within the window. You might want to leave the default arrangement of toolbars for now. When you become more familiar with PowerPoint, you can position the toolbars to suit your needs.

To move a toolbar, first place the mouse pointer within the borders of the toolbar, but not on top of any button. Then hold down the left mouse button and drag the toolbar to a new location on the screen. When you release the mouse button, the toolbar drops into its new position, and, if necessary, the presentation window inside the PowerPoint window adjusts to make room. If you drag a toolbar to one side of the PowerPoint window, the toolbar automatically changes shape to fit the space. If you drag the toolbar toward the middle of the screen, the toolbar becomes a box. After you drop a toolbar into place, you can reshape it by dragging its borders just as you reshape a window. Figure 1-12 shows the Drawing toolbar as a box within the Power-Point window.

FIGURE 1-12

The floating
Drawing toolbar.

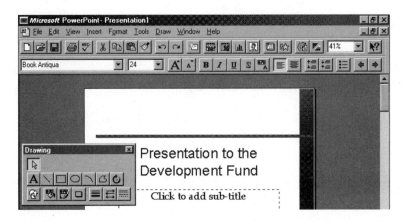

ToolTips

PowerPoint provides a handy feature called ToolTips to help you keep track of all those toolbar buttons. To see a description of any toolbar button or of any button on the screen, simply place the mouse pointer on the button and pause. A small ToolTip box pops up nearby, displaying the button's name; a brief description of the button appears in the status bar at the bottom of the PowerPoint window. Whenever you display a new toolbar in PowerPoint, use ToolTips to get acquainted with its buttons. To turn off ToolTips, choose Toolbars from the View menu, and deselect the Show ToolTips option at the bottom of the Toolbars dialog box.

Moving Through Slides

In Slide view, you see only one slide at a time, but the presentation may contain many slides. To move to another slide in your presentation, use any of the following methods:

■ Press PgDn to move forward one slide, or press PgUp to move back one slide.

■ Click the Next Slide button at the bottom of the presentation window's vertical scroll bar (see Figure 1-13) to move forward one slide, or click the Previous Slide button to move back one slide.

■ Drag the scroll box down or up in the presentation window's vertical scroll bar (see Figure 1-13) to move forward or backward through the presentation. As you drag the scroll box, the current slide number and title appear next to the scroll bar.

To practice moving through slides in a ready-made presentation, click the Open button on the Standard toolbar or choose the Open command from the File menu. When the File Open dialog box appears, select Presentation Templates from the Files of type drop-down list, and locate the Presentations folder in the MSOffice Templates subfolder in the Name list. Double-click the GENERAL presentation filename to open one of the sample presentations. Now try moving through the slides in the sample presentation by using any of the methods listed above. When you finish viewing the slides, choose Close from the File menu to close the presentation window.

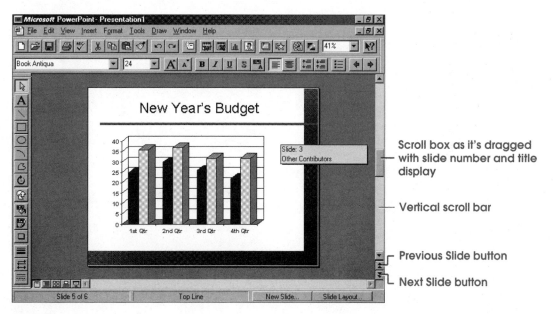

FIGURE 1-13

The vertical scroll bar and scroll box and the Previous Slide and Next Slide buttons in Slide view.

Saving Your Work

You've heard it before, but it always bears repeating: Save your work often. Don't wait until you've finished a presentation to save it. Save a presentation after you create the first slide. Save it again a little while later. The more frequently you save your work, the less you stand to lose if you fall victim to a power failure, a coffee spill, or a rambunctious child who decides to play piano on your keyboard.

To save a file, click the Save button on the Standard toolbar (that little picture on the button is a disk, not a TV) or choose Save from the File menu. If you have not yet named the file (if the presentation title bar still displays the name *Presentation* and a number), the File Save dialog box appears. As shown in Figure 1-14, you enter a filename in the File name edit box. The filename can be one word, a few words, or up to 255 letters and spaces. Use something that will make sense to you later when you want to find this presentation. The Save in box indicates where PowerPoint wants to save the file. You can change where the file is saved by clicking the arrow at the right end of the Save in box and moving to the folder you want.

Specify the storage location here

FIGURE 1-14

The File Save
dialog box.

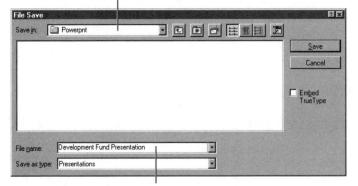

Enter the filename here

After you enter a filename and click Save, PowerPoint displays the Summary tab of the Presentation Properties dialog box. As shown in Figure 1-15, you can enter information in this dialog box to help you search for files later. For example, if you always enter the project name for all presentations belonging to a particular project in the Keywords edit box, you can later use these Keywords to extract a list of those presentations. (See the tip on the facing page.) You can also save a preview picture of your presentation, in case you find it easier to remember faces than names.

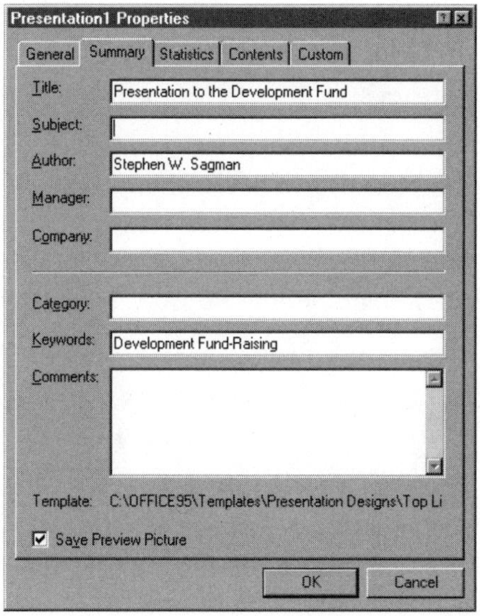

FIGURE 1-15
You can use the information in the Presentation Properties dialog box to search for specific files.

To enter information in the Summary tab of the Presentation Properties dialog box, type text directly in the edit boxes, using the Tab key to move to the next edit box and Shift+Tab to move to the previous edit box. When you've filled in as many edit boxes as you want, click OK to close the dialog box.

> **TIP** To search for a presentation, click the Open button on the Standard toolbar or choose Open from the File menu. In the Look in box, locate the drive or folder you want to search by clicking the down arrow and making your selection. At the bottom of the File Open dialog box, specify part of the filename or, if you know it, either an approximate time when the presentation was last modified, or some text that should appear within the presentation. Then click the Find Now button. If the search is successful, the filename appears in the Name list. If the search isn't successful, you can refine the search to look for information you entered in the Presentation Properties dialog box, by clicking the Advanced button, selecting a category (such as Author or Keywords) from the Property drop-down list, and entering the information in the Value edit box.

Getting Help

PowerPoint's online Help system is extensive and easy to use. Help includes three types of information: How Do I? topics that give step-by-step instructions, Tell Me About topics that give details and background information, and Troubleshooting topics that help diagnose and correct problems.

To access Help, press F1 while PowerPoint is displayed, or choose Microsoft PowerPoint Help Topics from the Help menu. The Help Topics window shown in Figure 1-16 appears.

FIGURE 1-16

The PowerPoint Help Topics window.

Clicking the Contents tab displays a set of book icons, and double-clicking a book icon displays its contents—either more book icons or topic icons that look like a page with a question mark. When you find the topic you want, double-click the topic icon to open it.

Clicking the Index tab in the Help Topics window displays a list of words associated with PowerPoint Help topics. Type the first few letters of the word you are looking for. As you type, the list of words advances to match the letters you type. You can also scroll through the word list until you find the word you want. Once you find the desired word, select it and click Display to see the topic.

Clicking the Find tab displays the Find Setup Wizard, which walks you through the process of creating a list of all of the words in PowerPoint Help so that you can locate the information you are searching for. You can choose whether to include all of the Help files associated with PowerPoint or only some of them by clicking the Customize Search Capabilities option. After the list is created, you can use the options on the Find tab to locate specific words in Help.

Clicking the Answer Wizard tab displays an edit box where you can type a question or a request for information. After you click the Search button, the wizard presents you with a list of possible topics that might answer your question. (You can also choose Answer Wizard from the Help menu to display this tab.)

As you read a Help topic, you'll see words with dotted underlines and words with solid underlines. A dotted underline indicates that when you click the word, a pop-up definition of the word is displayed. A solid underline indicates that when you click the word, the Help topic for the word is displayed. To see other related topics, click the Related Topics button at the end of a topic.

Within a Help topic, you may see a picture of a toolbar button or other object that you can click for more information. Within an instruction, you may see a shortcut button that you can click to open the dialog box you need to complete that step. Some topics may also have a small button that you can click to open another topic with more details.

Some Help topics have an Examples and Demos button at the top of their window. When you click this button, Help displays a graphical representation of the topic or gives you a step-by-step demonstration of how to carry out a corresponding task.

While in the Help system, you can click the Back button at the top of the Help window to return to the previous topic, or you can click the Help Topics button to redisplay the Help Topics window.

Clicking the Options button in the Help window displays a list of commands. Choose Annotate to read an existing note or to type a new note. When a topic has an annotation attached to it, a paper clip is displayed next to the topic title. To copy the information in the Help window, select the text you want to copy, and then choose Copy from the Options menu. You can also press Ctrl+C to copy selected text. Choose Print Topic to print the current topic. Choose Font to set the Help font to small, normal, or large size. Choose Keep Help on Top to display Help on top of the PowerPoint window while you work. Choose Use System Colors to change the colors that are used to display Help.

TIP   When you find a Help topic pertinent to the task you are trying to accomplish, you can keep the topic on your screen and refer to it while you work in PowerPoint. In the Help window, select the Options button, choose Keep Help on Top, and then choose On Top from the submenu. Choose Not On Top if you want Help to close when you work in PowerPoint.

Other Ways of Getting Help

To get help about a button or a menu command, use the Help button on the Standard toolbar. Just click the Help button (or press Shift+F1), and when the pointer displays a large question mark, click the button or menu command you want information on. Help then displays the corresponding topic for the button or menu command you've chosen.

You can get a description of any item in a dialog box by simply pointing to the item and clicking the right mouse button to display a "What's This?" topic. Or you can click the Help button next to the Close button in the dialog box's title bar and then click the item you want information about.

Chapter 2

The Essential Steps

Step 7: Saving Your Work

Your presentations won't be disposable, so here's how to save them for use at another time.

Step 8: Generating Printed Output, Slides, and Electronic Presentations

Unless you plan to show the presentation on your screen, you'll need to generate printed output or 35-mm slides.

Step 9: Collecting Accolades

In this step, you'll sit back and relax as cheers and laurels come your way for a job well done.

L ike any good software, PowerPoint offers a cornucopia of resources that were designed for a broad range of needs. Uses for the software are limited only by your time and imagination. Yet there's one well-trodden path that most users follow, taking excursions into the finer points of the program only when required. This chapter focuses on the steps that form the basic presentation-making process. Follow these footsteps, and you'll never get lost in the woods.

As you learn to use PowerPoint, you'll discover that it always guides you through the process of creating a presentation. After you start a slide, for example, PowerPoint displays a prompt that tells you to *Click here to add a title*. Simply follow PowerPoint's lead. Remember, the software was written with ease of use in mind. Whenever PowerPoint's designers could anticipate your next logical move, they instructed the software to do the same.

Although this chapter covers the nine steps involved in creating a presentation, you won't actually create one yet. Instead, you'll become familiar with the sequence of the steps, which also forms the structure of this book.

Step 1: Starting the Presentation

The presentation process gets under way as soon as you launch PowerPoint and start a new presentation. (As mentioned in Chapter 1, the first time you use PowerPoint, you can opt to see a Quick Preview of the software. To skip the preview, click the Cancel button.)

After the PowerPoint window opens and you read the Tip of the Day, the PowerPoint dialog box, shown in Figure 2-1 on the next page, is displayed. The first option in the PowerPoint dialog box activates the AutoContent Wizard. This option asks you to select a presentation type from a list of seven predefined types and then loads a set of slides with relevant text already in place. Of course, the text is generic, such as *Details about this topic*, but it nevertheless guides you in structuring the presentation.

The second option, labeled Template, displays a list of design templates you can choose from. You won't use this option until you're more familiar with PowerPoint. The third option, Blank Presentation, starts a blank presentation devoid of any design or sample text. You can, however, select a slide layout to get started.

FIGURE 2-1
The PowerPoint
dialog box.

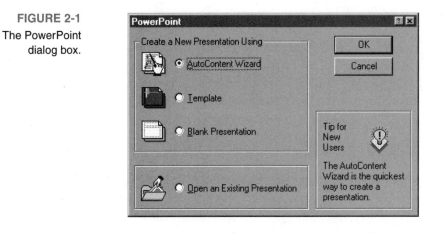

If you've already used PowerPoint to create a presentation, you can select the last option, Open an Existing Presentation. When you select this option, PowerPoint displays the File Open dialog box so that you can open a presentation that has already been created and filed away.

If you are already working in PowerPoint, you can always click the New button on the Standard toolbar or choose New from the File menu to start a new presentation.

Step 2: Choosing the Content and Appearance

Step 2 consists of two tasks that you can perform in either order: entering the presentation content and establishing its design. You can focus on the text of the slides first and leave the design for later, or you can select a design and have it applied to each new slide as you enter the text. The simplest way to take care of both tasks is to use the AutoContent Wizard. This wizard lets you select sample content for a set of presentation slides, as shown in Figure 2-2. One caveat, though: The AutoContent Wizard also institutes a presentation design. Of course, you can always change the design at Step 6, "Tweaking the Presentation."

As mentioned, you won't use the Template option in the PowerPoint dialog box until you're more familiar with PowerPoint and you've had a chance to develop your own logos and color schemes for custom design templates.

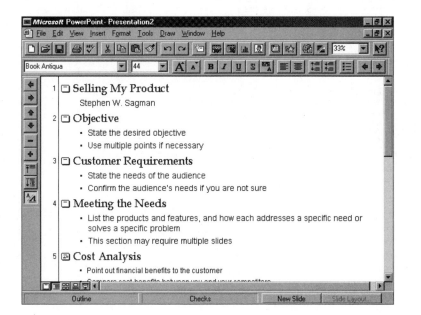

FIGURE 2-2

You can use
the AutoContent
Wizard to help you
choose the content
and design of your
presentation.

Step 3: Entering
and Editing the Text

Even if you use the AutoContent Wizard rather than type in your own text,
you still need to replace the wizard's generic text with your own. You can step
through the presentation slide by slide and substitute your words for Power-
Point's, or you can work in Outline view as shown in Figure 2-3, where you
can focus on the overall flow of the text as well as the text on individual slides.
In Outline view, you can enter and edit text, rearrange text, and copy or move
text from slide to slide.

FIGURE 2-3

Outline view
lets you focus on
the flow of your
presentation.

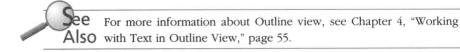

**See
Also**   For more information about Outline view, see Chapter 4, "Working
with Text in Outline View," page 55.

Step 4: Adding Graph, Organization Chart, and Table Slides

Not every topic is best communicated with written statements. Sometimes pictures or charts are the ticket, and sometimes tables are most effective. You can add a graph, chart, or table to a text slide, or you can create a new slide devoted to a graph, chart, or table. When you request a new slide or begin a blank presentation, PowerPoint displays the New Slide dialog box, which offers a variety of slide autolayouts, as shown in Figure 2-4. Some slide autolayouts have text only—a slide title and a block of text below, usually with bulleted lines of text—and others have graphs, organization charts, and tables in addition to a title. Some even have combinations of text and graphics on the same slide. You simply click the autolayout you want, and then click OK. The autolayout appears full-screen in Slide view, as shown in Figure 2-5.

FIGURE 2-4

The New Slide dialog box with a graph autolayout selected.

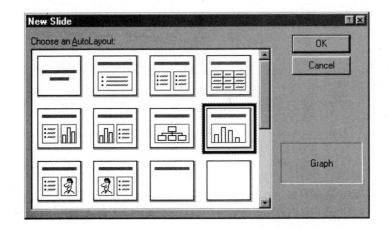

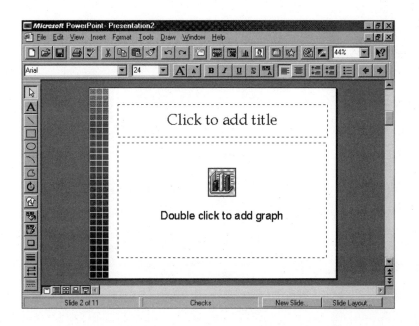

FIGURE 2-5
After you select
an autolayout, it
appears full-screen
in Slide view.

As you can see, an autolayout contains a combination of *placeholders*, which are dashed, rectangular boxes with text prompts. (Some placeholders, such as graph placeholders, contain icons as well as text prompts.) The text prompt in each placeholder tells you how to use the placeholder. For example, in Figure 2-5 one placeholder tells you to *Click to add title*. Another tells you to *Double click to add graph*. The autolayout shown in Figure 2-6 on the next page has three placeholders: one for a title, one for bulleted text, and one for a graph. With placeholders, you can't go wrong. When you click a text placeholder, such as *Click to add title*, PowerPoint displays an insertion point so that you can type text directly in the placeholder. If you double-click a graph placeholder, PowerPoint loads the special module you use to create graphs.

> **NOTE** PowerPoint can be set up so that you see the New Slide dialog box instead of the PowerPoint dialog box whenever you start a new PowerPoint session. If this is the case, you can redisplay the PowerPoint dialog box by choosing Options from the Tools menu, selecting the Show Startup Dialog option on the General tab of the Options dialog box, and clicking OK. (Notice that you can also control the display of the New Slide dialog box.)

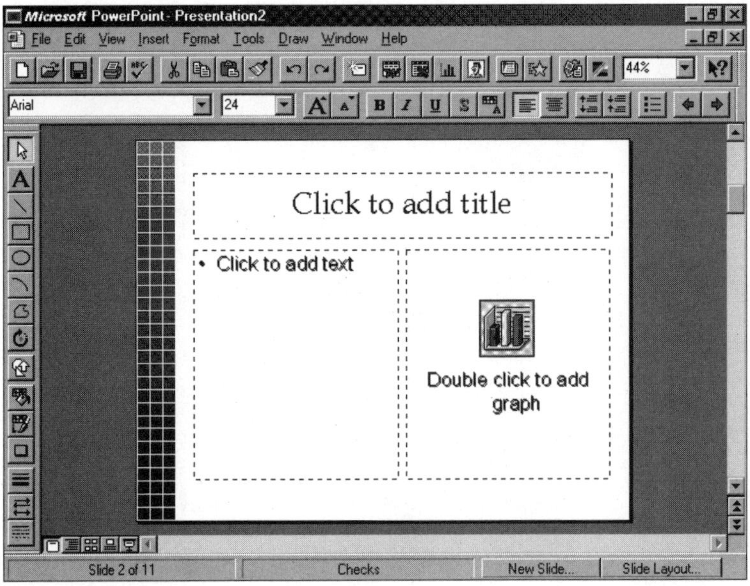

FIGURE 2-6

An autolayout
with title, bulleted
text, and graph
placeholders.

Autolayouts and placeholders are the keys to making your way through a presentation. When you select an autolayout and then click one of its placeholders, PowerPoint displays all the tools you need so that you don't have to hunt around for specific commands or toolbars.

Step 5: Adding Annotations and Graphic Embellishments

By step 5, you're ready to add the finishing touches to your presentation. The text and charts are complete, but you should take a moment to review each slide before continuing. On some slides, a little additional explanation might help the audience. With the Text Tool button on the Drawing toolbar, you can add free-floating blocks of text as annotations that highlight or explain a special feature. You can also use the Drawing toolbar to add graphics to accompany an image or text on a slide. The simplest case is a line that connects a text annotation to the subject it describes, such as the line connecting the label to the pie chart in the slide shown in Figure 2-7. But you can also draw more complex images with PowerPoint's drawing tools and commands.

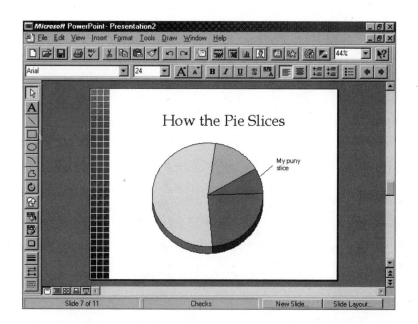

If drawing is not your thing, you can take advantage of the ClipArt Gallery—PowerPoint's extensive library of ready-made images—or you can use the AutoClipArt command on the Tools menu to help you select a drawing. Power-Point organizes the images by category in the gallery, as shown in Figure 2-8.

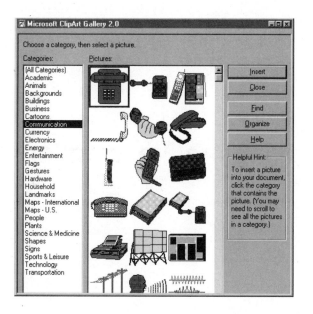

As Figure 2-9 below shows, you can increase the effectiveness of a slide by adding a clip art image to the text.

FIGURE 2-9

Adding a clip art image can add impact to a slide.

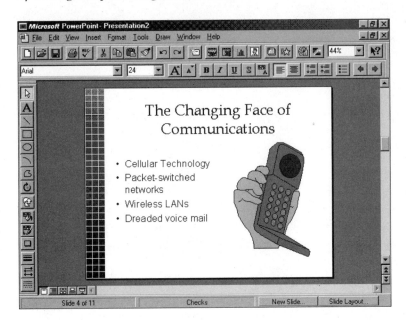

In addition to using clip art, you can also incorporate pictures you've drawn in other software programs and display photos you've scanned with a scanner. PowerPoint can import and display both drawings and bitmapped graphics from other applications.

See Also For more information about clip art, see "Using the ClipArt Gallery," page 362.

Step 6: Tweaking the Presentation

What would you do with all that extra time if it weren't for last-minute changes? Because your presentation is stored electronically in PowerPoint rather than drawn on paper, you can make changes as easily as you edit a document in a word processor or update numbers in a spreadsheet.

If you started with the AutoContent Wizard, which applies its own design template, or if you started with a blank presentation that had no template attached, you might also want to make more discretionary modifications to the presentation at the last minute. Whatever the circumstances, PowerPoint's Slide Sorter view, shown in Figure 2-10, is the best place to see and make sweeping changes to your slides because you can view an entire segment of the presentation at once. While in Slide Sorter view, you can also adjust the order of the slides or delete extraneous slides.

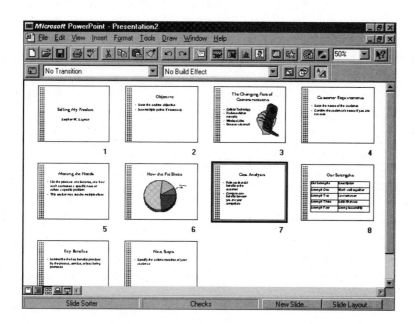

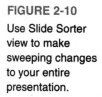

FIGURE 2-10

Use Slide Sorter view to make sweeping changes to your entire presentation.

Step 7: Saving Your Work

To store a completed presentation, you save it in a file by clicking the Save button on the Standard toolbar or by choosing Save from the File menu. Each PowerPoint file holds an entire presentation's worth of slides, so you don't have to worry about lost slides the next time you display a presentation.

Step 8: Generating Printed Output, Slides, and Electronic Presentations

Even if it's just for immediate gratification, you'll probably want to print a set of slides as soon as they're complete. PowerPoint can print your slides on paper with just about any printer you install in Windows. Laser and ink-jet printers, today's business standards, produce especially attractive printouts.

PowerPoint is equally adept at generating 35-mm slides. Unfortunately, slides do not pop out of a slide-making device the same way that pages emerge from a printer. You must either attach a film recorder, which records your slides onto slide film that must then be developed, or send the presentation file to a service bureau that can create and develop the slides for you.

A special form of output, the electronic presentation, is quickly overtaking even slides in popularity. An electronic presentation displays images on a computer screen or on a large screen with the aid of a computer projector. Electronic presentations can incorporate fancy fades and slick transitions between slides, and they can play sound and video, too. Electronic presentations can also be interactive, so you can control their flow during the presentation, stepping back to a previous slide or advancing to an additional topic. What's more, in an electronic presentation, you can "drill down" to the spreadsheet file that contains the figures for a graph so that the audience can see the original worksheet. Best of all, electronic presentations can be updated at the very last second. You'd be surprised by how many concluding slides are prepared even while a presentation is in progress.

Step 9: Collecting Accolades

The final step is the easiest. Leave your phone line clear and your door open for the flood of praise that will come your way. With a PowerPoint presentation, you'll not only enlighten an audience but entertain them as well. So say goodbye to the chalkboard, flip chart, and Orator ball.

Outstanding Achievement

This certificate is awarded to

Your name here

For the creation of
extraordinary presentations
that inspire and stimulate

Friday, May 26, 1995

Chief Financial Officer   President

Vice President   Vice President

In the next chapter, you'll get an opportunity to try the procedures you've learned about here.

Part 2

SELECT EDITION

Creating the
Basic Presentation

SELECT EDITION

Chapter 3

Getting Started on the Presentation

f you're new to preparing presentations, you'll find PowerPoint at your side, ready to help you through the process step by step. If you're a presentation veteran, on the other hand, PowerPoint provides easy-to-use tools for performing familiar tasks. If you're somewhere in between, PowerPoint offers as much assistance as you need.

PowerPoint recognizes that creating a professional presentation involves two initial tasks: drafting the content and coming up with a consistent design. Amazingly, PowerPoint can help you with both of these tasks. It's easy to find a presentation graphics program that comes with a selection of professionally designed templates. But it's rare to find a program that helps you work out what to say and how to say it.

In this chapter, you'll learn how to choose from among the options that PowerPoint presents whenever you start a new presentation. These options determine how much assistance PowerPoint provides as you get started creating the presentation. In the remaining chapters of this part of the book, you'll learn the next steps: working with the sample content PowerPoint provides, entering your own text, and adding graphs, organization charts, and other fancy visual effects.

Starting with the Presentation Content

When you have a good idea of the general content of your presentation, you can translate that idea into the beginnings of a PowerPoint presentation in three ways:

- You can use the AutoContent Wizard to help you select a ready-made presentation. It even helps you create the opening slide. The rest of the job—adapting the sample text; dropping in graphs, charts, and other elements; and revising the overall design—is up to you.

- If you've already created a presentation outline in Word, you can import it into PowerPoint's Outline view in one step. This option is often better than using the AutoContent Wizard because you start your work in PowerPoint with a specific outline instead of a generic sample. Adding graphs and other special elements and coming up with a design are still up to you.

■ You can start from scratch in PowerPoint, laying out the text in Outline view, and then dropping in graphs, pictures, annotations, and so forth in Slide view. After you complete the content, you can turn your attention to the design.

The first part of this chapter, which focuses on the content, explains each of these courses of action in more detail.

Using the AutoContent Wizard

PowerPoint can't possibly know what you need to say, but it does know how successful communicators organize their presentations. So, in the AutoContent Wizard, PowerPoint offers half a dozen tried-and-true predefined outlines as starting points for your own presentation. You can select one of these outlines:

■ Recommending a Strategy

■ Selling a Product, Service or Idea

■ Training

■ Reporting Progress

■ Communicating Bad News

■ General

To set up your presentation, the AutoContent Wizard does the following:

■ Asks for the title of the presentation (What are you going to talk about?)

■ Asks for other text for the title slide (a subtitle or footnote)

■ Asks you to select a presentation type

■ Asks you to select a visual style for the presentation and to estimate the length (in minutes) of the presentation

■ Asks you to specify the type of output (35-mm slides, for example) you want to generate and whether you want to print handouts

■ Displays a general outline for the presentation in Slide view

To activate the AutoContent Wizard, follow this procedure:

1. Start PowerPoint, and when the PowerPoint dialog box (shown earlier in Chapter 2) appears, double-click the AutoContent Wizard option. Or, if PowerPoint is already on your screen, choose New from the File menu to open the New Presentation dialog box, and then click the Presentations tab, as shown on the next page.

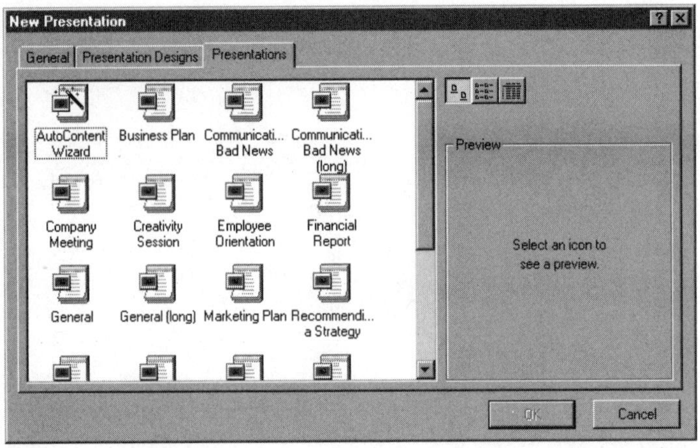

2. Double-click the AutoContent Wizard icon.

No matter how you activate the AutoContent Wizard, you see the dialog box displayed here:

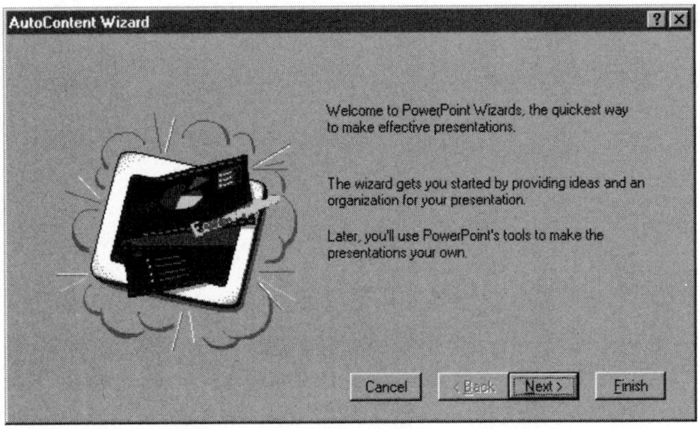

The AutoContent Wizard has six steps in the form of six dialog boxes. At the bottom of each dialog box is a set of navigation buttons. Click Next or press N on your keyboard to get to the next step, click Back or press B on your keyboard to get to the previous step, or click Cancel or press Esc to close the AutoContent Wizard. The wizard has a default choice for each step along the way, so you can click Finish or press F on your keyboard at any step to use all the defaults for the remaining steps.

Use the AutoContent Wizard by following these instructions:

1. The first dialog box introduces you to the AutoContent Wizard. Click Next or press N to move to the second dialog box shown here:

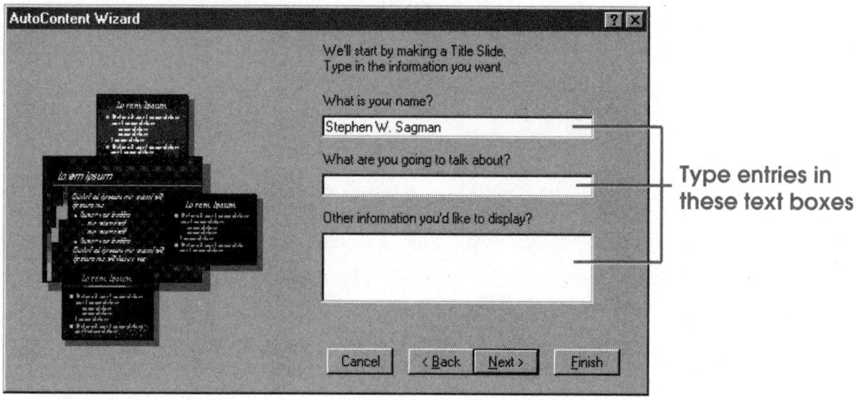

AutoContent Wizard

We'll start by making a Title Slide.
Type in the information you want.

What is your name?

Stephen W. Sagman

What are you going to talk about?

Other information you'd like to display?

Cancel   < Back   Next >   Finish

Type entries in these text boxes

2. Enter your name or your organization's name in the first edit box. The next time you use the AutoContent Wizard, PowerPoint will enter this name automatically. You can always type over the highlighted entry to change it.

3. Next answer the question *What are you going to talk about?* by typing a title for the presentation in the edit box. The text you enter will become the presentation title on the title slide.

TIP   You can replace the name in the first edit box with text you want to use for a presentation subtitle. The text you enter will appear below the title on the title slide. You can always put your name or your organization's name in the third edit box, under *Other information you'd like to display?*

---

4. Enter an optional third line of text for the title slide in the third edit box, under *Other information you'd like to display?* This line of text will appear as the third line on the title slide.

5. Click Next or press Alt+N to get to the third dialog box, shown on the next page, where you select a presentation type.

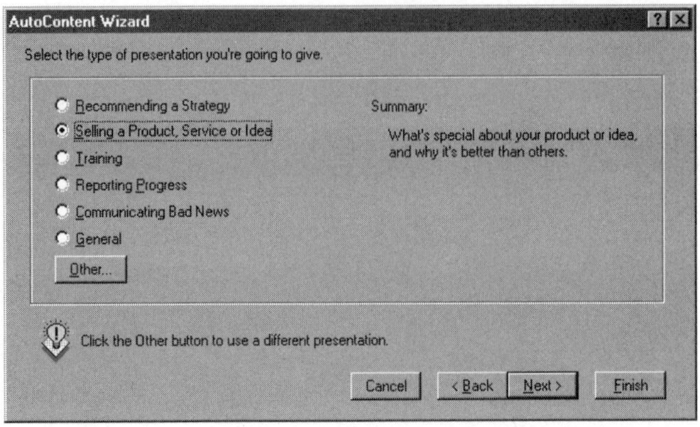

6. Click a presentation type to see a summary of that presentation's content. If you want to base your new presentation on an existing one, click Other, and then locate the existing presentation in the Select Presentation Template dialog box.

7. Click the presentation type you want, and then click Next or press N.

8. In the fourth dialog box, shown below, select a visual style to help the AutoContent Wizard determine whether your presentation will be a formal (Professional) or informal (Contemporary) one. If you don't want to specify a different style, leave the Default option selected.

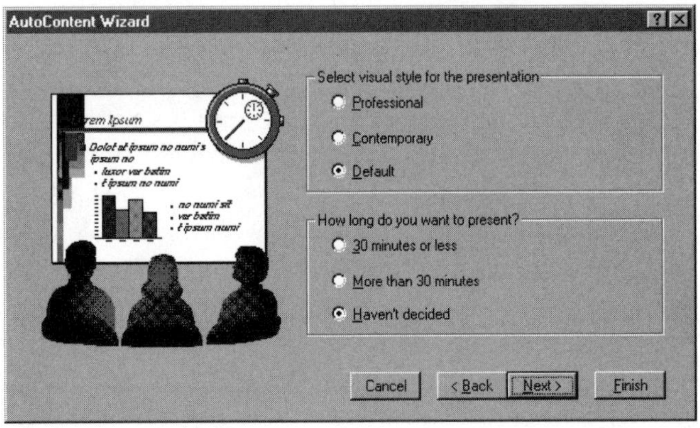

9. Next, to help the AutoContent Wizard determine the number of slides needed for your presentation, select an estimated time option, and then click Next or press N to display the fifth AutoContent Wizard dialog box, shown on the facing page.

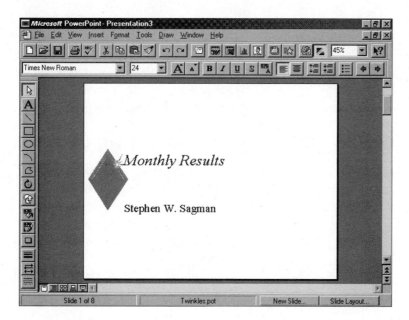

10. Select the type of output you want to generate for your presentation: black and white or color overheads; a slide show displayed on your computer; or 35-mm slides.

11. Click Yes if you intend to print your presentation to distribute as handouts to your audience, and then click Next or press N.

12. When the final AutoContent Wizard dialog box is displayed, click Finish or press F. The title slide of the new presentation appears in Slide view, as shown here:

You can click the Previous Slide and Next Slide buttons, press the PgUp and PgDn keys, or use the vertical scroll bar within the presentation window to scroll through the presentation. Notice that the presentation includes suggestions for the content of each slide in addition to the slide titles.

Behind the Scenes

The AutoContent Wizard is nothing more than a step-by-step procedure for using one of the presentation files stored in the Presentations subfolder of the Templates folder of the main folder where you keep Microsoft Office. You can accomplish the same task manually by using the New command on the File menu to open the New Presentation dialog box and then double-clicking one of the presentation icons on the Presentations tab. In addition to the six presentations offered by the AutoContent Wizard, you'll also find icons for other ready-made presentations, such as Creativity Session and Financial Report. When you have time, open some of these presentations and view the slides to get an idea of the range of presentation topics covered by PowerPoint.

TIP You can customize any presentation used by the AutoContent Wizard by modifying text on the slides or changing the template that gives the presentation its design. Simply open one of the presentations in the Presentations subfolder, and edit the text and/or change the design template. Then resave the Presentation in the same subfolder without renaming it. The next time you use the AutoContent Wizard, you'll get the same six presentation types, but they'll reflect your customized changes.

Using an Outline from Microsoft Word

If you've prepared an outline for your presentation in Microsoft Word, you can easily send the outline to PowerPoint by viewing the outline in Word and then clicking Word's Present It button. The Outline immediately shows up in PowerPoint's Outline view exactly as it appeared in Word. Level 1 headings become slide titles, and lower-level headings become indented bulleted items on the slides.

See Also For more information about using existing outlines, see "Importing Outlines," page 85.

For more information about the Present It button, see "Installing the Present It Button in Word," page 87.

Entering the Text from Scratch

When you know what you want to say and you just want to create the slides, you can always jump right into a new presentation and start entering the text from scratch. Simply start PowerPoint and select Blank Presentation in the PowerPoint dialog box. Then select an autolayout from the New Slide dialog box. Or, if PowerPoint is already on your screen, do one of the following:

- Click the New button on the Standard toolbar, and select an auto-layout in the New Slide dialog box.

- Choose New from the File menu, double-click the Blank Presentation icon on the General tab of the New Presentation dialog box, and select an autolayout from the New Slide dialog box.

- Choose New from the File menu, click the Presentation Designs tab, double-click one of the design template icons, and then select an autolayout from the New Slide dialog box. You'll learn more about design templates in the next section.

No matter which procedure you follow, PowerPoint displays the first slide of a new presentation in Slide view. You can switch to Outline view and concentrate on the text, or you can stay in Slide view and add slides one by one, entering text and graphics as you go.

See Also For more information about Outline view, see Chapter 4, "Working with Text in Outline View," page 55.

For more information about Slide view, see Chapter 5, "Working with Text in Slide View," page 91.

Starting with the Presentation Design

If you want to see the presentation's design while working on its content, you can select a design template first. Each slide you create picks up the design of the template so that your presentation has a consistent look. You can choose from among PowerPoint's many ready-made design templates, or, if you're feeling creative, you can create your own design.

To select one of PowerPoint's ready-made design templates, follow the steps below:

1. Choose New from the File menu, and when the New Presentation dialog box appears, click the Presentation Designs tab to display template options similar to the ones shown below:

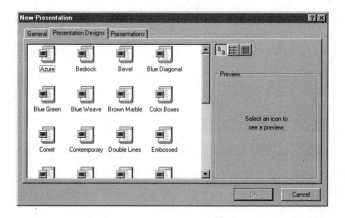

2. Click each template icon to see a sample of the template design in the Preview box on the right. (You can also use the arrow keys to move from one template to the next.) When you find the template you want, click its icon once and then click OK, or double-click its icon.

To use an existing presentation as a template for the design of a new presentation, follow this procedure:

1. Open the existing presentation, and make any changes you want to the design.

2. Choose Save As from the File menu, and when the Save As dialog box appears, select Presentation Templates from the Save as type drop-down list.

3. Double-click the Presentation Designs folder in the folder's list, enter a name for the new template in the File name edit box, and click Save.

Now all you have to do to use the new template is double-click its icon on the Presentation Designs tab of the New Presentation dialog box.

> **TIP** If you want your template to appear on the General tab of the New Presentation dialog box, save it in the Templates folder. If you save a template in a new *folder* in the Templates folder, the name of the new folder appears as a separate tab in the New Presentation dialog box. For example, you can create a special folder to hold your company-specific templates.

See Also For more information about creating a template, see Chapter 9, "Making Overall Changes," page 213.

Starting a Design from Scratch

If none of the templates suits your fancy or if you need to create a special presentation with a unique appearance, you can start with a blank presentation and then custom design the background, color scheme, and font choices.

To start with a blank presentation, follow these steps:

1. Choose New from the File menu.

2. On the General tab of the New Presentation dialog box, click the Blank Presentation icon and then click OK, or double-click the Blank Presentation icon.

3. When the New Slide dialog box appears, select an autolayout and then click OK.

See Also For information about changing the background, color scheme, and fonts of your presentation, see Chapter 9, "Making Overall Changes," page 213.

No matter what choices you make when starting a presentation, your next stop will probably be Outline view, where you can enter and edit the text that will form the backbone of your presentation. Chapter 4, "Working with Text in Outline View," is devoted to this next logical step. But if you want, you can skip Outline view and head straight to Slide view, where you can work on the slides of your new presentation one by one. In that case, Chapter 5, "Working with Text in Slide View," will give you the guidance you need.

Chapter 4

Working with Text in Outline View

C hapter 3 introduced the three ways of producing the text of a presentation: using the AutoContent Wizard; importing an outline created in Microsoft Word 7 for Windows 95 (or another application); and creating an outline from scratch in Outline view. The second and third methods are the topics of this chapter.

Starting a presentation in Outline view lets you mull over the themes and topics of the presentation, hone the flow of your arguments before you worry about how the presentation will look, and build a case that will be overwhelmingly persuasive. That, after all, is the purpose of a presentation.

If you don't start the presentation in Outline view, you can always switch to it to gain these advantages:

- In Outline view, you see only the presentation text—you don't see graphs, tables, or the design elements of the presentation, such as the background design. So you can concentrate on the content of the presentation—what it says—without being distracted by its appearance.

- In Outline view, you can easily enter the list of main topics of your presentation. Entering the main topics generates all the presentation slides you need because each main topic becomes the title of a slide in other views.

- In Outline view, you can easily rearrange the topics, thereby changing the order in which you will address issues in the presentation. You can enter supporting statements that will become bulleted items on the slides, and you can move the statements from topic to topic until you are sure a discussion point is addressed in just the right spot during the presentation.

Figure 4-1 on the next page shows the topics and supporting statements of a presentation in Outline view. Figure 4-2, also on the next page, shows the resulting titles and bulleted items on slides in Slide Sorter view.

FIGURE 4-1

A presentation
outline in
Outline view.

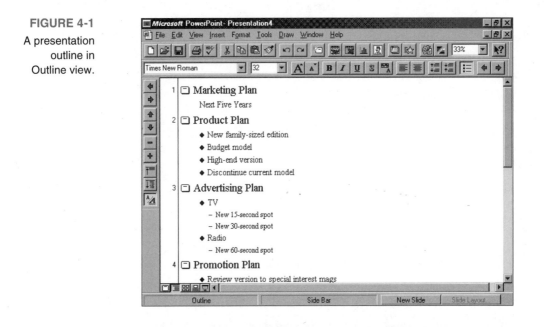

FIGURE 4-2

The slides in
Slide Sorter view.

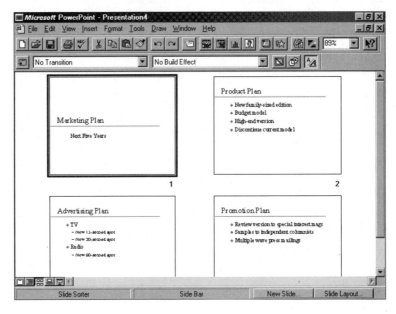

Switching to Outline View

When you start a new presentation using any of the options in the New Presentation dialog box, PowerPoint automatically opens the presentation in Slide view. If you want to concentrate on the topics you'll cover in the presentation and enter text to support each topic, you can easily switch to Outline view. After you finish with the text in Outline view, you can return to Slide view and add graphs and tables for information that is not readily communicated with words.

Assuming that you have launched PowerPoint and started a new presentation, here's how to switch to Outline view at any time: With the title slide displayed on your screen, click the Outline View button in the lower left corner of the presentation window or choose the Outline command from the View menu.

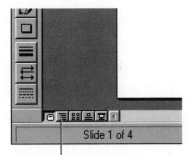

Outline View

When you switch to Outline view to begin a new presentation, the insertion point is positioned beside blank slide number 1, as shown in Figure 4-3 on the next page. When you begin typing, PowerPoint inserts your text at the insertion point. Also, when Outline view is active, a special Outlining toolbar replaces the Drawing toolbar on the left side of the presentation window, as shown in Figure 4-3.

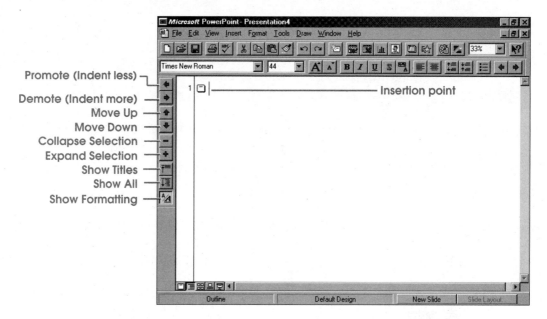

FIGURE 4-3

Starting a new presentation in Outline view, where the Drawing toolbar is replaced by the Outlining toolbar.

Entering the Main Topics

The first step in creating a presentation in Outline view is to enter a title for the presentation and a list of the topics you plan to discuss. The title and topics become your preliminary slide titles. Don't worry about entering the topics in exact order. You can always rearrange them later.

To enter the topics you'll cover in your presentation, follow these steps:

1. Type the presentation title on the first line of the outline, and then press Enter to move to the second line, where slide number 2 appears, as shown on the facing page:

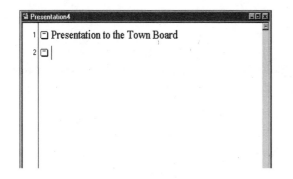

2. Type the first topic, and press Enter. If you don't yet have a topic precisely pinned down, type a two- or three-word placeholder. You can always edit it later.

3. Type the next topic, and press Enter.

4. Type the topic for each successive slide, pressing Enter after each one except the last.

Figure 4-4 shows a completed list of topics for a presentation about the construction of a new store.

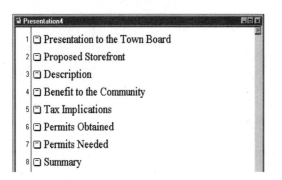

FIGURE 4-4

A list of topics for the slides of a new presentation.

TIP On each slide, use the fewest words possible to communicate your message. The fewer words used, the more impact the text has, and the larger and more readable it can be. Try to write newspaper-like headlines, not whole sentences. Write *Profits up 26%* rather than *Our profits increased by 26%.*

Next, examine your list of topics to determine the best way to communicate to your audience. Some topics are best conveyed with a few bulleted items you can add below the topics. Other topics involve numeric data. Later, you can switch to Slide view and add graphs or tables to these slides to bring the numbers to life. You can also add organization charts and drawings.

> **TIP** If your presentation outline has many topics, you may want to use the Zoom Control box on the Standard toolbar or the Zoom command on the View menu to reduce the magnification of the text so that more of it fits on the screen. For more information about zooming, see the sidebar titled "Zooming In and Out," page 71.

The Outline View–Slide View Connection

Each main topic entered in a presentation in Outline view becomes a title on a slide in Slide view. Similarly, each supporting statement entered under a main topic in Outline view becomes a bulleted item on a slide in Slide view. This connection between Outline view and Slide view is a two-way street. If you edit a title or bulleted item in Slide view, the changes you make show up in Outline view as well.

Adding Bulleted Items

After entering a list of topics, you're ready to enter the supporting statements for those topics.

To add bulleted items under a topic, follow these steps:

1. In Outline view, move the insertion point to the end of the topic that requires bulleted items. (The fastest way is to click at the end of the line, but you can also move the insertion point to the desired line with the Up or Down arrow key, and then press the End key.)

2. Press Enter to create a new line. PowerPoint thinks you want to insert a new topic, so it adds a slide icon and renumbers the existing topic, as shown here:

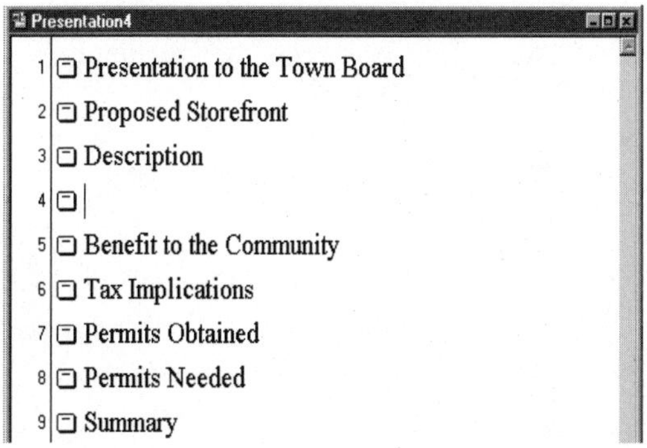

```
Presentation4                              _ □ ✕
  1 □ Presentation to the Town Board
  2 □ Proposed Storefront
  3 □ Description
  4 □ |
  5 □ Benefit to the Community
  6 □ Tax Implications
  7 □ Permits Obtained
  8 □ Permits Needed
  9 □ Summary
```

3. Click the Demote button on the Outlining toolbar or press the Tab key to move the insertion point one level to the right. PowerPoint removes the slide icon, readjusts the numbers, and inserts a bullet, as shown here:

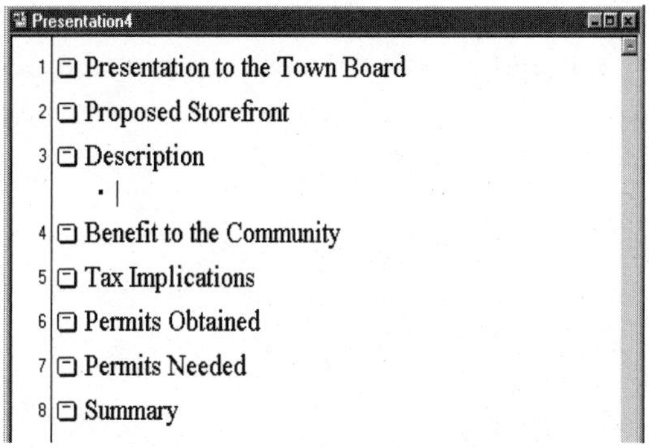

```
Presentation4                              _ □ ✕
  1 □ Presentation to the Town Board
  2 □ Proposed Storefront
  3 □ Description
        • |
  4 □ Benefit to the Community
  5 □ Tax Implications
  6 □ Permits Obtained
  7 □ Permits Needed
  8 □ Summary
```

4. Type the first bulleted item. If you type more text than will fit on one line, the text wraps to the next line.

5. Press Enter to start another bulleted item.

6. Repeat steps 4 and 5 until you've added all the bulleted items you need.

Figure 4-5 shows the completed set of bulleted items for the third slide of the store-construction presentation.

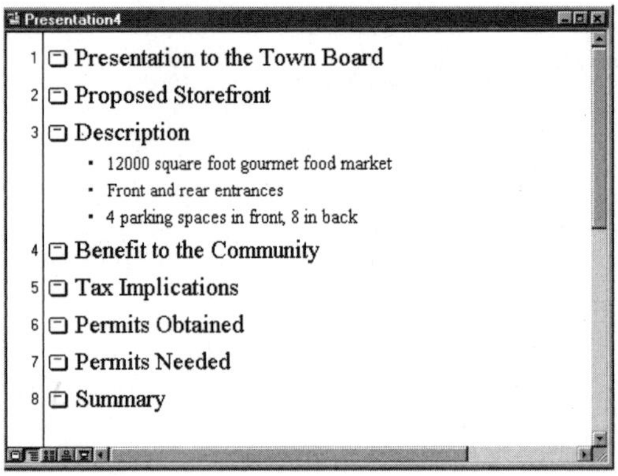

FIGURE 4-5

A complete set of bulleted items.

NOTE Text indented under the presentation title on slide 1 is not given a bullet; it becomes a subtitle on slide 1.

If you add bulleted items below the last topic of your outline and then you want to add a new topic, press Enter at the end of the last bulleted item, and then click the Promote button on the Outlining toolbar or press Shift+Tab to move the insertion point one level to the left. Then type the new topic. For example, Figure 4-6 shows the store-construction presentation with a new topic added after the bulleted items for slide number 8.

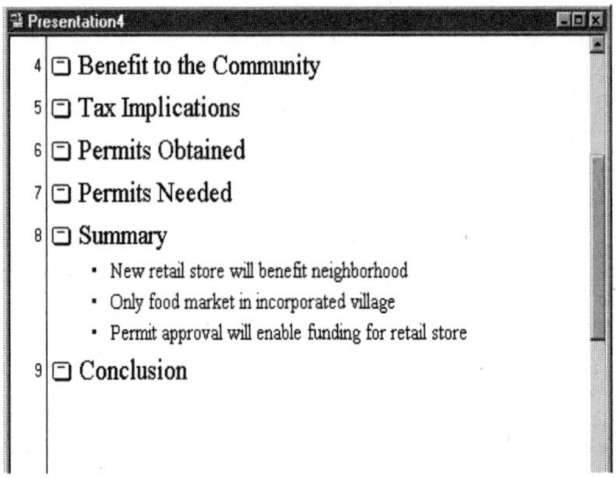

FIGURE 4-6

Press Enter and click the Promote button after typing a bulleted item to add another slide.

You can have five levels of bulleted items on a slide, as shown in Figure 4-7. Each level is indented from the preceding level and has its own default bullet style. To demote a bulleted item by one level, thereby indenting it farther to the right, click the Demote button on the Outlining toolbar or press Tab before typing the bulleted item. To promote a bulleted item by one level, click the Promote button on the Outlining toolbar or press Shift+Tab. With five indent levels, you can have points under the main topics, subpoints under the points, and so on. But don't get carried away. Remember, when it comes to presentations, less is more.

7 ☐ **Permits Needed**
- State Permits
  - Retail Certificate
    - Food Handling Approval
      - Servers
      - Food Preparers
        - Chefs
        - Sous Chefs
- County Permits
  - Retail Certificate

FIGURE 4-7

The five levels of bulleted items.

TIP To demote or promote an existing bulleted item, place the insertion point anywhere in the item, and click the Demote or Promote button or press Tab or Shift+Tab.

TIP Typing all the topics and then adding bulleted items is one approach to creating the outline. The advantage of this approach is that you can reorganize the list of main topics before adding any detail to the presentation. (For information about reorganizing the outline, see "Reorganizing Text in Outline View," page 77.) Another approach is to enter a topic and then press Tab to enter its supporting bulleted items. Then, after the last bulleted item, press Shift+Tab and type the next topic. When you finish the last topic, you can still reorganize the presentation before switching to Slide view, where the topics become slide titles and where you can add graphs, tables, and other elements.

Editing Text in Outline View

After you've entered topics and bulleted items, you can revise the text to reword entries or make corrections. To edit text in Outline view, you must first move the insertion point to the spot that needs editing. The simplest way is to click where you want the insertion point to be in the text. For example, clicking to the left of the *B* in *Board* positions the insertion point as shown in Figure 4-8.

FIGURE 4-8

An insertion point appears where you click.

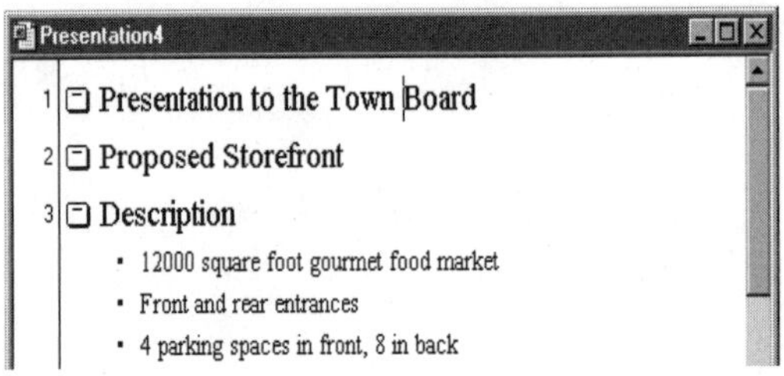

```
┌─────────────────────────────────────────────────────┐
│ Presentation4                                 _ □ X   │
├─────────────────────────────────────────────────────┤
│ 1 □ Presentation to the Town │Board                   │
│                                                        │
│ 2 □ Proposed Storefront                                │
│                                                        │
│ 3 □ Description                                        │
│       • 12000 square foot gourmet food market          │
│       • Front and rear entrances                       │
│       • 4 parking spaces in front, 8 in back           │
└─────────────────────────────────────────────────────┘
```

You can also move the insertion point with the keyboard by using one of the keys or key combinations listed in Table 4-1.

TABLE 4-1

Keys and key combinations for moving the insertion point.

Key or Key Combination	Moves the Insertion Point
Left, Right, Up, or Down arrow key	One character left or right or one line up or down
Ctrl+Left arrow key	To the beginning of the previous word
Ctrl+Right arrow key	To the beginning of the next word
Ctrl+Up arrow key	To the beginning of the current topic (or to the beginning of the previous topic if the insertion point is already in a topic)
Ctrl+Down arrow key	To the beginning of the next topic
Home	To the beginning of the current line
End	To the end of the current line
Ctrl+Home	To the top of the outline
Ctrl+End	To the bottom of the outline

After correctly positioning the insertion point, simply start typing to insert text. You can press the Backspace key to delete the character to the left of the insertion point, or press the Delete key to delete the character to the right of the insertion point. You can also press Ctrl+Backspace to delete the word to the left, or press Ctrl+Delete to delete the word to the right.

NOTE Unlike Microsoft Word, PowerPoint is always in Insert mode. Anything you type is inserted at the insertion point. You cannot press the Insert key to switch to Overtype mode.

Selecting Text for Editing

In PowerPoint, the easiest way to make more drastic editing changes is to select the text you want to modify so that your changes affect the entire selection rather than single characters.

To select a block of text with the mouse, click to the left of the first character in the block, hold down the left mouse button, and then drag across the text past the last character in the block. PowerPoint highlights the text as the mouse pointer passes across it, as shown in Figure 4-9. To select more than one line, drag down to the next line. Note that if you select a single word in one topic and then drag down to the next line, the entire first topic is selected.

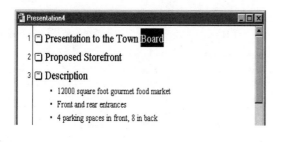

FIGURE 4-9

Selected text.

TIP   You can select a single word and its trailing space by double-clicking the word. You can select a series of words by double-clicking the first word, holding down the mouse button on the second click, and dragging across the remaining words. To select all of the text that follows a bullet, click the bullet once; to select a topic and all of its bulleted items, click the slide icon to the left of the topic text. You can select the entire presentation by choosing Select All from the Edit menu or by pressing Ctrl+A.

A special editing option called Automatic Word Selection makes it easy to select multiple words with the mouse. When you drag across any part of a word and continue to drag to the next word, PowerPoint selects both the first and second words. If you want to select an entire sentence, all you have to do is click anywhere in the first word and then drag to anywhere within the last word. PowerPoint then highlights the first and last words and all of the words in between. This option is on by default. To disable Automatic Word Selection, choose the Options command from the Tools menu, deselect the Automatic Word Selection option on the Edit tab, and click OK.

If you have trouble dragging across the text without also selecting part of the line above or below, you're not alone. You may want to use this technique instead: Click anywhere in the first word you want to select, hold down the Shift key, and then click anywhere in the last word of the block you want to select. PowerPoint highlights the first word, the last word, and all of the text in between. This technique does not work if the Automatic Word Selection option is turned off.

> **TIP**   You can select text with the keyboard by moving the insertion point to the beginning of the text you want to select, holding down the Shift key, and then using the keys and key combinations listed earlier in Table 4-1 to move the insertion point to the end of the desired text block.

To practice selecting and editing text, try the following: Start a new presentation, and use the AutoContent Wizard to load the presentation called *Selling a Product, Service or Idea*. When the presentation appears, switch to Outline view and click an insertion point in the *Objective* topic. Press the End key to move the insertion point to the end of the line, and then type an *s* to change the title of the slide to *Objectives*. Next, click the bullet in front of *State the desired objective* to select the entire line, and then type *To make you happy* to replace the selected text.

Later in this chapter, you'll make further changes to the outline, so you might want to save the presentation now by choosing Save As from the File menu and entering a filename.

Moving and Copying Text

Want to take the easiest and most direct approach to moving or copying selected text to another position within the outline? Then drag-and-drop editing is for you.

To move text using drag and drop, follow these steps:

1. Select the text you want to move or copy.

2. Point to the selected text. The I-beam changes to a hollow arrow, as shown here:

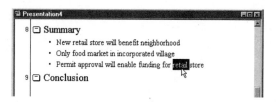

3. Hold down the mouse button, drag the pointer to the destination for the selected text, and release the mouse button. The text appears in its new location, as shown here:

To copy text using drag and drop, follow the same procedure, but hold down the Ctrl key while dragging the pointer. With drag and drop, you can drag text clear to another slide.

In addition to using the drag-and-drop techniques, you can move or copy selected text using the following methods:

■ To *move* selected text, start by clicking the Cut button on the Standard toolbar, choosing Cut from the Edit menu, or pressing Ctrl+X. Then move the insertion point to the destination for the text (even if it's on another slide), and click the Paste button on the Standard toolbar, choose Paste from the Edit menu, or press Ctrl+V.

■ To *copy* selected text, start by clicking the Copy button on the Standard toolbar, choosing Copy from the Edit menu, or pressing Ctrl+C. Then move the insertion point to the destination for the text, and click the Paste button, choose Paste from the Edit menu, or press Ctrl+V.

The Cut, Copy, and Paste commands are available on the text shortcut menu as well as on the Edit menu. To use a shortcut menu, select an object or text, and then click the right mouse button. A menu pops up with options that are relevant to the object or text.

For example, to use the shortcut menu to move or copy a text selection, follow these steps:

1. Select the text you want to move or copy.

2. Click the right mouse button. A shortcut menu appears, as shown below:

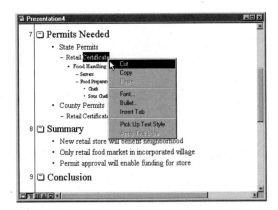

3. Choose Cut or Copy.

4. Move the insertion point to the destination for the text.

5. Click the right mouse button to open the shortcut menu again, and then choose Paste.

Zooming In and Out

While working in Outline view, you can use the Zoom Control box on the Standard toolbar, shown below, to change the magnification level, or zoom percentage, of your view of the outline. When you use a higher zoom percentage, the text becomes larger. Use a smaller zoom percentage to fit more text on the screen.

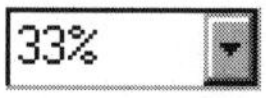

To change the zoom percentage, click the current percentage number in the Zoom Control box on the Standard toolbar, type a new zoom percentage, and press Enter. To select a preset magnification level, click the arrow to the right of the Zoom Control box, and then select one of the zoom percentages from the drop-down list.

You can also change the zoom percentage by first choosing Zoom from the View menu to display this Zoom dialog box:

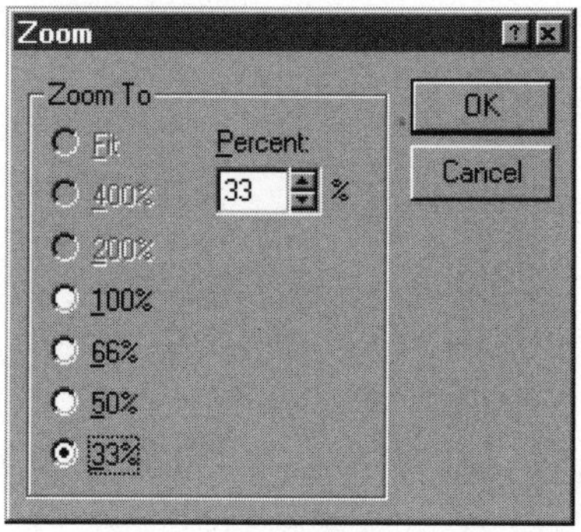

Then select one of the Zoom To percentages or edit the number in the Percent edit box. You can also click the arrows to the right of the Percent edit box to adjust the percentage up or down by one. Click OK to implement the new zoom percentage.

By default, Outline view uses a smaller zoom percentage than Slide view so that you can see more of your outline on the screen at one time. If you make Outline view's zoom percentage the same as Slide view's, the text size is identical in both views.

Deleting Text

To delete selected text, simply press the Delete key or the Backspace key. You can also delete selected text by clicking the Cut button on the Standard toolbar, choosing Cut or Clear from the Edit menu, or pressing Ctrl+X.

Undoing Editing

Retrieving something you've deleted is as simple as clicking the Undo button on the Standard toolbar, choosing Undo from the Edit menu, or pressing Ctrl+Z.

By repeatedly clicking the Undo button, you can undo up to your last 20 actions in PowerPoint. (If you want to increase—up to 150—or decrease this number, choose Options From the Tools menu, and change the Maximum Number of Undos setting on the Advanced tab of the Options dialog box.)

When you use the Undo button or command to reverse an action, the Repeat button on the Standard toolbar and the Repeat command on the Edit menu change to the Redo button and the Redo command, respectively. You can then quickly redo the last change you made in a presentation by clicking the Redo button or choosing the Redo command. For example, after applying bold format and then clicking the Undo button to remove the bold formatting, you can click the Redo button to reapply the bold formatting.

Repeating Actions

You can repeat many of the actions you take in PowerPoint—editing, formatting, or checking spelling, for example—by clicking the Repeat button on the Standard toolbar or by choosing the Repeat command from the Edit menu. The name of the command changes, depending on your last action—for example, Repeat Typing or Repeat Bold. If you cannot repeat your last action, the Repeat command changes to Can't Repeat.

Finding and Replacing Text

While editing an outline, you can search for a word or a string of characters and replace it with another. For example, you can use the Find command to find a former client's name in a presentation, and then use the Replace command to replace that name with a new client's name throughout the presentation.

To search for specific text, follow these steps:

1. Choose Find from the Edit menu or press Ctrl+F. PowerPoint displays the Find dialog box shown here:

2. Enter the text you want to find in the Find What edit box.

3. Then click Find Next or press Enter.

To have PowerPoint find only those words or strings of characters that match the capitalization entered in the Find What edit box, select the Match Case option. (Then PowerPoint will not find *Man* when you enter *man.*) To have PowerPoint find the text you've entered only when it is a whole word rather than part of a word, select the Find Whole Words Only option. (Then PowerPoint will not find *constitutional* when you enter *constitution.*)

To replace text, follow these steps:

1. Choose Replace from the Edit menu or press Ctrl+H. (Or, if the Find dialog box is open, you can click the Replace button.) PowerPoint displays the Replace dialog box shown here:

2. Enter the text you want to replace in the Find What edit box.

3. Enter the replacement text in the Replace With edit box.

4. Click the Find Next button.

5. After PowerPoint locates the Find What text, click the Replace button to substitute the Replace With text.

To replace every occurrence of the Find What text throughout the presentation, click the Replace All button instead of the Find Next button and the Replace button. You may want to use the Match Case option and the Find Whole Words Only option to be sure you do not inadvertently replace text that does not exactly match the Find What text.

PowerPoint keeps a log of the text you have searched for or used as a replacement. To perform the same search or replace again, open the Find dialog box or the Replace dialog box, click the down arrow next to the Find What edit box or Replace With edit box, and then select a previous entry from the drop-down list.

Checking the Spelling of Presentation Text

Before your presentation goes public, take a moment to use PowerPoint's very capable spelling checker. Nothing looms larger than a silly little typo when it is projected full-screen.

To spell-check a presentation, follow these steps:

1. Click the Spelling button on the Standard toolbar, choose Spelling from the Tools menu, or press F7. PowerPoint checks each word against two dictionaries: the main dictionary and a supplemental dictionary called CUSTOM.DIC, which is empty until you add words to it. When PowerPoint finds a word it considers misspelled, it displays the Spelling dialog box shown here:

The questionable word is displayed in the Not in Dictionary edit box. The first and most strongly suggested replacement is highlighted in the Suggestions list and appears in the Change To edit box.

2. Indicate what you want PowerPoint to do next:

    ❏ If you know that the word is spelled correctly—if the word is a company name, for example—click the Ignore button.

    ❏ If the word is spelled correctly and occurs frequently in this presentation, you may want to click Ignore All instead of Ignore.

    ❏ If the word is spelled correctly and occurs frequently in other presentations, you can click Add to add the word to a custom dictionary. In future spelling checks, the word will not be flagged as a misspelling.

    ❏ If the word is misspelled and you want to change it to the word in the Change To edit box, click Change.

    ❏ If the word is misspelled and you want to make the same change throughout the presentation, click Change All instead.

Using Custom Dictionaries

When you click the Add button to add a word to a custom dictionary, the word is added to the dictionary file listed in the Add Words To box in the Spelling dialog box. The default custom dictionary is CUSTOM.DIC, the same custom dictionary file used by Microsoft Word and other Microsoft Office applications. If you have created custom dictionaries in another Microsoft Office application, you can select one of those dictionaries from the Add Words To drop-down list. If you enter words in a custom dictionary while working in another Microsoft Office application, those words won't be flagged as incorrect in PowerPoint either.

---

3. When PowerPoint completes the spelling check of the presentation, it informs you with an on-screen message. Click OK to remove the message and return to your outline.

    WARNING PowerPoint cannot check the spelling of text in graphs, organization charts, and tables. It also cannot check the spelling of text in objects created in other applications that are embedded in PowerPoint.

Using AutoCorrect

If you frequently transpose the same letters in the same words while typing, you can use the AutoCorrect feature to recognize and then correct your mistakes. For example, if you type *captial* instead of *capital,* AutoCorrect can change the incorrect spelling to the correct one. In addition, you can use AutoCorrect to change two consecutive capital letters to one and to capitalize the names of the days of the week. Best of all, PowerPoint's AutoCorrect feature already contains a large list of commonly misspelled words (such as *teh*), which are corrected the instant you press the Spacebar or type punctuation.

To add a word to the AutoCorrect list, follow these steps:

1. Choose AutoCorrect from the Tools menu. The AutoCorrect dialog box appears as shown below:

AutoCorrect		? X
☑ Correct TWo INitial CApitals		OK
☑ Capitalize Names of Days		Cancel
☑ Replace Text as You Type		
Replace:	With:	
(c)	©	Add
(r)	®	
(tm)	™	Delete
...	...	
accesories	accessories	
accomodate	accommodate	
acheive	achieve	

2. Be sure the Replace Text as You Type option is selected to enable PowerPoint to automatically correct your misspelling.

3. Enter the misspelled word in the Replace edit box, enter the correctly spelled word in the With edit box, and then click OK.

The next time you type the word incorrectly, PowerPoint will correct the misspelling as soon as you press the Spacebar or type punctuation. If you want to add more than one word to the list in the AutoCorrect dialog box, click the Add button after you complete the Replace and With edit boxes for each entry. If you want to delete a word in the AutoCorrect list, select the word and then click Delete.

If the presentation you are creating is strictly text, as most presentations are, and you do not need to reorganize the text, your basic presentation is now complete. You can skip ahead to Chapter 9 and beyond. But if you want to format your slides or add graphs, organization charts, or tables to your presentation, take a close look at the next four chapters.

Reorganizing Text in Outline View

The power of Outline view becomes obvious as soon as you need to reorganize the text of a presentation. You can change the order of the topics covered in the presentation, change the order of bulleted items under individual topics, and even move bulleted items from one topic to another. You can also delete topics, duplicate topics, and insert new topics.

Selecting Topics and Bulleted Items

Before you can reorganize a presentation, you must select the element you want to work with. You can select an entire topic (the topic text and its bulleted items), several topics, or one or more bulleted items within a topic.

To select an entire topic, you can use any of the following methods:

- Click the slide number or click the space to the left of the slide number.

- Click the slide icon to the left of the topic.

- Triple-click the topic text.

- Click the topic text, and press Ctrl+Shift+Down arrow key.

Whichever method you use, the result is similar to that shown below in Figure 4-10.

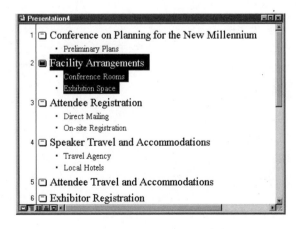

FIGURE 4-10
A selected topic.

To select multiple slides, you can use one of these methods:

- Hold down the Shift key while clicking each slide's icon.

- If the slides are consecutive, point to the left of the title on the first slide, hold down the mouse button, and drag downward in the space to the left of the slides you want to select.

To select a bulleted item, as shown in Figure 4-11, do one of the following:

- Click in the space to the left of the text but to the right of the vertical line that separates the slide number and the slide icon. This method selects the bulleted item and any items indented below it.

- Triple-click a word in the bulleted item to select the entire bulleted item. Any items indented below it are also selected.

- Drag through the text of the bulleted item with the mouse.

- Click the first word of the bulleted item, hold down the Shift key, and then click the last word.

- Position the insertion point at the beginning of the bulleted item, hold down the Shift key, and press the End key to move the insertion point to the end of the bulleted item.

FIGURE 4-11
A selected
bulleted item.

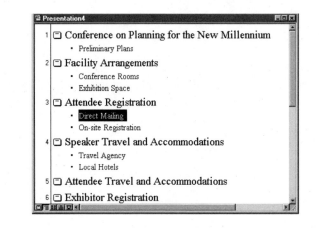

Reordering Topics and Bulleted Items

After you select a topic or a bulleted item, you can move it up or down in the outline to solidify the logic of your presentation. For example, you can move a touchy topic to the front of a presentation to get it over with early. Then move some good news to the end so that your audience can leave on a high.

To move an entire topic, follow these steps:

1. Point to the slide icon for the selected topic.

2. Hold down the mouse button, and drag up or down. When you drag, the pointer becomes a double-headed arrow, and a horizontal line indicates where the topic will drop when you release the mouse button.

3. Release the mouse button. The topic and its bulleted items move to the new position.

For example, Figure 4-12 shows the result after the Attendee Registration topic was moved down in the New Millennium Conference presentation.

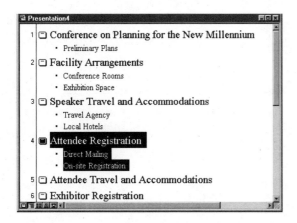

FIGURE 4-12

Dragging a selected topic's slide icon moves the topic within the presentation.

You can also move the selected topic up or down by clicking the Move Up or Move Down button on the Outlining toolbar at the left side of the presentation window. In fact, if you've selected multiple topics, you *must* use the Move Up or Move Down button to move them.

You can change the order of entire topics just as easily in Slide Sorter view. But what makes Outline view special is that you can reorder bulleted items under a topic and move them from topic to topic, as well as reorder entire topics. To move a bulleted item up or down, follow these steps:

1. Select the bulleted item.

2. Click the Move Up button or the Move Down button until the bulleted item is positioned where you want it. Alternatively, point to the left of the bulleted item, hold down the mouse button, and drag up or down in the outline. Release the mouse button when the bulleted item is in the correct position.

Using either the mouse or the button technique, you can move the selected bulleted item all the way to another topic if you want. Working this way in Outline view saves you from having to cut and paste text from one slide to another in Slide view.

TIP   If you want to use the keyboard to organize an outline, you can press Alt+Shift+Up arrow to move selected text up and Alt+Shift+Down arrow to move selected text down. (These are the same key combinations used to reorganize outlines in Microsoft Word.)

Now try reorganizing the outline you've started. Load the presentation you created earlier in this chapter, and click the slide icon for slide 2. All the text related to the *Objectives* topic is now selected. Point to the slide icon, hold down the mouse button, and drag down to just below the last text item on slide 3. As you drag, a horizontal line shows where the text will drop. Release the mouse button. *Objectives* becomes slide 3, and *Customer Requirements* becomes slide 2.

Now try moving a bulleted text item from one topic to another. Click the bullet at the beginning of *This section may require multiple slides,* on slide 4. Drag the bullet up and drop it under *Customer Requirements* on slide 2. Be sure to save the presentation again because you'll have the opportunity to make further changes later in this chapter.

Promoting and Demoting Topics and Bulleted Items

Earlier in the chapter, you learned that *promoting* text moves it one level to the left and *demoting* text moves it one level to the right. If you need to split a topic into two slides, you can promote one of the bulleted items to the main topic level to start a new slide. When an existing topic should be a supporting statement for the previous topic, you can demote it to a bulleted item.

To promote a bulleted item, select it and then do one of the following:

- Click the Promote button.

- Click just to the left of the item, hold down the mouse button, and drag to the left.

- Press Shift+Tab or Alt+Shift+Left arrow.

Figure 4-13 shows the result after the second bulleted item under *Facility Arrangements* in the New Millennium Conference presentation is promoted to a topic. As you can see, a new slide number and slide icon appear to the left of the promoted text, which becomes the title of a new slide in Slide view.

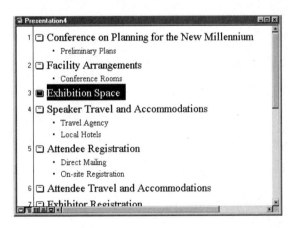

FIGURE 4-13

Promoting a bulleted item creates a new topic on a new slide.

To demote a topic or a bulleted item, select it and do one of the following:

- Click the Demote button.

- Click to the left of the selected text, hold down the mouse button, and drag to the right.

- Press Tab or Alt+Shift+Right arrow.

All of the promotion and demotion techniques discussed so far promote or demote not only the selected text but also bulleted items below the selected text. What if you want to promote or demote a line but leave any subpoints at their current levels? You can click once anywhere in a topic or bulleted item, and then press the Tab key to demote the line, or press Shift+Tab to promote the line without affecting any subordinate text.

Be aware when you are organizing topics and bulleted items that you can fit only a certain amount of text on any one slide. For example, in the presentation on the left in Figure 4-14, the list of bulleted items under the topic *What I Love About New York* is far too long. To get all these points across, move the insertion point to the end of *The action,* and press Enter to start a new bulleted item. Then type *What I Love to Do in New York* as a new bulleted item. Finally, drag the bullet in front of the new bulleted item one level to the left so that the bulleted item becomes a new main topic. The outline then looks as shown on the right in Figure 4-14.

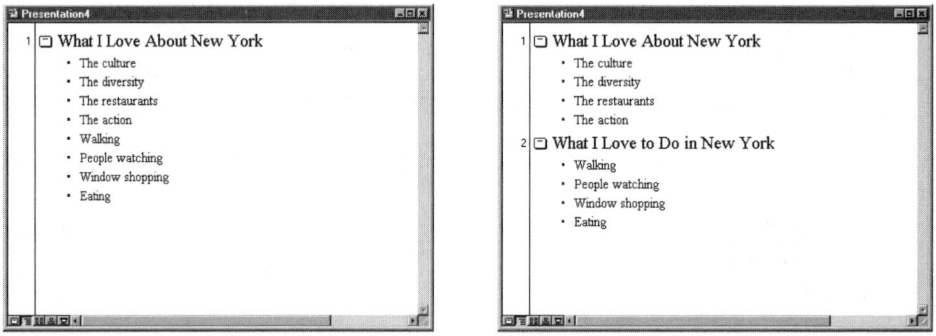

FIGURE 4-14

A long list of bulleted items (left) divided between two slides for greater impact (right).

Hiding and Revealing Detail

Sometimes you need to step back to see the big picture while working on a presentation outline. If the entire outline is displayed, the volume of detail can muddle the big themes. By *collapsing* bulleted items, you can temporarily hide them from view and show only the larger topics. To redisplay the bulleted items, you *expand* them. You can collapse and expand outlines using the Collapse Selection button and the Expand Selection button on the Outlining toolbar.

To collapse bulleted items under a topic, follow these steps:

1. Click anywhere in the topic or click the slide icon that is to the left of the topic.

2. Click the Collapse Selection button or press Alt+Shift+Minus. Power-Point draws a gray line under the topic to indicate the presence of collapsed bulleted items, as shown here:

TIP   When you collapse bulleted items under a topic, they remain an intrinsic part of the topic. If you move that topic, the collapsed bulleted items also move. In fact, you may find it easier to reorganize a presentation with many bulleted items if you collapse them under their topics and then reorder the topics.

To expand the collapsed bulleted items, follow these steps:

1. Click anywhere in the topic.

2. Click the Expand Selection button or press Alt+Shift+Plus.

To quickly collapse all bulleted items under their topics, click the Show Titles button or press Alt+Shift+1. Then to expand all of the items again, click the Show All button or press Alt+Shift+A.

Try hiding detail in this chapter's sample presentation. With the presentation displayed on your screen in Outline view, click the Show Titles button on the Outlining toolbar to show only the main topics. Drag topic 2, *Customer*

Requirements, to just after topic 3, *Objectives.* Then click the Expand Selection button on the Outlining toolbar to see that the collapsed bulleted items have come along for the ride. Finally, click the Show All button on the Outlining toolbar to redisplay all the presentation text.

You may want to save the sample presentation you've made for posterity, but you'll be making no further changes to it in this chapter.

Formatting Text in Outline View

Slide view is usually the best place to format the text of a presentation because you can see how the text fits with the background design. However, while entering and editing the presentation in Outline view, you can format any words or characters that are sure to need it. For example, you can italicize a special term or change a character in a formula name to superscript.

To format text in Outline view, you must first select it. Then you can use the character formatting buttons on the Formatting toolbar or the character formatting commands on either the Format menu or the shortcut menu. For example, choosing the Font command from the Format menu or the shortcut menu displays the Font dialog box shown in Figure 4-15. The character formatting buttons and commands work the same way in both Outline view and Slide view.

FIGURE 4-15
The Font dialog box.

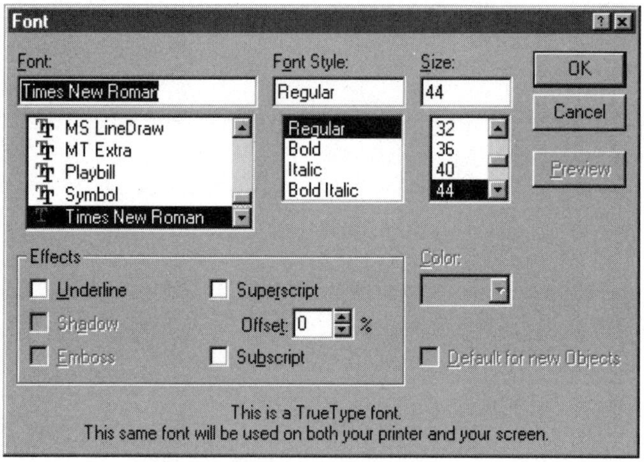

NOTE The Shadow option and the Emboss option in the Font dialog box are not available in Outline view. These effects can only be applied in Slide view.

Whether you apply character formatting in Outline view or in Slide view, you can display the outline in Outline view without character formatting. Just click the Show Formatting button on the Outlining toolbar or press the slash key above the numeric keypad on your keyboard. The Font Face box and the Font Size box on the Formatting toolbar still show accurate information about the selected text, but the entire outline is displayed in a standard font and size (Arial, 28 points). To redisplay the character formatting in Outline view, click the Show Formatting button or press the slash key again.

See Also For more information about selecting text, see "Selecting Text for Editing," page 67.

For more information about formatting text, see "Formatting Text in Slide View," page 102.

Importing Outlines

If you have already created a perfectly good outline in another application, it would be tedious to have to recreate it in PowerPoint. And you don't have to. You can import the outline as a starting point for your presentation.

Importing an Outline from Microsoft Word

You can generate a presentation outline in Microsoft Word and then easily export the outline to PowerPoint. Developing the outline in Word lets you take advantage of Word's sophisticated text capabilities. For example, you can use the thesaurus to replace ordinary outline words with vibrant, vigorous, pulsating, dynamic, energetic words.

Because PowerPoint imports Word outlines so easily, anyone can generate an entire text presentation in Word and hand the file over to you. You can then import the outline, give the presentation a distinctive look, and generate slides in no time.

To import a Word outline:

1. Open the outline in Word.

2. Click the Present It button. (If you don't see the Present It button, you must install it on the Standard toolbar by following the procedure described in the next section.) Word opens PowerPoint if necessary, opens a new presentation in Outline view, and exports the outline to PowerPoint.

For example, Figure 4-16 shows an outline in Word. Figure 4-17 shows the same outline after it has been imported into PowerPoint.

FIGURE 4-16

An outline in
Microsoft Word.

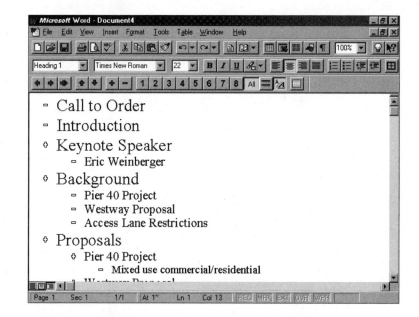

FIGURE 4-17

The Word outline in
PowerPoint.

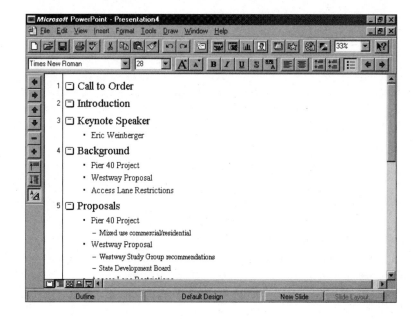

> **TIP** A super-slick method you can use to create a new PowerPoint presentation from a Word outline is to drag and drop the Word outline file from Windows Explorer to the PowerPoint window. A new presentation opens in PowerPoint with the Word outline in place.

NOTE Imported outlines can have up to nine indent levels. However, when you import an outline into PowerPoint, levels beyond level five are converted to fifth-level entries.

Installing the Present It Button in Word

The Present It button does not appear on a Word toolbar until you put it there. The fairly long installation procedure involves copying the PresentIt macro from a template called *Present7* and then adding a button to Word's Standard toolbar. To make the Present It button available whenever you are working in Word, you copy the macro to the Normal template.

To copy the macro to the Normal template, you must first open the Present7 template. Follow these steps:

1. Start Word.

2. From the File menu, choose the Open command, and in the Open dialog box, select Document Templates from the Files of type drop-down list.

3. Locate the Winword folder in the MSOffice folder on your hard drive. Then double-click the Winword folder to open it.

4. In the list box, double-click the Macros folder, and then double-click Present7.

Next, copy the PresentIt macro from Present7 to Normal by following these steps:

1. From the Tools menu, choose Macro.

2. In the Macro dialog box, click the Organizer button.

3. On the Macros tab of the Organizer dialog box, select PresentIt from the In Present7 list.

4. Click the Copy button, and then click the Close button.

5. From the File menu, choose Close to close the Present7 template.

Now you must open the Normal template, and then create a Present It button on Word's Standard toolbar. Follow these steps:

1. From the File menu, choose Open, and in the Open dialog box, select Document Templates from the Files of type drop-down list.

2. Locate the Templates folder in the MSOffice folder on your hard drive. Double-click the Templates folder, and then double-click Normal.

3. From the View menu, choose Toolbars, and then click the Customize button in the Toolbars dialog box.

4. Be sure the Toolbars tab of the Customize dialog box is displayed, and then select Macros from the Categories list.

5. Hold down the Alt key, and drag the PresentIt macro to any location on the Standard toolbar. A blank button appears on the toolbar, and the Custom Button dialog box is displayed.

6. Select a button from the Button section of the Custom Button dialog box to represent the macro, and then click Assign. Click Close to close the Customize dialog box.

Importing an Outline from Another Application

You can import an outline from just about any word processing program as well as from other presentation applications that can export their presentation outlines. If the application can generate an RTF (Rich Text Format) file, you should use that format when saving the outline to disk. When you import the file, PowerPoint uses the styles in the file to determine the outline structure. For example, a Heading 1 style becomes a slide title, a Heading 2 style becomes an indented bulleted item, and so on. If the file contains no styles, PowerPoint uses the paragraph indents to determine the outline structure.

If the application cannot generate an RTF file, you should generate a plain ASCII text file. PowerPoint then picks up the outline structure from the tabs at the beginning of paragraphs. A paragraph preceded by no tabs becomes a slide title, a paragraph preceded by one tab becomes an indented bulleted item, and so on.

To import an outline file, follow these steps:

1. Click the Open button on the Standard toolbar or choose Open from the File menu.

2. In the File Open dialog box, select All Outlines from the Files of type drop-down list.

3. Navigate through the folders list, select the file you want to import, and then click Open. PowerPoint opens the file and displays it as a PowerPoint outline.

Inserting an Outline in an Existing Presentation

As a starting point for a presentation, in addition to importing an outline created in an application such as Word you can also insert an outline file created with another application into an existing PowerPoint presentation.

To supplement a PowerPoint outline with an imported outline, follow these steps:

1. In Outline view, click the topic after which you want the imported outline to appear.

2. Choose Slides from Outline from the Insert menu. PowerPoint displays the dialog box shown here:

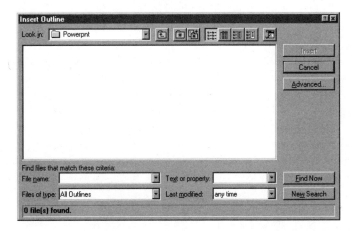

3. In the Insert Outline dialog box, navigate through the folders and filenames, select the outline file you want to insert, and then click Insert. PowerPoint inserts the imported outline in the current outline, assigning numbers, slide icons, and indent levels to create a seamless presentation. If you import an outline with more than five levels, PowerPoint converts all levels beyond five to fifth-level entries.

NOTE You can also import an outline in Slide view. First move to
the slide after which you want the outline to appear, and then
follow steps 2 and 3 above. PowerPoint imports the outline into the
presentation as slides.

After you import an outline from another application as a new presentation or insert an imported outline in an existing PowerPoint presentation, you
can manipulate it just like an outline created from scratch in Outline view.

In this chapter, you learned how to develop and modify a presentation
outline in Outline view—the best place for concentrating on the text and the
flow of ideas. In the next chapter, you'll learn how to create the text for a
presentation in Slide view, where you can see the design of each slide, but
you cannot easily see the progression of the presentation from one slide to
the next.

Chapter 5

Working with Text in Slide View

reating and organizing a presentation in Outline view may be the best way to focus on the text of your presentation, but you may prefer to create the slides of your presentation one by one in Slide view—especially if you know what you want to say and how you want to say it. In Slide view, you can devote your creative energy to crafting a single slide at a time. Slide view may also be the best place to start when your job is not to conceive a presentation but to produce slides for someone else from hand-written notes and napkin sketches. Figure 5-1 below shows a completed slide as it appears in Slide view.

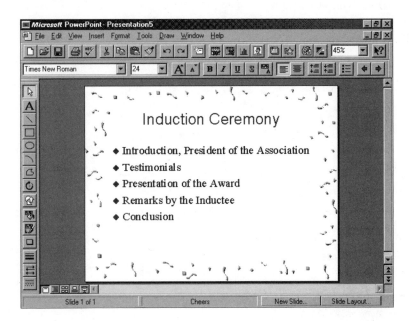

FIGURE 5-1

A slide in
Slide view.

In this chapter, you'll learn how to create text slides in Slide view. By the time you finish, you'll be just as far along as if you'd entered the presentation text in Outline view and then switched to Slide view. The task still remaining is to drop in the graphs, tables, and drawings you want to include in the presentation. You'll learn how to do this in the next several chapters.

Creating a New Presentation in Slide View

After you start a new presentation by using the AutoContent Wizard, you are dropped off in Slide view with a sample title slide displayed on your screen. When you start a new presentation by clicking the New button on the Standard toolbar or by selecting the Blank Presentation option in the PowerPoint dialog box or the New Presentation dialog box, PowerPoint displays the New Slide dialog box. The first autolayout in the first row, called the Title Slide autolayout, is selected by default, so you can simply click OK to move to Slide view with a blank title slide displayed. If PowerPoint is correct in assuming that you plan to create a complete presentation, you should fill out this title slide.

> **NOTE** If you're using PowerPoint to create a single slide, you may want to use a slide layout other than the Title Slide layout. To work with a graph chart layout or organization chart layout, for example, click the Slide Layout button in the lower right corner of the PowerPoint window, and select a different slide layout in the Slide Layout dialog box. (For more information about selecting a slide layout, see "Adding a New Slide," page 97.)

If you need to switch to Slide view from another view, click the Slide View button in the lower left corner of the presentation window or choose Slides from the View menu.

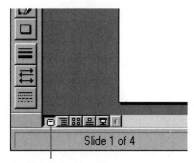

Slide 1 of 4

Slide View

Creating the Title Slide

As shown in Figure 5-2, the Title Slide layout displays two text *placeholders*—dashed boxes that show the location for an object on a slide. All placeholders contain a prompt that tells you to click (or double-click) to add text, a graph, or another presentation element. In this case, you're prompted for a title and a subtitle for the new presentation.

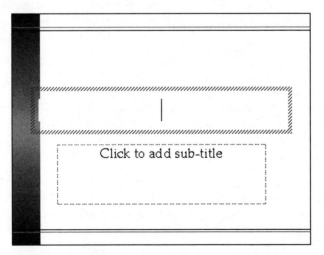

FIGURE 5-2

The Title Slide layout that appears when you create a new presentation based on the Black template.

To enter a presentation title in the Title Slide layout, follow these steps:

1. Click the *Click to add title* placeholder. The dashed box disappears, a gray bar surrounds the placeholder frame, and the insertion point appears within the frame, as shown below.

NOTE When you add a new slide, you can start typing without clicking the *Click to add title* placeholder. The first text you type is automatically entered in the placeholder.

2. Type the presentation title.

3. If you want to enter a subtitle, click the *Click to add sub-title* place-holder, and type the subtitle.

4. Click anywhere outside the placeholder frame to see a completed slide, like the one shown below.

NOTE The formatting of the text (its font, size, color, and so on) is determined by the formatting of the text on the title master and slide master. To change the appearance of the text on any single slide, you can apply your own formatting, which overrides the title master's and slide master's formatting. (For more information, see "Formatting Text in Slide View," page 102.) To change the appearance of the text on all the slides of a presentation, you must change the formatting of the title master or slide master. (For more information, see "Editing the Title Master or Slide Master," page 226.)

If you want to try creating the sample title slide shown in Figure 5-3, start a new presentation by choosing New from the File menu. In the New Presentation dialog box, click the Presentation Designs tab, and then double-click the Side Bar template. When the New Slide dialog box appears, select the Title Slide autolayout, and click OK. Then click the *Click to add title* placeholder, and type *Person to Person.* Click the *Click to add sub-title* placeholder or press Ctrl+Enter, and type *Our New Care-Giving Partnership.* Finally, click anywhere outside the subtitle frame to see the completed title slide.

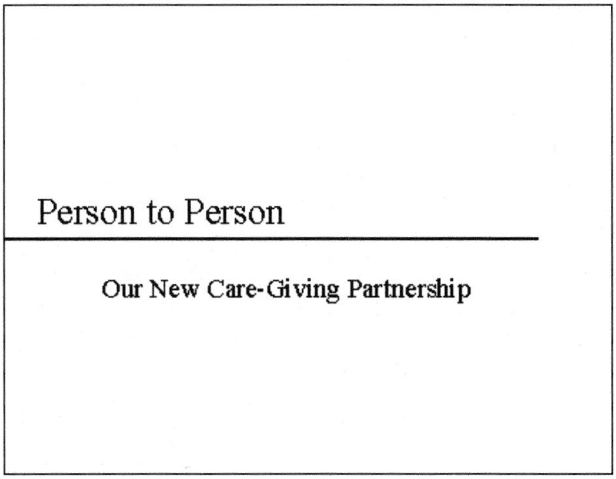

Person to Person

Our New Care-Giving Partnership

FIGURE 5-3
A sample title slide.

TIP   After typing text in a placeholder, you can press Ctrl+Enter to move to the next placeholder. If the current slide has no more placeholders, PowerPoint creates a new slide and puts the insertion point in the *Click to add title* placeholder on that slide.

Adding a New Slide

After completing the title slide, you are ready to add the next slide. Before you add a slide, however, you must select an autolayout from the New Slide dialog box. Like the Title Slide autolayout, PowerPoint's other autolayouts also contain placeholders. For example, the Bulleted List autolayout has a *Click to add title* placeholder and a *Click to add text* placeholder; the Graph autolayout has a *Click to add title* placeholder and a *Double click to add graph* placeholder; and so on. PowerPoint offers 24 autolayouts that should meet nearly all your presentation needs.

To add a new slide to your presentation, follow these steps:

1. Click the New Slide button at the bottom of the PowerPoint window. The New Slide dialog box appears, as shown here:

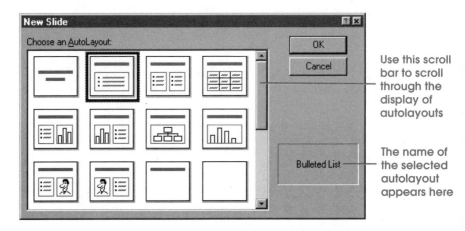

Use this scroll bar to scroll through the display of autolayouts

The name of the selected autolayout appears here

2. Scroll through the display of autolayouts using the scroll bar. To see the name of an autolayout, click the autolayout once to display its name in the box in the lower right corner.

3. When you've decided which autolayout you want, either double-click it or click it once and then click OK. A new slide with the selected autolayout appears on the screen.

The rest of this chapter focuses on entering text in text slides. When you finish one slide, you can repeat the previous steps to create the next one. If you need to look at a slide you've already completed, you can move back to the slide by pressing the PgUp key. Press the PgDn key to move forward through your slides. You can also move from one slide to another by dragging the scroll box in the vertical scroll bar up or down.

Entering Text in a Bulleted List AutoLayout

If you add a new slide with a layout that has bulleted text, such as the Bulleted List autolayout or the 2 Column Text autolayout, a *Click to add title* placeholder appears on the new slide along with one or more *Click to add text* placeholders. Figure 5-4 shows a Bulleted List layout as it appears on a new slide.

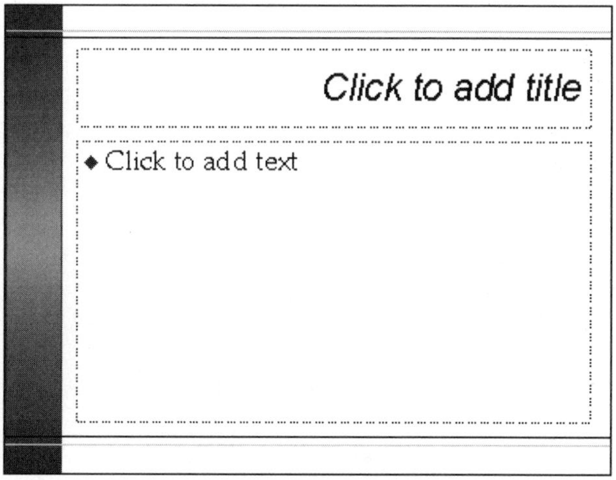

FIGURE 5-4

The Bulleted List autolayout on a new slide.

To complete a slide with bulleted items, follow these steps:

1. Type a slide title. (You don't have to click the *Click to add title* placeholder first.)

2. Click the *Click to add text* placeholder or press Ctrl+Enter.

3. Type the first bulleted item, press Enter, type the next item, and so forth.

4. After typing the last bulleted item, click outside the placeholder frame to see the completed slide.

   NOTE If you want text without bullets (for a paragraph that is a quote, for example), never fear. You can turn off the bullets at any time. For more information about turning off bullets, see "Adding and Removing Bullets," page 110.

As an example, try adding the bulleted slide shown in Figure 5-5 to the slide you created earlier using the Side Bar template. Click the New Slide button, and then double-click the Bulleted List autolayout—the second layout in the first row. Type *Activities* in the title placeholder frame. Then click the *Click to add text* placeholder or press Ctrl+Enter, type *Home visits*, and press Enter. Type *Hospital bedside visits,* and press Enter. Finally, type *County Community Center work*, and click outside the placeholder frame.

FIGURE 5-5

A sample slide with bulleted items.

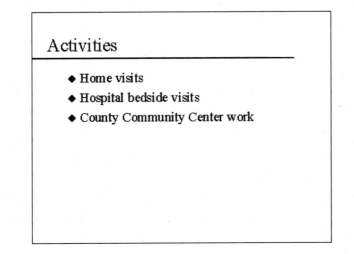

> ## Activities
>
> ◆ Home visits
> ◆ Hospital bedside visits
> ◆ County Community Center work

As in Outline view, you can create up to five levels of bulleted items in Slide view, using the same buttons and keystrokes that you use in Outline view. The Demote and Promote buttons are available on the Formatting toolbar, and you can also press Alt+Shift+Right arrow to demote an item and Alt+Shift+Left arrow to promote it.

Editing Text in Slide View

While creating presentation text in Slide view, you can use all the text editing techniques available in Outline view. In fact, everything you type flows through to the presentation outline; you see the presentation as an outline if you switch to Outline view.

To edit text directly on a slide in Slide view, first position the insertion point in the spot you want to edit. The keyboard methods of moving the insertion point in Slide view are nearly the same as those used in Outline view. The notable exceptions: Pressing Ctrl+Up arrow or Ctrl+Down arrow moves the insertion point to the previous or next paragraph, respectively, rather than to the previous or next topic; and pressing Ctrl+Home or Ctrl+End moves the insertion point to the beginning or end of the current *text object* (all the text in a single placeholder) rather than to the beginning or end of the entire outline.

After clicking an insertion point or positioning the insertion point with the keyboard, you can type to insert text, press the Backspace key to delete characters to the left of the insertion point, or press Delete to delete characters to the right of the insertion point. As in Outline view, you can make larger edits most efficiently by first selecting the text you want to edit.

Selecting text with the mouse is the same as it is in Outline view: Position the insertion point at the beginning of the text, hold down the left mouse button, and drag to the end of the text. (Automatic Word Selection is active in Slide view, so when you drag across any part of a word, the entire word is selected.) Selecting text with the keyboard is also the same: Move the insertion point to the beginning of the text, hold down the Shift key, and then use the appropriate keys to move the insertion point to the end of the text. To select all the text in one bulleted item, click the bullet. Any text indented under that bulleted item is also selected, as shown on the left side of Figure 5-6.

To select an entire text object, click anywhere in the object, and choose Select All from the Edit menu or press Ctrl+A. PowerPoint highlights all the text in the current placeholder, as shown on the right side of Figure 5-6. (By the way, the slide on the right has the 2 Column Text autolayout.)

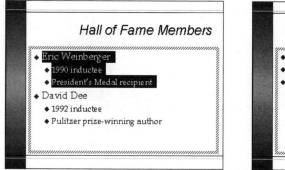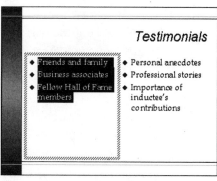

FIGURE 5-6
A selected bulleted item (left) and a selected text object (right).

After you select text on a slide, you can delete, move, or copy it using the same buttons, commands, and key combinations you use in Outline view. You can also use drag-and-drop editing to move text within one placeholder or to move text from one placeholder to another.

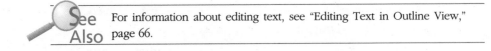

See Also   For information about editing text, see "Editing Text in Outline View," page 66.

Reorganizing Text in Slide View

Reorganizing bulleted items is not as easy in Slide view as it is in Outline view, but it's not that difficult, either. Because the Outlining toolbar, with its Move Up and Move Down buttons, is not present, you must select bulleted items and then press Alt+Shift+Up arrow or Alt+Shift+Down arrow to move them.

See Also   For more information about reorganizing text, see "Reorganizing Text in Outline View," page 77.

Formatting Text in Slide View

The appearance of the text on all text slides is determined by the slide master for that particular presentation. By editing the slide master, you can change the formatting of text throughout the presentation. You can also override the slide master's control of the text on any individual slide by applying your own formatting. This section discusses formatting that you apply to individual slides.

Many of PowerPoint's text formatting options are available as buttons on the Formatting toolbar or as key combinations. Others are available only as menu commands. You'll soon get a feel for the quickest way to apply specific types of formatting.

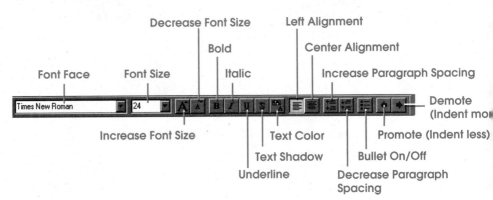

See Also For more information about changing the slide master, see "Editing the Title Master or Slide Master," page 226.

Selecting Text for Formatting

You can apply two types of formatting to the text on your slides: character formatting that affects individual characters, and a broader type of formatting that affects an entire text object. Selecting text for character formatting is just like selecting text for editing. You drag across characters to select them, and then make your formatting changes.

You can also drag to select entire text objects, but you might want to take advantage of a special technique to select all the text in the object containing the insertion point. Either press Ctrl+A to highlight all the text within the object, as shown on the left side of Figure 5-7, or press F2 to select the text object itself, as shown on the right side of Figure 5-7. When you press F2 to select a text object, the object is surrounded by handles. Press F2 again to select the text within the object. After you select a text object, you can press Tab to select the next text object on the slide either before or after you make formatting changes. (You can select the previous text object by pressing Shift+Tab.)

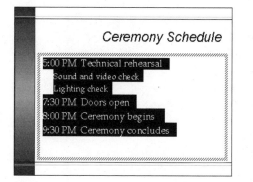
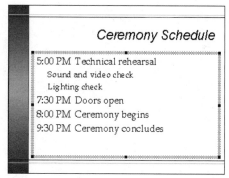

FIGURE 5-7
Selected text within a text object (left) and a selected text object (right).

> **TIP** Instead of pressing F2 to select the object, you can click the fuzzy gray border that surrounds the text object.

Changing the Font, Font Style, Size, Color, and Font Effects

You can emphasize individual characters, words, or phrases by changing their font, font style, size, or color. You can even apply special font effects, such as shadows or embossing, to selected text. All of these options are available in the Font dialog box.

To make formatting changes using the Font dialog box:

1. Select the text you want to format. You can select an individual character, you can place the insertion point in a word to format the entire word, or you can select several words or sentences.

2. Choose Font from the Format menu, or click the right mouse button and choose Font from the shortcut menu to display the Font dialog box shown below:

3. Select a Font, Font Style, and Size from the lists in the Font dialog box. The Font list includes the fonts installed on your Windows 95 system. The sizes are measured in points (with 72 points comprising 1 inch).

4. Select any combination of Effects options by clicking the appropriate check boxes. If you turn on Superscript or Subscript, you can change the percentage by which the text is set above or below the line by increasing or decreasing the Offset setting.

5. To change the color of the selected text, first click the down arrow next to the Color box. Then click one of the eight colors available for the current color scheme, or click Other Color to select from the full palette of available colors.

6. Click the Preview button if you want to see the changes you've made. (If necessary, drag the title bar of the Font dialog box to move the box out of the way.)

7. Click OK to implement the changes.

TIP Limiting the number of fonts on a slide is as important as limiting the number of fonts in a document. Try to stick to two fonts. Also, remember to use a light text color against a dark background and vice versa for legibility.

Try formatting some text on the bulleted slide you created earlier in this chapter. Select *County Community Center work*, click the right mouse button, and choose Font from the shortcut menu to display the Font dialog box. Then select Bold Italic as the Font Style option, and click OK.

The choices you make for the selected text in the Font dialog box are cumulative. You might make certain changes during one pass, such as changing the font and font style, and then come back later and make more changes, such as changing the color. When you select already formatted text and return to the Font dialog box, all the changes you've made to the formatting up to that point are reflected in the dialog box's settings.

After you select the text you want to format, you can also change the font and font size by using the Font Face and Font Size drop-down lists on the Formatting toolbar. The Increase Font Size or Decrease Font Size button increases or decreases the font size by specific increments. The increments become larger as the font size increases. The largest theoretical font size is 4000 points, but you will probably run out of paper long before you can print a character that large.

You can apply the bold or italic font styles by clicking the Bold button or the Italic button on the Formatting toolbar, and you can apply the underline or shadow effects by clicking the Underline button or the Text Shadow button. Clicking the Text Color button drops down a palette of the eight colors available with the current color scheme. Most text formatting options are available as keyboard shortcuts, too. Rather than using menus or the Formatting toolbar, you can select the text and then use one of the keyboard shortcuts listed in Table 5-1 on the next page.

TABLE 5-1

Text formatting
keyboard shortcuts.

Text Formatting	Keyboard Shortcut
Change font	Ctrl+Shift+F
Change font size	Ctrl+Shift+P
Increase font size	Ctrl+Shift+>
Decrease font size	Ctrl+Shift+<
Bold	Ctrl+B or Ctrl+Shift+B
Underline	Ctrl+U or Ctrl+Shift+U
Italic	Ctrl+I or Ctrl+Shift+I
Subscript	Ctrl+=
Superscript	Ctrl+Shift+=
Plain text	Ctrl+Shift+Z
Restore default formatting	Ctrl+Spacebar

TIP You can replace all instances of a certain font with another font—for example, replacing Times New Roman with Arial—by using the Replace Fonts command on the Tools menu. In the Replace box, select the font you want to replace and then in the With box, select the font you want to use instead. Click the Replace button, and all of the instances of the Replace font are immediately changed to the With font.

Changing the Indents, Alignment, and Spacing

You can perform certain types of text formatting only on entire text objects, not individual characters or words. These formatting types include changing the left and first-line indents of paragraphs, changing the alignment of paragraphs, and changing the spacing between and within paragraphs.

Remember, a text object includes all the text in a single placeholder. For example, a bulleted list slide has only two text objects, the title and the bulleted list, even though the bulleted list probably consists of more than one paragraph. Any change you make to a text object affects all the paragraphs within it.

Changing the Left Indent and First-Line Indent

Increasing the left indent of a bulleted list text object pushes all the text to the right, increasing the space between the bullets and the text for each bullet. To change the indents of a text object, you must click anywhere in the text object and then drag the corresponding markers in the top ruler.

First-line indent

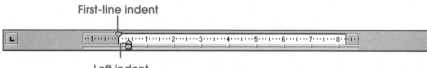

Left indent

If the ruler is not visible, you can display it in one of the following ways:

■ Choose Ruler from the View menu.

■ Point to the slide background, click the right mouse button, and choose Ruler from the shortcut menu.

NOTE If a text object has bulleted items at two or more levels, the ruler contains a pair of markers (a left indent marker and a first-line indent marker) for each level.

To increase the space to the right of the bullets, follow these steps:

1. Click any of the text in the object.

2. Drag the left indent marker to the right.

TIP Be sure to drag the lower, triangular marker that points upward. Dragging the rectangular marker located below the left indent marker moves the first-line indent marker and the left indent marker at the same time.

Dragging the first-line indent marker (the upper, triangular marker that points downward) to the left or the right changes the starting position of the first line relative to the rest of the paragraph. Because a bullet starts the first line of a bulleted list paragraph, dragging the first-line indent marker to the right moves the bullet to the right. Figure 5-8 on the next page shows the indent settings on several rulers and the corresponding indents of the text below. If a text object contains paragraphs that have no bullets, dragging the first-line indent marker to the left creates a hanging indent, as shown in Figure 5-9 on the next page.

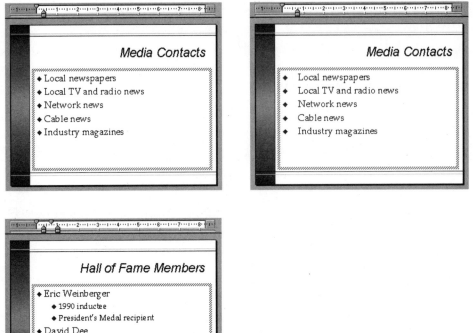

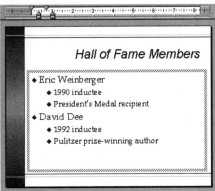

FIGURE 5-8

Notice how the ruler settings correspond to the text on these three slides.

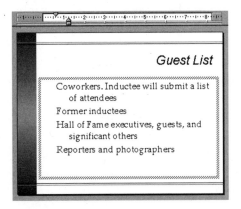

FIGURE 5-9

Paragraphs with hanging indents.

Changing Paragraph Alignment

The *alignment* of a text object determines the horizontal placement of its lines. The alignment options are as follows:

Option	Effect
Left	Text within a text object is flush with the left edge of the object.
Center	Text within a text object is centered horizontally within the object.
Right	Text within a text object is flush with the right edge of the object.
Justify	Extra spaces are added between the words within a text object to make the text flush with both the left and right edges of the object.

To change the alignment of the paragraphs in a text object, follow these three steps:

1. Select the text object.

2. Choose Alignment from the Format menu, or click the right mouse button and choose Alignment from the shortcut menu.

3. Select the alignment option you want from the Alignment submenu.

To left-align or center text, you can click the Left Alignment or Center Alignment button on the Formatting toolbar. You can also use one of the keyboard shortcuts listed in Table 5-2 to align text in various ways.

Alignment	Keyboard Shortcut
Left-align	Ctrl+L
Center	Ctrl+E
Right-align	Ctrl+R
Justify	Ctrl+J

TABLE 5-2
Alignment keyboard shortcuts.

Changing Line and Paragraph Spacing

The *line spacing* value determines the amount of vertical space between lines within a paragraph, and the *paragraph spacing* value determines the amount of space between paragraphs within a text object. You may want to add extra space between paragraphs to separate them or add extra space between the lines of a paragraph to make the paragraph easier to read, for a design effect, or to make the text fill more vertical space on the page.

To change the line spacing in a text object, follow these steps:

1. Select the text object.

2. Choose Line Spacing from the Format menu. This dialog box appears:

3. In the Line Spacing dialog box, you can change the line spacing by hundredths of a line or by a single point. First select either Lines or Points from the drop-down list in the Line Spacing section of the dialog box, and then enter a new number in the edit box to the left. You can click the up or down arrows to increase or decrease the number.

The other two options in the Line Spacing dialog box allow you to add extra space before or after each paragraph. By using the Before Paragraph and After Paragraph options, you can spread out the paragraphs vertically. You can also use the Increase Paragraph Spacing or Decrease Paragraph Spacing button on the Formatting toolbar to adjust the spacing.

Adding and Removing Bullets

Each bullet that appears at the beginning of a text line emphasizes the statement that follows. In addition, bullets are only appropriate when a slide contains a series of statements. As a result, there may be times when you don't need bulleted text, such as when a slide contains a single phrase. Fortunately, you can easily add and remove bullets in PowerPoint by using the Bullet On/Off button on the Formatting toolbar.

To remove the bullet from a line of text:

1. Click anywhere in the line.

2. Click the Bullet On/Off button on the Formatting toolbar.

For example, in Figure 5-10, the bullet has been removed from the second of two text statements. To remove the bullets from all the text in a placeholder, first select the text by pressing Ctrl+A, or select the placeholder's text object by pressing F2 or by clicking the object's gray border, and then click the Bullet On/Off button. The Bullet On/Off button is a toggle, so if you select the text and press the Bullet On/Off button again, PowerPoint restores the bullets.

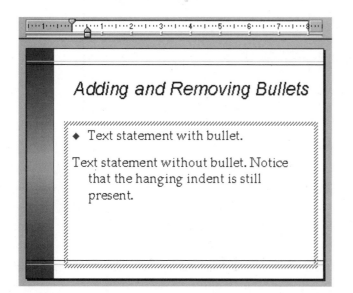

FIGURE 5-10
The bullet has been removed from the second text statement.

Another way to add or remove bullets is to select the text to the right of the bullets, and choose Bullet from the Format menu or the shortcut menu. Then, when the Bullet dialog box appears, select or deselect the Use a Bullet option to turn the bullets on or off.

When you remove the bullet from a bulleted paragraph that contains more than one line of text, you'll notice that the first line of text shifts to the left. The paragraph's hanging indent is still present, as you can see in the second text statement in Figure 5-10. To remove the hanging indent in a nonbulleted paragraph, follow these steps:

1. Check that the ruler is visible. (If it is not, choose Ruler from the View menu or the shortcut menu.)

2. Drag the left indent marker to the left so that it aligns with the first-line indent marker, as shown on the next page. Be careful to drag the triangular part of the left indent marker, not the rectangular part, which moves both the first-line and left indent markers simultaneously.

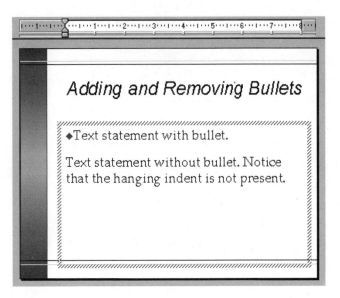

Notice that the text in the second bulleted item is now properly left-aligned, but the top bulleted item has been affected, too. As we've said before, changing indents affects all the paragraphs in a text object.

Changing the Bullet Shape, Color, and Size

The default bullets that precede the text on your slides are only one of the almost limitless options for bullet shape, color, and size. You can use any character from any TrueType font on your system, and you can change the color and size of the bullets on any slide.

To select a special bullet character, follow these steps:

1. Select the text following the bullet or bullets you want to change.

2. Choose Bullet from the Format menu, or press the right mouse button and choose Bullet from the shortcut menu. The Bullet dialog box appears, as shown on the facing page.

3. Select a font from the Bullets From drop-down list. The special characters available for the selected font are then displayed in the dialog box. As you can see, the Wingdings font is a good source of graphic bullet shapes.

4. Click any of the characters displayed. The character will be magnified temporarily so that you can see it better.

5. If you want to change the bullet color, select a color from the Special Color drop-down list.

6. If you want to change the bullet size, type a new size in the Size edit box, or click the up or down arrows at the right end of the edit box to increase or decrease the size of the bullet as a percentage of the text size.

7. Click the Preview button at the bottom of the Bullet dialog box to see the changes you've made, or click OK to implement the changes.

Figure 5-11 shows a bulleted list slide with bullets that are far more interesting than the defaults.

FIGURE 5-11
Check boxes used as bullets.

Creating Numbered Lists

PowerPoint cannot automatically number paragraphs in a text object. You must first turn off the bullets, and then type a number at the beginning of each paragraph. After the number, press the Tab key. Then align the text of the numbered paragraph by changing the first tab marker on the ruler. For more information about tabs, see the following section.

Setting and Removing Tab Stops

Creating tables in PowerPoint is so easy that you'll probably want to use a table whenever you need to place text in columns on a slide. But you can also place tab stops in a text object and follow a more traditional approach for spacing text horizontally across a slide.

As described in Table 5-3, PowerPoint provides four different types of tab stops. All of these are available on the ruler.

TABLE 5-3
PowerPoint's
tab stops.

Tab Button	Tab Stop	Description
L	Left-aligned tab stop	Aligns the left edge of text with the tab stop
⊥	Centered tab stop	Aligns the center of text with the tab stop
⌐	Right-aligned tab stop	Aligns the right edge of text with the tab stop
⊥·	Decimal tab stop	Aligns the decimal points of numbers with the tab stop

To switch from one tab type to the next, click the Tab Alignment button at the left end of the ruler until the tab type you want appears on the face of the button. Figure 5-12 shows the location of the Tab Alignment button and the appearance of text entered at a set of tab stops.

To enter tab stops, follow these steps:

1. Click anywhere in the text within a text object. (All of the text in the object will be formatted with the same tab stops.)

2. Click the Tab Alignment button until the type of tab stop you want appears.

Tab Alignment button

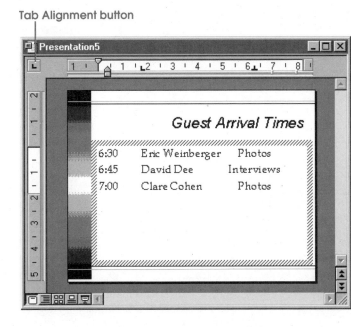

FIGURE 5-12

The Tab Alignment button and text entered at various tab stops. (The ruler shows the current tab stops.)

3. On the ruler, click the position for the tab stop.

4. Continue clicking different positions in the ruler to add tab stops of the same type, or select a different tab type and then click the ruler.

    NOTE To remove a tab stop you have set, point to the tab stop, hold down the left mouse button, and drag the tab stop all the way to the left end of the ruler.

Changing the Case of Text

To change the capitalization of text on a slide, select the text you want to modify, and then, from the Format menu, choose Change Case. Figure 5-13 shows the Change Case dialog box, which offers five case options for the selected text. You might want to take a moment and try out each of the options to see their effects. Simply select an option, and then click OK. You can also

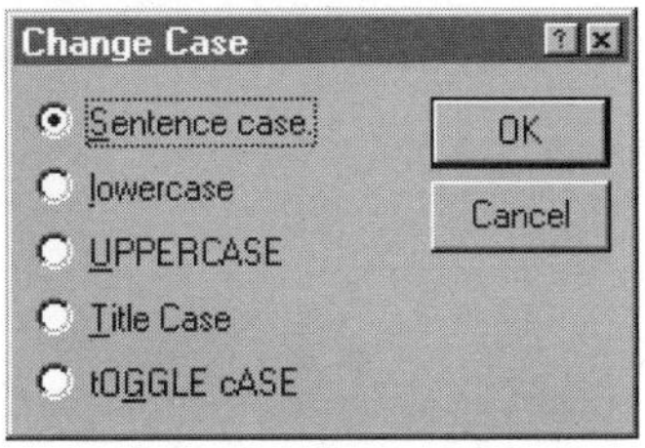

FIGURE 5-13

The Change Case dialog box.

cycle between uppercase, lowercase, and title case for the selected text by pressing Shift+F3.

Adding and Removing Periods

To add or remove periods from the text on a slide, select the text, and then, from the Format menu, choose Periods. In the Periods dialog box, shown in Figure 5-14, select either Add Periods or Remove Periods, and click OK.

Periods
In Selected Paragraphs
Add Periods
Remove Periods
OK
Cancel

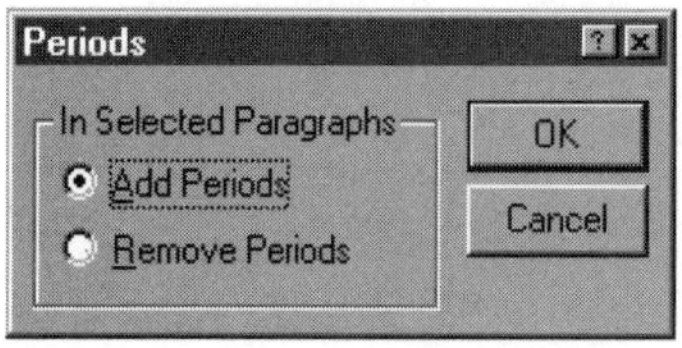

FIGURE 5-14
The Periods dialog box.

You can also use the Periods command in Outline view. But no matter what view you're in, you cannot use the Periods command to add or remove periods from a slide title.

Transferring Text Styles

After you format one selection of text, you can transfer the same formatting, called the *text style,* to another selection of text. By transferring a text style, you save time because you don't have to reopen menus, reselect options, and so on.

To transfer the formatting of one text selection to another text selection, follow these steps:

1. Select the text whose formatting you want to transfer, as shown below.

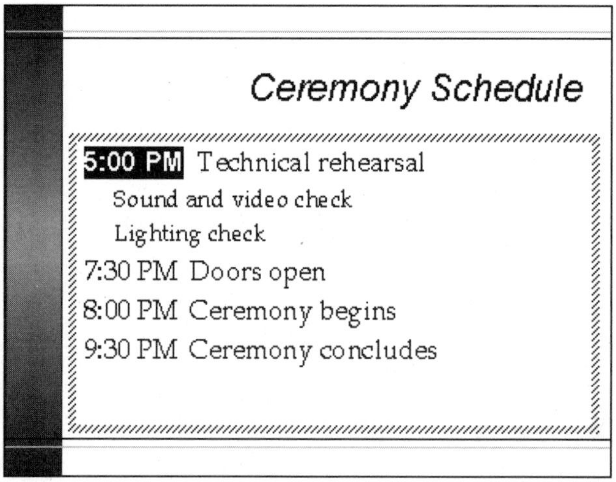

Ceremony Schedule
5:00 PM Technical rehearsal
Sound and video check
Lighting check
7:30 PM Doors open
8:00 PM Ceremony begins
9:30 PM Ceremony concludes

2. From the Format menu, choose Pick Up Text Style, or click the right mouse button and choose Pick Up Text Style from the shortcut menu.

3. Select the text that you want to transfer the formatting to.

4. From the Format menu, choose Apply Text Style, or click the right mouse button and choose Apply Text Style from the shortcut menu. As shown below, the formatting of the original text selection is transferred to the other text selection.

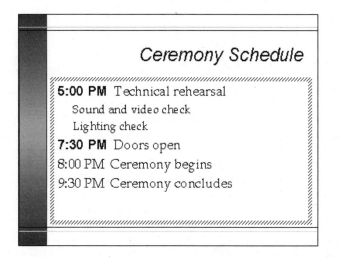

Moving and Resizing Text Objects

The text you enter in a placeholder appears at the position of the placeholder text. But after you enter all the text you need, you may want to move the text object or change its size, perhaps to make room on the slide for a chart or graphic.

To move or resize a text object, you must select the object with one of these procedures:

- Choose Edit Object from the Edit menu.
- Press F2.
- Click the fuzzy gray border that surrounds the object.

In each case, a set of handles appears around the selected object, as shown in Figure 5-15 on the next page.

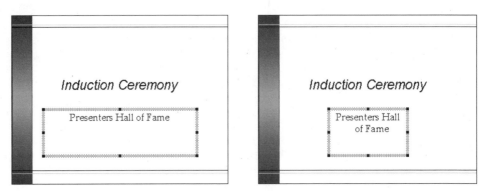

FIGURE 5-15

Handles around a selected text object allow you to move and resize the object.

After you select the text object, position the mouse pointer on the object's border, hold down the left mouse button, and drag the object to a new position; or press the arrow keys to move the object incrementally. To resize the object, drag one of the object's handles.

NOTE By holding down the Shift key and dragging one of the object's corner handles, you can change the object's scale. That is, both the object's width and height are resized proportionally.

Turning Word Wrap On or Off

When you resize an object, the text inside wraps to fit the new size, as shown in Figure 5-15. Words in a paragraph that can no longer fit on a line within the object move to the following line. Words in a paragraph that can fit on the previous line after the object is resized move to the previous line.

You can turn word wrap off by first selecting the text object or any of the text within the object, and then choosing Text Anchor from the Format menu. The Text Anchor dialog box appears, as shown in Figure 5-16.

FIGURE 5-16

The Text Anchor dialog box.

118

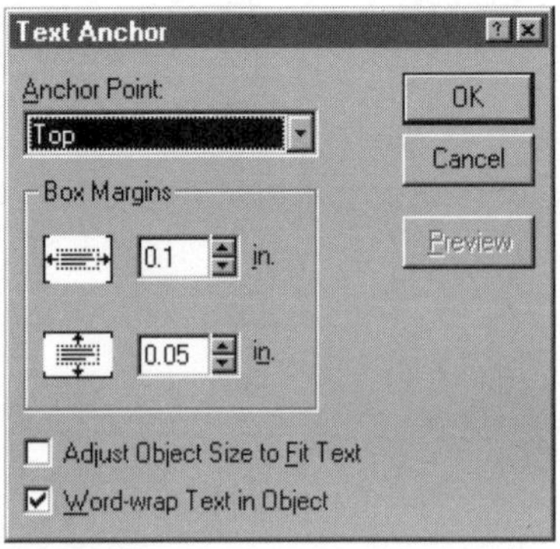

The Word-wrap Text in Object option controls word wrapping. Click the option's check box to turn word wrapping on or off.

When word wrapping is turned off, any text you add to a paragraph continues across the slide, beyond the borders of the text object, and even beyond the edge of the slide if necessary.

Changing the Box Margins

The two Box Margins settings in the Text Anchor dialog box, shown in Figure 5-16, let you adjust the horizontal and vertical margins of the text object. When you increase the margins, you add space within the object, between the text and the borders of the object.

Increasing the box margins is helpful when you add an actual graphic box to the borders of a text object, as you'll learn in the section titled "Special Text Object Formatting." Larger margins pad the interior of the box so that the text does not appear so cramped in the box. Figure 5-17 shows the same text within two text objects. The text object in the right box has larger box margins.

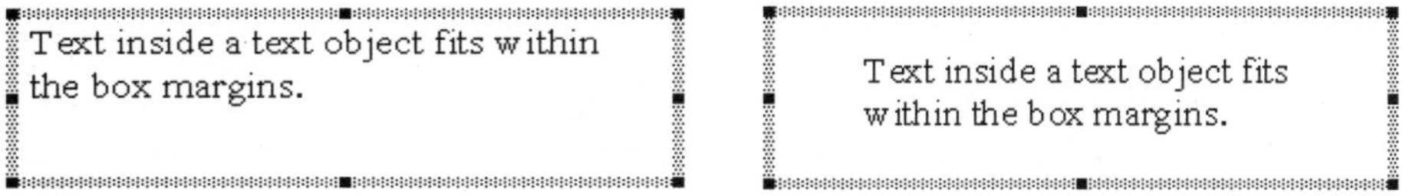

FIGURE 5-17

The text object on the right has larger box margins.

Fitting Text Objects to the Text

Sometimes, the text you enter in a placeholder does not completely fill the placeholder. For example, the bottom border of the text object shown on the left in Figure 5-18 on the next page is some distance from the text. To automatically shrink the text object to fit the text you've entered, select the text, and then select the Adjust Object Size to Fit Text option in the Text Anchor dialog box. The text object immediately shrinks to fit the text inside. If you enter additional text, the text object will grow vertically to accommodate the new text, as shown on the right in Figure 5-18.

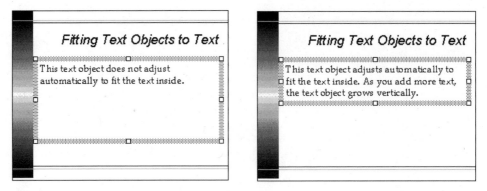

FIGURE 5-18

The size of the text object on the left is not automatically adjusted to fit the text. The text object on the right grows vertically to accommodate any new text you add.

When the Adjust Object Size to Fit Text option is turned on, you can stretch the sides of a text object horizontally, but the bottom border of the object always snaps to fit the last line of the text. When Adjust Object Size to Fit Text is turned off, newly typed text overruns the bottom border of the text object, and you have to resize the object manually.

Decreasing the box margins while the Adjust Object Size to Fit Text option is turned on brings the borders of the text object closer to the text.

Special Text Object Formatting

Because a text object is just like any other object on a PowerPoint slide, you can surround it with a line, add a shadow to it, fill it with color, rotate it, and scale it. In fact, you can use any of the commands that you use to change the appearance of other objects (such as drawings) to change the appearance of a text object. For example, you can add a border to a text object by first selecting the object and then choosing the Colors and Lines command from the Format menu. Or you can add a shadow to a text object by choosing the Shadow command from the Format menu.

One special command you may find helpful is Scale. After selecting a text object, you can change its size by choosing Scale from the Draw menu and then revising the Scale To percentage setting in the Scale dialog box shown in Figure 5-19. You can reduce a text object to 90 percent of its former size, for example, to make room for a graphic.

FIGURE 5-19

The Scale
dialog box.

Microsoft WordArt

When your presentation title needs a little pizzazz, you can use Microsoft WordArt to create spirited titles with one or more eye-catching special effects. WordArt can create shadowed, stretched, rotated, and skewed text of any size, and text that has been contoured to fit a number of predefined shapes.

To add WordArt text to a title slide, or to any slide, choose Object from the Insert menu, select Microsoft WordArt 2.0 from the Insert Object dialog box, and click OK. (Before you choose the Object command, you can delete the *Click to add title* placeholder on the title slide so that it doesn't get in your way.) When WordArt's menus and toolbar appear on the screen, type the desired text in the Enter Your Text Here dialog box, and then click Update Display. Next, use WordArt's Format menu and toolbar to add special formatting effects. For example, click the arrow next to the first box on the WordArt toolbar to display a palette of shapes that you can use to contour the text.

To return to PowerPoint after you finish formatting the text, click outside the WordArt frame. To return to WordArt, double-click any WordArt text.

If the presentation you are creating is strictly text, as most presentations are, then you have now done everything required to create the presentation, and you can skip ahead to Chapter 9. But if you want to add graphs, organization charts, and tables to your presentation, go on to the next three chapters.

Chapter 6

Adding Graph Slides

Y ou can reel off numbers until you're blue in the face, but nothing gets your message across like a graph. PowerPoint's powerful Graph module offers 14 different chart types with all the pizzazz you could want, and it makes the process of creating graphs simple and automatic. In this chapter, you'll learn how to use the Graph module to create the graphs you need and add them to presentation slides. You'll also learn how to enter and edit the data that supports your graphs, and you'll make the acquaintance of the AutoFormat command. Finally, you'll discover ways to incorporate data and graphs from other sources into your PowerPoint graph slides.

Because a graph is a visual representation of data, it can have a much greater impact than words alone. For example, the statement "We outproduced our nearest competitors by 2 to 1" is impressive, but not nearly as impressive as this graph:

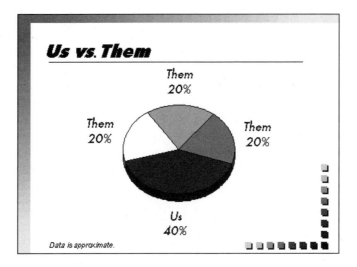

A graph can communicate any information that can be quantified, so don't hesitate to pull a graph from your arsenal whenever your message is numeric—even if your numbers aren't precise.

Graphs are your best bet for illuminating trends, deviations, and other measurements that don't require a great deal of explanation. If an explanation is needed, you can simply add text to the graph or include a text slide. By the time you finish this chapter, you'll probably think of new ways that you can use graphs to enhance your PowerPoint presentations.

See Also For information about creating custom graphs, see Chapter 10, "Formatting Graphs," page 243.

What Is Microsoft Graph?

Microsoft Graph 5 is a special module that creates graphs for use in Windows-based applications such as Microsoft Word, Microsoft Excel, and, of course, PowerPoint. If you're already familiar with graphing in Excel, you'll find it easy to jump to graphing in PowerPoint because both programs use the same Graph module. If you're not familiar with graphing in Excel, don't worry. At every step of the way, Graph guides you through the process of converting raw numbers into professional, colorful, and illuminating graphs.

When you create or modify a graph, Graph's menus and Standard toolbar replace PowerPoint's menus and toolbars, as shown in Figure 6-1, so only the commands and controls you need are on the screen.

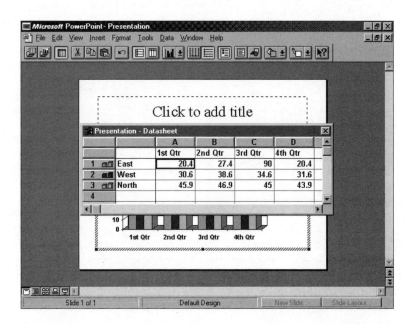

FIGURE 6-1

Graph's menus and Standard toolbar take over the screen when you create a graph.

The graph you are creating in Graph appears on the current slide. When you are entering or editing the graph's data, a datasheet containing the numbers overlays the graph. Any change to the numbers in the datasheet is reflected immediately in the graph.

Graph Basics

When it's time to back up an assertion with numeric data, you can create a special graph slide devoted to an entire graph, or you can add a graph to an existing slide to enhance a text message. Then you can select from 14 different chart types to ensure that the graph presents your data effectively.

NOTE The words *graph* and *chart* are used interchangeably throughout this chapter. In general, the word *chart* is reserved for option and button names.

Creating a Graph Slide

To create a graph slide in an existing presentation, follow these steps:

1. In Slide view, switch to the slide that the new slide should follow, and click the New Slide button at the bottom of the PowerPoint window or choose New Slide from the Insert menu to display the New Slide dialog box shown below:

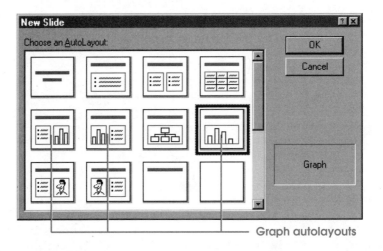

Graph autolayouts

2. In the New Slide dialog box, click the fourth autolayout in the second row if you want only a graph on a slide, or click the first or second autolayout in the second row if you want a bulleted list along with a graph. These are the only autolayouts that provide graph placeholders.

3. Click OK. A graph placeholder on the new slide displays the text *Double click to add graph*.

4. Double-click the graph placeholder to start Microsoft Graph. A sample graph appears within the placeholder, and the datasheet window, which contains the sample data for the graph, overlays the graph as shown in Figure 6-1 on page 125.

Adding a Graph to an Existing Slide

To add a graph to an existing slide, click the Insert Graph button on Power-Point's Standard toolbar or choose Microsoft Graph from the Insert menu. Either way, Graph loads and displays a sample graph and datasheet on the current slide. Don't worry about the positioning or size of the graph at this point. After you enter your data, you can move and size the graph as needed.

Selecting a Chart Type

After you create a graph slide or add a graph to an existing slide, you can select a chart type from PowerPoint's 14 chart options. Selecting a chart type before you begin entering data is a good first step because you are compelled from the start to consider the message your data conveys. It also modifies the appearance of the datasheet window to show how the data will be represented. You'll see bars in the datasheet window if you select a bar chart, or pie slices if you select a pie chart. Of course, because PowerPoint always lets you change your mind at any time, you can always begin with the default chart type and change to any other chart type later.

Keep in mind that PowerPoint can produce stock variations, called *subtypes*, of most of the 14 basic chart types. You can also go way beyond these subtypes and modify any chart to a virtually unlimited degree. You can even mix chart types within the same graph, showing some data with lines and some with bars, for example.

To select a chart type for a graph, follow these steps:

1. Select the sample graph on your slide.

2. Click the down arrow to the right of the Chart Type button on Graph's Standard toolbar. A palette of chart types appears, as shown on the next page.

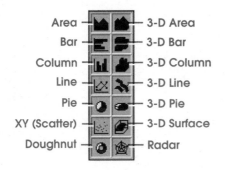

Area — 3-D Area
Bar — 3-D Bar
Column — 3-D Column
Line — 3-D Line
Pie — 3-D Pie
XY (Scatter) — 3-D Surface
Doughnut — Radar

3. Click the chart type you want.

TIP You can "tear off" the palette of chart types and drop it on an unused part of the screen for easy access later. Simply click the arrow next to the Chart Type button to drop down the palette. Next, position the mouse pointer over the palette, hold down the left mouse button, and drag the palette away from Graph's Standard toolbar. You can close the Charts palette by clicking the Control button at the left end of the palette's title bar.

You can also use the Chart Type command on Graph's Format menu or shortcut menu to select a chart type. When you choose this command, Graph displays the Chart Type dialog box shown in Figure 6-2. Note that the names of the chart types and their pictures appear in large, easy-to-see panes. Click 2-D or 3-D in the Chart Dimension section, and then select a chart type from the display of chart options.

FIGURE 6-2

The Chart Type
dialog box.

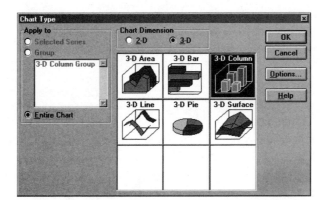

You can further refine your selection by clicking the Options button in the Chart Type dialog box and selecting a chart subtype. For example, Figure 6-3 shows the Format Column Group dialog box that appears when you select the 3-D Column chart option and then click Options. You can select one of the subtypes displayed in large panes on the Subtype tab of the dialog box. After you select a subtype, a preview of your data plotted according to the selected chart subtype appears in the bottom section of the dialog box. You can then click OK to implement the selected chart subtype, or click another Subtype option and click OK. To return to the Chart Type dialog box, simply click the Chart Type button.

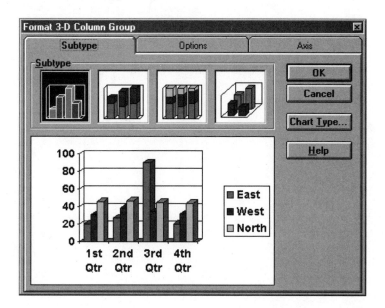

FIGURE 6-3

You can use the Format Column Group dialog box to select a chart subtype.

TIP You can select a chart type, a subtype, and special chart formatting options all at once by choosing AutoFormat from Graph's Format menu or shortcut menu. For more information, see "Selecting an AutoFormat," page 141.

The following sections discuss PowerPoint's 14 basic chart types and explain how each chart type presents information. Figure 6-4, which starts on the next page, provides an example of each chart type.

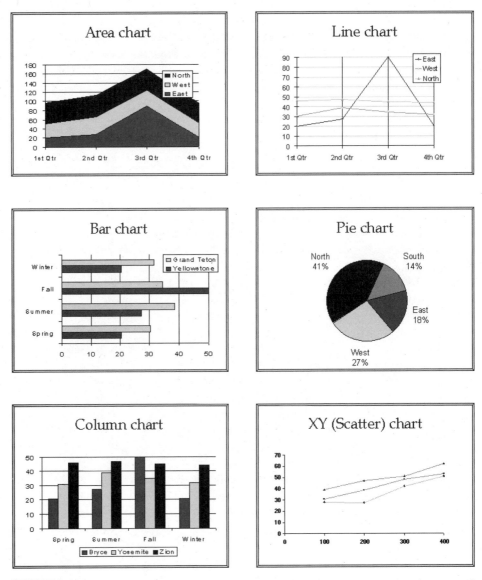

FIGURE 6-4   *(continued)*

PowerPoint's 14 basic chart types.

FIGURE 6-4 *continued*

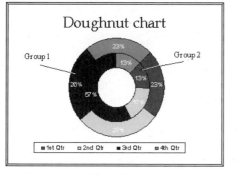

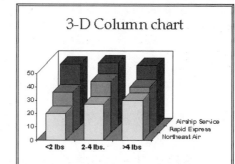

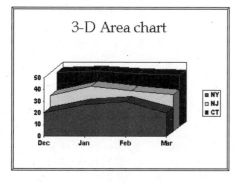

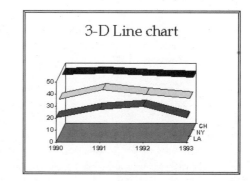

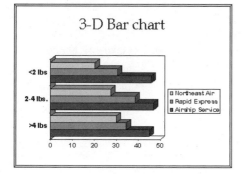

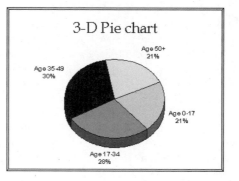

(continued)

FIGURE 6-4 *continued*

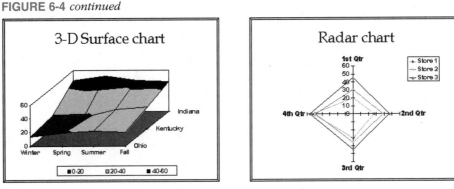

Area Charts

Area charts show the amount of change in a set of values during an interval of time. Line charts are similar, but they emphasize the *rate* of change rather than the *amount* of change.

Bar Charts

Bar charts compare measurements at intervals. They emphasize measurements at discrete times rather than the changes over time. Their bars run horizontally. The stacked bar subtype shows the relative contributions of several measurements to a whole. The 100% stacked bar subtype shows the relative percentage of contributions of several measurements to the whole without identifying specific numeric contributions.

Column Charts

Column charts are much like bar charts except their bars run vertically rather than horizontally. Like bar charts, they compare measurements at intervals and provide snapshot views of data taken at specific moments rather than offer a depiction of the change of data over time. Column charts also have stacked and 100% stacked subtypes.

Line Charts

Line charts show changes in data or trends over time. You can show the same data using bars or columns, but lines emphasize change rather than comparisons at intervals. Two subtypes of line charts, high-low-close and open-high-low-close, are used to depict stock prices and other types of data that have a high and a low during an interval, such as the temperature or barometric pressure.

Pie Charts

Pie charts show the breakdown of a total. You can separate slices of the pie to emphasize certain values. The values depicted by slices are contained in a single series on the Graph datasheet.

XY (Scatter) Charts

XY (scatter) charts show the degree of correspondence between two series of numbers. Generally used for scientific data, XY charts also let you depict two sets of numbers as one set of XY coordinates.

Doughnut Charts

Like pie charts, doughnut charts show breakdowns of totals, but they let you depict several breakdowns in successive rings around a doughnut hole.

3-D Area Charts

3-D area charts are area charts depicted in three dimensions. The third dimension has no significance except to make the chart more interesting.

3-D Bar Charts

3-D bar charts are bar charts shown in three dimensions. Again, the third dimension has no significance except to make the chart more visually appealing than a standard 2-D bar chart.

3-D Column Charts

3-D column charts come in two varieties. The standard 3-D column chart, shown in Figure 6-4, is a three-dimensional view of a column chart. The 3-D perspective column chart, shown in Figure 6-5, is far more visually striking; however, beware of potential problems interpreting 3-D perspective column charts. Gauging the true relative and absolute heights of the bars can be very difficult. Use this chart type to give a general impression of the data, not the specific values.

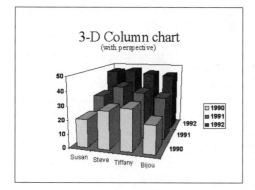

FIGURE 6-5
A 3-D perspective column chart.

3-D Line Charts

3-D line charts display lines as ribbons. They provide a more interesting view than 2-D line charts, but like 3-D bar charts, 3-D line charts make it difficult to interpret change over time.

3-D Pie Charts

3-D pie charts offer a more visually appealing view of a breakdown than standard 2-D pie charts. Otherwise, they are identical. You can separate slices of 3-D pie charts from the pie just as easily as you can in 2-D pie charts.

3-D Surface Charts

3-D surface charts emphasize the relationships among large quantities of numbers. Colors or patterns designate areas with the same value. Two subtypes—contour charts and wire-frame charts—show a 2-D view of the surface chart from above and the surface chart without color, respectively.

Radar Charts

Radar charts simultaneously compare the relationship of several different values of a subject. Each value is measured on an axis that radiates from the center of the chart and depicts another aspect of the subject.

Entering the Data

The generic set of data you see in the datasheet window when you start Microsoft Graph provides an example of how text and numbers should be arranged in a datasheet. The graph peeking out from behind the datasheet window displays the text and numbers graphically, and it is updated immediately as you enter and edit data in the datasheet. Figure 6-6 shows the datasheet.

FIGURE 6-6
The datasheet.

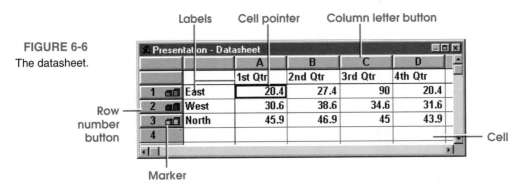

The datasheet is made up of *cells,* which are the rectangular spaces at the intersections of the rows and columns. In Figure 6-6, text labels appear in the leftmost and topmost cells of the datasheet. The actual numbers to be graphed occupy the cells below and to the right of the labels. Each cell in this section has an *address* that consists of a column letter and row number. For example, the address of the cell at the intersection of column A and row 1 is *A1*.

NOTE In most spreadsheet programs, every cell in a worksheet has an address. But in Microsoft Graph, the cells reserved for text labels in the datasheet (the leftmost and topmost cells) do not have cell addresses.

To create a proper graph, PowerPoint must know whether the *series* (the sets of related numbers) are entered in rows or columns. By default, PowerPoint assumes that the series are arranged in rows. If you've arranged the series in columns instead, you can click the By Column button on Graph's Standard toolbar. To return to a by-row arrangement, simply click the By Row button.

PowerPoint places small pictures of the *markers* that will be used in the graph (the bars, columns, lines, or other graphic shapes) on either the row number or column letter buttons in the datasheet. If the markers are on the row number buttons, the data is organized in the graph by row. If the markers are on the column letter buttons, the data is organized by column.

Entering the Labels

Your first step in entering the data for a graph is to replace the text labels in the first row and first column of cells. To replace a label, use the mouse or the arrow keys to move the *cell pointer*—the highlight surrounding a single cell—to the cell containing the label, and then type over the existing entry. You can also double-click or press F2 to place an insertion point in a selected cell and then edit its contents. Keep in mind that you can use the same text editing techniques that you use elsewhere in PowerPoint to edit the contents of a cell in the datasheet.

Because PowerPoint's default setting arranges graph data by row, each label entered in the leftmost cell of a row appears in the graph's legend. (Displaying the legend is optional.) The labels entered in the topmost cells of columns often have time or date designations, such as a specific year or month, but they can be any other text that distinguishes the individual data points in a series of numbers. Remember, if you want the column labels to appear in the graph's legend rather than in the row labels, you can click the By Column button on Graph's Standard toolbar.

To try your hand at entering labels, start by creating a new graph:

1. Click the New Slide button at the bottom of the PowerPoint window.

2. In the New Slide dialog box, select an autolayout that includes a graph placeholder.

3. In Slide view, double-click the *Double click to add graph* placeholder to start Microsoft Graph.

Stick with the default chart type when the graph and datasheet appear, and then follow these steps, using the suggested labels or your own:

1. Select the first cell in row 1 (the cell that contains the label *East*).

2. Type *Regular mail* and press Enter. Don't worry that the label is too long to fit in the cell. The length of the label won't affect the resulting graph, and you can widen the entire column to accommodate the label at any time (see the sidebar titled "Changing the Widths of Columns," on the facing page).

3. Now replace *West* with *Overnight* and press Enter.

4. Replace *North* with *Courier,* and then select the first cell in column A, and replace *1st Qtr* with *Package*.

5. Press Tab to move to the cell to the right, replace *2nd Qtr* in column B with *Box*, and press Tab again.

6. Replace *3rd Qtr* in column C with *Letter*. Leave the text in Column D as is—you'll plot only three columns of data in the graph. Here's how the datasheet should look now:

Presentation - Datasheet		A	B	C	D
		Package	Box	Letter	4th Qtr
1	Regular m	20.4	27.4	90	20.4
2	Overnight	30.6	38.6	34.6	31.6
3	Courier	45.9	46.9	45	43.9
4					

Changing the Widths of Columns

When the label you enter in a cell exceeds the width of the cell, you won't be able to see the entire label. To widen the entire column, place the mouse pointer between the current column letter button and the column letter button to the right (the pointer changes to a double arrow). Then hold down the left mouse button, and drag to the right. In the datasheet shown below, the first column is being widened to accommodate the longest label.

		A	B	C	D	
		Package	Box	Letter	4th Qtr	
1		Regular m	20.4	27.4	90	20.4
2		Overnight	30.6	38.6	34.6	31.6
3		Courier	45.9	46.9	45	43.9
4						

Presentation - Datasheet

To change the width of more than one column, click the column letter button for the first column, hold down the mouse button, and drag across the other column letter buttons. Then, when you widen the first column using the technique described above, the other selected columns are also widened.

In addition, you can double-click between two column letter buttons to automatically adjust the width of the first column to accommodate the column's longest entry. Select several columns and double-click between any two to automatically fit them all to their longest entry.

Entering the Numbers

After you enter the labels to create a framework for the data, you must replace the sample numbers with your own. You can select any single cell, type over the cell's contents, and then move to the next cell. However, the best way to quickly enter all the numbers is to select the range of cells that will contain the numbers, and then begin typing columns of replacement numbers. To select a range of cells, place the mouse pointer on the first cell, hold down the mouse button, and then drag across to the cell at the opposite corner of the range. You can also move the cell pointer to the first cell, hold down the Shift key, and then use the arrow keys to move to the cell at the opposite corner.

When you type a number and press Enter, the cell pointer moves to the cell below. When you type a number in the last cell of a selected range of cells and press Enter, the cell pointer returns to the first cell in the range.

To enter the data for the graph you've created, follow these steps. (Again, you can use the suggested data or supply your own.)

1. Place the mouse pointer on cell A1, which is located at the intersection of column A and row 1.

2. Hold down the left mouse button, and drag the pointer to cell C3.

3. Release the mouse button. The rectangular range of cells from A1 to C3 is selected, as shown here:

Presentation - Datasheet		A	B	C	D
		Package	Box	Letter	4th Qtr
1	Regular mail	20.4	27.4	90	20.4
2	Overnight	30.6	38.6	34.6	31.0
3	Courier	45.9	46.9	45	43.9
4					

4. Type the columns of numbers shown below, pressing Enter after each number. Be sure to enter the numbers by column, *not* by row.

8.60	10.75	.32
17.90	22.00	9.95
48.00	56.00	17.50

The datasheet now looks like this:

Presentation - Datasheet		A	B	C	D
		Package	Box	Letter	4th Qtr
1	Regular mail	8.6	10.75	0.32	20.4
2	Overnight	17.9	22	9.95	31.6
3	Courier	48	56	17.5	43.9
4					

NOTE To use the quick data-entry technique, you must enter the numbers in columns, even if you're charting the data by rows.

TIP You can control whether the cell pointer moves to the next cell or remains on the selected cell when you press Enter by first choosing Options from Graph's Tools menu. Then click the check box next to the Move Selection after Enter option to deselect it, and click OK.

Formatting the Labels and Numbers

You can use Graph's Formatting toolbar (shown below) to select a different font and numeric format for a datasheet. The changes you make to the font are displayed only in the datasheet, whereas the changes you make to the numeric formatting appear in both the datasheet and the graph.

NOTE If Graph's Formatting toolbar is not present, choose Toolbars from Graph's View menu, select the Formatting option, and then click OK.

Text formatting buttons   Number formatting buttons

From Graph's Formatting toolbar, you can select a font, a point size, and character formatting attributes such as bold, italic, and underline for the text and numbers in your datasheet. You cannot change the alignment while working in the datasheet because the paragraph alignment buttons are inactive, but you should keep in mind that text is always left-aligned in the datasheet and numbers are always right-aligned.

In addition to Graph's Formatting toolbar, you can use the Font command on Graph's Format menu or shortcut menu to change the formatting of the data in the datasheet. When you choose the Font command, the Font dialog box is displayed so that you can make your formatting selections.

To change the numeric formatting of the numbers in a datasheet, you must first select the numbers, and then either use the number formatting buttons on Graph's Formatting toolbar or choose the Number command from

Graph's Format menu or shortcut menu. You can select one set of numbers and format them as decimal and then select another set and format them as percentages, for example.

The five number formatting buttons are located at the right end of Graph's Formatting toolbar. You use the first three buttons to apply a general format to your numbers, and the last two buttons to increase or decrease the number of decimal places. For additional number formatting options, choose Number from Graph's Format menu or shortcut menu. Then in the Number Format dialog box, shown in Figure 6-7, select a formatting category from the list at the left, and select a formatting code from the list at the right. The code you select appears in the Code edit box, and a sample number at the bottom of the dialog box shows the effect of your selection. Click OK to implement your changes.

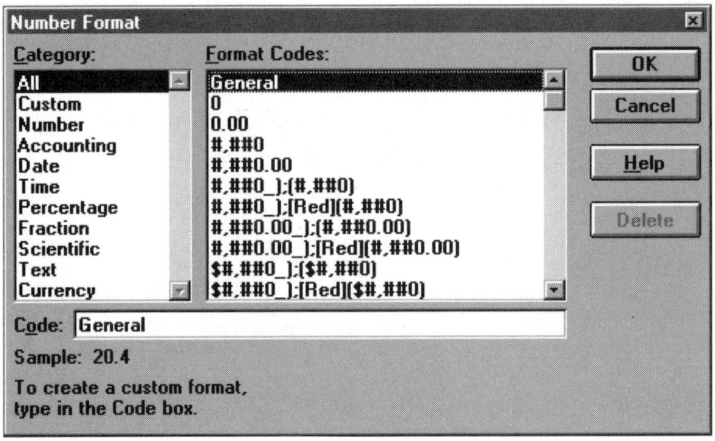

FIGURE 6-7

The Number Format dialog box.

Number Format

Category:	Format Codes:	
All	General	OK
Custom	0	Cancel
Number	0.00	
Accounting	#,##0	Help
Date	#,##0.00	
Time	#,##0_);(#,##0)	
Percentage	#,##0_);[Red](#,##0)	Delete
Fraction	#,##0.00_);(#,##0.00)	
Scientific	#,##0.00_);[Red](#,##0.00)	
Text	$#,##0_);($#,##0)	
Currency	$#,##0_);[Red]($#,##0)	

Code: General

Sample: 20.4

To create a custom format, type in the Code box.

To format the numbers in your sample graph, follow these steps:

1. Select the rectangular range of numbers from cell A1 to cell C3.

2. Click the Currency Style button on Graph's Formatting toolbar. The numbers should look like this:

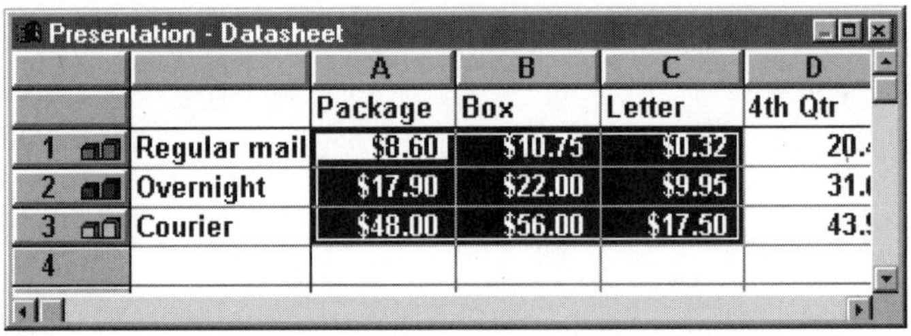

Presentation - Datasheet

		A	B	C	D
		Package	Box	Letter	4th Qtr
1	Regular mail	$8.60	$10.75	$0.32	20.4
2	Overnight	$17.90	$22.00	$9.95	31.0
3	Courier	$48.00	$56.00	$17.50	43.5
4					

To remove formatting from the data in your datasheet, select the data, choose Clear from Graph's Edit menu, and choose Formats from the Clear submenu. Choosing Contents from the Clear submenu removes the data from selected cells without deleting the cells. (You can also remove the data from selected cells by choosing Clear from Graph's shortcut menu.)

See Also For more information about formatting graphs, see Chapter 10, "Formatting Graphs," page 243.

Viewing the Graph

As you revise the data in the datasheet, the graph adjusts to reflect the changes. To see the graph, close the datasheet window by clicking the View Datasheet button on Graph's Standard toolbar, by double-clicking the Control button at the left end of the datasheet's title bar, or by clicking any visible part of the graph window. Figure 6-8 on the next page shows the graph created from the sample datasheet. If you close the datasheet window, you can always reopen it by clicking the View Datasheet button again or by choosing the Datasheet command from Graph's View menu.

> **NOTE** Before closing the sample datasheet window, we double-clicked the column letter button at the top of column D to exclude the data in column D from the graph. For more information about excluding data, see "Excluding Data," page 145.

The numbers along the vertical axis of the graph in Figure 6-8 are formatted with the currency style you specified earlier in the datasheet window. Other aspects of the graph's appearance are controlled by the template that formats the current presentation and by the chart type you selected. The template gives the graph its color scheme and font selections. The chart type gives the graph its overall design and special option settings. If necessary, you can now start revising the content of the graph and adjusting the appearance of the graph. To do the latter, you can select one of PowerPoint's autoformat options rather than make individual formatting choices for different parts of the graph.

Selecting an AutoFormat

An autoformat is a combination of a chart type, a subtype, and special formatting options for each part of a graph, such as the placement of the legend or the location of the data labels. Selecting an autoformat gives a graph a

FIGURE 6-8
The graph based
on the data
entered in the
sample datasheet.

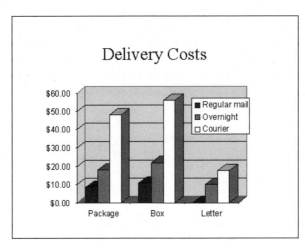

complete top-to-bottom design overhaul and can relieve the tedium of making detailed formatting changes to individual graph elements. Graph comes with a broad selection of autoformats for each of the 14 basic chart types. You can also create custom graph designs and save them as user-defined autoformats.

To select an autoformat for a graph, choose AutoFormat from Graph's Format menu or shortcut menu. The AutoFormat dialog box appears, as shown in Figure 6-9.

The AutoFormat dialog box contains a gallery of chart designs for each of the chart types in Graph. Select a chart type from the Galleries list, and then select a format by double-clicking one of the options in the Formats section. The graph will immediately reflect the autoformat you select. If you have created custom graph formats, you can select the User-Defined option in the Formats Used section, and then double-click the custom format you want.

FIGURE 6-9
The AutoFormat
dialog box.

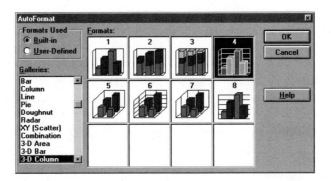

See Also For information about creating custom autoformats, see Chapter 10, "Formatting Graphs," page 243.

Editing the Data

PowerPoint offers a variety of ways to edit the data displayed by the graph, including moving, copying, inserting, and deleting. Before you can put any of these techniques to work, however, you must activate the datasheet by clicking the View Datasheet button on Graph's Standard toolbar or by choosing the Datasheet command from Graph's View menu.

Moving and Copying Data

You might want to move the data in your datasheet to make room for new data. Or you might want to rearrange the data so that the graph becomes more meaningful. For example, by ordering the data in your datasheet from largest to smallest or vice versa, you can enhance the impression the graph makes. As in Outline view and Slide view, you can move or copy data in the datasheet window by selecting it and then using the Cut, Copy, and Paste buttons on Graph's Standard toolbar; the Cut, Copy, and Paste commands on Graph's Edit menu or shortcut menu; or the corresponding key combinations. You can also use the drag-and-drop method to drag the data to a new location.

To move data with drag and drop, select a rectangular region of cells in your datasheet, place the pointer on the border of the selected cells (the pointer changes to an arrow), hold down the mouse button, and then drag. Release the mouse button when the cells are in the correct position.

By holding down the Ctrl key as you drag, you can copy the selected cells and then drop the copy in a new location on the datasheet. A small plus sign appears next to the pointer when you hold down the Ctrl key.

> **NOTE** Graph displays a warning if you inadvertently try to drop data on a cell that already contains data. To continue the drag-and-drop operation, just click OK in the message box.

Now try using drag and drop to rearrange the data in your sample graph:

1. Select the three columns of data you've entered by dragging across column letter buttons A, B, and C, as shown on the next page.

Presentation - Datasheet		A	B	C	D
		Package	Box	Letter	4th Qtr
1	Regular mail	$8.60	$10.75	$0.32	20.4
2	Overnight	$17.90	$22.00	$9.95	31.0
3	Courier	$48.00	$56.00	$17.50	43.5
4					

2. Place the pointer on the outline of the selected range, and when the pointer changes to an arrow, hold down the mouse button and drag the outline to the right, until it's over columns E, F, and G. Then release the mouse button to drop the data into place. (Be careful not to over-write the contents of column D.)

3. Next, click the column G button to select the contents of column G.

4. Drag the outline of column G to the left until it's over column A, and then release the mouse button. (Is this beginning to sound like "Insert tab A into slot B?")

5. Finally, select columns E and F, and drag them to columns B and C. Now the data is arranged sequentially from least expensive to most expensive.

Presentation - Datasheet		A	B	C	D
		Letter	Package	Box	4th Qtr
1	Regular mail	$0.32	$8.60	$10.75	20.4
2	Overnight	$9.95	$17.90	$22.00	31.0
3	Courier	$17.50	$48.00	$56.00	43.5
4					

Inserting and Deleting Data

To insert a row or column of cells in the datasheet, click a row number or column letter button, and then choose Cells from Graph's Insert menu. To remove a row or column from the datasheet, click the row number or column letter button for the row or column you want to delete, and then choose Delete from Graph's Edit menu or shortcut menu. To add or remove more than one row or column at a time, drag across the row number or column letter buttons for as many rows or columns as you want to add or remove before you choose the Cells command or the Delete command. For example, to add three columns, drag across three column letter buttons, and then choose Cells from Graph's Insert menu.

When you select only some of the cells in a row or column and then choose Cells from Graph's Insert menu or shortcut menu, the Insert dialog box shown in Figure 6-10 appears. Here you can specify whether you want to push aside (shift) the other cells in the row or column or insert an entire row or column. If you want to push the cells aside, select Shift Cells Right or Shift Cells Down. If you want to insert an entire row or column, select Entire Row or Entire Column. Then click OK.

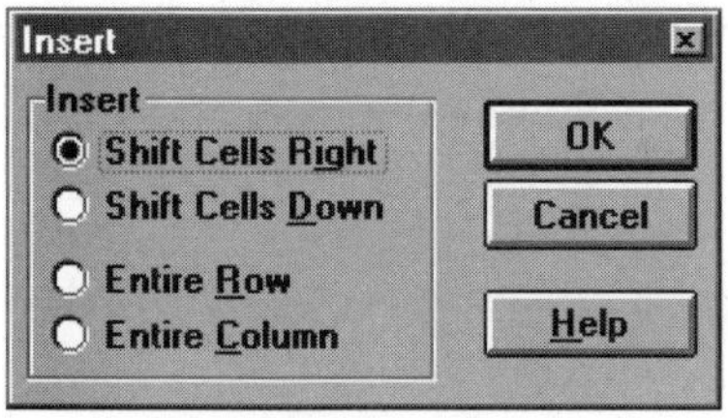

FIGURE 6-10
The Insert
dialog box.

Excluding Data

You can temporarily exclude data from a graph without deleting the data from the datasheet. Excluding data can be helpful when you want to use the same set of data to create several graphs. In one graph, you can compare only certain sets of data, and then, in another graph, you can compare different sets of data from the same data pool.

To exclude a row or column of data, double-click the corresponding row number or column letter button. The selected data in the row or column is dimmed, and the graph adjusts immediately. To include the data once again, double-click the same row number or column letter button.

You can also exclude multiple adjacent rows or columns of data by first selecting one or more cells in the rows or columns you want to exclude. Then choose the Exclude Row/Col command from Graph's Data menu. When the Exclude Row/Col dialog box appears, as shown in Figure 6-11 on the next page, select the appropriate option and click OK.

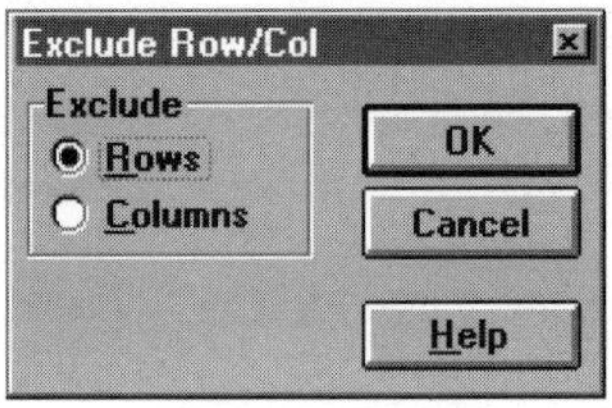

FIGURE 6-11

The Exclude
Row/Col
dialog box.

To return excluded data to a graph, select the excluded row or column, and choose the Include Row/Col command from Graph's Data menu.

Data Arrangements for Special Chart Types

For each chart type, Graph expects you to follow certain rules when it comes to arranging the data in the datasheet. Otherwise, the graph may deliver a message that is different from the one you intended.

Area, Bar, Column, Line, and Surface Charts

Charts with areas, bars, columns, lines, or a surface as their markers all require the same arrangement of data in the datasheet. You enter each series of numbers in a row or a column, and then allow Graph to create the chart. By default, Graph interprets each row of numbers as a series. If you want Graph to interpret each column of numbers as a series, you must click the By Column button on Graph's Standard toolbar or choose the Series in Columns command from Graph's Data menu.

Clicking the By Column button after you've entered numbers in rows can give you an equally legitimate view of the data, whether you create a bar chart or column chart. In fact, you may want to try both options to see which makes your case more clearly. For example, Figure 6-12 on the facing page shows a chart plotted by row. Figure 6-13 shows the same chart plotted by column. The chart in Figure 6-12 emphasizes the comparison of results from quarter to quarter, whereas the one in Figure 6-13 emphasizes the comparison of results by region.

Pie Charts

A pie chart can plot only one series, with each number in the series represented by a pie slice. To plot more than one series, you must use a doughnut chart, which plots multiple series in two dimensions as concentric rings in the chart.

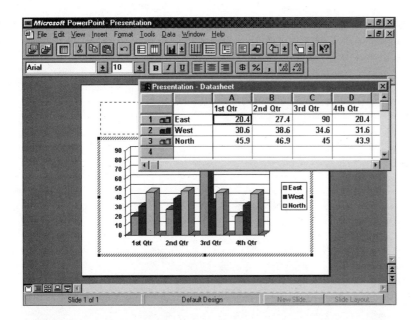

FIGURE 6-12

A chart plotted by row.

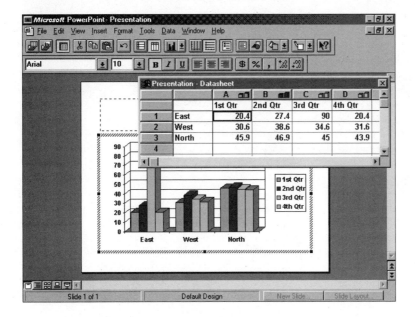

FIGURE 6-13

The same chart plotted by column.

To show multiple breakdowns in three dimensions, you might want to consider using the stacked or 100% stacked subtype of a 3-D bar or column chart. Each bar or column can show the breakdown of a different series.

If you've entered more than one series in the datasheet for a pie chart, the chart plots the first series only. To plot a different series, exclude the earlier series. For example, to plot the third series in a datasheet, exclude the first and second series. Figure 6-14 shows a pie chart that plots the data in row 3 of the datasheet. Notice that rows 1 and 2 have been excluded and that a pie chart marker appears on the row 3 button.

FIGURE 6-14

This pie chart plots the numbers in the third series, row 3, in the datasheet.

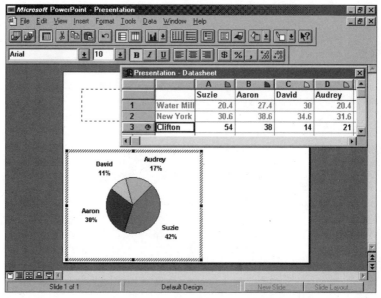

Radar Charts

The numbers in a series are represented as data markers on different radial axes of a radar chart. All the data markers in the same series are connected by a line that forms a ring around the center of the chart.

148

When you enter series in rows, each column is represented by a different radial axis. (The labels at the top of the columns identify the axes.) Figure 6-15 shows a radar chart and its datasheet.

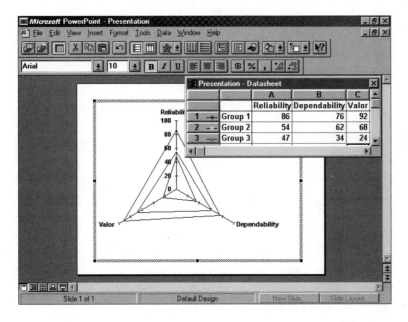

FIGURE 6-15

A radar chart and its datasheet.

High-Low-Close and Open-High-Low-Close Charts

To create these two line chart subtypes, which are most often used to depict stock prices, you must enter all the high numbers in one series, all the low numbers in another series, and so forth. The order in which you enter the numbers is important. If the chart depicts data series in rows, follow one of these patterns:

Row	High-Low-Close Chart	Open-High-Low-Close Chart
1	High value	Opening value
2	Low value	High value
3	Closing value	Low value
4		Closing value

Figure 6-16 on the next page shows an open-high-low-close chart and the datasheet that underlies it.

FIGURE 6-16

An open-high-low-
close chart and
its datasheet.

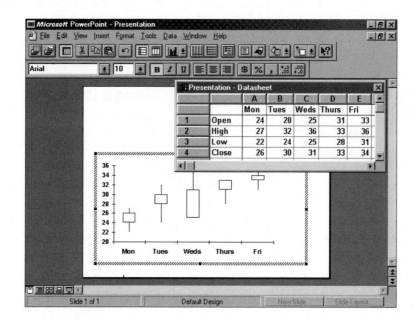

Using Data and Graphs from Microsoft Excel

If you've already typed the numbers for a chart in a Microsoft Excel worksheet, the last thing you want to do is retype the numbers in PowerPoint. Fortunately, there's an easy way to transfer your Excel data to PowerPoint. In fact, you can set up a link between the original numbers in Excel and the copies in Power-Point. Then, if you change the numbers in Excel, the numbers in PowerPoint are updated automatically. You can also import Excel charts into PowerPoint; and you can even drag a chart from an Excel window onto a PowerPoint slide.

Importing Excel Data into Graph

To perform a simple transfer of data from an Excel worksheet to Graph, you can use the Import Data command on Graph's Edit menu. You can then specify the Excel file and the range that contains the data you want to import.

> **NOTE** Use the Import Data command when you want to copy data from an Excel worksheet. To establish a link between the Excel data and the PowerPoint graph, however, you must use a different procedure, as described in the next section.

To import data from an Excel worksheet like the one shown here, follow the steps below.

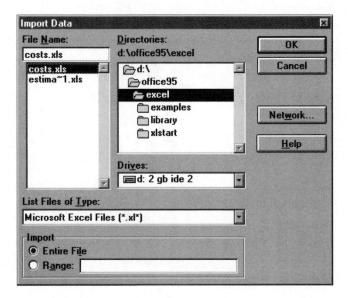

1. Switch to the Graph datasheet by clicking the View Datasheet button on Graph's Standard toolbar or by choosing Datasheet from Graph's View menu.

2. In the datasheet, click the cell located in the upper left corner of the area into which you want to import the data.

3. From Graph's Edit menu, choose the Import Data command. The Import Data dialog box appears, as shown here:

4. Use the Directories list and File Name list to navigate to the Excel file containing the data you want to import.

5. At the bottom of the dialog box, select Entire File to import all the data in the file, or select Range to import only the data in the range you specify. (If you select Range, be sure to enter the range address or the range name in the Range edit box.)

6. Click OK to import the data.

7. If the destination cells in the datasheet already contain data, Graph displays a message warning you that the data will be overwritten. Click OK to proceed, or click Cancel to cancel the import operation. If you click Cancel, you can then select a different destination in the datasheet and begin the procedure again. When the data is successfully imported, it appears in the Graph datasheet like this:

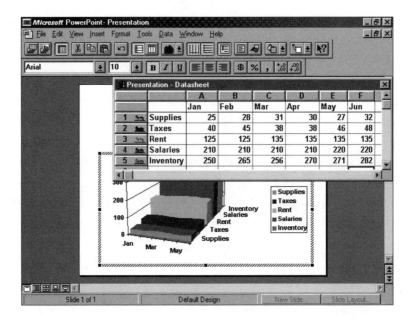

NOTE To import data from an Excel workbook, the data must reside in the first worksheet in the workbook. If it does not, you must reorder the worksheets in the workbook.

TIP You can use the Import Data command to consolidate data from several Excel worksheets into a single Graph datasheet. After you import data from the first worksheet, select another location in the datasheet, import data from the second worksheet, and so on.

Creating a Link Between Excel and Graph

Establishing a link between the data in an Excel worksheet and the data in a Graph datasheet allows you to update the numbers in Excel and then see the changes automatically reflected in PowerPoint.

To create a link, you use a special feature of Windows called OLE. Windows takes care of all the behind-the-scenes complexity. Simply by copying the data to the Windows Clipboard in Excel and then using the Paste Link command in Graph to paste the data from the Clipboard to the datasheet, you automatically establish the link you need. Then, after the link is created, PowerPoint's ChartWizard appears to help you complete the transfer of data.

To create a link, follow these steps:

1. In Excel, select the range of data you want to link to PowerPoint, as shown here:

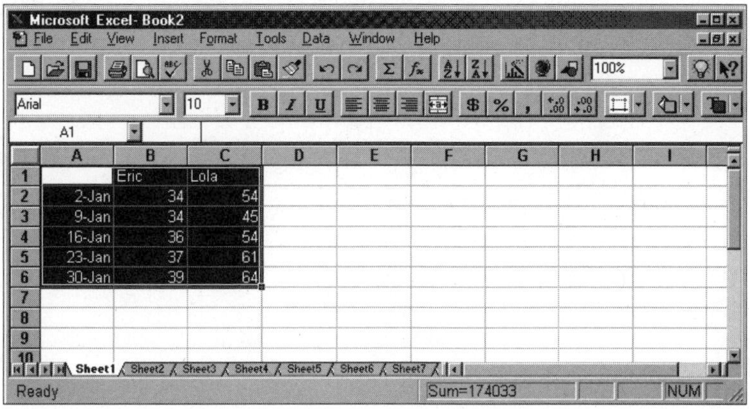

2. Choose the Copy command from Excel's Edit menu to copy the data to the Windows Clipboard.

3. Switch to the datasheet window in PowerPoint, and then select the cell in the upper left corner of the area into which you want to paste the data.

4. From Graph's Edit menu, choose the Paste Link command. If Graph displays a message box cautioning you about overwriting existing data, click OK to continue or click Cancel. When you click OK, the ChartWizard dialog box opens in its own window, as shown here:

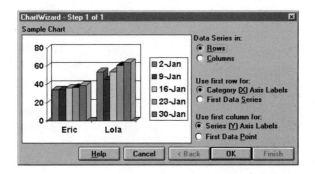

The ChartWizard has only one step, as you can see in the title bar of the dialog box, and it provides several options you can use to determine how data is arranged in the resulting graph. The Sample Chart on the left side of the dialog box displays the results of the options you select.

Use the options in the Data Series in section to specify whether the data series in the Excel worksheet are arranged by row or by column. Use the other options to specify how the information in the first row and first column of the Excel worksheet should be treated. If you want to import both the labels and the data from the Excel worksheet, select the Category (X) Axis Labels option and the Series (Y) Axis Labels option.

5. In the ChartWizard dialog box, select the options you want and then click OK. The data appears in the Graph datasheet, as shown on the facing page.

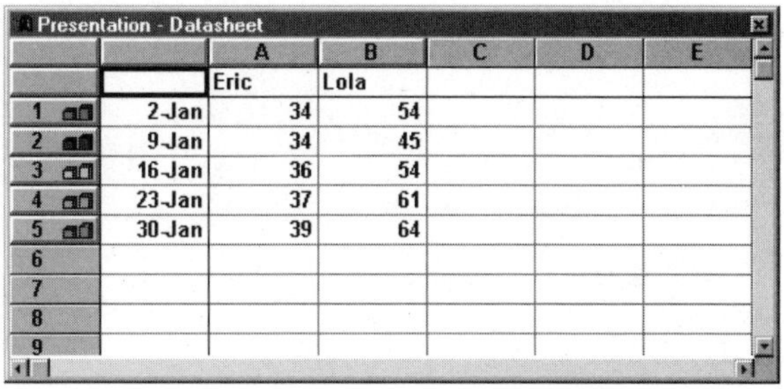

Updating the Link

After you create a link between Excel and PowerPoint, the link will be updated automatically unless you change it to a manual update link. Just for interest's sake, you can arrange the Excel and PowerPoint windows side by side to see the link in action; when you change a number in Excel, you can immediately see the number updated in PowerPoint.

To change the characteristics of the link, choose the Link command from the Graph Edit menu. The Link dialog box appears, as shown in Figure 6-17. To change the link so that it updates only when you click the Update Now button, select the Manual option at the bottom of the Link dialog box. Other options in this dialog box allow you to open the original data in Excel for editing; select a different data source—perhaps a different range in the Excel worksheet; or break the link between Excel and PowerPoint. If you break the link, the data remains in the Graph datasheet, but it is no longer updated when you make changes in the Excel worksheet.

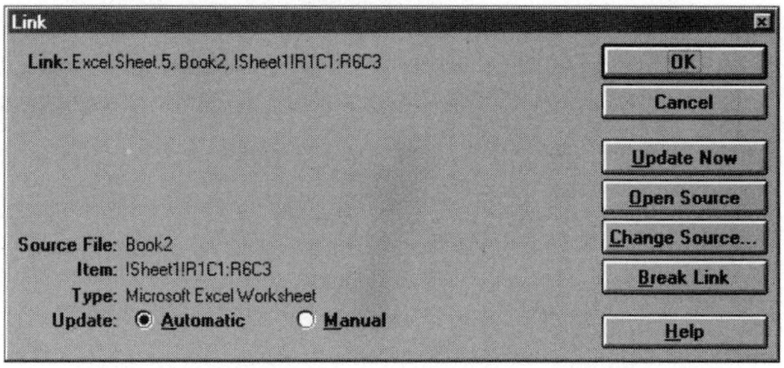

FIGURE 6-17

The Link
dialog box.

Importing an Excel Chart

If you've already created a graph in Excel, you can import the graph into PowerPoint. The graph arrives as a standard graph that you can edit in Graph as if you'd created the graph in PowerPoint rather than in Excel.

155

> **TIP** Another way to bring a Microsoft Excel graph into a presentation is to drag the graph from Excel to a Power-Point slide (press the Ctrl key while you drag to copy the graph into PowerPoint rather than move it) or copy and paste the graph from Excel to PowerPoint. However, both methods produce a picture of the graph rather than an actual graph that you can modify in PowerPoint.

To import a graph that you have created in Excel, follow these steps:

1. From Graph's Edit menu, choose the Import Chart command to display the Open Chart dialog box shown below:

2. In the List Files of Type drop-down list, select either Microsoft Excel 4.0 Charts (*.xlc) or Microsoft Excel 5.0 Charts (*.xls).

3. Use the Directories and File Name lists to navigate to the Excel file you want to import, and then double-click the filename.

The Excel graph data appears in the Graph datasheet, and the graph appears on the slide with the same formatting it had in Excel. You can then use Graph's features to reformat the graph.

> **NOTE** PowerPoint imports the graph on the first chart sheet it finds in an Excel workbook. You may have to rearrange the sheets to bring the chart sheet you want to the front.

Using Text and Data from Data Files

When the data you need for a graph is stored in an ASCII text file (a text file without formatting), you can import the file into Graph using the Import Data command. The columns of data in the file should be separated by tabs, semicolons, commas, or spaces.

To import an ASCII text file, follow these steps:

1. In the Graph datasheet, click the cell in the upper left corner of the destination area for the data.

2. Choose the Import Data command from Graph's Edit menu, and when the Import Data dialog box appears, select Text Files (*.prn, *.txt, *.csv) in the List Files of Type drop-down list.

3. Use the Directories and File Name lists to navigate to the file you want to import, and then double-click the filename. The Text Import Wizard opens, as shown below:

If the columns of data are separated by tabs, semicolons, or commas, the file is *delimited*, and by default the Delimited option is selected as the file type. If the columns of data are separated by spaces, the Fixed Width option is selected. A preview at the bottom of the first Text Import Wizard dialog box shows the data to be imported.

4. Click the Next button to move on to step 2, shown here:

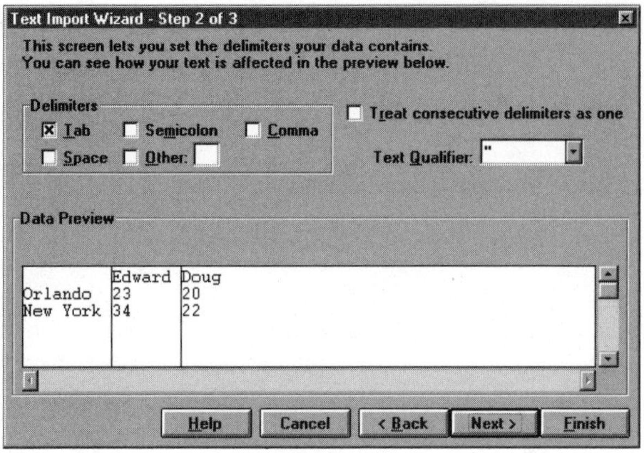

5. If the Text Import Wizard has not properly identified the delimiter used in the file (tabs or commas, for example), select the correct delimiter in the Step 2 dialog box. Vertical lines should properly separate the columns of data in the Data Preview box.

6. Click the Next button to get to step 3, shown below:

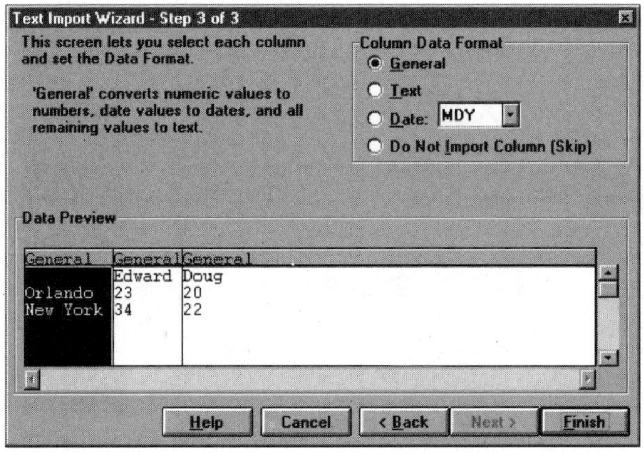

7. Select each column of data in the Data Preview box by clicking anywhere in the column. Then check the Column Data Format section that appears in the upper right corner of the Step 3 dialog box. If the Text Import Wizard has selected the incorrect data format, select the correct format now.

8. Click the Finish button to complete the import procedure. The data appears in the Graph datasheet, and you can then format the resulting graph to suit your needs.

That completes your introduction to creating graphs and graph slides. In Chapter 10, "Formatting Graphs," you'll learn how to create custom graphs that you can tailor to meet even the most demanding requirements. For now, you might want to spend a little time reviewing PowerPoint's graphing features before moving on to the next chapter, where you'll learn how to add organization chart slides to your presentations.

Chapter 7

Adding Organization Chart Slides

An organization chart, or *org chart*, shows the hierarchy of an organization using a series of boxes and connecting lines. A classic hierarchy is the military's structure of commanding officers, officers, and enlisted men and women. But an org chart can also depict the structure of a company, a division within a company or a government department, or even groups of organizations that are affiliated in a "top-down" arrangement.

This chapter introduces you to PowerPoint's built-in organization chart module. You'll learn how to create an org chart slide from scratch, how to add an org chart to an existing slide, and how to incorporate an existing org chart in a presentation. In addition, you'll learn how to create and modify the org chart's structure and how to format its text, boxes, and connecting lines.

Org Chart Basics

The procedure you use to add an org chart to your presentation depends on where you want the chart to appear. If you want the org chart to be on a new slide that is dedicated to the chart, you can create a new slide and then select a layout that includes an org chart placeholder. If you want the chart to be on an existing slide or if you want to use an existing org chart, you can add an org chart object to a slide.

Creating an Org Chart Slide

PowerPoint's autolayouts make it easy to create an org chart slide for a presentation. When you click the New Slide button and select the Organization Chart autolayout, PowerPoint creates a new slide with an org chart placeholder.

Here are the specific steps for creating an org chart slide:

1. In Slide view, move to the slide that you want the org chart slide to follow.

2. Click the New Slide button at the bottom of the PowerPoint window.

3. In the New Slide dialog box, select the Organization Chart autolayout, as shown on the facing page:

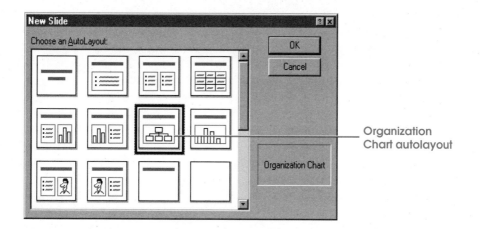

Organization
Chart autolayout

4. Click OK or double-click the Organization Chart autolayout. Power-
Point creates this new slide with an org chart placeholder:

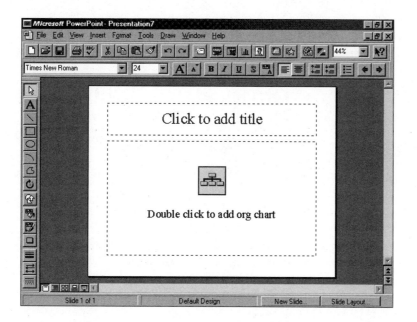

5. Double-click the org chart placeholder. The Microsoft Organization
Chart module opens, as shown on the next page. (We reduced the
size of the org chart and maximized the Org Chart window so that the
entire org chart is visible.)

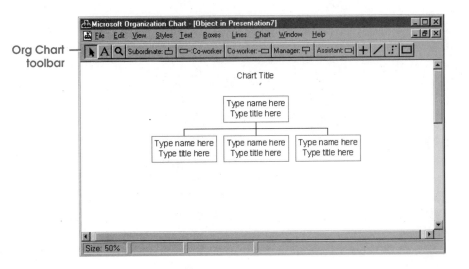

Org Chart toolbar

As you can see, the org chart contains a number of placeholders to simplify the task of entering information in the chart. And the Microsoft Organization Chart module comes equipped with a menu bar and a toolbar so that you can edit and format the org chart.

Adding an Org Chart to an Existing Slide

To include both an org chart and another object, such as a group of bulleted text items or a graph on a slide, you can add an org chart to an existing slide. The bulleted text items can help explain the org chart, and a graph can depict a numeric achievement that resulted from a change in the organization's structure.

TIP   Org charts should be large enough that viewers can clearly see the boxes and the text inside. If the chart is too small, viewers won't be able to make out the detail. You might consider breaking the structure into separate charts that show divisions, or you might want to place the chart on a new slide in order to give it plenty of space.

The easiest way to add an org chart to an existing slide is to display the slide in Slide view, and click the Insert Organization Chart button on the Standard toolbar. (If you don't see the Insert Organization Chart button, you can add it to the Standard toolbar using the procedure described on page 459.) The Microsoft Organization Chart module opens in a window, as shown above.

Here's another method for adding an org chart to an existing slide:

1. In Slide view, move to the slide you want to add the org chart to.

2. Choose Object from the Insert menu to display the Insert Object dialog box, shown below:

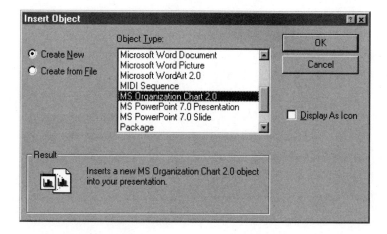

3. Make sure the Create New option is selected, and then double-click MS Organization Chart 2.0 in the Object Type list. (You'll probably have to scroll down to it.)

The Microsoft Organization Chart module opens in a window so that you can create the org chart.

See Also For more information about entering text in org charts, see "Filling in the Boxes," page 167.

Using an Existing Org Chart

If you've already created and saved an org chart, you can pull it into a presentation by inserting the chart as an object. If you follow the procedure below, you can double-click the chart to edit it from within PowerPoint:

1. In Slide view, move to the slide you want to add the org chart to.

2. Choose Object from the Insert menu.

3. In the Insert Object dialog box, select the Create from File option.

4. Enter the org chart's pathname in the File edit box. If you can't remember the pathname, click the Browse button to display the Browse dialog box, where you can search for the org chart file. After you find the file, simply double-click it to enter its pathname in the Insert Object dialog box.

5. Select the Display As Icon check box only if you want an icon to represent the chart on the slide. During an electronic presentation, you can then "drill down" to the Microsoft Organization Chart module by double-clicking the icon. The org chart opens in the module, and you can modify it right in front of your audience.

6. Click OK to add the org chart to the current slide.

> **NOTE** If you want to establish a link between the original org chart file and the picture of the org chart that will be displayed in PowerPoint, select the Link option in the Insert Object dialog box. Linking allows the chart in the presentation to reflect any subsequent changes that are made in the original org chart file. But be careful: If you select Link and then move the presentation to another computer, the chart will not come along for the ride. That's because the data for the chart is stored in the external org chart file rather than in PowerPoint. To store the data for the org chart in PowerPoint, you must leave the Link option unselected in the Insert Object dialog box.

Creating the Org Chart Structure

When the Microsoft Organization Chart window (hereafter known as the *Org Chart window*) opens, the beginning of a hierarchy (one manager and three subordinates) is displayed in four boxes. (If you see only one box in the Org Chart window, you can choose Options from the Org Chart Edit menu, select the Use standard 4-box template for new charts option, and click OK. Then close the Org Chart window, and click No when the program asks whether to update the presentation. You can then create a new org chart with four boxes.)

Before you begin entering text in the org chart's boxes, you may want to give the chart a title. Select the text *Chart Title* at the top of the chart, and type a new title, such as *Our Division*. You can press Enter at the end of the title line to add a line for a subtitle. In fact, you can create a series of subtitles, but then you'll have little room left for the chart!

Filling in the Boxes

To start entering names in the org chart's boxes, follow these steps:

1. Click the box at the highest level.

2. Type a name in the box, and press Enter. You can also press Tab or the Down arrow key. As shown below, when you begin typing, the box opens to reveal spaces for two comments in addition to the name and the title.

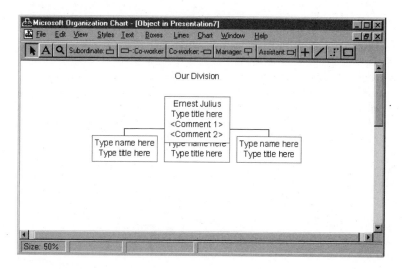

3. Type the title and press Enter.

4. If you want to include comments, type them in, pressing Enter after each one. If you don't want to include comments, go on to step 5.

5. Press Ctrl+Down arrow key to move to the first subordinate box.

6. Follow steps 2 through 4 above to fill in the box.

7. To move to the next box, simply press Ctrl+Right arrow key. You can also press Ctrl+Left arrow key to move to the box to the left, and you can press Ctrl+Up arrow key to move to the top box.

Editing the Text

After you enter text in an org chart box, you can edit the text by clicking the box once to select it and then clicking an insertion point in the text you want to edit. You can use all the same text selection and editing techniques you use elsewhere in PowerPoint.

> **TIP** After you enter text in a box, you can press Esc to complete the entry but leave the box selected. Then you can immediately edit the text if necessary.

You can also edit the text in an org chart by clicking the Enter Text button on the Org Chart toolbar and then clicking any of the text in the chart. As you'll learn later, the Enter Text button is useful for typing text directly on the chart background as well.

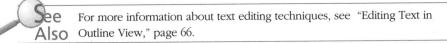

See Also For more information about text editing techniques, see "Editing Text in Outline View," page 66.

Adding and Deleting Boxes

Chances are, your organization has more than three members, so you need to know how to add more boxes to the org chart. Fortunately, adding boxes is easy. On the Org Chart toolbar, click the button for the type of box you want to add, and then click the box that you want to connect the new box to. To add more than one box at a time, click the appropriate toolbar button the desired number of times, and then click an existing box.

The boxes you can add to an org chart are shown in Table 7-1, along with their corresponding buttons and a description of each button's function.

To add a subordinate to one of the three subordinates already in the chart, follow these steps:

1. Click the Subordinate button on the Org Chart toolbar.

2. Click one of the three boxes in the second row of the chart. A new box appears, ready for you to type in a name, title, and comments, as shown on the facing page.

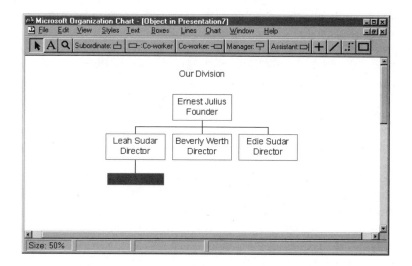

Box	Toolbar Button	Function
⊓	Subordinate	Adds a box at the level below the selected box.
⊏⊐	Left Co-worker	Adds a box to the left of the selected box at the same level.
⊏⊐	Right Co-worker	Adds a box to the right of the selected box at the same level.
⊓	Manager	Adds a box at the level of the selected box and moves the selected box down one level. The selected box is attached to the new box as a subordinate.
⊏⊐	Assistant	Adds a box below the selected box. The new box is attached to the line of command but is not a part of it (a staff position).

TABLE 7-1

The org chart boxes and their corresponding toolbar buttons.

TIP   You may want to diagram each division of a complicated organizational structure in a separate chart to avoid overcrowding. You can create a preliminary organization chart that depicts the broad picture (the branches of the organization without any of the "leaves"), and then show each division in detail in a separate chart.

Deleting an org chart box is as easy as adding one. Simply select the box you want to delete, and then press the Delete key or choose Clear from the Org Chart Edit menu. To delete two or more boxes, first select the boxes by clicking one box, holding down the Shift key, and clicking the other boxes. Then press Delete to delete all the selected boxes.

TIP   If the org chart boxes you want to delete are adjacent to one another, you can use the Select button on the toolbar to drag a selection box around the boxes. Then you can press Delete to delete the selected boxes.

A Sample Org Chart

To try your hand at creating an org chart with an assortment of boxes, follow this example: Imagine that you need to diagram the structure of a nonprofit organization and its regional affiliates. If you've been following along by creating an actual chart, choose Exit and Return to *Presentation* from the Org Chart File menu, and then click No when you are asked if you want to update the chart. When you return to PowerPoint, start a new org chart either by double-clicking the org chart placeholder or by clicking the Insert Organization Chart button (if you have added it to the Standard toolbar), and then follow these steps:

1. After the Org Chart window opens, choose 50% of Actual from the Org Chart View menu to reduce the size of the chart. Then select the text *Chart Title* at the top of the new chart, and type *League of Lefties*.

2. Click the topmost box once, type *Renee A. Gauche* as the name, press Enter, and type *National Director* as the title.

3. For the first comment, type *Wash., D.C.* You won't enter a second comment, so press Ctrl+Down arrow key to move to the first subordinate box. The org chart should appear as shown on the facing page.

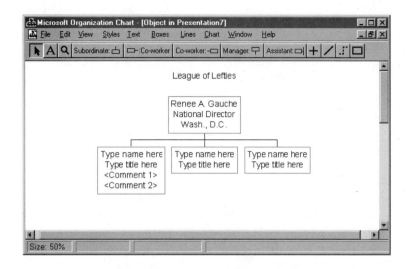

4. In the first subordinate box, type *Greta Links,* press Enter, and type *Director* as the title and *California* as the first comment. Then press Ctrl+Right arrow key to move to the second subordinate box.

5. In the second subordinate box, type *Leanora Izquierda,* press Enter, and type *Director* as the title and *New York* as the first comment.

6. The League of Lefties does not have a third individual at the Director level, so click the third subordinate box, and press Delete. The chart now looks like this:

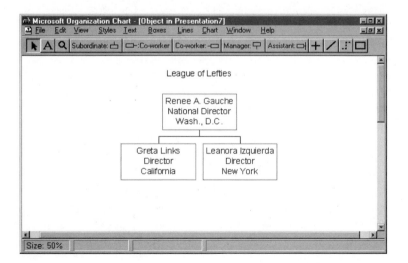

7. Greta Links has two subordinates, so click the Subordinate button on the toolbar twice, and then click Greta's box. Two subordinates appear.

8. Leanora Izquierda has three subordinates, so click the Subordinate button three times, and then click Leanora's box.

9. Renee A. Gauche has an assistant, so click the Assistant button, and then click Renee's box. Next, type *Sylvia Southpaw* as the name, type *Assistant* as the title, and then click anywhere outside the org chart.

10. Enter the names of the subordinates under both Greta and Leanora. Click the first subordinate box under Greta, type *Tiffany,* press Ctrl+Right arrow key, and type *Brent.* Type *Sal, Howie,* and *Clarice* as the subordinates under Leanora. Here are the results:

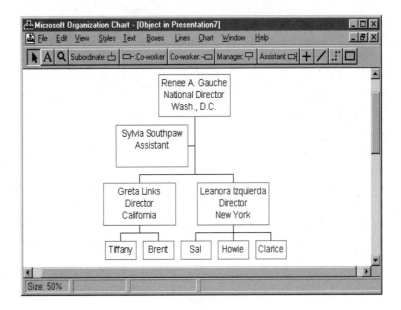

Later in this chapter, you'll modify the structure and change the formatting of the org chart you've just created. For now, return with the chart to Power-Point by first choosing Update *Presentation* from the Org Chart File menu and then choosing Exit and Return to *Presentation* from the File menu. In a moment, the chart appears on the current PowerPoint slide. Save the PowerPoint presentation with a name of your choosing so that you can retrieve it later.

Moving Boxes

The ease with which you can modify the structure of an org chart suits today's dynamic organizations. But fortunately or unfortunately, depending on your place in the organization, restructuring an actual org chart in PowerPoint is far easier than restructuring an actual organization.

Restructuring an organization in real life often results in moving people from one manager to another. The counterpart in PowerPoint is dragging a box from one place in the org chart to another. You can drag boxes to other positions at the same level in the chart, or move them up or down within the organization's structure.

To move a box in an org chart, follow these steps:

1. Open the org chart in the Org Chart window.

2. Place the mouse pointer on the box you want to move.

3. Hold down the left mouse button, and drag the box's frame to another box, as shown below:

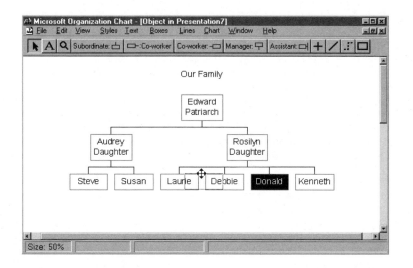

4. When the frame is in position, release the mouse button.

When you drag a box's frame near the left or right inside edge of another box and release the mouse button, the moved box appears to the left or right of the other box, at the same level. When you drag the frame near the bottom inside edge of another box, the moved box appears below the other box, as a subordinate.

When you drag the frame onto another box, an indicator appears inside the frame. As shown in Figure 7-1, the indicator is a left arrow when the moved box will appear at the left side of the existing box. The indicator is a right arrow when the moved box will appear at the right side of the existing box. The indicator is a subordinate box when the moved box will appear below the existing box, as a subordinate.

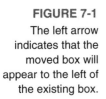

FIGURE 7-1

The left arrow indicates that the moved box will appear to the left of the existing box.

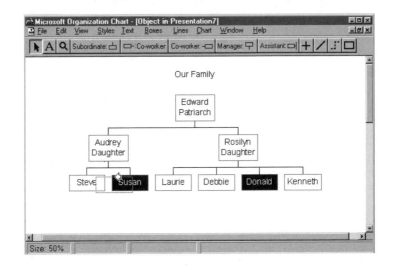

Try moving a box in the org chart you created earlier by first opening the presentation file (if necessary), double-clicking the org chart to open the Org Chart window, and then placing the mouse pointer on Sal's box. Next, hold down the left mouse button, and drag Sal's box onto Greta's box without releasing the mouse button. Then move Sal's box toward the bottom of Greta's box, and when the subordinate indicator appears, release the mouse button to drop Sal's box into place. (Sal now appears to the right of Brent.) Next move Sal between Tiffany and Brent by clicking anywhere outside the chart to de-select Sal's box and dragging Sal's box onto Brent's box. Notice the left arrow inside Sal's box when you drag it onto Brent's box. The arrow indicates that Sal's box will drop to the left of Brent's box, just as you want. Release the mouse button to see the results shown in Figure 7-2.

Finally, return to the presentation by choosing Update *Presentation* from the Org Chart File menu and then choosing Exit and Return to *Presentation* from the File menu. Resave the presentation file with the changes by clicking the Save button on the Standard toolbar, choosing Save from the File menu, or pressing Ctrl+S.

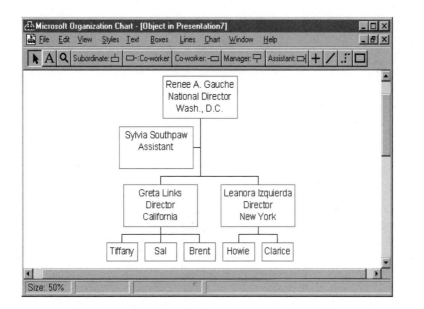

FIGURE 7-2
The revised
org chart.

Changing the Style of Groups and Branches

The subordinates under a manager are called a *group*. By default, PowerPoint displays a group in boxes that are side by side. But, from the Styles menu, you can choose several other ways to display a group. For example, the members of a group can be shown as a vertical list, or they can be depicted as leaves that emanate from a central branch.

Before you can change the style of an org chart group, you must select the group. So your first step is to double-click any member of the group, or click a member and then press Ctrl+G (*G* for *Group*) to select the entire group. You can also select a group by selecting one member of the group and choosing Select and then Group from the Org Chart Edit menu. Figure 7-3 on the next page shows the members of a group after they have been selected. Note that the group members report to the same manager.

After you select a group, open the Styles menu, and click one of the six group style buttons at the top of the menu. For a group at the lowest level of a chart, a useful style is that shown on the second button in the second row of styles. Arranging a group in this style can reduce the horizontal space needed by a chart whose organizational structure is wide rather than deep.

Just as you can change the style of an org chart group, you can also change the style of an org chart *branch*. A branch consists of a manager and

FIGURE 7-3
The members of a
selected group.

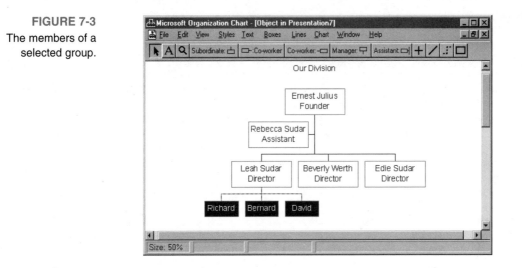

all the manager's subordinates. To select a branch, select the manager at the top of the branch, and then press Ctrl+B (*B* for *Branch*), or choose Select and then Branch from the Org Chart Edit menu. After you select a branch, you can choose one of the styles from the Styles menu.

TIP   You can also select an org chart group or branch by clicking the Select button on the toolbar and dragging a selection box around the group or branch.

Two special styles at the bottom of the Styles menu let you change the rank of members of a group. The first style, Assistant, changes selected members of a group to assistants. For example, Figure 7-4 displays two org charts on a slide. The left chart shows three subordinates under a manager. The right chart shows the result after two of the subordinates are converted to assistants with the Assistant style.

The second style at the bottom of the Styles menu is the Co-manager style. You can use this style to indicate two or more members of the organization who report to the same manager and share power. After you select the members you want to make comanagers, click the Co-manager style on the Styles menu. Figure 7-5 shows two subordinates who have become comanagers.

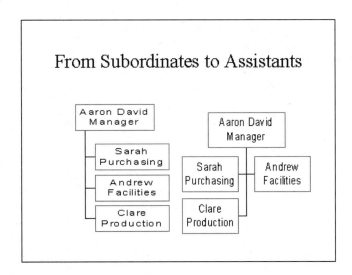

FIGURE 7-4

Subordinates
converted to
assistants with the
Assistant style.

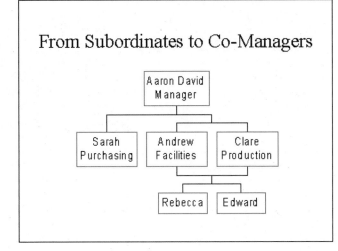

FIGURE 7-5

Subordinates
converted to
comanagers with
the Co-manager
style.

Try changing the style of the groups in the org chart you created earlier, by first opening the presentation file, if necessary, and then double-clicking the org chart to open the Org Chart window. Next, click one of the subordinates under Greta, and press Ctrl+G to select the entire group of subordinates who report to Greta. Open the Styles menu, and click the second style in the second row. The three side-by-side boxes of the group change to a small ladder that lists the three subordinates. You can try other styles or choose the same style for Leonora's group of subordinates. Figure 7-6 on the next page shows Greta's group with its new style.

FIGURE 7-6

The new style
applied to the
group of
subordinates
who report to
Greta Links.

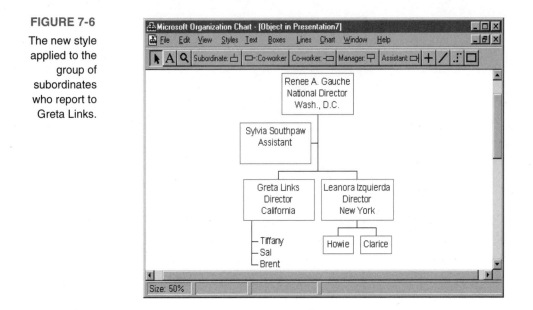

Formatting the Org Chart

An org chart inherits the design characteristics of the template that you attached to the current presentation. For example, the template determines the font of the text and the color of the boxes in the org chart. But, as you'll learn in this section, after you complete an organizational structure, you can still make changes to the appearance of the chart. For instance, you can emphasize the titles of the organization members with a special color or change the borders of the boxes.

Zooming In and Out

Before you start formatting an org chart, you should get acquainted with the Org Chart zoom feature. That way, you can see exactly what you're doing when you make changes to a chart.

To zoom in on an org chart, click the Zoom button on the toolbar, and then click the area of the org chart you want to zoom in on. To zoom out, click the Zoom button again (the Button now displays a miniature org chart instead of a magnifying glass), and then click the org chart. You can also use the following commands to change the zoom percentage of the chart: Choose Size to Window from the View menu or press F9 to fit the entire chart within the Org Chart window; choose 50% of Actual or press F10 to reduce the chart to 50 percent of its actual size, which, in turn, is approximately 50 percent of its printed size; and choose 200% of Actual or press F12 to enlarge the chart so that you can focus on some of the chart detail.

Formatting the Text

The procedures for formatting the text in an org chart are similar to the procedures for formatting text elsewhere in PowerPoint. Rather than use commands on the Format menu, however, you use commands on the Org Chart Text menu. These commands allow you to change the font, color, and alignment of the text in org chart boxes.

Of course, before you can use the commands on the Text menu, you must select the text you want to format. To select all the text in a box, click the box. To select all the text in several boxes, hold down the Shift key as you click each box. You can also select specific boxes by using the Select commands on the Org Chart Edit menu. Table 7-2 on the next page describes each of the Select commands.

> **TIP**   You can also select several adjacent boxes by clicking the Select button on the toolbar and dragging a selection box around the boxes.

To format specific text in a box, such as the title only, click the box, and then click an insertion point in the text that you want to format. Next, use any of the standard text selection techniques to select the text in the box. For example, drag across the text with the mouse, double-click a word, or hold down the Shift key as you press the Left or Right arrow key. By selecting only certain text within a box, you can change the appearance of as little or as much text as you want. You can even format a single character with a special font or color.

Unfortunately, PowerPoint offers no easy method to select all names or all titles in an org chart. You must move from box to box, selecting the name or the title, if you want to apply special formatting to only those elements.

TABLE 7-2
The Select
commands.

Command	Function
All	Selects all boxes in the org chart.
All Assistants	Selects all assistants.
All Co-Managers	Selects all members who have been made comanagers with the Co-manager style.
All Managers	Selects only members who have subordinates.
All Non-Managers	Selects only members who do not have subordinates.
Group	Selects the other members of a group. You must have one group member selected first.
Branch	Selects the other members of a branch. You must have one branch member selected first.
Lowest Level	Selects only the boxes at the lowest level of the org chart.
Connecting Lines	Selects only the connecting lines between boxes.
Background Objects	Selects only the boxes and lines drawn with the drawing tools.

Formatting the Boxes

By selecting an org chart box and then using the commands on the Boxes menu, you can change the box's color, add a shadow, and modify the box's borders. Before you can make any of these changes, however, you must select the box or boxes you want to format using the techniques described in the previous section. Then simply choose the desired commands from the Boxes menu. For example, to format a box with the color red and an extra-thick border, first click the box to select it, choose the Color command from the Boxes menu, click the red color option in the Color dialog box, and then click OK. Next choose the Border Style command from the Boxes menu, and click the second border option in the second column of the Border Style submenu.

The Color command allows you to apply any of the colors in the current color palette to the interior of the selected box or boxes. (After you finish creating the org chart, you'll see it on the slide, against the slide background, and you'll be able to determine whether the box interior color clashes with the slide background color.)

The Shadow command allows you to apply a shadow that extends in one or more directions behind the selected box or boxes. Shadows give boxes a three-dimensional look. Figure 7-7 shows shadows added to the boxes in the sample org chart.

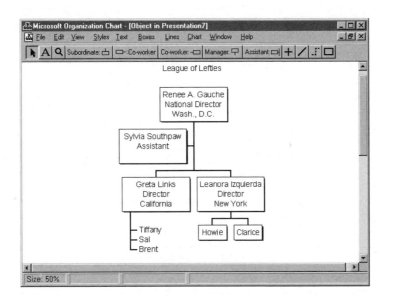

FIGURE 7-7

The sample org chart with shadows added.

To change the style, color, and line style of a selected box's border, use the three Border commands on the Boxes menu. Figure 7-8 shows the sample org chart formatted with thick, dashed borders.

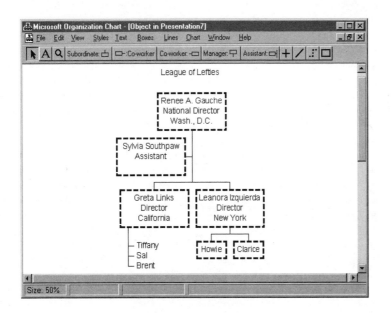

FIGURE 7-8

The sample org chart formatted with thick, dashed borders.

Formatting the Lines

You can change the thickness, style, and color of the lines that connect org chart boxes just as easily as you change the formatting of the boxes. Before you can change the formatting of a line, you must select the line by clicking it. The line then changes to a dashed light gray to show that it is selected. You can select multiple lines by holding down the Shift key as you click each line, or you can select all the lines by choosing Select and then Connecting Lines from the Edit menu.

 TIP You can also select multiple lines by clicking the Select button on the toolbar and dragging a selection box around the lines.

After you select the line or lines you want to format, choose the Thickness, Style, or Color command from the Lines menu. Each command offers a set of options that are fairly self-explanatory. Figure 7-9 shows the the sample org chart formatted with thicker connecting lines. Figure 7-10 shows the chart's connecting lines with the dotted line style.

FIGURE 7-9

The sample org chart formatted with thicker connecting lines.

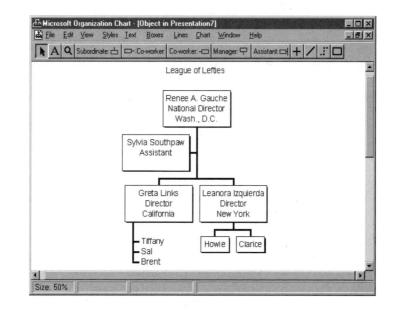

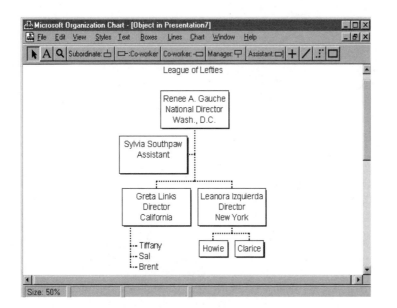

FIGURE 7-10

The sample org chart formatted with dotted connecting lines.

Drawing Boxes and Lines with the Drawing Tools

Sometimes the built-in box arrangements (subordinates under managers, assistants below managers, and comanagers sharing power) simply cannot describe the complicated, spaghetti-like reporting structures in an organization. Fortunately, you can add new boxes and lines easily with the Microsoft Organization Chart module's drawing tools, shown below.

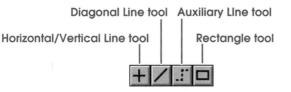

NOTE If you don't see four drawing tools to the right of the Assistant button on the toolbar, choose Show Draw Tools from the View menu or press Ctrl+D.

To draw a horizontal or vertical line or a diagonal line on the chart, click the Horizontal/Vertical Line or Diagonal Line tool, respectively, place the cross-hair pointer at the starting point for the line, hold down the left mouse button, and then drag to draw the line. After you add a line, you can select the line by clicking it with the mouse. You can then delete the line with the Delete key, format the line with the commands on the Lines menu, or change the line's length by dragging the handles at either end. You can also move a selected line by dragging it with the mouse.

To connect two boxes with a line, click the Auxiliary Line tool, place the pointer at the edge of the first box, and then drag to the edge of the second box, as shown in Figure 7-11. As you drag, you'll see the connecting line appear. If the connecting line has three segments (like the one in Figure 7-11), you can drag the middle segment to change the size or shape of the line. You may have to move the middle segment if the connecting line overlaps an existing line or box.

FIGURE 7-11

A new connecting line has been added to the sample org chart.

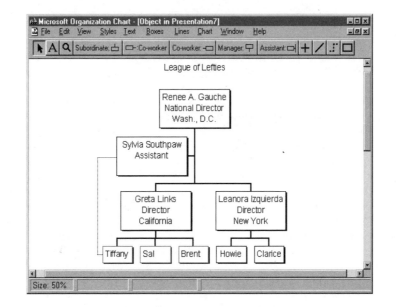

To draw a new box, as shown in Figure 7-12, click the Rectangle tool, place the cross-hair pointer where you want the box to appear, and then drag to create the new box. To adjust the size or shape of the new box, drag one of the handles at the sides or corners of the box. To move the box, place the mouse pointer on the border of the box, between two handles, and drag in the desired direction.

You cannot use the Auxiliary Line tool to connect new boxes with existing chart boxes or with other new boxes. To connect new boxes, you must draw lines with the Horizontal/Vertical Line tool or the Diagonal Line tool.

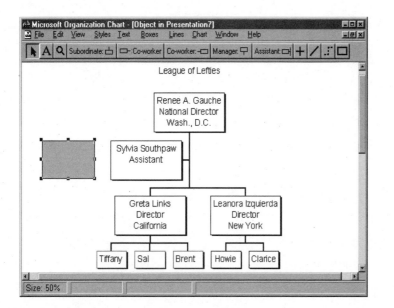

FIGURE 7-12
A new box has
been added to the
sample org chart.

Returning to PowerPoint

When the org chart is complete, choose Update *Presentation* from the Org Chart File menu, and then choose Exit and Return to *Presentation* from the File menu. If you choose Exit and Return without choosing Update first, Power-Point displays a dialog box asking whether you want to update the chart. Click Yes to proceed.

The new org chart appears on the current PowerPoint slide. You can move the entire chart or drag a corner handle to resize the chart, but the chart always remains the same shape.

To edit the chart, double-click it. The Microsoft Organization Chart window reopens with the chart inside, ready for editing.

In this chapter, you've learned to create another special type of object that you can place on PowerPoint slides: organization charts. You learned about graph slides in the previous chapter, and in the next chapter, you'll complete the survey of slide types by learning about table slides.

Chapter 8

Adding Table Slides

When you want to display text paragraphs side by side—to lay out the pros and cons of an issue, for example—you can use the row-and-column format of a table. PowerPoint's table slides are quick to make and easy to modify, especially when compared to the alternative, which is to align text in columns with tab stops.

Table slides often hold text only, but they can hold numbers just as easily. When you don't need the power of a graph to illustrate a result, a table can do quite nicely. Tables are also useful as a backup to a graph, when the audience needs to see the raw data.

This chapter focuses on how to create a slide devoted entirely to a table and how to add a table to an existing slide. Because PowerPoint uses the table-making module from Microsoft Word 7 for Windows 95, not everyone can create a table in PowerPoint. If you do not have Word 7, you must create a table in another application and import it into PowerPoint as an object, which is a more complex process.

By borrowing Word's table-making module, PowerPoint gives you all of Word's advanced text handling and formatting capabilities as you create tables. For example, you can use Word's thesaurus to find a synonym. In fact, you gain access to all of Word's menus and tools without ever having to leave PowerPoint.

Table Basics

When you need to include a table in a presentation, you can create a new slide with the Table autolayout or you can add the table to an existing slide that already contains other objects, such as a group of bulleted text items.

Creating a Table Slide

Creating a table slide for a presentation is easy. Just follow these steps:

1. In Slide view, move to the slide that you want the table slide to follow.

2. Click the New Slide button at the bottom of the PowerPoint window.

3. In the New Slide dialog box, double-click the Table autolayout:

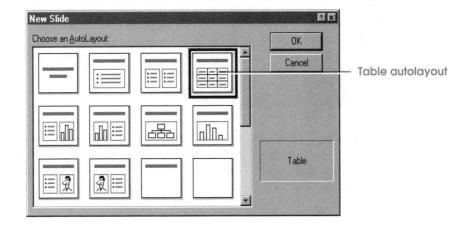

— Table autolayout

As you can see in the figure below, the new slide contains two placeholders: one for the slide title and one for the table.

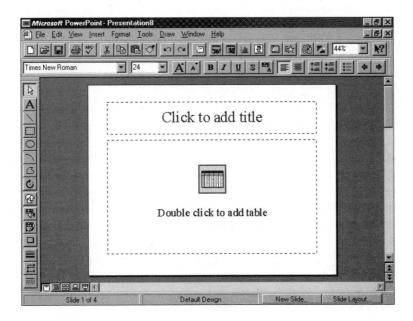

4. Double-click the table placeholder to display this dialog box:

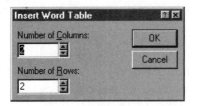

5. In the Insert Word Table dialog box, enter the number of columns and the number of rows you want to include in the table by typing new numbers in the Number of Columns and Number of Rows edit boxes or by clicking the up or down arrows next to the edit boxes. Then click OK to create the table.

Using a Microsoft Excel Table

If the data for a graph comes from Microsoft Excel, you might want to reserve a slide to display the Excel table as a backup slide. (That way, if someone asks for clarification of the table's data, you can produce the original Excel table.) When you embed an Excel table in a PowerPoint slide, the table appears just as it does in Excel, plus you gain all the advantages of Excel's data calculation powers from within PowerPoint. For example, Excel tables (actually small worksheets embedded in PowerPoint slides) can include formulas that carry out complicated calculations, and the formula results are updated automatically when any of the numbers change. For information about embedding an Excel table, see "Using PowerPoint with Microsoft Excel," page 445.

Adding a Table to an Existing Slide

You can use either of two methods to add a table to an existing slide. Here are the steps for the first method:

1. Click the Insert Microsoft Word Table button on the Standard toolbar to display the following 4 x 5 grid of empty cells as shown on the facing page:

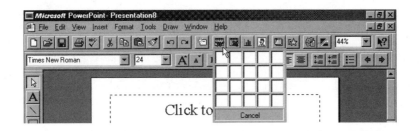

2. Position the mouse pointer on the cell in the upper left corner of the grid, hold down the left mouse button, and drag across the number of columns (up to 12) and down the number of rows (up to 6) you want in the table. For example, the result of the grid selected below would be a table with five rows and three columns.

3. Release the mouse button to add the table to the current slide.

The second method you can use to add a table to an existing slide involves the following steps:

1. Choose the Microsoft Word Table command from the Insert menu.

2. When the Insert Word Table dialog box appears, as shown earlier, enter the number of columns and rows you want in the table, and click OK.

TIP If you've already created a table in Word, you can drag and drop the table onto a PowerPoint slide, as you'll learn in "Using PowerPoint with Microsoft Word," page 435.

Entering Text in a Table

When you create a new table slide, an empty table appears within a gray frame on the slide. Vertical and horizontal rulers adjoin the table, and dotted lines called *gridlines* mark the boundaries of the columns and rows of cells in the table. Figure 8-1 shows a slide with a brand-new table.

FIGURE 8-1

A slide with a
new table.

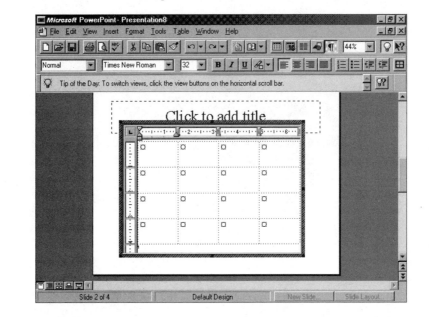

When the new table appears on the current slide, the menus and toolbars from Word replace the PowerPoint menus and toolbars. (Word's Tip Wizard also appears, just below the Formatting toolbar. To reduce screen clutter, you can turn off the Tip Wizard by right-clicking it and deselecting Tip Wizard from the shortcut menu.) In fact, if it weren't for *PowerPoint* in the title bar, you might think you had switched to Word entirely. PowerPoint's chameleon-like ability to transform itself, provided by OLE, lets you use all of Word's menus and tools without leaving PowerPoint.

After you finish the table, you must click outside the gray frame. Only the section of the table within the gray frame is placed on the slide, and PowerPoint's menus and toolbars reappear.

WARNING If you move a table's gray frame before you add the table to a slide, you may not see the entire table on the slide.

If you have created a table in Word before, you know exactly what to do after you specify the dimensions of the table. The close partnership among all the Microsoft Office 95 applications makes it easy to move from one application to another. But if you haven't used Word's table features, don't worry. This chapter leads you through everything you need to know.

The first thing you should consider is the structure of the table. For example, you'll probably want to use the cells at the tops of columns or beginnings of rows for table headings. Then, after you enter the table headings, you can enter data in the remaining cells. As you'll learn later in the chapter, it's not necessary to know exactly how many columns and rows you need from the start because you can easily add columns and rows at any time.

When you start a table, the insertion point flashes in the first cell in the upper left corner of the table. As always, you type to enter text at the location of the insertion point. To move the insertion point to another cell, press the Tab key or click the destination cell. Press Shift+Tab to move back one cell.

As you type, the text wraps within the current width of the cell. In other words, when you've typed all the way across a cell, the next word you type moves to a second line within the cell, as shown in Figure 8-2. In fact, as shown in Figure 8-3 on the next page, the entire table row grows vertically rather than horizontally to accommodate its longest text entry. Later in this chapter, you'll learn how to change the height of rows, as well as the width of columns, manually.

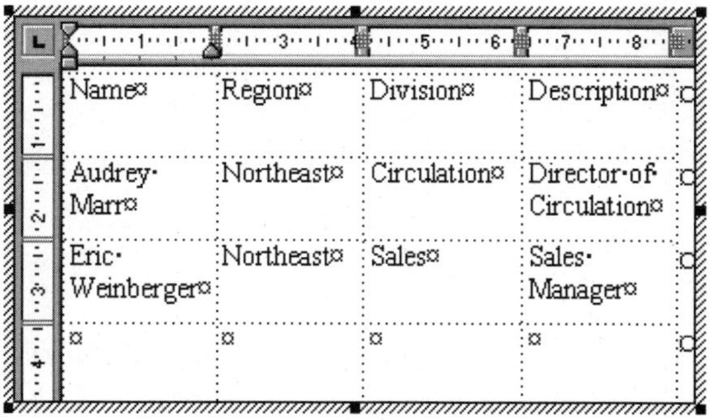

FIGURE 8-2
The text in four cells of this table has wrapped to the second line.

FIGURE 8-3

A table row grows
vertically to
accommodate its
longest text entry.

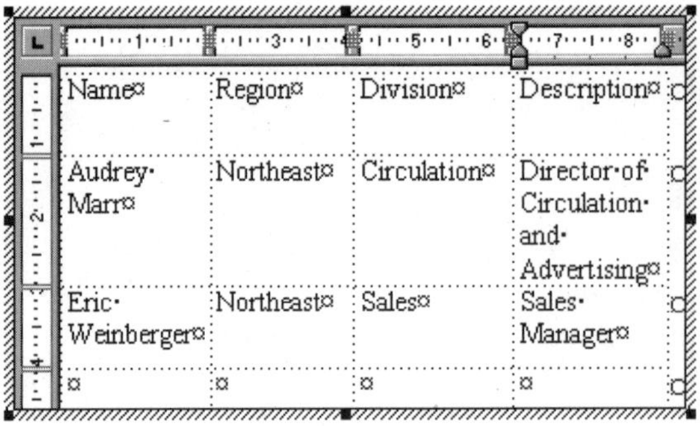

> **TIP** Although a cell can accommodate lengthy text
> entries, try to use short text entries to avoid overwhelm-
> ing the screen with words. Type a word or two rather than
> a sentence. Keep in mind that in tables, as in charts, less
> is more.

You can use a variety of keys and key combinations to move around in
a table. For example, to move quickly to the end of a row, press Alt+End. To
move to the first cell in a column, press Alt+PgUp. Table 8-1 summarizes the
keystrokes you can use to move around in a PowerPoint table.

TABLE 8-1

The navigation
keys for a
PowerPoint table.

To Move...	Press...
To the next cell	Tab
To the previous cell	Shift+Tab
To the first cell in a row	Alt+Home
To the last cell in a row	Alt+End
To the first cell in a column	Alt+PgUp
To the last cell in a column	Alt+PgDown

NOTE When you press Tab to move to a cell that contains text,
the text is highlighted. You can then replace the highlighted
text by simply typing new text. (Remember, any selected text
is instantly replaced when you type.)

As you enter text in a cell, you can end a paragraph and start a new
paragraph by pressing Enter. When you get to the end of the last cell in the
last row, you can add a new row at the bottom of the table by pressing Tab.

A Sample Table

You can try your hand at creating a sample table. Imagine that you need to compare two vendors who want to supply coffee for your office kitchen. You can start by creating a new presentation, or you can use an existing presentation. Then follow the steps below.

1. Click the New Slide button to start a new slide. When the New Slide dialog box appears, double-click the Table autolayout.

2. On the new slide, double-click the table placeholder to start the table. When the Insert Word Table dialog box appears, enter *3* in the Number of Rows edit box, and then click OK to create the empty 3 x 2 table.

3. With the insertion point in the first cell of the table, type *The Coffee Pot,* press Tab to move to the next cell, and type *Roast and Brew.* Now you can begin typing the benefits provided by each service in the cells below.

4. Press Tab to move to the second cell in the first column, and type *Freshly ground beans each week.* Then press Tab to move to the second cell in the second column, and type *Free donuts on Fridays.*

5. Press Tab again to move to the third cell in the first column, and type *Daily 7 AM service.* Then press Tab one more time, and type *Jelly donuts, too.* Your table should now look something like the table shown below.

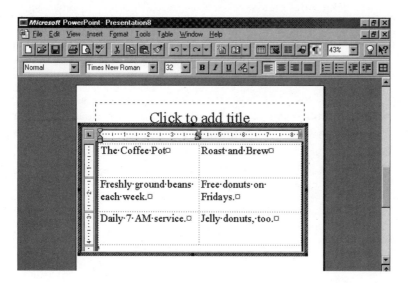

6. Click anywhere outside the gray frame surrounding the table to place the table on the current slide.

As you can see, this table could use a little formatting. The text is too large, the rows are too tall, and the column headings are not distinguished in any way. Later in this chapter, you'll learn how to make these improvements, and others as well. But first, you need to learn how to make basic modifications to the structure of the table, such as inserting a new column if a third vendor makes a bid.

Modifying the Table

After you've created a table, you can modify its structure by adding, deleting, moving, and copying cells, columns, and rows. You can also change the widths of columns, the heights of rows, and merge and split cells to accommodate the contents of your table. All these changes are easy to accomplish. (If you've already clicked outside the gray frame to place a table on a slide, you must double-click the table to reactivate it for modifications.)

Selecting Cells, Columns, and Rows

As always, if you want to modify something in PowerPoint, you must select it first. This section discusses the various ways you can select cells, columns, and rows in a table.

Clicking the middle of a cell places an insertion point inside the cell, so the usual approach of clicking something to select it doesn't work in tables. Instead, you must carefully position the mouse pointer near the left inside edge of the cell you want to select, and when the pointer changes to a right arrow, click the cell. To select adjacent cells in the same column, click anywhere in the first cell, and drag down the column. To select adjacent cells in the same row, click anywhere in the first cell, and drag across the row. Word's Automatic Text Selection feature ensures that everything in the cells is also selected. In addition, you can click one cell, hold down the Shift key, and then click another cell to select both cells and any cells in between. Figure 8-4 shows a table with all the cells in one row selected.

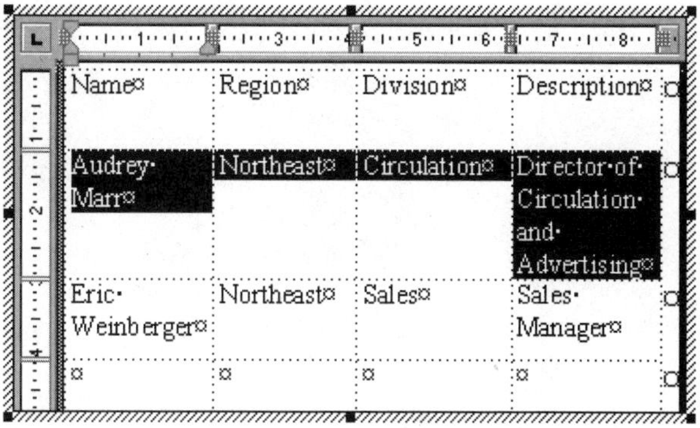

FIGURE 8-4
All the cells in the second row have been selected.

A shortcut for selecting a column of cells is to first position the mouse pointer on the top border of the column. Then, when the pointer changes to a down arrow, click the left mouse button to select the entire column, as shown in Figure 8-5.

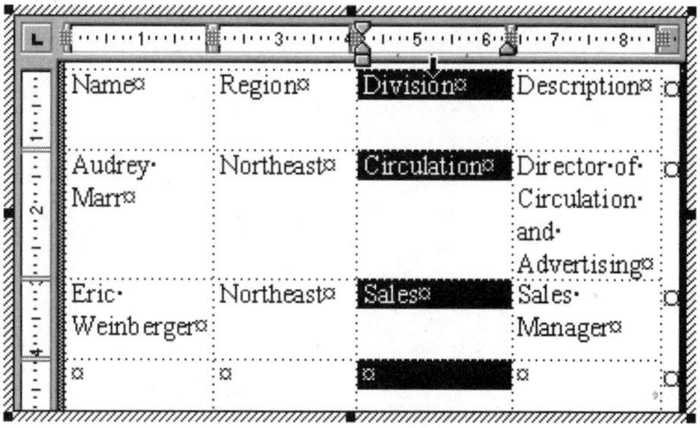

FIGURE 8-5
The third column in this table has been selected. (Note the down arrow at the top of the column.)

Just to make things a bit complicated, there's a difference between selecting all the cells in a row and selecting a row. You select all the cells in a row when you want to modify the contents of all the cells. You select a row when you want to add a new row or delete the current row. As shown in Figure 8-6 on the next page, to select a row, you must also select the end-of-row marker that sits just to the right of the last cell in the row.

197

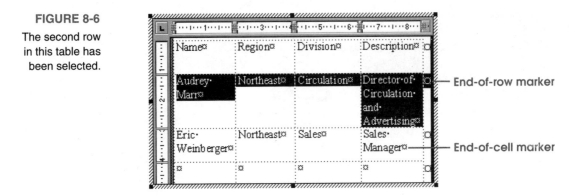

FIGURE 8-6

The second row in this table has been selected.

End-of-row marker

End-of-cell marker

If you don't see any end-of-row markers in your table, click the Show/Hide ¶ button on the Standard toolbar. (You may also need to drag the right side of the table's gray frame a little to the right.) When the end-of-row markers appear, you'll also see end-of-cell markers that mark the end of the contents of each cell.

TIP   If you have trouble selecting rows and columns with the mouse, you can use Table menu commands instead. First use the arrow keys and the Tab key to move the insertion point to a cell in the row or column you want to select, and then choose Select Row or Select Column from the Table menu. After you place the insertion point in a cell at one end of a range of cells that you want to select, you can also hold down the Shift key, and press the arrow keys to select adjacent cells.

Adding and Deleting Cells, Columns, and Rows

Depending on whether you've selected a cell, column, or row, the first command on the Table menu becomes Insert Cells, Insert Columns, or Insert Rows. When you insert new cells, the Insert Cells dialog box appears, as shown in Figure 8-7. You can then specify where the currently selected cell (or cells) should be moved in order to accommodate the new cell (or cells).

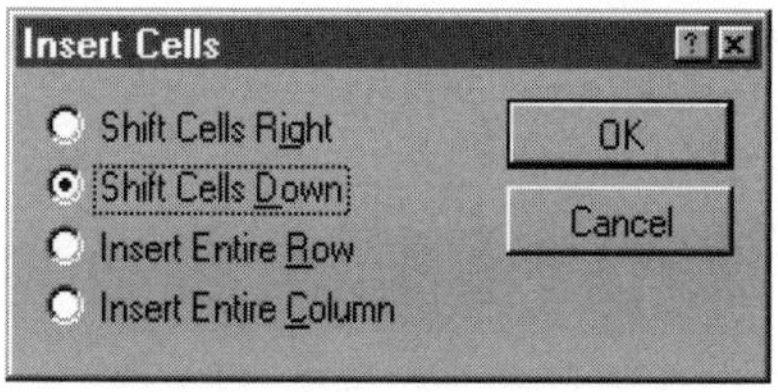

FIGURE 8-7
The Insert Cells
dialog box.

When you insert a new column, it appears to the left of the selected column. When you insert a new row, it appears above the selected row.

NOTE If you want to add a new row to the end of a table, click the last cell in the table, and then press Tab.

Like the Insert command, the Delete command on the Table menu becomes Delete Cells, Delete Columns, or Delete Rows depending on whether you've selected a cell, column, or row. When you delete a cell, the Delete Cells dialog box appears. The options in this dialog box are similar to those in the Insert Cells dialog box. When you delete a column or row, the contents of the cells in the column or row are also deleted.

TIP You can also use the Insert Cells and Delete Cells dialog boxes to insert and delete entire columns or rows. In addition, the Insert and Delete commands are available on the shortcut menu that appears when you select a cell, column, or row and then click the right mouse button.

Moving and Copying Cells

After you select the contents of a cell, you can move or copy the contents to another cell using the drag-and-drop techniques you learned in Chapter 4. As an alternative, you can use the Cut, Copy, and Paste buttons on the Standard toolbar or the commands on the Edit menu. The Cut, Copy, and Paste commands are also available on the shortcut menu that appears when you select the contents of a cell and then click the right mouse button.

Keep in mind that when you select only the contents of a cell without selecting the end-of-cell marker and then you move or copy the contents to a different cell, the contents of the destination cell are not overwritten. When you select both the contents of a cell and the end-of-cell marker, the contents of the destination cell are overwritten.

To move or copy a cell's contents using drag and drop, follow these steps:

1. Select the information you want to move or copy. If you want the contents of the cell to replace the contents of the destination cell, you should also select the end-of-cell marker. The figure on the left shows the contents of a cell selected without the end-of-cell marker selected. The figure on the right shows the contents of a cell selected with the end-of-cell marker selected, too.

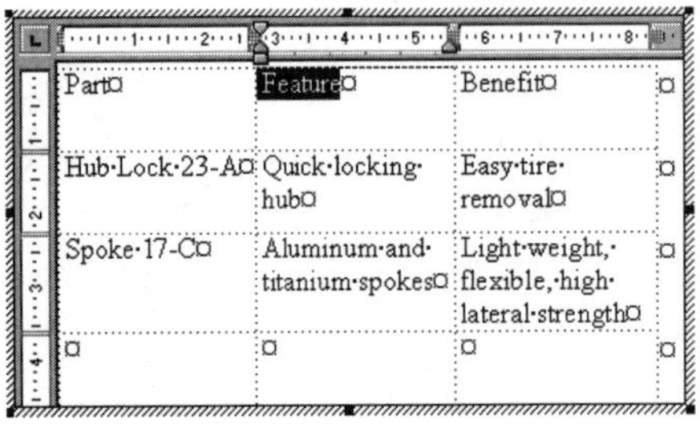

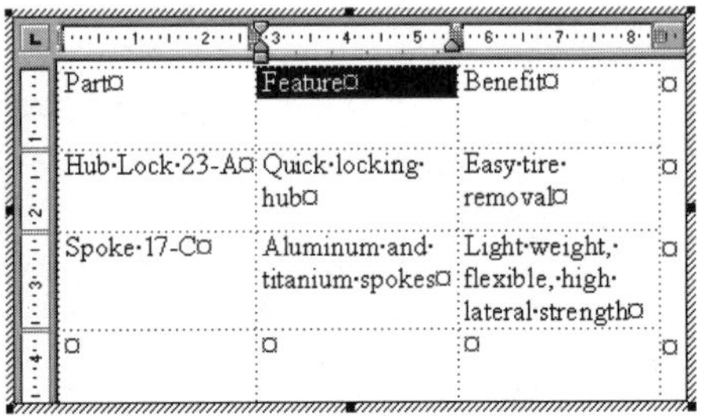

2. Position the mouse pointer over the selected information, hold down the left mouse button, and drag the information to the destination point in another cell. To copy rather than move the contents of a cell, hold down the Ctrl key as you drag the contents. The figure on the left shows the result when only the contents are selected. The figure on the right shows the result when the end-of-cell marker is dragged to another cell, too—the moved or copied contents replace the contents in the destination cell.

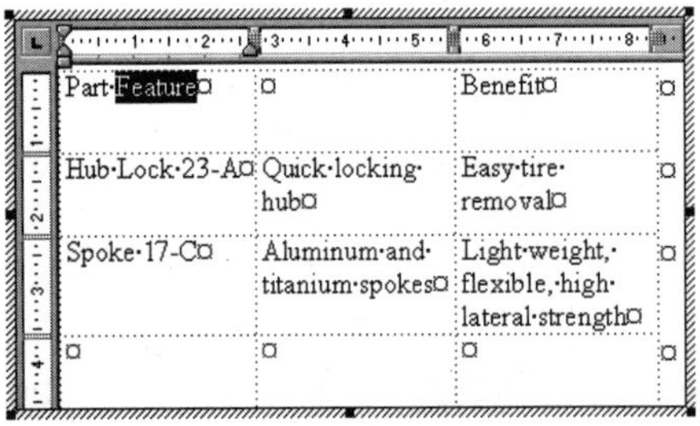

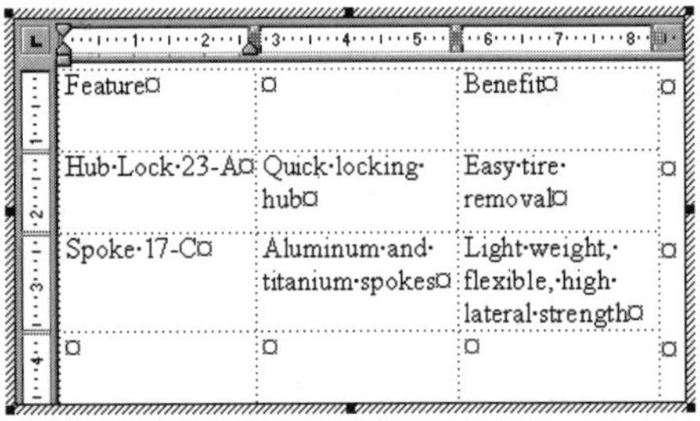

Moving and Copying Columns and Rows

To move a column or row in a table, select the column or row and drag it be-tween two other columns or rows. To copy a column or row in a table, simply hold down the Ctrl key as you drag the column or row. You can also move or copy multiple columns or rows by selecting all the columns or rows that you want to move before you drag.

When you select a row (or rows) to move or copy, you must be sure to select the end-of-row marker as well; otherwise, the contents of the moved or copied row will overwrite the contents of the destination row. In addition, when you move or copy a row (or rows), you must drag the row to the begin-ning of the first cell in the destination row. If you don't, the contents of the moved or copied row will be added to the destination row, overwriting its con-tents. Figure 8-8 shows a second set of rows created by copying the first set.

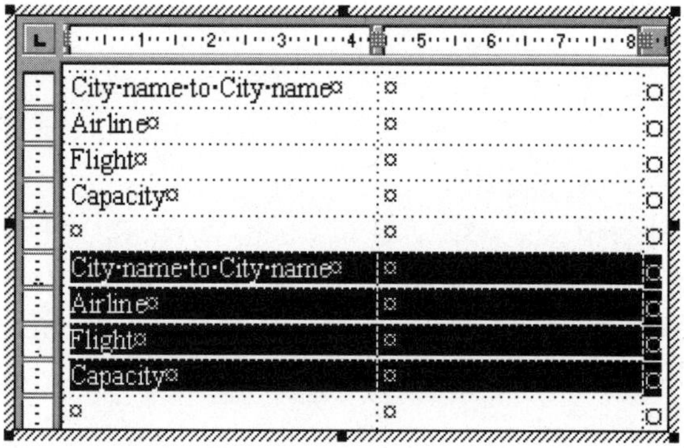

FIGURE 8-8
The second set of rows was copied from the first set.

Changing Column Widths and Row Heights

To decrease or increase the width of a column in a table, drag the dotted column border at the right side of the column to the left or right, respectively. You can also drag the column markers on the table's horizontal ruler, shown in Figure 8-9 on the next page, to the left or right to change the width of a column. When you reduce the width of a column so that some of the text no longer fits within the width of the column's cells, the extra text in each cell wraps to a second line.

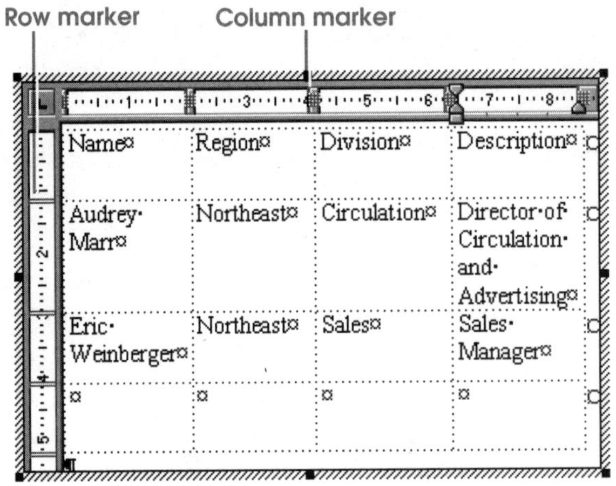

FIGURE 8-9

The column and
row markers on the
table rulers.

Row marker   Column marker

To decrease or increase the heights of rows in a table, drag the corresponding row markers on the table's vertical ruler up or down, respectively. As shown in Figure 8-9, the row marker for a row aligns with the bottom of the row. Changing the heights of rows is especially important because the default row height is determined by the number of rows in the table and the amount of space allotted for the table. Thus, the fewer the rows, the taller they must be. You may prefer shorter row heights that better fit the text height.

To change column widths and row heights in a table, you can also use the Cell Height and Width command on the Table menu. This command is also available on the shortcut menu that appears when you select a column or row and then click the right mouse button.

To change the widths of columns using the Cell Height and Width command, follow these steps:

1. Select as many columns as you want to modify.

2. Choose Cell Height and Width from the Table menu or from the shortcut menu.

3. Click the Column tab of the Cell Height and Width dialog box, shown on the facing page.

4. Enter a new width in the Width of Column edit box by typing directly in the edit box or by using the up and down arrows on the right side of the edit box. Then click OK.

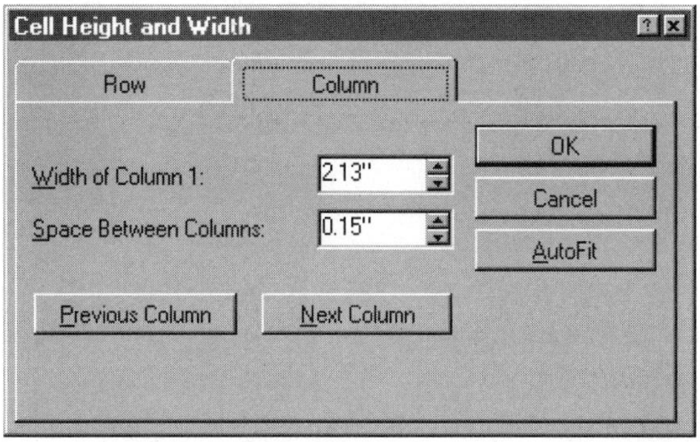

You can also use the Space Between Columns option on the Column tab to add a little breathing room to a crowded table. Or click the AutoFit button to set the width of each selected column to fit the longest text entry in the column. If you want to change the width of individual columns, click the Previous Column or Next Column button until the number of the column you want to change is displayed in the Width of Column option. Then enter a new width in the Width of Column edit box and click OK.

To change the heights of rows using the Cell Height and Width command, follow these steps:

1. Select as many rows as you want to modify.

2. Choose Cell Height and Width from the Table menu or from the shortcut menu.

3. Click the Row tab of the Cell Height and Width dialog box, shown below:

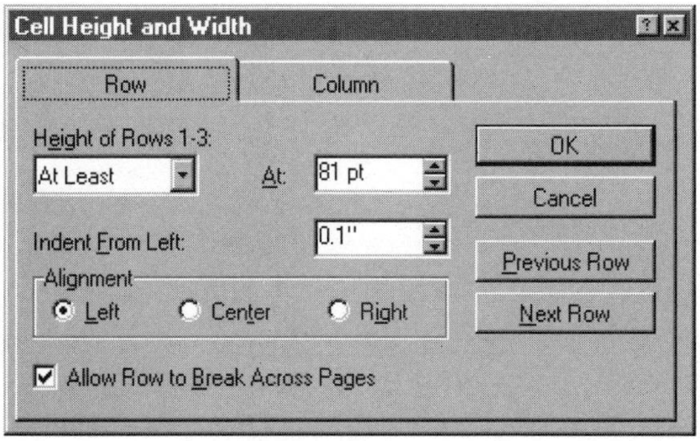

4. Click the arrow on the right side of the Height of Rows edit box to display a drop-down list of options. Select the Auto option to set the row height to the height of the tallest cell in the row. Select the At Least option to set a minimum row height. When you select At Least, the row becomes taller if the contents of the cells are taller than the row height. Select Exactly to set an exact row height. Any text that does not fit in the cells at the exact row height is cut off. Note that when you select the At Least or Exactly options, you can enter a point size in the At edit box to specify a particular row height.

You can also use the Indent From Left setting on the Row tab to indent the row from the left side of the table. In addition, you can select Left, Center, or Right to specify the alignment of the row. The Allow Row to Break Across Pages option lets you determine whether the contents of the row are split at an automatic page break or whether the entire row is moved to the following page. To format the previous or next row, you can click the Previous Row or Next Row button.

Dragging the column and row markers to change column widths and row heights is usually the easiest way to go, but you may want to select the entire table by clicking any cell and choosing Select Table from the Table menu. Then use the Cell Height and Width dialog box to set all the columns or rows to a uniform width or height, respectively.

Merging and Splitting Cells

To create one cell that spans two or more cells, you can merge adjacent cells. As shown in Figure 8-10, merging cells allows you to enter a column heading in one large cell that occupies the same width as several smaller cells below.

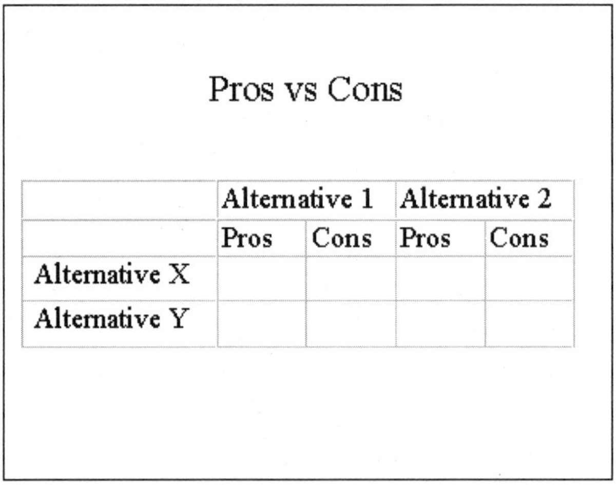

FIGURE 8-10

The cells in row 1 of columns 2 and 3 and columns 4 and 5 have been merged to accommodate the column headings.

Pros vs Cons

	Alternative 1		Alternative 2	
	Pros	Cons	Pros	Cons
Alternative X				
Alternative Y				

To merge two or more cells, simply select the cells, and then choose Merge Cells from the Table menu. Even when two or more cells have been merged, they retain their separate identities so that you can always select the merged cell and choose Split Cells from the Table menu to return to the original grouping of individual cells.

Formatting the Table

After you enter the contents of the table and make any necessary structural changes, you can turn your attention to the overall appearance of the table. By default, PowerPoint uses the current presentation template to format elements of the table such as text font and color. You can change the formatting of table text by using the same methods that you use to change the formatting of text elsewhere in PowerPoint. Simply select the text, and then use the buttons on the Formatting toolbar or the commands on the Format and shortcut menus.

In addition to the text, however, there are other elements that you should consider when you format a table, such as borders and shading. These elements are discussed in the next section.

Adding Borders and Shading with Table AutoFormats

The dotted gridlines that depict the boundaries of table cells on the screen do not appear when you view the completed table on the slide, so you must add borders to make the gridlines visible. You can also add shading to certain cells to give them a little emphasis.

PowerPoint provides both a Borders toolbar and a Borders and Shading command, but the easiest way to add borders and shading is to use one of the table autoformats. Each table autoformat (there are a total of 37) offers its own combination of cell borders, cell shading, fonts, and color selections. In addition, while applying a table autoformat, you can automatically size the table so that its columns and rows fit the contents of the cells perfectly.

To apply a table autoformat, follow these steps:

1. Click anywhere in the table.

2. From the Table menu or the shortcut menu, choose Table AutoFormat. Be careful not to choose the AutoFormat command from the Format menu by mistake.

3. In the Table AutoFormat dialog box, shown on the next page, select a format from the Formats list, and view the result in the Preview box.

```
┌─────────────────────────────────────────────────────────────────────────┐
│ Table AutoFormat                                                   ? ✕   │
│ ┌Formats:──────┐ ┌Preview──────────────────────┐  ┌──────────────┐      │
│ │[none]      ▲ │ │                              │  │      OK      │      │
│ │Simple 1    ▓ │ │         Jan  Feb  Mar  Total │  └──────────────┘      │
│ │Simple 2      │ │   East   7    7    5    19   │  ┌──────────────┐      │
│ │Simple 3      │ │   West   6    4    7    17   │  │    Cancel    │      │
│ │Classic 1     │ │   South  8    7    9    24   │  └──────────────┘      │
│ │Classic 2     │ │   Total  21   18   21   60   │                       │
│ │Classic 3     │ │                              │                       │
│ │Classic 4     │ │                              │                       │
│ │Colorful 1    │ │                              │                       │
│ │Colorful 2  ▼ │ └──────────────────────────────┘                       │
│ └──────────────┘                                                         │
│ ┌Formats to Apply────────────────────────────────────────────┐          │
│ │  ☑ Borders        ☑ Font           ☑ AutoFit                │          │
│ │  ☑ Shading        ☐ Color                                   │          │
│ └─────────────────────────────────────────────────────────────┘         │
│ ┌Apply Special Formats To────────────────────────────────────┐          │
│ │  ☑ Heading Rows              ☐ Last Row                     │          │
│ │  ☑ First Column              ☐ Last Column                  │          │
│ └─────────────────────────────────────────────────────────────┘         │
└─────────────────────────────────────────────────────────────────────────┘
```

As you click each option, the sample table in the Preview box changes to reflect your selections.

4. To format specific elements in your table, select any or all of the options in the Formats to Apply section.

Option	Effect
Borders	Applies the cell borders shown in the preview.
Shading	Applies the shading shown in the preview.
Font	Applies the fonts shown in the preview. Leave Font unselected to use a font that matches your presentation font.
Color	Applies the colors shown in the preview. Leave Color unselected to use shades of gray.
AutoFit	Automatically sizes columns and rows to fit the largest entry.

5. To add special formatting to other table elements, select any or all of the options in the Apply Special Formats To section. Again, as you select options, the sample table in the Preview box changes to reflect your selections. Depending on the options you select, the special formatting may be shading, a bold font, a wider column, or special cell borders.

Option	Effect
Heading Rows	Applies a special format to the heading rows of the table.
First Column	Applies a special format to the first column of the table.
Last Row	Applies a special format to the last row of the table.
Last Column	Applies a special format to the last column of the table.

6. Click OK to implement the table autoformat you have selected. The table below is formatted using the Simple 3 table autoformat.

Circulation and Sales Staff

Name	Region	Division	Description
Audrey Marr	Northeast	Circulation	Director of Circulation and Advertising
Eric Weinberger	Northeast	Sales	Sales Manager

NOTE To undo a table autoformat, choose Undo Auto Format from the Edit menu or press Ctrl+Z. You can also choose Table AutoFormat from the Table menu, and then select (none) in the Formats list.

Adding Custom Borders and Shading

Rather than use a table autoformat to apply a preset combination of borders and shading, you can add borders and shading to table cells by using the Borders toolbar and the Borders and Shading command on the Format menu.

To use the Borders toolbar, select the cells you want to add borders or shading to, and then click the Borders button on the Formatting toolbar. The Borders toolbar, shown on the next page, appears below the Formatting toolbar.

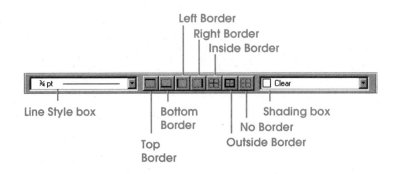

Line Style box · Top Border · Bottom Border · Left Border · Right Border · Inside Border · No Border · Outside Border · Shading box

On the Borders toolbar, click the arrow at the right end of the Line Style box to drop down a list of available line styles. You can then click the line style you want. After you select a line style, click one of the border buttons to apply the line style as a border for the selected cells. For example, to apply a border to the bottom of a group of selected cells, simply click the Bottom Border button.

To separate all the cells in a rectangular region with borders, click the Inside Border button on the Borders toolbar. To enclose all the cells within a border, click the Outside Border button on the Borders toolbar. To remove all the borders from the selected cells, click the No Border button.

To set a shading amount for the selected cells, click the arrow at the right end of the Shading box, and select an option from the drop-down list. The options at the top of the list give you various shades of gray. (Farther down the list, you can also select patterns to fill the selected cells.) For example, to fill the cells of a column with light gray, you select the cells, and then select 20% from the Shading drop-down list. Figure 8-11 shows the results.

FIGURE 8-11

The rightmost column has been formatted with a 20% shade.

Employee Performance

Employee	Years of Service	Start Date	Rating
Audrey Marr	10	11/15/84	98
Eric Weinberger	8	12/1/86	84

When you use the Borders and Shading command rather than the Borders toolbar, you can select a color for the borders as well as a foreground and background color for the shading. Simply select the cells you want to format, and then choose Borders and Shading from the Format menu. Next, click the Borders tab of the Cell Borders and Shading dialog box to set the borders of the selected cells, or click the Shading tab to set the shading of the selected cells. Figure 8-12 shows the Borders tab (top) and the Shading tab (bottom).

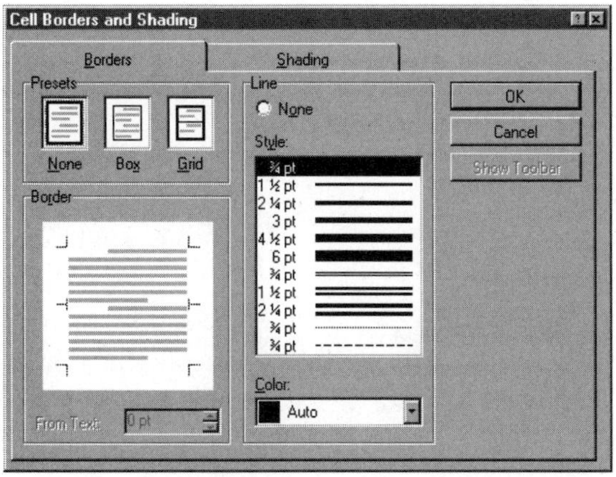

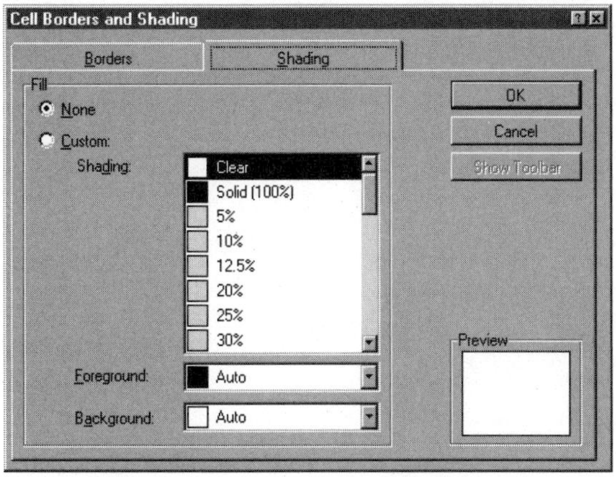

FIGURE 8-12

The Borders and Shading tabs of the Cell Borders and Shading dialog box.

On the Borders tab, you can select Box from the Presets section to add a border to the outside of the selected cells, or you can select Grid to add a border around each individual cell in the selection. You can also select one or more borders in the Border section by clicking in the border diagram (hold down the Shift key as you click to select multiple borders), and then select a line style from the Style list and a color from the drop-down Color list. To remove all borders from the selected cells, select None in the Presets section. To remove a specific border, simply click the border in the Border section.

When you click the Shading tab of the Cell Borders and Shading dialog box, you can select a shading percentage from the Shading list and a foreground and background color from the Foreground and Background drop-down lists. The selections you make are then displayed in the Preview box. The resulting shade is a percentage of the foreground color against the background color. For example, 50% mixes the foreground and background colors evenly. To see just the background color, select Clear from the Shading list. To see just the foreground color, select Solid. Because you can mix the foreground and background colors to any degree, you can create special colors. For example, you can create a color that is 20% dark blue against a light yellow background.

After you select a border, shading, or both, click OK to apply the border and shading to the selected cells.

Now that you've learned how to create table slides and add them to a presentation, you know how to work with all the basic presentation building blocks. In Part 3, you'll learn how to make overall changes to the presentation and how to add enhancements to strengthen its powers of communication.

Part 3

SELECT EDITION

Modifying
the Presentation

Chapter 9

Making Overall Changes

As you've seen, PowerPoint offers a sophisticated system for creating an entire presentation's worth of slides that share a common design. This chapter focuses on the central controls behind the presentation design process: the template, the color scheme, and the title master and slide master. You can use these controls to make overall changes to your presentation, such as redesigning the background or applying a different combination of colors to all the slides. The following list describes the elements that are managed by each of the three controls:

- The template contains a color scheme, a title master and slide master, and a set of autolayouts that control where objects are positioned on slides.

- The color scheme contains a background color and seven other colors that are applied to particular elements in the presentation.

- The title master and slide master contain a background design and default text formatting for the slide titles and main text items. The background design can contain graphic objects or can be shaded (with one or more colors), patterned, or textured. The default text formatting is applied to the slide titles and the bulleted text items.

What is so powerful—and potentially confusing—about these controls is the way they overlap. When you alter the title master or slide master, for example, you can change the current color scheme, which can change the background color. To make things even more interesting, you can also change the background color directly, without changing the color scheme. To help you understand how these controls interact, this chapter is organized from the big picture to the detailed picture. It begins with a discussion of the controls that have the broadest influence on a presentation and then goes on to cover the controls that affect a single aspect of a slide.

Applying a Different Template

The easiest—and most sweeping—step you can take when you want to change the appearance of a presentation is to apply a different template. Changing the template makes a wholesale change to just about every aspect of the presentation's appearance. Figure 9-1 shows a basic presentation, both before (top) and after (bottom) the Tridots template is applied.

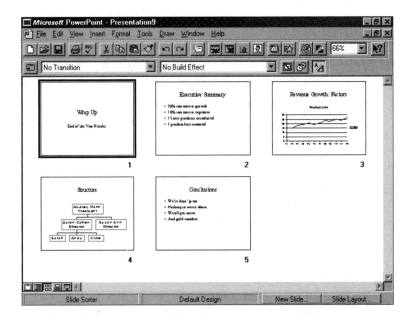

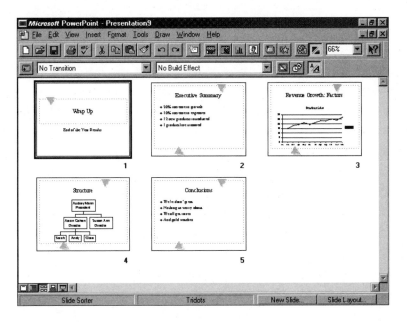

FIGURE 9-1

A basic presentation slide before (top) and after (bottom) a new template is applied.

Other Ways to Change the Design

By changing the template, you can give your presentation an entirely new look: All the slides in the presentation get the same new background and new color scheme, and even a new selection of text fonts. But you can control each of these design aspects individually without having to apply a new template. You can even make design changes on selected slides, leaving the other slides to conform to the template's design. Some of the overall changes you can make without changing the template are:

- Decorating the background with a company logo or project name

- Adding special text to the background that spells out the presentation's subject

- Modifying the presentation colors to match a client's corporate color scheme

- Changing the font and text formatting used in slide titles to give the presentation a more playful or more serious character

The template is the most powerful and far-reaching of the central controls. Among other things, changing the template:

- Changes the color scheme that controls the colors used in the presentation

- Changes the title master and slide master, which in turn change the background design and default text formatting

The templates that come with PowerPoint were created by professional artists, so they produce polished, attractive presentations. Therefore, you may not need to make further changes to the appearance of the presentation after you apply a template.

If someone else has created a unique new presentation design, he or she may have saved it in a template that you can use. When you apply the custom template to your presentation, you get the same special presentation design. Often, the chief PowerPoint user in an organization will create a template you can use to conform to the company look. In fact, the design guru may even have changed the characteristics of the default template so that each new presentation you create gets the standard, approved presentation design automatically.

> **TIP**   To find out which template is applied to the current presentation, you can check the status bar at the bottom of the PowerPoint window. The template name appears just to the right of the slide number.

Selecting an Existing Template

When you create a new presentation using the AutoContent Wizard, a template is automatically attached to the presentation. To select a template by name when you start a new presentation, click the Presentation Designs tab of the New Presentation dialog box, and then select a template.

To change the template for an existing presentation, follow these steps:

1. Click the Apply Design Template button on the Standard toolbar or choose Apply Design Template from the Format menu. The Apply Design Template dialog box appears, as shown below:

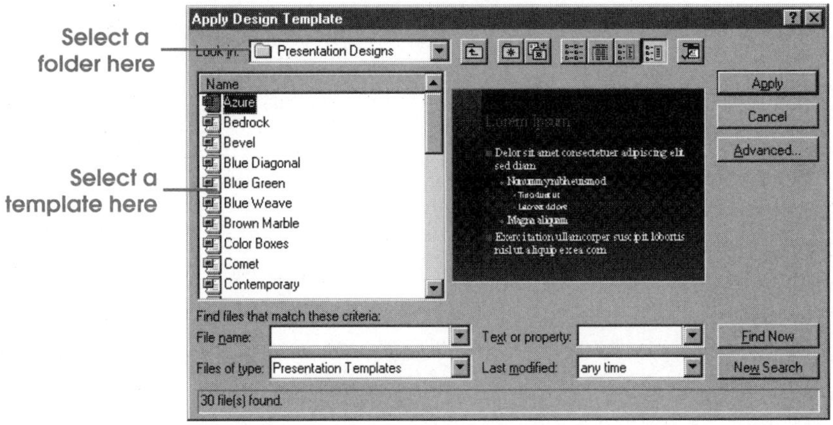

Select a folder here

Select a template here

2. Click any template to display its preview on the right side of the dialog box.

3. Double-click a template name to apply it to the current presentation, or click a template name and then click Apply. The new template reformats every slide in the presentation.

If you've never changed a template before, you can get some practice by creating a simple presentation. (You can use the AutoContent Wizard to quickly generate a multipage dummy presentation.) You can then click the Apply Design Template button and select a template name from the Apply Design Template dialog box. Notice the different effects that are created when you apply different templates.

Creating a New Template

To create a custom look for future presentations, you can create your own template based on the changes you've made to a presentation's color scheme and its title and slide masters. (Later in this chapter, you'll learn how to change the color scheme and the title and slide masters.) It's not a bad idea to model your template on an existing one. When you apply the template, the color scheme, background items, and text formatting will be the ones you use in the presentation.

To create a template, follow these steps:

1. Open or create a presentation that you want to use as the basis for a template.

2. Make any changes to the presentation that you want to save in the new template.

    NOTE All the existing text, clip art, and links will be saved in the template unless you remove them now.

3. From the File menu, choose Save As.

4. Locate the folder in which you want to save the template.

5. In the Save As type box, select Presentation Templates.

6. In the File name edit box, type a name for the template, and then click Save.

Changing the Color Scheme

Every template you apply contains a color scheme that provides the various parts of a presentation with a coordinated set of eight default colors. The most distinctive part of the presentation is the background, so the first color in the color scheme is the background color. The other seven colors tastefully match the background color and are applied to text, charts, and other objects that appear against the background. Whenever you choose a command that allows you to change the color of an object, such as the Font command, you can display the default color scheme by clicking the arrow at the right end of the Color box. Figure 9-2 shows the default color scheme displayed in the Font dialog box.

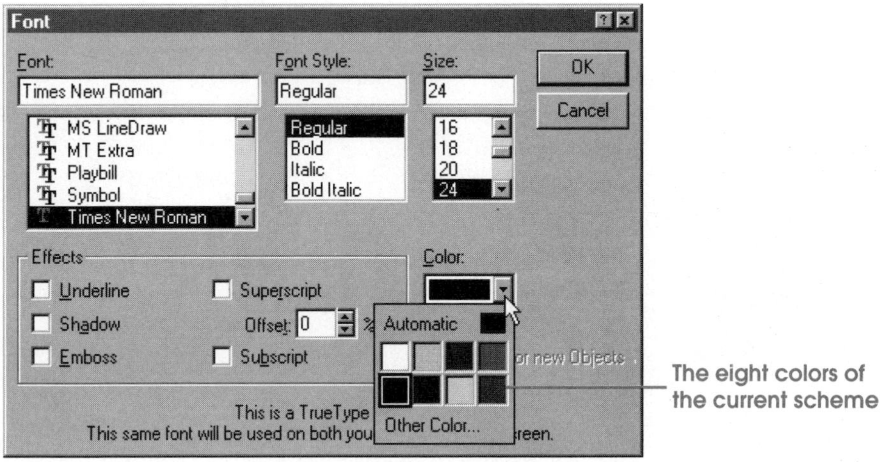

FIGURE 9-2
The default color scheme in the Font dialog box.

The eight colors of the current scheme

Changing the colors of the color scheme without making additional changes to the presentation can be enough to dramatically transform the look. When you modify the color scheme, you can apply the revised scheme to the entire presentation or to the current slide only. If you apply the color scheme to all the slides in a presentation, the new colors are applied to every object in the presentation as well. The only exceptions are objects to which you have assigned specific colors. For example, if you have selected a special color for certain words in a slide title, that color remains even when you change the overall color scheme.

As always, you can save a modified color scheme for future use. After you've carefully matched your organization's standard colors, for example, you can save the color scheme in a template and distribute the template to coworkers. That way, every presentation delivered by a representative of your organization can have the uniform look you desire. In addition, if you've modified the color scheme for one presentation, you can copy the color scheme directly to another presentation.

> **NOTE** You cannot save a color scheme in its own file. A color scheme is always part of a template, so you must save the template with a new name in order to save the revised color scheme.

PowerPoint also allows you to use a different color scheme for speaker's notes and audience handouts by revising the color schemes of their masters. The revised color schemes of the notes and audience handouts have no effect on the overall color scheme applied to the presentation.

 See Also For more information about transferring color schemes, see "Copying Color Schemes Among Slides," page 315.
For more information about speaker's notes, see Chapter 12, "Working with Text Annotations and Speaker's Notes, " page 321.
For more information about audience handouts, see Chapter 15, "Creating Printed Output and 35-mm Slides, " page 379.

Selecting a Standard Color Scheme

The easiest way to change the color scheme of a presentation is to select one of PowerPoint's standard color schemes, which were created by professional artists.

 **TIP** If you create a custom color scheme but then decide to apply a standard color scheme, before you apply the standard color scheme, you should click the Add as Standard Scheme button on the Custom tab of the Color Scheme dialog box to add your custom scheme to the list of schemes. That way, if you don't like the standard color scheme that you apply, you can always return to the custom color scheme by simply selecting it on the Standard tab.

To select a predefined color scheme, follow these steps:

1. Open the presentation whose color scheme you want to modify.

2. Choose Slide Color Scheme from the Format menu or the shortcut menu, and then click the Standard tab to display the Color Scheme dialog box shown below:

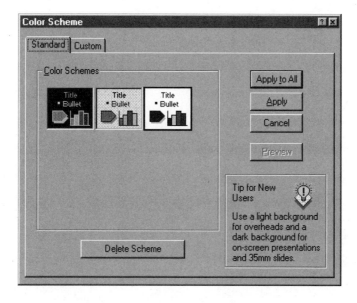

3. Click one of the color schemes, and then click Preview to see how the new colors will appear in the presentation. To preview a different scheme, click the color scheme, and then click Preview. (You may need to drag the Color Scheme dialog box to one side to preview the presentation.)

4. When you are satisfied with your choice of color scheme, click Apply to All to apply the new color scheme to the entire presentation, or click Apply to apply the color scheme to the current slide only.

   NOTE If you previously applied a color to a specific element in your presentation, that element will not be affected by the new color scheme.

Creating a Custom Color Scheme

Occasionally, the standard color schemes won't quite work for your presentation. You might want to vary the brightness or the shade of one or more colors, or you might want to select a different set of colors entirely. If this is the case, you can create a custom color scheme. You'll probably want to first select a template for your presentation that has a color scheme similar to the one you want to create.

To create a custom color scheme, follow these steps:

1. Click the Open button or choose Open from the File menu, and open an existing presentation.

2. Choose Slide Color Scheme from the Format menu or the shortcut menu to display the Color Scheme dialog box, and then click the Custom tab, shown below. (See Table 9-1 on the facing page for more information about the eight color boxes displayed at the top of the Color Scheme dialog box.)

Color Box	Description
Background	The color applied to the background of the slides. The background color can be shaded in a template from light to dark or dark to light, and, on selected slides, it can be superseded by a different background color that you select.
Text & Lines	The color applied to bulleted text and to text blocks typed onto the slides with the Text Tool. Also used for lines and arrows drawn with the Line Tool and as the outline color for autoshapes and objects drawn with the other drawing tools.
Shadows	The color applied to shadows created with the Shadow command.
Title Text	The color applied to slide titles and subtitles.
Fills	The color used to fill autoshapes and objects drawn with any of the drawing tools. Also the color used to fill the first series in a graph.
Accent	The color used as a second color in graphs, org charts, and other added elements.
Accent	The color used as a third color in graphs, org charts, and other added elements.
Accent	The color used as a fourth color in graphs, org charts, and other added elements.

TABLE 9-1

The eight color boxes in the Color Scheme dialog box.

3. To change one of the colors in the eight color boxes, double-click the box, or click the box once and then click Change Color. For example, to change the fill color, double-click the Fills box to open the Fill Color dialog box, and then click the Standard tab. The Fill Color dialog box, shown at the top of the next page, displays 126 color panes and several shades of gray from which you can select a new color. (Note that the current color's pane is highlighted.)

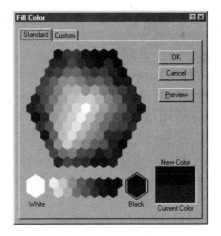

4. Select a color by clicking its pane, and then click OK. If you don't see the color you want, click the Custom tab shown here:

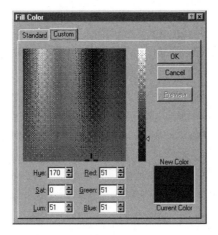

You can use the two controls in the upper part of the Custom tab to select a color. The large box has a cross hair that identifies the general color (the hue) and the intensity of the hue (the saturation level) when you drag it across the box. The vertical strip to the right of the box has a triangular marker that indicates how much black or white is mixed with the color (the luminance of the color) when you drag it up or down the strip. Two color boxes in the lower right corner show the new color and the currently selected color. The remaining boxes contain numeric values for the hue, saturation, and luminance (HSL) and for the red, green, and blue (RGB) of the color. You can use the HSL and RGB numbers to specify an exact color. For example, you can record the numbers of a color you like in one color scheme and then enter the numbers in another color scheme to reproduce the same color. (You can enter either the three HSL numbers or the three RGB numbers—you don't need both sets.)

5. On the Custom tab, drag the cross hair in the large box to the general color you want, and then drag the marker on the vertical strip to brighten or darken the color. Check the New Color box in the lower right corner of the tab to see the new color, or click Preview to see how the new color will appear in the presentation. (You may need to drag the Color Scheme dialog box to one side to preview the presentation.)

6. When you're satisfied with the new color, click OK to return to the Color Scheme dialog box.

7. Follow steps 3 through 6 to change any of the other colors in the eight color boxes. Then click Apply to All to apply the color scheme to the entire presentation, or click Apply to apply the scheme to the current slide only.

After you create a custom color scheme, you may want to add it to the presentation as a standard scheme. That way, if you change one or more slides to another color scheme, you can always return the slides to the custom color scheme you created.

To add a custom color scheme as a standard scheme, follow these steps:

1. Choose Slide Color Scheme from the Format menu or the shortcut menu to display the Color Scheme dialog box, and then click the Custom tab. The custom color scheme appears on the tab.

2. Click Add as Standard Scheme. PowerPoint copies the custom color scheme to the Standard tab.

PowerPoint's Color System

Although PowerPoint provides a broad palette of colors from which to choose, it does not follow the commonly used color matching systems for selecting and specifying colors, such as the Pantone system or the Trumatch system. To match a color, such as the dominant color in your company's logo, you must go through the trial-and-error process of selecting a color, sending it to your color output device, examining the output, and then adjusting the color in PowerPoint. The process can be time-consuming because most output devices produce colors that are lighter or darker than they appear on your screen. In addition, the number of colors you see on the screen and the precision with which they are displayed depend on the color capabilities of your hardware. Even the brightness control on your monitor affects how a color looks. When you do find the correct color, you might want to make note of its HSL or RGB number so that you can reproduce it later.

Editing the Title Master or Slide Master

In addition to the color scheme, the title master and the slide master are the other elements you can modify in a presentation. Changes you make to the title master affect only the slides that you add with the Title autolayout; changes you make to the slide master affect all the other slides in a presentation. Both masters contain:

- A background color that can be shaded
- A scheme of fonts and text formatting for the slide titles and bulleted text
- An optional group of graphic objects placed on the background and arranged to form a design

The title master and slide master give the presentation an overall look by providing the background and the design of the text, as well as saving you the tedium of having to format each slide individually. This section discusses how to open the title master and slide master and how to customize their background color and shading, title and text, and background design.

Opening the Title Master or Slide Master

Before you can actually edit the title master or slide master, you must display it on your screen.

To display the title master shown in Figure 9-3, first make sure that a title slide is displayed. (To determine whether the slide you are in is a title slide, click the Slide Layout button in the lower right on your screen to see which layout is selected. Click cancel to return to your slide.) Then, you can use one of these methods:

- Choose Master and then Title Master from the View menu.

- Hold down the Shift key, and click the Slide View button.

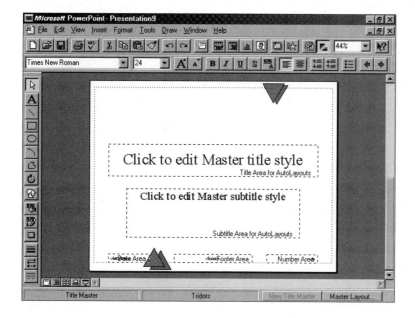

FIGURE 9-3
The title master.

To display the slide master shown in Figure 9-4 on the next page, first make sure that a slide other than the title slide is displayed. (If you're unsure, click the Slide Layout button and check which layout is selected, and then click Cancel.) Then, you can use one of these methods:

- Choose Master and then Slide Master from the View menu.

- Hold down the Shift key and click the Slide View button.

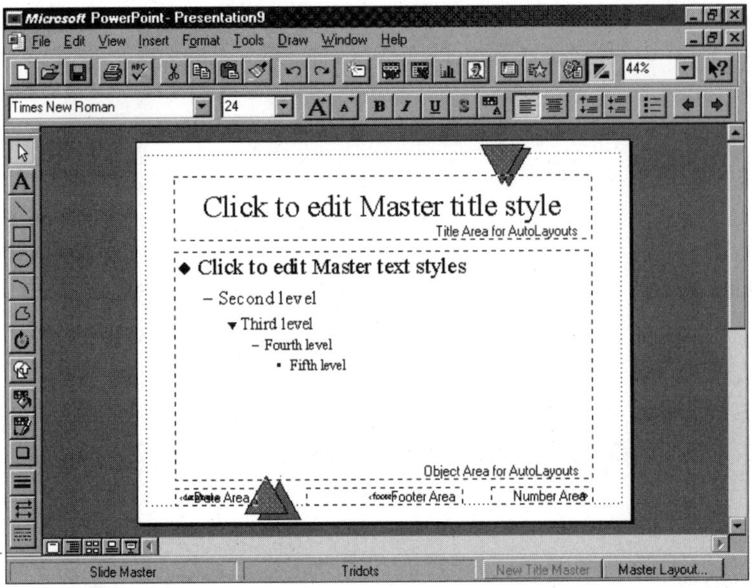

FIGURE 9-4

The Slide master.

As you can see, the title master or the slide master temporarily takes over the screen. In the lower right corner of the screen, the New Slide button becomes the New Title Master button, and the Slide Layout button is now the Master Layout button. The New Title Master button is dimmed when the Slide Master is displayed.

To close the master and return to another view, simply click one of the view buttons in the lower left corner of the presentation window or choose a view from the View menu.

Altering the Custom Background

Although the color scheme supplies a background color for a presentation, you can modify the background color when you change the slide background for the master. Modifying the background color on a master is just like modifying the background color in the color scheme. In fact, when you return to the Color Scheme dialog box, you'll see the background color you applied in the master.

In addition to the color, you can also make other changes to the master's background. For instance, you can set a shading for the background color and then lighten or darken the shading.

To make changes to the master's background, choose the Custom Background command from the Format menu or the shortcut menu. (Remember, the master must be displayed on your screen before you choose the command.) The Custom Background dialog box shown in Figure 9-5 appears. You use the controls in the drop-down list of the Custom Background dialog box to change the appearance of the background, including its shading, pattern, and texture. If you'd like, you can even insert a picture for a "watermark" effect. The current background appears in the drop-down list. To return to a background color that complements the color scheme, select Automatic or one of the eight colors that appear in the drop-down list.

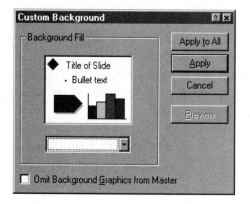

FIGURE 9-5

The Custom Background dialog box.

TIP You can click the Preview button in the Custom Background dialog box to preview the new background. After you click Preview, you may need to drag the dialog box aside to see the background. If you're not satisfied with the background shading, the Custom Background dialog box is still on the screen, so you can select a different setting.

After you select a background, click Apply to All to apply the settings to both the title master and the slide master, or click Apply to apply the settings to the current master only.

Applying Shading

You can shade the background of a title master or slide master using one color, two colors, or a preset color scheme. Shading can make the presentation look like it has been lighted from one side, the top or bottom, or even inside out or outside in. To apply shading to the background, first select Shaded from the drop-down list in the Custom Background dialog box.

To select a different background color altogether, first select the One Color, Two Color, or Preset option. Then use the drop-down lists to select a color or preset color scheme. You can also select Other Color to specify a different color using the techniques described earlier for selecting a standard or custom color scheme. If you are using just one color, try using the scroll bar under the Color drop-down list to vary the intensity of the shading.

Now you are ready to select a Shade Styles option and one of its variants—just click the options you want. For example, to create a background shade that runs vertically from dark to light, click Vertical as the shade style and then click the variant that shows a transition from dark to light. Other variants allow you to shade the background from light to dark, from light to dark to light, or from dark to light to dark. You get the idea.

Applying a Pattern

Rather than shade the background, you can apply a pattern made up of two colors. PowerPoint offers more than 35 patterns and many colors to choose from. To apply a pattern to the background, first select Patterned from the drop-down list in the Custom Background dialog box.

In the Pattern Fill dialog box, the patterns shown are composed of the foreground and background colors displayed in the Foreground and Background boxes. You can select a different pattern and different foreground and background colors to create the combination you want.

Applying a Texture

Yet another way to change the background of the title master or slide master involves applying a texture. Applying a texture can change the overall "feel" of your presentation. You can choose from several textures, including medium wood, white marble, cork, and paper. To apply a texture to the background, first select Textured from the drop-down list in the Custom Background dialog box, and then click the texture you want. Figure 9-6 shows a presentation formatted with a textured background.

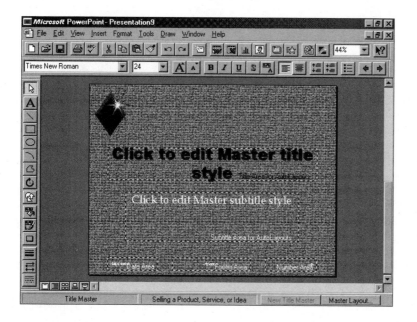

FIGURE 9-6

A presentation formatted with the Cloth texture.

Inserting a Picture

If you prefer, you can insert a picture into the background of either master. Select Picture from the drop-down list in the Custom Background dialog box to display the Insert Picture dialog box, where you can select a background picture. PowerPoint will scale the picture to fit the entire background area of the slide. Bright, bold pictures work well on title slides, such as the one in Figure 9-7 on the next page. Because text will be displayed over the picture on other slides, you may want to choose something simple rather than complex.

See Also For more information about inserting pictures, see Chapter 14, "Adding Clip Art Pictures and Bitmapped Images," page 361.

FIGURE 9-7
A bright, bold
picture works well
on title slides.

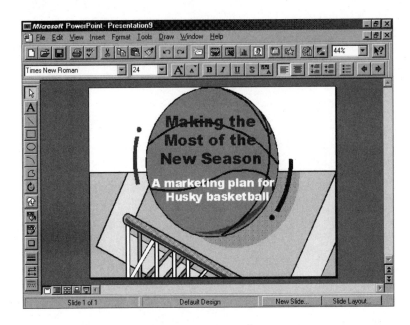

FIGURE 9-7
A bright, bold
picture works well
on title slides.

Formatting the Title Master or Slide Master

With the background set, you can turn your attention to the appearance of the text in the presentation.

Figure 9-8 shows the title master of the Travel template. As you can see, the title master displays text in two areas indicated by dashed boxes: The title area for autolayouts contains sample text for the title, and the subtitle area for autolayouts contains sample text for the subtitle. When you change the formatting of the sample text on the title master, only the formatting on the title slide changes. To change the formatting on the remaining slides, you must change the formatting of the text of the slide master.

FIGURE 9-8
The title master of
the Travel template.

As shown in Figure 9-9, the slide master, looks nearly identical to the title master, but it contains an object area for autolayouts instead of a subtitle area. The object area for autolayouts holds sample text at each of the five bulleted text levels. When you change the formatting of the sample text on the slide master, the formatting of the text on every slide—except for the title slide—changes accordingly.

FIGURE 9-9

The slide master of the Travel template.

The initial colors of the text in the title, subtitle, and object areas are determined by the colors of the color scheme. For example, the Title Text color of the color scheme sets the title area text color, and the Text & Lines color of the color scheme sets the object area and subtitle area text color. But changing the color of the sample text on the master overrides the color scheme. Even when you change the actual color scheme, the text colors on the title master or slide master are applied rather than the color scheme's text colors.

To change the appearance of the slide titles or subtitles, format the text in the title or subtitle area by selecting the text and then using buttons on the Formatting toolbar or commands on the Format menu or the shortcut menu. To change the font and color of the title, for example, click the title to select it, click the right mouse button to display the shortcut menu, choose the Font command, and then select options in the Font dialog box. To change all instances of a particular font to another font, choose the Replace Fonts command from the Tools menu.

If you want to make uniform changes to all the bulleted text in a presentation, click the object area of the slide master to select all the bulleted text, and then use the text formatting commands.

To change the formatting of the bulleted text at only one of the indent levels, select the text at that level, and then make a formatting change. For example, to change the font used by bulleted text lines at the second level, select the text *Second Level,* as shown in Figure 9-10, and then use the text formatting commands. Similarly, to change the bullet used at the second level, select the second level text, choose Bullet from the Format menu, and then select a different bullet shape, color, and size from the Bullet dialog box.

FIGURE 9-10

To change the formatting of the bulleted text at the second level, select the level, and then use the text formatting commands.

Click to edit Master title style

Title Area for AutoLayouts

◆ **Click to edit Master text styles**

— Second Level

• Third Level
    – Fourth Level
        • Fifth Level

Date Area   Footer Area   Number Area

> **TIP**   Although you can apply different formatting to the text at each level, you probably shouldn't deviate too much from the formatting of the first level. Otherwise, you might end up with a jumble of formatting. You might consider using the same font for each level, but make them distinctive by varying the size.

Creating a New Background or Modifying the Existing Background

You can create your own background design or modify an existing one by using PowerPoint's drawing tools to place graphic objects on the background of the title master or slide master. Professional artists can do wonders with simple drawing tools, creating entire scenes like those found in the templates that come with PowerPoint. If your artistic skills are not strong, you might prefer to add a few simple geometric shapes to the background. A line or two, or a row of small shapes that you create with the AutoShape tool, can look quite nice.

Rather than compose a background design of your own, you can make minor modifications to the background objects in one of the templates. Simply by moving some of the existing objects, duplicating objects, or changing the objects' positions, you can create a new background design with a unique look. Figure 9-11 shows a slide with a diamond picture in the upper left corner and a picture of an artist at his easel on the right of the slide.

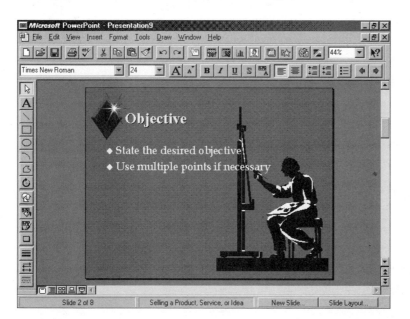

FIGURE 9-11

A custom background design.

NOTE Any graphic objects that are already a part of the title master or slide master have been grouped into a single object. You must select the group of objects and then use the Ungroup command on the Draw menu before you can work with the individual objects. You'll learn more about grouping and ungrouping objects in "Grouping Objects," page 351.

Text annotations, clip art, and scanned pictures saved as bitmapped files are other elements you can add to the background of the title master or slide master so that they appear on every slide. When you read about adding text annotations, clip art, and bitmaps to slides in Chapters 12 and 14, bear in mind that these elements can be added to the title master or slide master background as well.

See Also For more information about using PowerPoint's drawing tools to create and modify graphic objects, see Chapter 13, "Drawing Graphic Objects," page 331.

Adding a Header or Footer

PowerPoint makes it easy to add three special text elements to the background of every slide: the date, the time, and the slide number. You can display these elements when you display the presentation in a slide show or print the presentation as slides, handouts, or notes pages. To add a header or footer to your presentation, choose Header and Footer from the View menu, and then click the Slide tab. The Header and Footer dialog box appears, as shown in Figure 9-12.

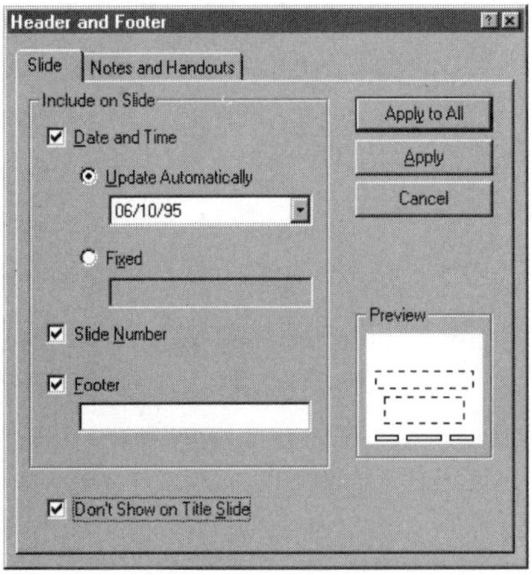

FIGURE 9-12

The Header and Footer dialog box for a slide with the date, slide number, and some text in the footer.

Header and Footer	
Slide	Notes and Handouts

Include on Slide

☑ Date and Time
   ⦿ Update Automatically
     06/10/95
   ○ Fixed

☑ Slide Number

☑ Footer

☑ Don't Show on Title Slide

Apply to All
Apply
Cancel

Preview

To add the date or time, select the Date and Time check box, and then select the Update Automatically option or the Fixed option. The format of the date and time is determined by the format you select in the corresponding drop-down list or the format you type in the edit box. The Preview window shows the placement of the options you select.

To add the slide number, select the Slide Number check box. You can also add some additional text to every slide by selecting the Footer check box and typing the text in the corresponding edit box. If you don't want the date, time, slide number, or footer text to appear on the title slide, be sure to select the Don't Show on Title Slide check box.

When you are satisfied with your choices, click Apply to All to apply the header or footer to the entire presentation, or click Apply to apply the header or footer to the current slide only.

If you want to add a header or footer to your notes or handouts, click the Notes and Handouts tab of the Header and Footer dialog box, and select the options you want. Then click Apply to All to apply the header or footer to the entire presentation.

You can position the date, time, slide number, and footer text anywhere on the slides. To reposition one of these elements, first open the title master or slide master and select the frame that contains the element you want to move. Then drag it to a new location.

TIP   You may want to use the date and time to keep track of versions while the presentation is in the draft stage, and then remove them when you're ready to display or print the final presentation. To remove the date and time, simply choose Header and Footer from the View menu, click the Slide tab, and deselect the Date and Time check box.

Inserting the Slide Number, Date, or Time on Selected Slides

If you want to add only the date, time, or slide number on a selected slide, first move to the slide and click an insertion point on it.

To insert the current slide number, choose Slide Number from the Insert menu. PowerPoint places the slide number at the insertion point. You can start slide numbering at a number other than 1 by choosing Slide Setup from the File menu and then altering the number in the Number Slides from edit box. Changing the starting slide number is helpful when the presentation you're creating is a continuation of an earlier presentation.

To add the date or time, choose Date and Time from the Insert menu to open the Date and Time dialog box shown in Figure 9-13 on the next page. The format of the date and time is determined by the format you select in the list box. If you'd like PowerPoint to automatically update the date and time each time you modify or print your presentation, be sure to select the Update Automatically (Insert as Field) check box.

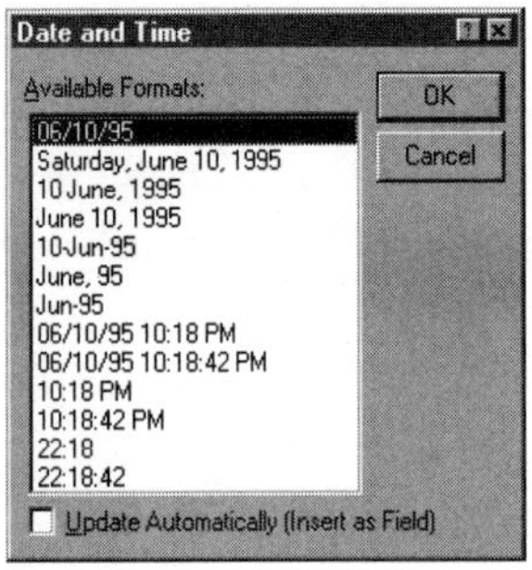

FIGURE 9-13
The Date and Time dialog box.

To add the date, time, or slide number to a title master or slide master, use the Header and Footer command on the View menu or select the Text Tool on the Drawing toolbar, and draw a text box outside the title, subtitle, and object areas of the title master or slide master. Then choose the Date and Time command or the Slide Number command from the Insert menu.

Checking Your Presentation's Style

After you've made all the changes to your presentation, you may want to use PowerPoint's handy Style Checker to ensure consistency across all your slides. With the Style Checker, you can do a final check on the spelling in your presentation, make sure your slides are easy to read, and verify that the case of bulleted text and titles and their end punctuation are the same throughout.

To open the Style Checker, shown in Figure 9-14, choose Style Checker from the Tools menu.

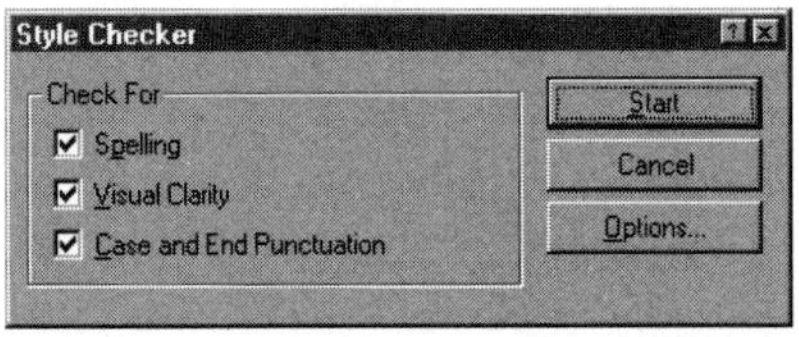

FIGURE 9-14
The Style Checker dialog box.

To start checking your presentation for inconsistencies, select the options you want to check, and then click Start. PowerPoint displays a dialog box for each slide in the presentation, similar to the one shown in Figure 9-15.

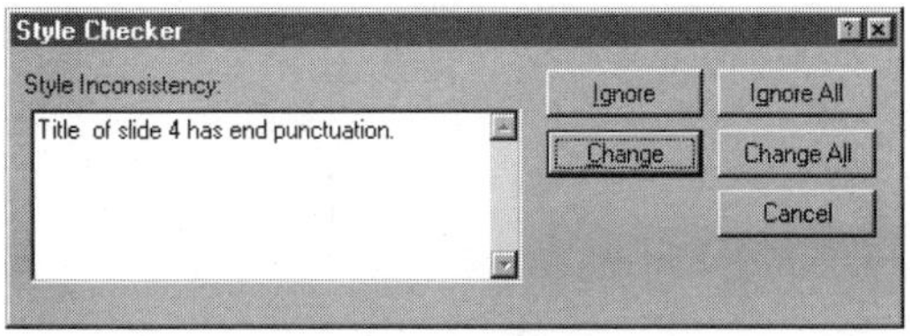

FIGURE 9-15
The Style Checker
checks each slide
for inconsistencies.

When the Style Checker has worked its way through each of the slides in your presentation, it displays the Style Checker Summary dialog box shown in Figure 9-16. The Style Checker Summary box lists other possible inconsistencies within your presentation and tells you which slides are affected.

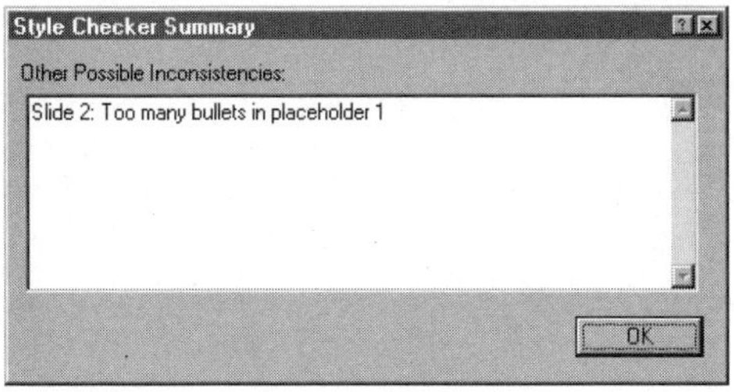

FIGURE 9-16
The Style Checker
summarizes
potential problems.

More often than not, the Style Checker's default settings for visual clarity, case, and end punctuation will work for most presentations. There are times, however, when you may want to change the settings. For example, you may need to comply with an in-house style guide that determines how many bulleted items you can have on a slide or that dictates a period at the end of each bulleted item.

To change the Style Checker settings, open the Style Checker dialog box, and click Options. Then click the Case and End Punctuation tab of the Style Checker Options dialog box, as shown in Figure 9-17 on the next page.

In the Case group, select from the drop-down lists how you want the titles and body text of your slides to appear. You can select sentence case, title case, uppercase, or lowercase. If you created a presentation with the Caps Lock key accidentally turned on, you can even ask the Style Checker to toggle the case in your presentation, changing uppercase to lower and lowercase to upper. If you want the Style Checker to ignore case when reviewing your slides, remember to deselect the Slide Title Style and Body Text Style options.

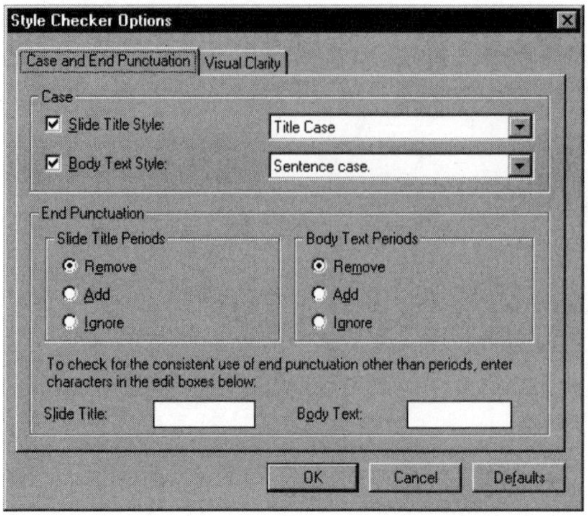

FIGURE 9-17

The Case and End
Punctuation tab of
the Style Checker
Options dialog box.

FIGURE 9-17

The End Punctuation group of the Case and End Punctuation tab lets you standardize the end punctuation for the titles and body text of your slides. You can ask the Style Checker to remove all end punctuation, add end punctuation, or ignore how your slides are punctuated. The default end punctuation is a period. If you want the Style Checker to use another type of punctuation, such as a semicolon or a comma, enter the punctuation in the Slide Title and Body Text edit boxes.

With PowerPoint's flexible formatting, it's easy to apply several different fonts and font sizes to text in your presentation. If more than one person works on a presentation and each person has a different formatting style, the Style Checker can check the presentation for visual clarity. The Visual Clarity tab of the Style Checker Options dialog box, shown in Figure 9-18, lets you tell the Style Checker how you want the presentation to look, ensuring that it can be easily read.

The Fonts group of the Visual Clarity tab lets you set the maximum number of fonts within a presentation. You can also set the size of the font used for title text and for body text. The Legibility group defines the maximum number of bullets per slide and the maximum number of lines per title and per bullet. The Style Checker can also check to make sure that your text doesn't overrun the edges of the slide. If you don't want the Style Checker to check a particular option, simply deselect it.

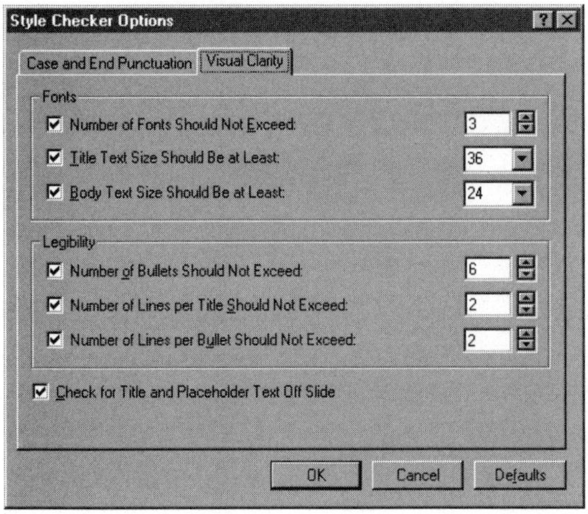

FIGURE 9-18
The Visual Clarity
tab of the Style
Checker Options
dialog box.

Once you've selected or modified all the options, click OK to return to
the Style Checker dialog box. Then click Start, and the Style Checker is off and
running!

The changes you have learned about in this chapter are broad in scope
and affect an entire presentation. They allow you to govern the overall
appearance of a presentation and to customize its look. In the next two
chapters, you'll learn to make further modifications to a presentation by formatting graphs you've added and using Slide Sorter view to rearrange the
presentation's slides.

Chapter 10

Formatting Graphs

When all you need is a standard-issue graph to get your message across, the basic steps of entering data and selecting a graph type or autoformat—covered in Chapter 6—are as far as you need to go. Graph 5, the graphing module used by PowerPoint, creates a professional-quality graph that accurately portrays your data and matches the design of your presentation.

But in many cases, simple accuracy is not sufficient. You want the graph to *communicate*—to accentuate a trend, de-emphasize an outcome, or call attention to a result. At times like these, creating the basic graph is only the first step. Formatting the graph to make it truly expressive is an equally important part of the process.

In this chapter, you'll learn how to emphasize patterns or trends in your graphs in a variety of ways, including changing the appearance of the markers that represent numbers, and changing the structure and design of the graph axes. You'll also learn how to format the titles, legend, gridlines, and other parts of the graph to communicate your data more effectively.

Activating a Graph for Formatting

After you create a basic graph by following the steps in Chapter 6, the graph appears on a slide with the default formatting prescribed by its particular chart type. For example, a new pie graph has the default formatting for pie graphs.

To activate the graph so that you can modify any aspect of its formatting, use one of these methods:

- Double-click the graph.
- Select the graph and press Enter. (Remember, you can cycle through the objects on a slide by pressing Tab.)
- Select the graph, choose Chart Object from the Edit menu, and then choose Edit from the submenu.

When you activate a graph, Graph's menus and Standard toolbar replace PowerPoint's menus and toolbars. The graph appears on a slide within a gray frame surrounded by black handles, as shown in Figure 10-1 on the next page. You haven't left PowerPoint, but you can now use any of Graph's Standard toolbar buttons to make changes to the entire graph. You learned about these buttons in Chapter 6, but they are shown on the next page for review.

FIGURE 10-1

An active graph
on a slide.

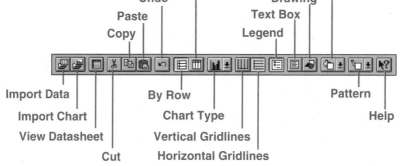

NOTE You can open the Graph module so that its menus and its toolbar appear within a separate Graph window that overlays the PowerPoint window. (This is how Graph worked in previous versions of PowerPoint.) First select the graph, and choose Chart Object and then Open from the Edit menu. When you finish editing in Graph, choose Update from Graph's File menu, and then choose Exit and Return to *Presentation* from the File menu.

After you finish formatting the graph, click outside the gray frame to exit Graph and to redisplay PowerPoint's menus and toolbars.

> **TIP**   To use the Zoom command on Graph's View menu, you must first select the graph in the PowerPoint window. Next, choose Chart Object and then choose Open from PowerPoint's Edit menu. The Graph module is loaded, and the Zoom command on Graph's View menu becomes available. You can also quickly zoom in on a graph in the PowerPoint window by using PowerPoint's Zoom Control box or Zoom command.

Selecting a Graph Object for Formatting

In addition to changing the entire graph, you can change individual components, called *graph objects*. To understand which graph objects you can change, you need to know a little about the anatomy of a graph. Figure 10-2 shows a typical graph and its graph objects. Don't worry if you can't remember the names of all the graph objects right now. You'll have plenty of opportunity to become familiar with them as you read the sections of this chapter, which cover each graph object in depth.

NOTE The words *graph* and *chart* are used interchangeably throughout this chapter.

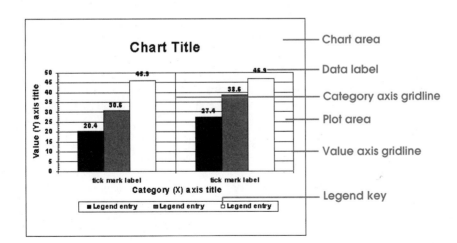

FIGURE 10-2

A typical graph and its graph objects.

To change a graph object, double-click the object after you've activated the graph. A dialog box opens with formatting options for the selected object. You can double-click each object in the graph in succession, and make formatting changes in a dialog box. You can double-click and format the bars in a bar graph, for example, and then double-click and format the legend.

To use the keyboard to select a graph object, first press the Up or Down arrow key to move from one group of graph objects to the next. Then, to select an individual graph object from the group, such as one of the columns of a column series or one of the legend entries of the legend, press the Right or Left arrow key. After you select an object in this way, you can choose the first command on the Format menu to display a dialog box with formatting options for the selected object. The name of the command changes depending on which graph object is selected. If you select an axis, for example, the command is Selected Axis. If you select a legend, the command is Selected Legend, and so on.

A third method for indicating which graph object you want to format is to click the object and then open the shortcut menu by clicking the right mouse button. Select the Format command halfway down the shortcut menu to open a dialog box with formatting options for the corresponding object. Like the Selected command on the Format menu, the name of the Format command on the shortcut menu reflects the graph object you've selected, such as Format Legend or Format Data Series.

> **TIP** When you have formatted as many graph objects as necessary to create a graph with the look you want, you can save the combination of formatted graph objects as an autoformat. Then you can select the custom autoformat to quickly apply its settings to all the graph objects in any new graph. For more information about saving a formatted graph as an autoformat, see "Saving Graph Formatting as an AutoFormat," page 297.

2-D Graph Formatting

Each graph object has its own special formatting options. This section, which covers these special options, assumes that you have already activated the graph and are ready to select a graph object for formatting.

Changing the Color of a Data Series

In a graph, a data series is represented by one or more markers: an area, a group of bars, a group of columns, a line, the slices of a pie, the rings of a doughnut graph, the lines of a radar graph, or the groups of points in an XY (scatter) graph. The color of a data series is the color displayed by the markers of that series. These markers can also contain a pattern of another color.

The easiest way to change the color of a data series is to click the series and then use the Color button and Pattern button on Graph's Standard toolbar. On the face of these buttons, small boxes display the current color and pattern settings—white is the default. To select a different color, click the down arrow to the right of the Color button, and then click a color in the palette of colors, which looks like this:

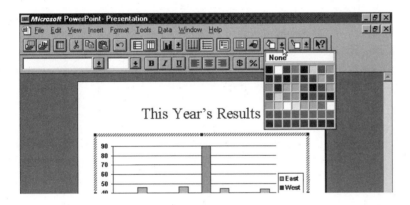

To select a different pattern, click the down arrow to the right of the Pattern button, and then click a pattern at the top and a pattern color at the bottom of the palette of patterns, which looks like this:

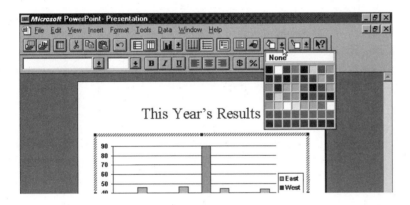

To select a color or pattern for the markers of a data series as well as a color for the border of the markers, you must use the Format Data Series dialog box instead. Follow these steps:

1. Double-click any of the markers in a data series to open the Format Data Series dialog box, as shown below.

The Format Data Series dialog box contains at least two tabs. The Patterns tab gives you options that change the patterns and colors of the series. The Data Labels tab lets you add numbers that show the numeric values of the data points. Other tabs in the dialog box provide advanced formatting options for types of graphs that are covered later in this chapter.

2. If you want to change the currently selected markers, click the Patterns tab. Then in the Border section, select a Style, Color, and Weight option from each of the Custom lists to change the appearance of the marker borders. (The Custom button is selected as soon as you change any of the default settings.) To remove the borders around the markers, click None. To reset the borders to the default setting, click Automatic.

NOTE If the series is represented by a line, the options in the Border section control the appearance of the line.

3. In the Area section, change the look of the markers themselves by clicking a color in the Color palette and selecting a pattern from the

Pattern drop-down list. From the Pattern list, you can select a pattern color, as well.

4. Click OK to close the Format Data Series dialog box.

If, for example, you want to surround an area marker in an area graph with a white line and fill the area marker with dark blue, first double-click the marker. Then, in the Format Data Series dialog box, select white as the Color option in the Border section and dark blue as the Color option in the Area section, and click OK.

> **TIP** When you change the color of a data series, be sure you select a color that properly contrasts with the background of the graph and with the other data series.

Adding and Formatting Titles

After you enter your data, the basic graph that PowerPoint draws displays no text other than the labels that mark increments along the axes and the text in the legend. Figure 10-3 shows a graph at this earliest stage. You may want to enter a title for each of the graph axes to identify what they measure. You may also want to add a title above the graph to describe the graph's purpose, especially if you've used the slide title to describe the slide in general rather than the graph in particular.

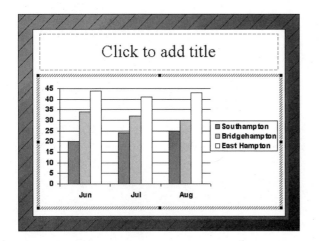

FIGURE 10-3
A basic graph without titles.

Adding the Titles

To add titles for the graph and its axes, follow these steps:

1. With the graph activated, choose Titles from the Insert menu or the shortcut menu. Graph displays the Titles dialog box, as shown here:

2. Click the check boxes to select the titles you want to add, and then click OK to display sample titles on the graph, as shown here:

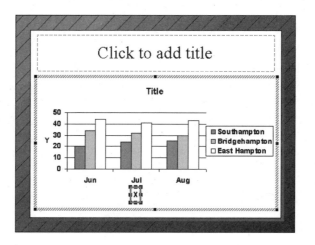

One of the titles—in this case the category (X) axis title—appears in a text box surrounded by handles, which shows that it is selected.

3. Click each title and type the actual text you want. The titles can be two or more lines; simply press Enter to start a new line.

To remove a title, select it, choose Titles from the Insert menu, and then deselect the title's check box. Alternatively, you can select the title and press Delete, or click the right mouse button and then choose Clear from the shortcut menu.

To replace a title, you simply click the title, and then type the replacement text. To edit a title, click the title once, and then click an insertion point in the text. Edit the text as you would edit any text in PowerPoint. Press Esc or click elsewhere on the graph to complete the editing process.

After you add a title, you can reposition it on the graph by following the steps below.

1. Click the title. Graph displays the title's text box surrounded by handles, as shown here:

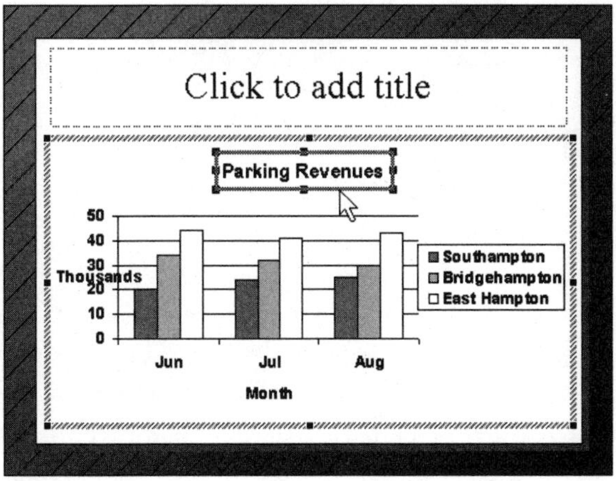

2. Place the pointer on the outline of the text box or on one of the handles, and drag to move the box.

   NOTE Dragging the handles does not stretch the box, as you might expect. Instead, the entire box moves.

Don't worry about the value (Y) axis title, *Thousands*. You'll learn how to rotate titles later in the chapter.

Formatting the Titles

The default formatting of the graph determines the formatting of the titles. However, you can select and format each title separately—making the chart title larger and the axis titles smaller, for example. You can format both the text of the title and the rectangle that contains the text. Unfortunately, you cannot select multiple titles for formatting; you must select and format each title in turn.

To format both a title and its box, double-click the title. A Format dialog box for the selected object appears, as shown in Figure 10-4. (If the title is already selected, be sure to click elsewhere first, and then double-click the title outline, or you will end up clicking an insertion point in the text.)

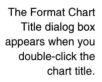

FIGURE 10-4

The Format Chart Title dialog box appears when you double-click the chart title.

Alternatively, you can click the title and display the Format dialog box by choosing the first command from the Format menu, which is either Selected Chart Title or Selected Axis Title; by pressing Ctrl+1; or by clicking the right mouse button and choosing the Format command from the shortcut menu.

To format only the text of a title or a selected part of a title, click the title and select the text you want to format. Then display the Format dialog box by choosing Selected Chart Title or Selected Axis Title from the Format menu; by pressing Ctrl+1; or by choosing the Format command from the shortcut menu. (The Format dialog box consists of only the Font tab when you select part of the title and choose either of the Format menu commands.)

To format the title's text box rather than its text, you use the options on the Patterns tab in the Format dialog box. The Border settings control the appearance of the border of the text box. The Area settings control the color and pattern of the interior of the text box. A sample in the lower right corner shows the results of the Border and Area settings. You can select the appropriate None option if you want the text box to have no border or a clear interior. To restore the defaults for the Border or Area settings, select the Automatic option.

TIP   When you select an Area color for the text box, be careful to select a color that properly contrasts with both the plot area of the graph and the text of the title. You may have to change the text color to contrast with the text box color, as described below.

To add a border, select a Style, Color, and Weight option from the drop-down lists under Custom in the Border section. To add a shadow, click the Shadow check box. The color of the shadow is determined by the Shadow color of the color scheme.

To change the appearance of the title's text, select the title and then click the Font tab of the Format dialog box. Figure 10-5 shows the Font tab options. Use the Font, Font Style, Size, Underline, and Color options to change the look of the text. Leaving the Color option set to Automatic applies the Window Text Color specified by the color option of the Windows Control Panel. This color is probably black, but you can select any other text color.

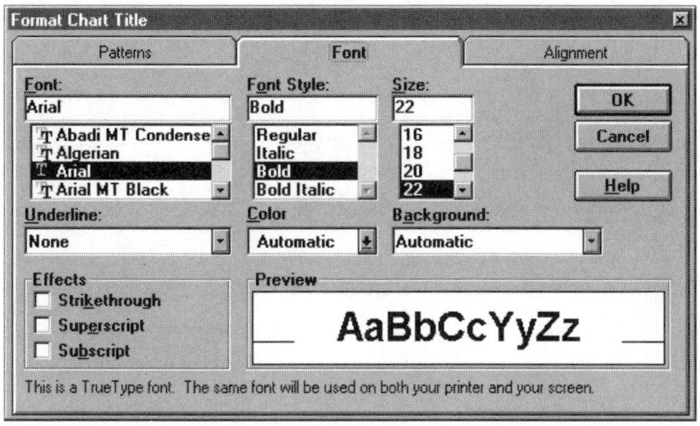

FIGURE 10-5

The Font tab of the Format Chart Title dialog box.

TIP   You can also format the text of a title by selecting the text and then using the text formatting buttons on Graph's Formatting toolbar. Display this toolbar by choosing Toolbars from Graph's View menu, selecting the Formatting option in the Toolbars dialog box, and then clicking OK.

The Background option on the Font tab is a fine-tuning control. Leave it set to Automatic to let Graph select a background that contrasts properly with the foreground text color. If the text and text box are the same color, the Automatic setting fills the area behind the letters of the text with a contrasting color to ensure that the text is readable. You can select Transparent to make the area behind the letters transparent so that the text box color shows through, or you can select Opaque to make this area a solid color. When you select Opaque, any pattern is removed from the area behind the letters of the text.

The Effects options on the Font tab let you turn on Strikethrough (a horizontal line through the text), Superscript, or Subscript. Figure 10-6 shows an axis title with a subscript character.

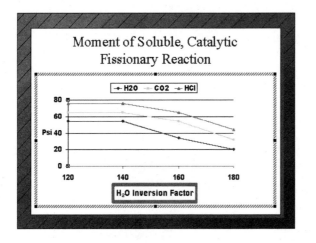

To change the alignment of the text in the text box, click the Alignment tab of the Format dialog box. (Figure 10-7 on the facing page shows the Alignment tab options in the Format Axis Title dialog box.) You can then position the text within the text box by selecting options in the Text Alignment section. For example, selecting Left for Horizontal and Center for Vertical aligns the text against the center-left interior edge of the text box.

The Orientation option is especially useful for rotating the value (Y) axis title of the graph, as shown in Figure 10-8 on the facing page.

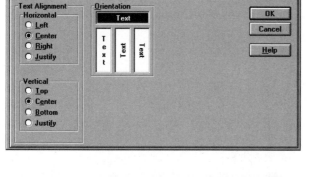

FIGURE 10-7

The Alignment
tab of the
Format Axis Title
dialog box.

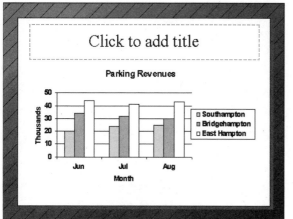

FIGURE 10-8

The value (Y) axis
title, *Thousands,*
rotated 90 degrees.
(Compare this
graph with the one
on page 253.)

Formatting All the Graph Text

By double-clicking the chart area, you can display the Format Chart Area dialog box. You can then use the Font tab of this dialog box to make changes to all the text in the graph. This is an efficient way to set the font for all the graph text, for example.

Adding and Formatting a Legend

If the graph you've created does not already have a legend, you can add one by clicking the Legend button on Graph's Standard toolbar or by choosing Legend from the Insert menu. The plot area of the graph shrinks, moving in from the right to allow space for the legend. If you change your mind, you can quickly remove the legend by clicking the Legend button again or by selecting the legend and pressing the Delete key.

Repositioning the Legend

If you want the legend to appear above, below, or to the left of the graph instead of to the right, you can select a preset legend location by choosing a menu command, or you can drag the legend into position. The advantage of using the menu command is that Graph adjusts the plot area to make room for the legend and adjusts the shape of the legend to fit its new location. The advantage of dragging the legend is that you can place it anywhere you want—even within the graph, if you can find a position that won't obscure the graph's data. Placing the legend within the graph allows you to recover the space formerly occupied by the legend. You can then stretch the plot area of the graph to make the graph larger and easier to see.

To reposition a legend using a menu command, follow these steps:

1. Select the legend, and then choose Selected Legend from the Format menu, press Ctrl+1, or choose Format Legend from the shortcut menu.

2. When the Format Legend dialog box appears, click the Placement tab, as shown below.

3. Click one of the Type options to select a placement, and then click OK. The legend jumps to the new placement, and its shape adjusts to fit the space.

4. If you want to recover the space that is now empty, select the plot area of the graph, and drag its right handle to the right.

When you drag a legend above, below, or to the left of the graph, the plot area of the graph does not adjust to make space. Also, the legend does not automatically change shape to fit its new location. You must perform these steps by dragging the handles of the plot area and the legend. You can reshape a legend by dragging one of its corner handles. As the boundaries of the legend move, dotted boxes in the legend show the new arrangement of the legend entries. For example, when you stretch the legend horizontally, the boxes indicate that the legend entries will be arranged side by side, as shown in Figure 10-9.

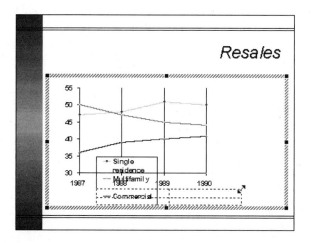

FIGURE 10-9

Stretching a vertical legend horizontally.

TIP   When you move a legend from the right or left of the graph to the top or bottom, you can widen the graph to reclaim the legend's space. But when you widen an area, bar, column, or line graph, you decrease the impression of change over time. The lines of a line graph, for example, do not appear to climb or fall as rapidly. You can use this fact to your advantage. To emphasize positive change, place the legend on the left or right side of the graph; to de-emphasize negative change, place the legend above or below the graph.

Formatting the Legend Entries

You can format the legend box, the text within the legend, and even an individual legend text entry or legend key (the small box within the legend that shows the identifying color or pattern). To format the legend box and all the text within it, double-click the legend to display the Format Legend dialog box. To format a legend entry or legend key, double-click the legend entry or legend key to display the corresponding dialog box. You can also select the legend, legend entry, or legend key and then choose the corresponding Selected command from the Format menu, press Ctrl+1, or choose the Format command from the shortcut menu.

> **NOTE** When you change the color or pattern of a legend key, the color or pattern of the corresponding data series changes, too.

In the Format Legend dialog box, you use the options on the Patterns tab to format the legend box and legend key, and you use the options on the Font tab to format the legend text. Both tabs work the same way with legends as they do with chart titles.

See Also   For more information about using the Patterns tab and the Font tab, see "Formatting the Titles," page 253.

Formatting the Axes and Tick Marks

The axes of an area, bar, column, line, XY (scatter), or radar graph are the scales against which the values of the markers in the graph are measured. Pie and doughnut graphs do not have axes. By scaling the axes (changing the minimum or maximum values), you can emphasize or de-emphasize the graph's data. By adding, removing, and formatting tick marks and tick mark labels, you can make the graph easier to interpret—or harder, if that's your goal.

Showing or Hiding the Axes

By default, axes are displayed on the basic graph that Graph creates, but you can turn off one or both axes if you need to display only the markers of the graph. For example, you may not need to give your audience a scale against which to measure the actual values in the graph. Or you may prefer to omit the axes and instead display data point labels, which specify the exact value of each data point.

To turn off an axis, follow these steps:

1. Choose Axes from the Insert menu. The Axes dialog box for a 2-D graph appears, as shown below.

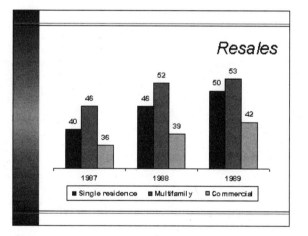

2. Deselect one or both of the Primary Axis check boxes, and click OK. For example, deselecting the Value (Y) Axis option and adding data point labels (you'll learn how later in this chapter) produces the graph shown here:

To remove an axis, you can select the axis, and then press the Delete key or choose Clear from the shortcut menu. (The Insert Axes command, which opens the Axes dialog box, is also available on the shortcut menu.)

Formatting the Axes

To change the color or line style of an axis, start by double-clicking the axis. Alternatively, select the axis and then choose Selected Axis from the Format menu, press Ctrl+1, or choose Format Axis from the shortcut menu. When the Format Axis dialog box appears, click the Patterns tab, shown in Figure 10-10.

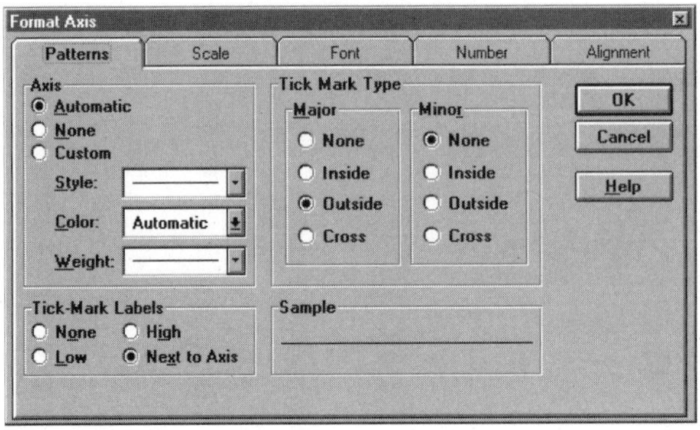

FIGURE 10-10

The Patterns tab of the Format Axis dialog box.

Format Axis

Patterns | Scale | Font | Number | Alignment

Axis
- ● Automatic
- ○ None
- ○ Custom

Style:
Color: Automatic
Weight:

Tick Mark Type

Major
- ○ None
- ○ Inside
- ● Outside
- ○ Cross

Minor
- ● None
- ○ Inside
- ○ Outside
- ○ Cross

OK
Cancel
Help

Tick-Mark Labels
- ○ None ○ High
- ○ Low ● Next to Axis

Sample

TIP   If you have trouble double-clicking the axis, you can double-click any of the labels along the axis to open the Format Axis dialog box.

You can select a line style, line color, and line weight from the three drop-down lists under Custom in the Axis section. The Sample box shows the result of your changes. Click OK to return to the graph, or click a different tab to make other changes to the axis.

Scaling the Axes

Graph automatically determines appropriate axis scaling for the numbers you entered in the datasheet. The maximum value of the value axis is set to the next major interval above the largest value in the data. However, you might want to change the automatic settings to achieve specific effects. To accentuate change in a line graph, for example, you can reduce the maximum value and increase the minimum value.

To change the scale of an axis, start by double-clicking the axis. Alternatively, select the axis and then choose Selected Axis from the Format menu, press Ctrl+1, or choose Format Axis from the shortcut menu. When the Format Axis dialog box appears, click the Scale tab. Figure 10-11 shows the Scale tab for a value (Y) axis. Figure 10-12 shows the Scale tab for a category (X) axis. If the graph is an XY (scatter) type, it has two value axes.

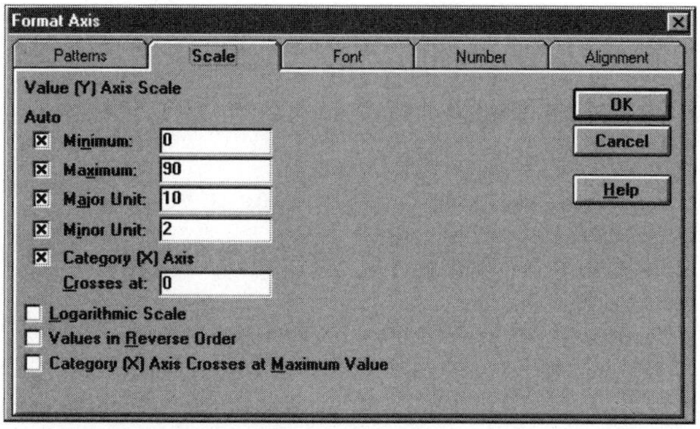

FIGURE 10-11

The Scale tab options in the Format Axis dialog box when a value (Y) axis is selected.

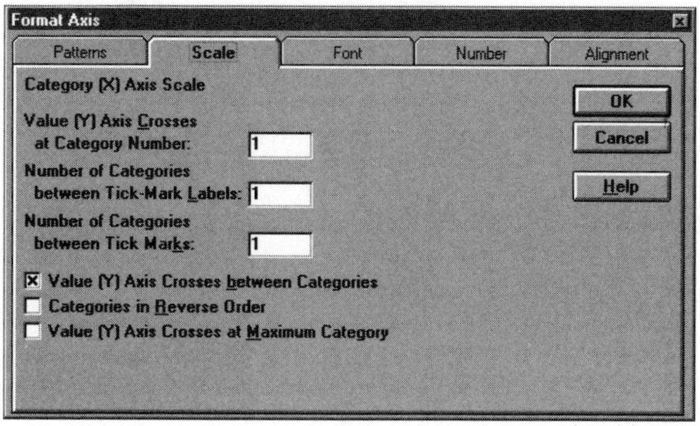

FIGURE 10-12

The Scale tab options in the Format Axis dialog box when a category (X) axis is selected.

If you've selected a value axis, the Scale tab shows the current settings for the Minimum, Maximum, Major Unit, Minor Unit, and Category (X) Axis Crosses at options, which are described in Table 10-1 on the next page. The Auto check box to the left of each option is checked to show that Graph has automatically supplied a standard setting. When you change a setting, Graph clears the Auto check box.

263

Option	Description
Minimum	The minimum value along the axis.
Maximum	The maximum value along the axis.
Major Unit	The increment between the major units along the axis.
Minor Unit	The increment between the minor units that appear between the major units along the axis.
Category (X) Axis Crosses at	The point on the value axis at which the category axis intersects. This setting might be less than 0 if your data includes negative values.

NOTE The minimum value of a bar or column graph must always be 0. Anything other than 0 hides the full lengths of the bars or columns. If you can't see the full bars or columns, you can't gauge their relative lengths, and the graph is truly misleading.

The other three options on the Scale tab for a value axis serve special purposes. To use a logarithmic scale along the value axis when your data has vast variations, click the Logarithmic Scale option. Then each successive interval along the axis is 10 times the previous interval. To invert an entire graph, click the Values in Reverse Order option. Figure 10-13 shows an inverted graph.

FIGURE 10-13

An inverted graph created by selecting the Values in Reverse Order option on the Scale tab of the Format Axis dialog box.

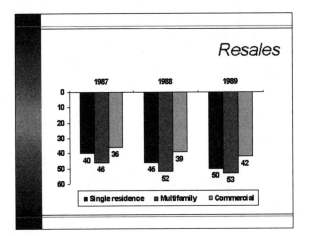

To invert a graph without inverting the value axis, click the Category (X) Axis Crosses at Maximum Value option. You can use such a graph to show the amount of progress still needed to reach a goal by setting the Maximum option to the value of the goal and entering the progress so far on the datasheet. Figure 10-14 shows such a graph.

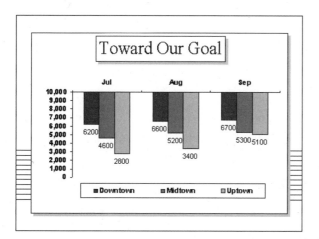

FIGURE 10-14

An inverted graph created by selecting the Category (X) Axis Crosses at Maximum Value option on the Scale tab of the Format Axis dialog box.

If you've selected a category axis, the Scale tab shows the three edit boxes described in Table 10-2.

Option	Description
Value (Y) Axis Crosses at Category Number	Moves the value axis to the right along the category axis to the category number in the edit box.
Number of Categories between Tick-Mark Labels	Determines the number of labels along the category axis. Enter 2, for example, to show every other label.
Number of Categories between Tick Marks	Determines the number of tick marks along the category axis. Enter 2, for example, to show every other tick mark.

TABLE 10-2

The Category (X) Axis Scale options.

Deselecting the Value (Y) Axis Crosses between Categories option draws the value axis in the middle of a category rather than between categories. Selecting the Categories in Reverse Order option reverses the order of the categories along the category axis. For example, if the categories are chronological, they appear in reverse chronological order. Selecting the Value (Y) Axis Crosses at Maximum Category option moves the value axis to the right side of the graph (or to the left side if the categories are reversed).

Formatting the Tick Marks Along the Axes

Major and minor tick marks are the tiny notches that appear along the value axis of a graph to indicate the major and minor units specified on the Scale tab of the Format Axis dialog box. Tick marks also appear between categories on the category axis.

An axis can have major and minor tick marks inside, outside, or crossing the line of the axis. These tick marks automatically have the same color and pattern as the axis to which they are attached. You can change the position of the tick marks by changing the Tick Mark Type options on the Patterns tab of the Format Axis dialog box, shown in Figure 10-15. Figure 10-16 on the facing page shows a graph with major tick marks that appear outside the value axis and minor tick marks that appear inside the axis.

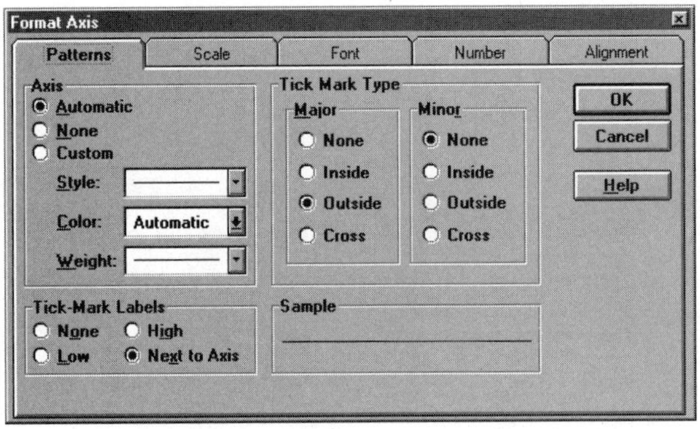

FIGURE 10-15

The Patterns tab of the Format Axis dialog box.

Formatting the Labels Along the Axes

Tick mark labels appear at the major tick marks of the value axis and between tick marks on the category axis. You control the formatting of these labels by using options on the Patterns, Font, Number, and Alignment tabs of the Format Axis dialog box.

To change the location of the tick mark labels, use the Tick-Mark Labels options on the Patterns tab of the Format Axis dialog box, shown in Figure

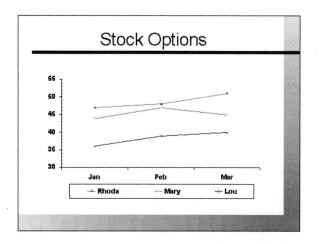

FIGURE 10-16

An axis with major tick marks outside and minor tick marks inside.

10-15. The default setting, Next to Axis, places the labels near their own axis. To place them near the maximum or minimum values of the other axis, select High or Low, respectively. For example, selecting High moves the tick mark labels to the opposite side of the graph, adjacent to the maximum value on the other axis, as shown in Figure 10-17.

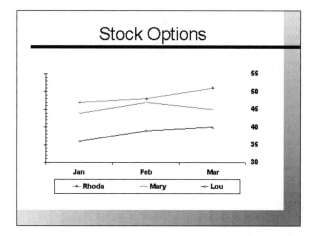

FIGURE 10-17

A graph for which the Tick-Mark Labels option is set to High.

To remove tick mark labels, click None, but unless you want to show only relative values in a graph, be sure to use data point labels to specify the absolute values.

> **NOTE** The Font tab options for formatting the text of tick mark labels work just like the Font tab options for formatting titles. For more information about the Font tab options, see "Formatting the Titles," page 253.

The options on the Number tab, shown in Figure 10-18, let you modify the formatting of the numbers along a numeric axis. If the Linked to Source option is selected, these numbers have the same formatting as the numbers in the datasheet. To change the formatting, select a category from the Category list, and then select an option from the Format Codes list. The Sample number in the dialog box reflects the selected formatting.

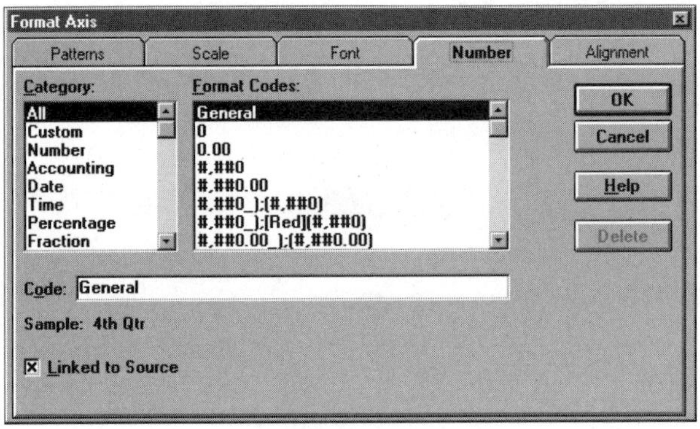

FIGURE 10-18

The Number tab of the Format Axis dialog box.

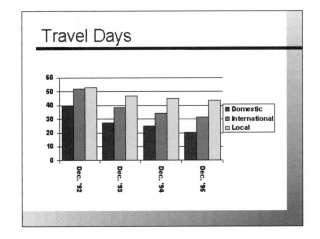

The options on the Alignment tab let you change the orientation of the tick mark labels. The Automatic setting (horizontal) usually works best for the value tick mark labels, but you may want to select one of the vertical orientations for the category tick mark labels if the labels are long. Figure 10-19 shows a graph with vertical tick mark labels along the category axis.

FIGURE 10-19

A graph with vertical tick mark labels along the category axis.

TIP Be aware that setting the tick mark label orientation to vertical leaves less vertical space for the graph, so the graph becomes shorter without a corresponding change in its width. Changing a graph only vertically or only horizontally increases or decreases the impression of change in the graph.

Showing or Hiding Gridlines

Gridlines extend from major unit tick marks and help you gauge the heights of areas and lines, the lengths of bars and columns, and the position of data points. The easiest way to turn gridlines on or off is to click the Vertical Gridlines and Horizontal Gridlines buttons on Graph's Standard toolbar. Click once to turn on gridlines, and click again to turn them off. You can also choose Gridlines from the Insert menu or choose Insert Gridlines from the shortcut menu to turn gridlines on or off.

Formatting the Gridlines

After you turn on gridlines, you can format them by double-clicking any gridline to display the Format Gridlines dialog box. Then use the options on the Patterns tab to set the style, color, and weight of the gridlines. You can click Automatic to return to the default settings.

NOTE The options on the Scale tab in the Format Gridlines dialog box allow you to set the scaling of the axis from which the gridlines emanate.

Modifying the Graph Background

A graph has two background areas you can format: the plot area immediately behind the markers, axes, and axis tick mark labels; and the chart area within the heavy border surrounding the graph, including the area occupied by the legend and the chart title.

Formatting the Plot Area

To format the plot area, first double-click within the graph but away from the axes or markers. If the graph is three-dimensional, you must double-click just outside the graph, but away from the axes or axis labels. You can also click once to select the plot area and, when you see a border appear around the plot area, choose Selected Plot Area from the Format menu, press Ctrl+1, or choose Format Plot Area from the shortcut menu. The Format Plot Area dialog box contains only the Patterns tab. Use the options in the Border and Area sections to change the look of the plot area. Figure 10-20 shows the plot area of a graph filled with a medium gray.

FIGURE 10-20

The plot area of a graph filled with a medium gray.

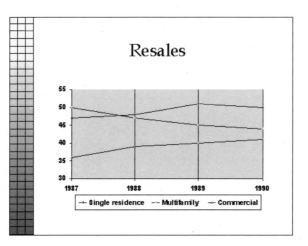

Formatting the Chart Area

To format the chart area, double-click within the heavy border of the graph but outside the plot area, or click once to select the chart area and then choose Selected Chart Area from the Format menu, press Ctrl+1, or choose Format Chart Area from the shortcut menu. (Be careful not to click the legend or the chart title.) The Format Chart Area dialog box appears, as shown in Figure 10-21.

FIGURE 10-21

The Format Chart Area dialog box.

Use the options in the Border and Area sections of the Patterns tab to change the look of the border and the interior of the chart area. You can select a border style, color, and weight, and you can fill the chart area with a background color and pattern. Use the Font tab options to change the look of all the text in the graph. Figure 10-22 shows a line graph with contrasting formatting in the plot and chart areas.

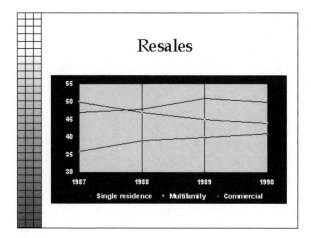

NOTE The Replace Fonts command on the Tools menu, which changes the fonts used throughout a presentation, does not affect the fonts used by the text in graphs. After changing the presentation font, you can quickly change a graph's font to match by using the options on the Font tab of the Format Chart Area dialog box. That way, you don't have to select and format each graph text object individually.

Adding and Formatting Data Labels

The markers of a data series provide only an approximate representation of the numbers in the datasheet. To show the actual numbers, you must provide a table of numbers or place the numbers directly on the markers as data labels.

To add data labels to a data series, start by double-clicking the series. When the Format Data Series dialog box appears, click the Data Labels tab, which is shown in Figure 10-23 on the next page.

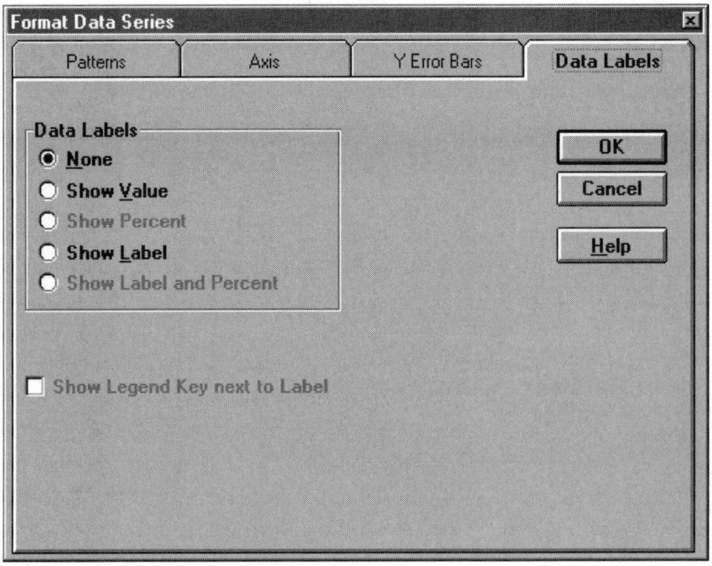

FIGURE 10-23

The Data Labels
tab of the
Format Data
Series dialog box.

FIGURE 10-23

The Data Labels tab of the Format Data Series dialog box.

To add data labels to all the markers in the graph, you can select the graph and then choose Data Labels from the Insert menu or choose Insert Data Labels from the shortcut menu. The Data Labels dialog box shows the same options as the Data Labels tab of the Format Data Series dialog box.

When you have displayed the dialog box, click Show Value to display the numeric value of each data point in the series. Click Show Percent if the graph is a stacked bar, stacked column, pie, or doughnut graph and you want to show the percentages represented by the segments or slices. Click Show Label to display the category assigned to the data point. (In an area graph, clicking Show Label displays the series names.) Click Show Label and Percent to display both the category or series names and the percentages.

If an Automatic Text check box appears on the Data Labels tab, the data labels of the datasheet are being used. Click this check box to synchronize the data labels with those on the datasheet. If the Show Legend Key next to Label check box is available, you can check it to place the legend key, which displays the color of the series, next to the data label.

TIP You can add a data label to a single marker—an outstanding result, for example—by clicking the marker to select it and then double-clicking the marker to open the Format Data Point dialog box, which contains the same Data Labels and Patterns tabs as the Format Data Series dialog box. Alternatively, you can select a single marker and choose Data Labels from either the Insert menu or the shortcut menu. Then select one of the Show options in the Data Labels dialog box, and click OK.

To format the data labels on a graph, double-click any data label in a series. The Format Data Labels dialog box appears. The options on the four tabs of the dialog box (Patterns, Font, Number, and Alignment) work just as they do when you format any other text in a graph. For example, you can use the Patterns options to create a filled box around each data label and the Number options to change the number of decimal places shown in the data labels.

To format a single data label, select the data labels for the series, and click the data label you want. Then double-click the same data label, and use the options in the Format Data Labels dialog box as usual. You can also select a single data label, click an insertion point in it, and then edit or add text. For example, you might want to delete the number and enter a note about the data point, as shown in Figure 10-24.

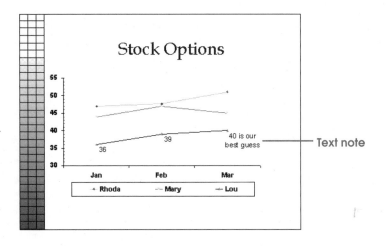

FIGURE 10-24

A text note attached to a data point.

TIP   Don't try to crowd too many data labels on a graph. You might prefer to add a table to the slide or to the following slide showing the numbers.

Moving and Resizing Graph Objects

You've already seen that you can move a graph's title or legend by dragging its border. You can also drag the border of the entire graph to move it on the slide and drag the plot area to move or resize the area of the graph bounded by the axes and axis labels. (Enlarging the plot area of a graph can make interpreting the markers easier, but changing the shape of the plot area alters the impression of change in the graph.) You can even drag each data label to reposition it relative to its data point or marker.

To move or resize a graph object, click the object and then drag the object's border. To drag a data label, for example, first click the data label to select it, and then drag the border surrounding the data label.

After you finish formatting the graph, click outside the graph's border to redisplay PowerPoint's menus and toolbars. Later, if you want to make additional changes to the graph, you can open the Graph module by simply double-clicking the graph.

3-D Graph Formatting

PowerPoint's 3-D chart types are almost always worthy replacements for their 2-D equivalents. They portray the same data with the added touch of depth and, if you want, perspective. The third dimension also adds more formatting possibilities, which are the subject of this section.

Adjusting the 3-D View

PowerPoint provides 3-D versions of area, bar, column, line, and pie graphs, in addition to 3-D surface graphs which are by definition three-dimensional. You can slant, rotate, and change the height of 3-D graphs by changing their 3-D view. For all types other than 3-D bar and 3-D pie graphs, you can also increase the illusion of depth by adding perspective.

To change both the elevation (the forward slant) and the rotation of a 3-D graph, you don't even have to use a dialog box. You can simply drag the corners of the graph by following these steps:

1. Click one of the corners of the graph. A handle appears at every corner of an imaginary box that encloses the graph. (If you see handles only at the corners of the back wall, try clicking the corner again or click a different corner.)

2. Place the mouse pointer on one of the corner handles, hold down the mouse button, and drag the mouse slightly. The outlines of the imaginary box appear. If you hold down the Ctrl key as you drag, you see outlines of the markers, too, as shown below:

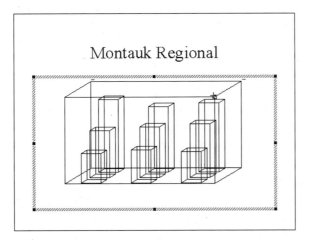

3. Still holding down the mouse button, drag the corner up or down to change the elevation, or drag the corner left or right to rotate the graph.

4. Release the mouse button to redraw the graph at its new elevation and rotation.

You can use the options in the Format 3-D View dialog box to accomplish the same task. Select the graph and then choose 3-D View from the Format menu or the shortcut menu to open the dialog box shown in Figure 10-25 on the next page. As you can see, additional options in the dialog box let you change the height of 3-D graphs and add perspective to those graphs that can show perspective.

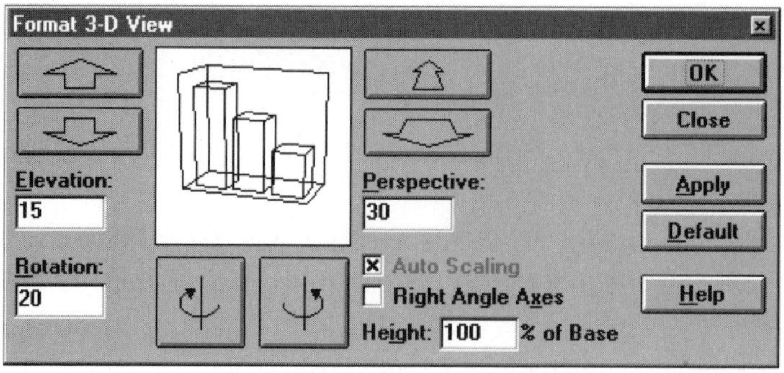

FIGURE 10-25

The Format 3-D
View dialog box.

In the Format 3-D View dialog box, a model of the 3-D graph shows the current option settings. By viewing the model as you change the options, you can determine how the actual graph will look when you click OK.

To change the elevation of the graph, enter a number in the Elevation edit box or click the Increase Elevation or Decrease Elevation button to the left of the model. Each click changes the elevation by 5 degrees. To change the rotation, enter a number in the Rotation edit box or click the Rotate Left or Rotate Right button below the model. Each click changes the rotation by 10 degrees.

To change the height of the graph, deselect the Auto Scaling option, and then edit the number in the Height edit box. (You cannot change the height of 3-D pie graphs.) The height of the graph is specified as a percentage of the length of the base. To let PowerPoint select a height that is appropriate for the graph, turn on Auto Scaling by clicking the option again.

To add perspective, deselect the Right Angle Axes option. (You cannot add perspective to 3-D bar graphs or 3-D pie graphs.) Then edit the number in the Perspective edit box or click the Decrease Perspective or Increase Perspective button to the right of the model. Each click changes the perspective by 5 units. (Valid perspective numbers are 0 to 100.) The default perspective setting of 30 is just enough to give the graph a true sense of depth without the kind of distortion shown in Figure 10-26 on the facing page.

After you change the options in the Format 3-D View dialog box, click Apply to apply the new settings without removing the dialog box, or click OK to return to the graph. If you click Apply, you can drag the dialog box aside to see the revised graph. You can also click Default to return the graph to its default 3-D view settings.

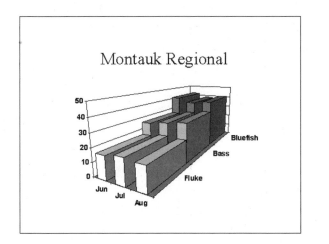

FIGURE 10-26

A rotated, 3-D column graph distorted by a Perspective setting of 60.

To change the depth of a 3-D graph, select the graph and then choose either the 3-D Group command from the bottom of the Format menu or the Format 3-D Group command from the bottom of the shortcut menu. Figure 10-27 shows the Options tab of the dialog box that appears when a 3-D column graph is selected. Then change the Chart Depth option and click OK. (The minimum and maximum chart depths are 20 and 2000, respectively.)

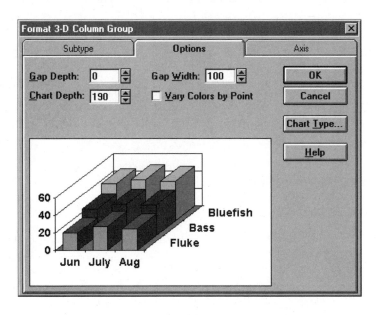

FIGURE 10-27

The Options tab of the Format 3-D Column Group dialog box.

Formatting 3-D Graph Objects

3-D graphs have unique graph objects that 2-D graphs do not have. Figure 10-28 identifies the graph objects that are unique to 3-D graphs.

FIGURE 10-28

The unique graph objects of a 3-D column chart.

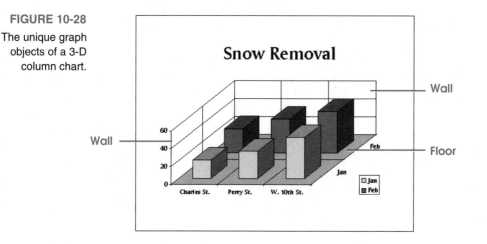

Formatting the Axes

When the series in 3-D graphs appear behind one another at various depths in the graph, a third axis—the series (Y) axis—extends along the floor of the graph from front to back. The category axis remains the X axis, but the value axis rises from the floor and is called the Z axis. The graph shown in Figure 10-28 shows all three axes.

Formatting the value axis of a 3-D graph is just like formatting the value axis of a 2-D graph. You double-click the value axis or select the axis and then choose Selected Axis from the Format menu, press Ctrl+1, or choose Format Axis from the shortcut menu. All three methods display the Format Axis dialog box. The options on the Patterns, Font, Number, and Alignment tabs of this dialog box are the same as those for 2-D graphs. However, the Scale tab has a new option, Floor (XY Plane) Crosses At, that lets you change the position of the floor within a 3-D area, bar, column, line, or surface graph.

When you change the vertical position of the floor, markers in 3-D area and column graphs extend either above the floor or below the floor, but they do not cross the floor to reach their proper length along the value axis. Figure 10-29 shows a graph with the floor set at 35. Such a graph can show an excess above or deficiency below a budget or target value. In 3-D bar graphs, the floor runs vertically, so markers extend to the left or right of the floor. In 3-D line and 3-D surface graphs, the floor appears as a transparent panel within the graph and has no effect on the display of the lines or surface.

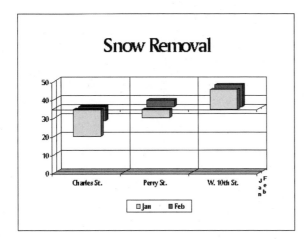

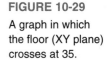

FIGURE 10-29

A graph in which the floor (XY plane) crosses at 35.

You can click the Floor (XY Plane) Crosses at Minimum Value option to place the floor at the minimum value of the value axis.

Formatting the Walls and Floor

All 3-D chart types, except 3-D pie graphs, have walls and a floor. The walls are behind and to the side of the markers, and the markers rest on the floor.

By double-clicking the walls of a 3-D graph, you can open the Format Walls dialog box shown in Figure 10-30 on the next page, which displays only Patterns options. Use the options in the Border and Area sections to change the border and surface color and pattern of the walls. Figure 10-31, also on the next page, shows a 3-D area graph with black walls. The floor must be formatted separately. Double-click the floor to open the Format Floor dialog box, which contains the same options as the Format Walls dialog box.

FIGURE 10-30

The Format Walls
dialog box.

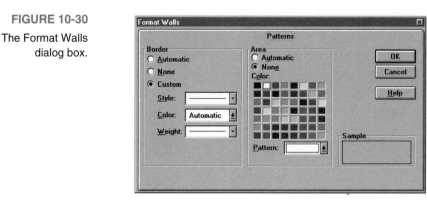

FIGURE 10-31

The walls of a 3-D
area graph with
the Area section's
Color option set
to black.

Formatting the Gridlines

When a graph has three axes, you can add major and minor gridlines to all
three axes. When you choose Gridlines from the Insert menu, the Gridlines
dialog box appears, as shown in Figure 10-32 on the facing page. The options
in this dialog box let you turn on major and minor gridlines for the category,
series, and value axes.

> NOTE When 3-D graphs contain markers that look three-
> dimensional but are not at planes of different depths, you can
> display 2-D walls and gridlines by clicking the 2-D Walls and
> Gridlines option at the bottom of the Gridlines dialog box.

FIGURE 10-32
The Gridlines dialog
box for a 3-D graph.

Formatting Area, Bar, Column, and Line Graphs

In Chapter 6, where you created basic graphs, you learned about selecting a chart type and subtype. Each subtype has a unique style and arrangement of markers that convey a different message; changing the subtype is the quickest way to dramatically change the look of a graph.

To change the subtype of a graph, select the graph, choose Group from the bottom of the Format menu or choose Format Group from the bottom of the shortcut menu, and then select one of the subtypes from the dialog box that appears.

> **NOTE** If you select the 2-D stacked bar or 2-D stacked column subtype, you can click Series Lines on the Options tab of the Format Column Group dialog box to connect the series in the columns with lines.

Creating Combination Graphs

PowerPoint allows you to mix 2-D chart types, selecting the best chart type for each series or group of series in the graph. You might use a line for one series and columns for another to compare the fluctuating change of a series (for example, sales volume) in response to incremental adjustments in another series (for example, price). Figure 10-33 on the next page shows such a graph.

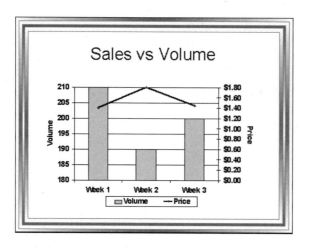

NOTE You can't mix chart types in a 3-D graph.

The easiest way to change the chart type of one or more series is to select the series, click the down arrow to the right of the Chart Type button on Graph's Standard toolbar, and then select a different 2-D chart type from the palette of chart types. You can also choose Chart Type from the Format menu or the shortcut menu, and then double-click one of the 2-D chart types in the Chart Type dialog box. After you change the chart type of one or more series, you can use the Group command at the bottom of the Format menu to apply different formatting to each chart type.

If you want to change one of the chart types in a combination graph, choose Chart Type from the Format menu. Each chart type group is listed in the Chart Type dialog box's Group list. You can select a group and then change its appearance by selecting a different chart type. To change all the groups back to the same type, click the Entire Chart option in the Apply to section of the Chart Type dialog box, and then double-click the chart type you want.

When a graph has two or more series or groups of series with different chart types, you can add a secondary category or value axis against which you can plot one or more of the chart type groups. A secondary axis appears on the opposite side of the graph and is scaled according to the chart type group assigned to it. As a result, the same graph can show two chart type groups that have very different ranges of values. For example, you might plot the price of a product over time against the primary axis, which ranges from 39 to 49 cents, and plot the units sold against the secondary axis, which ranges from 250,000 to 350,000.

To add a secondary axis, select one of the groups in the graph, and choose Axes from the Insert menu. The Axes dialog box appears, with two Secondary Axis options: Category (X) Axis and Value (Y) Axis. Select one or both options to add one or two axes to the graph.

To assign a group to a secondary axis, first select the group and choose the Group command from the bottom of the Format menu or shortcut menu. Then click the Axis tab of the Format Group dialog box to display the options shown in Figure 10-34, click either the Primary Axis or Secondary Axis option, and click OK.

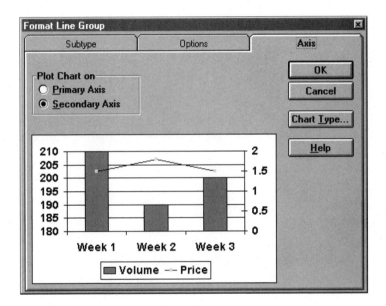

FIGURE 10-34

The Axis tab of the Format Line Group dialog box.

Adjusting the Spacing of Areas, Bars, Columns, and Lines

With the Gap Depth and Gap Width settings on the Options tab of the Format Group dialog box, you can modify the spacing between 2-D and 3-D areas, bars, and columns, and between 3-D lines. Figure 10-35 on the next page shows these options for a 3-D bar graph. For 2-D bar and column graphs, you can also use the Overlap option, which is not available for 3-D graphs.

FIGURE 10-35

The Options tab
of the Format
3-D Bar Group
dialog box.

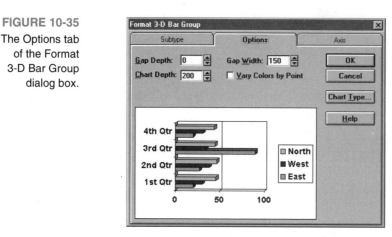

The bars or columns of a default graph are arranged in clusters along the category axis. To change the spacing between clusters, change the Gap Width setting, which can range from 0 to 500 percent of the width of a single bar or column. A setting of 0 percent creates a step graph or histogram. The default setting of 150 percent leaves 1.5 times the width of a bar or column between each cluster. As you increase the gap width, the width of the bars or columns decreases.

To separate the areas, bars, columns, or lines along the Y axis of a 3-D graph, change the Gap Depth setting on the Options tab. The gap depth, like the gap width, is a percentage of the depth of a single marker.

To change the spacing of 2-D bars or columns within a cluster, rather than between clusters, change the Overlap setting. At 0 percent, the bars or columns are side by side without overlapping. At 100 percent, they overlap completely. Figure 10-36 shows a column graph with a 50-percent overlap and a 100-percent gap width.

TIP   To separate the bars or columns within a cluster, you can enter a negative overlap percentage. An overlap setting of –50 percent, for example, separates the columns within a cluster by half the width of a single column.

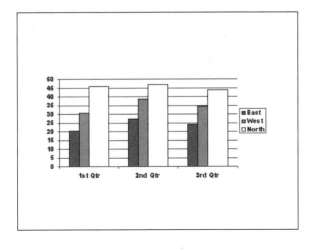

FIGURE 10-36

A column graph
with a 50-percent
overlap and a 100-
percent gap width.

Adding Drop Lines
to Area and Line Graphs

Drop lines are vertical lines that help identify the data points of 2-D and 3-D
area and line graphs. They run from the data points of the areas or lines to the
category axis of the graph. In Figure 10-37, a 3-D line graph with drop lines
is shown.

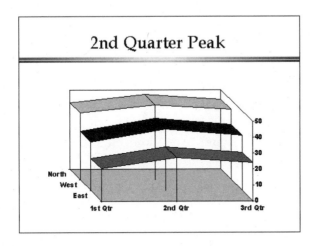

2nd Quarter Peak

FIGURE 10-37

A 3-D line graph
with drop lines.

To turn on drop lines, choose the Group command from the bottom of the Format menu or shortcut menu, click the Drop Lines option on the Options tab of the Format Group dialog box, and click OK.

Adding High-Low Lines to Line Graphs

High-low lines can be added to individual lines or to all lines in a 2-D line graph to depict the range over which a measurement varies, such as the high and low temperature of the day or the high and low test scores of different groups of people. Figure 10-38 shows high-low lines added to all the data series in a temperature fluctuation graph.

FIGURE 10-38
High-low lines added to a temperature fluctuation graph.

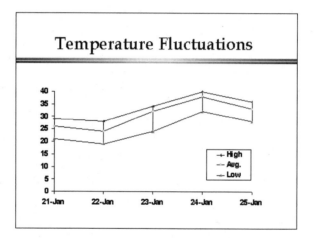

To create a graph that shows discrete ranges of measurements instead of connected series, you can set the Line option on the Patterns tab of the Format Data Series dialog box to None. Figure 10-39 shows the temperature fluctuations graph with this setting.

To change the style, color, and weight of drop lines and high-low lines, first double-click a line. Or select a line and choose the Selected command from the Format menu, press Ctrl+1, or choose the Format command from the shortcut menu. Then change the Line options in the dialog box that appears.

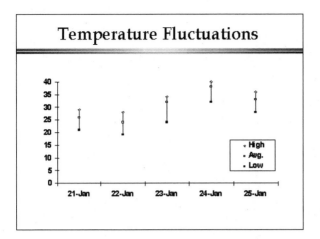

FIGURE 10-39

A 2-D line graph with high-low lines, and the Line option on the Patterns tab of the Format Data Series dialog box set to None.

A Sample Stock Tracking Graph

To create an open-high-low-close graph with up-down bars, like those used by stock watchers, follow these steps:

1. Enter four series of stock data in the datasheet in this order: the opening values, the high values, the low values, and the closing values.

2. Plot the data as a 2-D line graph.

3. To form the familiar stock chart, add up-down bars and high-low lines to the graph by first choosing the Line Group command from the bottom of the Format menu or by choosing the Format Line Group command from the shortcut menu. Then select the Up-Down Bars and High-Low Lines options on the Options tab of the Format Line Group dialog box, and click OK.

4. Next, remove the lines connecting the data points by selecting each line (or data series) in turn and setting the Line option to None on the Patterns tab of the Format Data Series dialog box.

Figure 10-40 on the next page shows a sample open-high-low-close graph. Up bars (when the stock's closing value is greater than the opening value) are filled with white. Down bars are filled with black, as is the case in the bar for Wednesday.

FIGURE 10-40

A typical stock
tracking graph
created with
up-down bars and
high-low lines.

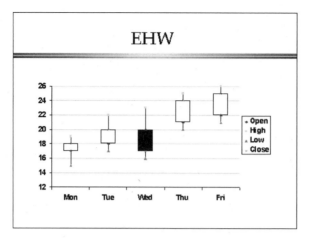

To change the appearance of the up-down bars in the graph, select one of them and then choose the Selected Up Bars command from the Format menu, press Ctrl+1, or choose the Format command from the shortcut menu. If the graph contains both up bars and down bars, you must select and format the up bars and down bars separately.

Showing and Predicting Trends with Trendlines

When working with area, bar, column, line, and XY (scatter) graphs, you can add an automatic regression line that depicts the general trend of the numbers in a data series and allows you to predict approximate future data points based on the existing data. The regression line, called a *trendline*, overlays the series markers. The default trendline is a linear regression that depicts a "best fit" straight line passing nearest to all the data points. You can select one of five other regression types, each based on a different mathematical regression formula. You can also format the trendline to set the intercept; change the number of forecast periods; or display the trendline name, the R-squared value, or the regression equation on the graph. (If terms like "intercept" and "R-squared value" puzzle you, you might want to stick with a simple linear regression trendline and leave the higher math to the statisticians.) Figure 10-41 shows standard linear regression lines on a column graph.

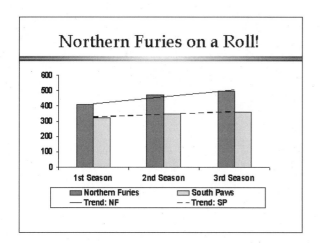

FIGURE 10-41

Linear regression
lines on a column
chart.

To add a trendline to a graph, select a data series and then choose Trendline from the Insert menu or choose Insert Trendline from the shortcut menu. On the Type tab, shown in Figure 10-42, select an option in the Trend/Regression Type section and click OK.

FIGURE 10-42

The Type tab
of the Format
Trendline
dialog box.

To delete a trendline quickly, select the line and then press the Delete key or choose Clear from the shortcut menu.

To format a trendline, first double-click it or select it, and then choose the Selected Trendline command from the Format menu, press Ctrl+1, or choose the Format Trendline command from the shortcut menu. When the Format Trendline dialog box appears, click the Options tab, shown in Figure 10-43 on the next page.

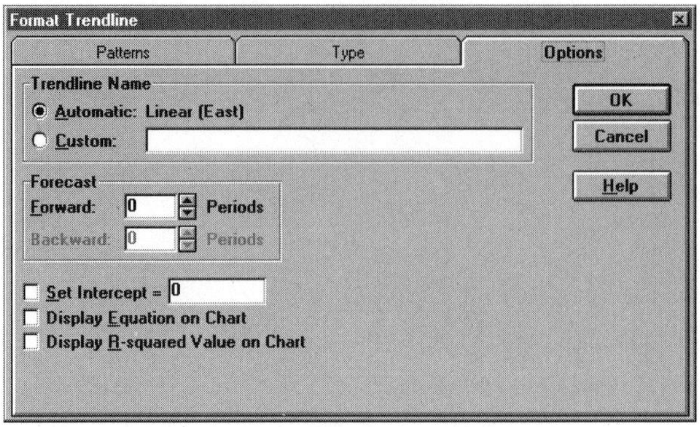

FIGURE 10-43

The Options tab
of the Format
Trendline
dialog box.

In the Custom edit box in the Trendline Name section, you can enter a custom trendline name that will replace the default name in the legend. The options in the Forecast section allow you to extend the trendline beyond the actual data by adding a number of forecast periods forward and backward. If regressions are the stuff of your daily life, you will want to vary the intercept by entering values in the Set Intercept edit box and display the math behind the trendline by clicking the Display Equation on Chart and Display R-squared Value on Chart options.

To change the line style, color, and weight of the regression line, use the options on the Patterns tab of the Format Trendline dialog box.

Allowing for Error with Error Bars

Error bars in a graph allow you to depict the minor deviations that you expect in your data. You can enter this "margin of error" as a fixed number, a percentage, the number of standard deviations from the mean of plotted values, or the standard error. You can also add a custom plus and minus error value. 2-D area, bar, column, and line graphs have Y error bars that apply to the Y axis only. XY (scatter) graphs can have both X error bars and Y error bars. Figure 10-44 shows a column graph with Y error bars.

To add error bars that extend from each data point in a series, select each series in turn and then choose Error Bars from the Insert menu or choose Insert Error Bars from the shortcut menu.

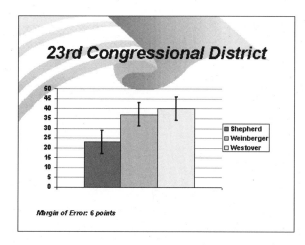

FIGURE 10-44

A column graph
with Y error bars.

On the Y Error Bars tab of the Error Bars dialog box, shown in Figure 10-45, select a display type by clicking the Both, Plus, Minus, or None option in the Display section, and select an error type and amount in the Error Amount section. If the graph is an XY graph, the Error Bars dialog box has two tabs, one to set the X error bars and another to set the Y error bars.

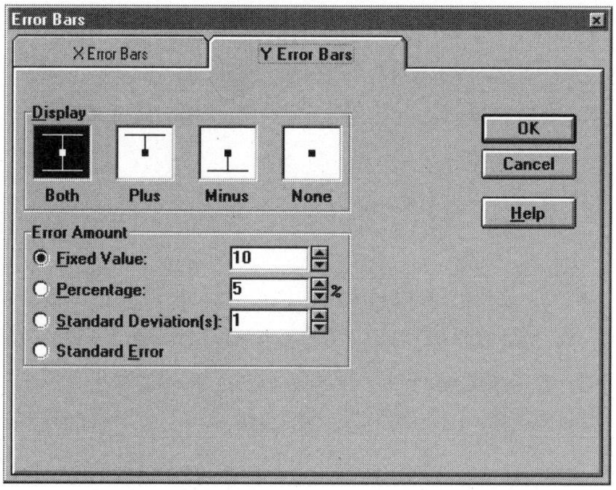

FIGURE 10-45

The Y Error Bars
tab of the
Error Bars
dialog box.

To format the error bars, double-click one of the error bars, and click the Patterns tab of the Format Error Bars dialog box. You can then select the style, color, and weight of the bars, and you can select one of two marker styles: a T or a straight line extending from the data point.

Varying the Colors of a Single Series Graph

When a graph displays only one series, you can have each marker in the series display a different color rather than the same color. Double-click the series, and in the Format Data Series dialog box, select Vary Colors by Point on the Options tab. The Vary Colors by Point option is not available for 2-D area, 3-D area, or 3-D surface graphs.

> **NOTE** A related option, Vary Colors by Slice, applies a different color to each slice in a pie or ring in a doughnut graph. This option is turned on by default.

Formatting Pie and Doughnut Graphs

Pie and doughnut graphs offer special formatting options that are unique to their chart types. You can select and format the entire pie or doughnut group, or you can select and format a pie slice, a doughnut ring, or a segment of a doughnut ring.

Separating Slices

To call attention to certain pie slices, you can separate them from the rest of the pie by dragging them away from the center one by one. You can also separate segments of the outermost doughnut ring by dragging them.

Labeling Slices

The easiest way to label the slices of a pie is to apply an autoformat with the type of labels you want. To apply an autoformat, select the pie, choose AutoFormat from the Format menu or the shortcut menu, and then select one of the seven autoformats shown in Figure 10-46. Autoformats 2 and 5 show slice labels, autoformat 6 shows percentages, and autoformat 7 shows both labels and percentages.

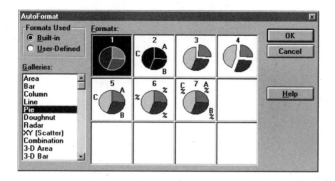

FIGURE 10-46

The autoformats
available for pie
graphs.

You can also label the slices by selecting the pie and choosing Data Labels
from either the Insert menu or the shortcut menu. (To label a single slice,
select that slice before choosing Data Labels.) Selecting Show Value in the
Data Labels dialog box places the value of each slice next to the slice. Selecting
Show Percent shows the calculated percentage of each slice. Selecting Show
Label shows the name of the slice. (You may prefer to show slice names rather
than a legend so that the viewer can see what each slice represents without
having to match up the legend key with the slice colors.) Selecting Show Label
and Percent shows both the name and percentage next to each slice, as shown
in the example in Figure 10-47.

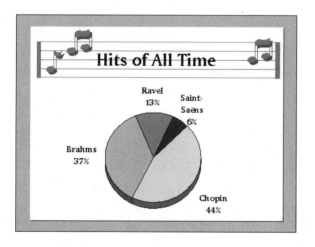

FIGURE 10-47

A pie with data
labels created by
turning on the
Show Label and
Percent option in
the Data Labels
dialog box.

 **TIP** You can drag the values, percentages, or labels onto their corresponding pie slices. But if you have turned on the Show Label and Percent option, you cannot drag the percentages onto the slices and leave the labels off to the side unless you convert the pie to graphic objects. For more information, see "Converting a Graph to Graphic Objects," page 302.

Varying Colors by Slice

By default, the Vary Colors by Slice option on the Options tab of the Format Pie Group dialog box is turned on. When you turn off Vary Colors by Slice, all slices get the same color, and the legend is no longer helpful unless the slices are filled with different patterns.

Changing the Angle of the First Slice

On the Options tab of the Format Pie Group dialog box or the Format Doughnut Group dialog box, you can set the Angle of First Slice option to rotate the entire pie or doughnut. Slices or segments start in the location specified by the Angle of First Slice option and are plotted clockwise to the pie. The default setting is 45 degrees. To rotate the pie 90 degrees to the right, for example, you would change the Angle of First Slice setting to 135 degrees.

NOTE You can also rotate a 3-D pie graph by changing the Rotation setting in the Format 3-D View dialog box. For more information about rotating a 3-D graph, see "Adjusting the 3-D View," page 274.

Changing the Hole Size of a Doughnut Graph

Reducing the hole size of a doughnut graph enlarges the segments so that they are easier to see. The default hole size, specified as a percentage of the width of the graph, is 50 percent. To change the hole size, simply modify the Doughnut Hole Size percentage setting on the Options tab of the Format Doughnut Group dialog box.

Formatting Radar and 3-D Surface Graphs

The size of the ring of each data series in a radar graph shows the aggregate of the values in the series. Where the ring bulges from the center, the series shows the greatest measurements. For example, Figure 10-48 shows a radar graph in which each ring represents the yearly sales, by month, of a store in a three-store chain. As you can see, the sales of all three stores swelled during the months before Christmas. The store with the largest ring, E. 23rd St., had the greatest overall sales.

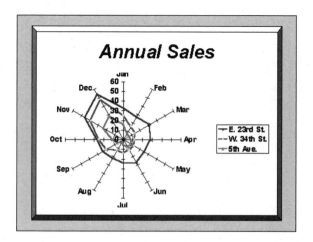

FIGURE 10-48

A radar chart showing the monthly sales of three stores.

In a radar graph, value (Y) axes extend from the center of the graph, evenly spaced, in different directions. Each data point in the series has its own value axis. Double-clicking any axis and changing a setting in the Format dialog box formats all of the axes, except that changing the tick mark label options affects only the axis that rises vertically from the center of the graph.

Most of the formatting options for radar graphs are available as auto-formats, and you are likely to find an autoformat that suits your need. If you don't, double-click the graph and then change the settings in the Format Radar Group dialog box. To label the axes of the radar graph, click the Category Labels option on the Options tab. To display markers at each data point, select the first subtype on the Subtype tab. To display each series as a filled ring, select the second subtype.

To change the formatting of a data series, double-click the data series and then change the options in the Format Data Series dialog box.

Formatting 3-D Surface Graph Intervals

In a 3-D surface graph, each height interval along the vertical (Z) axis—the 3-D axis—has its own color, as shown in the graph's legend. The color of a 3-D surface graph region indicates the height interval along the Z axis that the region has reached. If you want to change the colors of the Z axis intervals, you cannot do it by selecting the surface or the intervals themselves. Instead, you must double-click the legend keys and then change the Color and Pattern options in the Area section of the Patterns tab in the Format Legend Key dialog box. (Remember, the legend keys are the small boxes that show colors within the legend.)

Creating Picture Graphs

By replacing the markers of a graph with pictures, you can create a picture graph, also called a *pictograph*. The pictures can identify the series and communicate more information at a glance, as shown in Figure 10-49.

FIGURE 10-49

A picture graph.

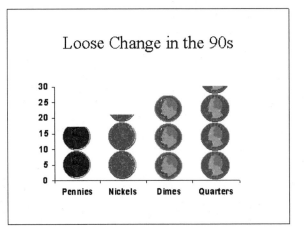

To turn a regular graph into a picture graph, select a picture in another application, and copy it to the Windows Clipboard using the Copy command. When you return to PowerPoint, activate the graph and then select one of the series of markers you want to replace with pictures. Click the Paste button or choose Paste from the Edit menu to replace all the markers of that data series with the picture.

To change the appearance of the pictures, double-click a picture, and then change the options on the Patterns tab of the Format Data Point dialog box, shown in Figure 10-50.

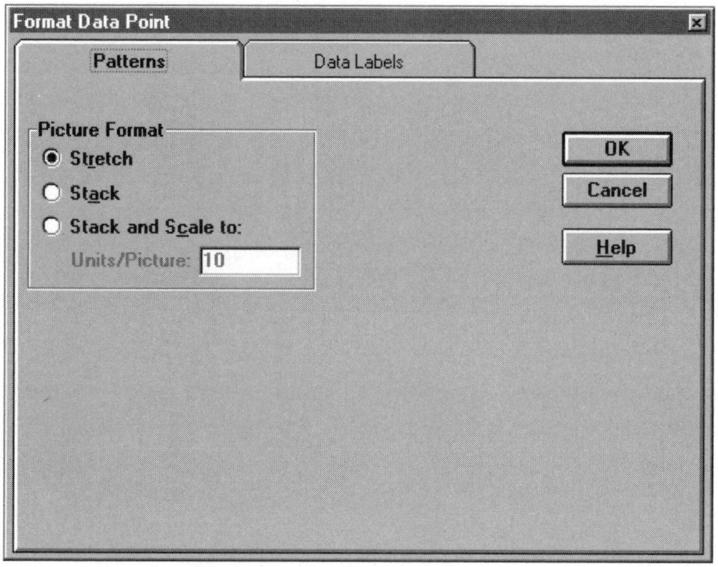

FIGURE 10-50

The Patterns tab options for a picture graph in the Format Data Point dialog box.

When you replace bar or column markers with pictures, the pictures stretch to fill the markers. You can tell PowerPoint to stack the pictures instead, using as many copies of the picture at its original size as necessary to fill the marker. You can also tell PowerPoint to stack the pictures at a size you specify.

When you replace the markers of a line, XY, or radar graph with pictures, the pictures always appear at their original size. They cannot be stretched, stacked, or scaled.

Saving Graph Formatting as an AutoFormat

After you've created a special combination of graph formatting, you can save the combination as an autoformat that you can then apply to other graphs. To create a new autoformat, follow the steps on the next page.

1. Activate a completed graph, and then choose AutoFormat from the Format menu or shortcut menu. The AutoFormat dialog box appears.

2. Click the User-Defined option in the Formats Used section. The dialog box changes to look like this:

3. Click the Customize button, and in the User-Defined AutoFormats dialog box, click the Add button. The Add Custom AutoFormat dialog box appears, as shown here:

4. In the Format Name edit box, enter a name. (You can include spaces.) If you want, enter a description by pressing Tab and then typing in the Description edit box.

5. Click OK; the selected graph appears in the Format Sample dialog box.

6. Click Close to close the dialog box and return to the graph.

To delete an autoformat, display the User-Defined AutoFormats dialog box, select the autoformat, click the Delete button, and then click OK.

Adding and Formatting Text Boxes

You can add a free-floating text box to contain a note that describes or highlights some aspect of a graph. The text box becomes an intrinsic part of the graph. If you resize or move the graph, or copy it between slides or presentations, the text box goes along for the ride.

Adding a Text Box

To add a text box to a graph, follow these steps:

1. Click the Text Box button on Graph's Standard toolbar.

2. Position the mouse pointer approximately where you want the upper left corner of the text box to be, hold down the mouse button, and drag down and to the right to create a text box of approximately the correct shape and size. When you release the mouse button, an insertion point appears within the text box.

3. Enter the text. The text will wrap within the boundaries of the invisible text box, as shown below.

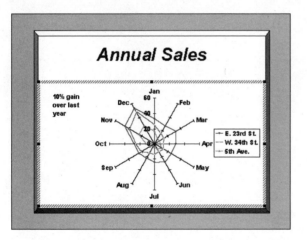

To reposition the text box, click the edge of the text, and drag the box to a new position. To resize the text box, click the edge of the text, and drag one of the handles.

Formatting a Text Box

To format the text box and the text within it, start by double-clicking the border of the text box. The Format Object dialog box appears, as shown in Figure 10-51. You can also select the text box, and then choose Font from the Format menu or choose Format Object from the shortcut menu to display this dialog box.

Format Object

| Patterns | Font | Alignment | Properties |

Border
- ○ Automatic
- ● None
- ○ Custom
  - Style: _____
  - Color: Automatic
  - Weight: _____
- ☐ Shadow
- ☐ Round Corners

Fill
- ○ Automatic
- ● None

Pattern: _____

OK
Cancel
Help

Sample

Use the options on the Patterns tab of the dialog box to change the formatting of the text box containing the text. Use the options on the Font tab and Alignment tab to change the formatting of the text.

The Properties tab of the dialog box holds a single option you can use to set whether text should resize when the graph resizes. The default Don't size with chart option prevents the text from becoming too small to read when you reduce the size of the graph.

 **TIP** To change the formatting of selected words or characters within a text box, click an insertion point in the text box, select the text you want to format, and then choose Font from the Format menu or choose Format Object from the shortcut menu.

Adding and Formatting Arrows

After you add a text box containing a note about an item in the graph, you can connect the text box to the item with an arrow, as shown in Figure 10-52.

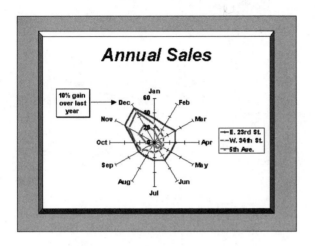

FIGURE 10-52
An arrow points to the item described by the text in the text box.

To add an arrow, follow these steps:

1. Click the Drawing button on Graph's Standard toolbar to display Graph's Drawing toolbar.

2. Click the Arrow button on the Drawing toolbar.

3. Position the mouse pointer near the text box, hold down the mouse button, and drag to the item in the graph to which you want the arrow to point. When you release the mouse button, an arrow appears.

To format the arrow, start by double-clicking it. The Format Object dialog box appears, as shown in Figure 10-53 on the next page.

On the Patterns tab of the dialog box, use the Line options to change the appearance of the arrow's line. Use the Arrowhead options to change the appearance of the arrowhead. On the Properties tab, select the Object Positioning option if you want the arrow to be resized with the graph.

See Also For more information about using the tools on Graph's Drawing toolbar, see Chapter 13, "Drawing Graphic Objects," page 331.

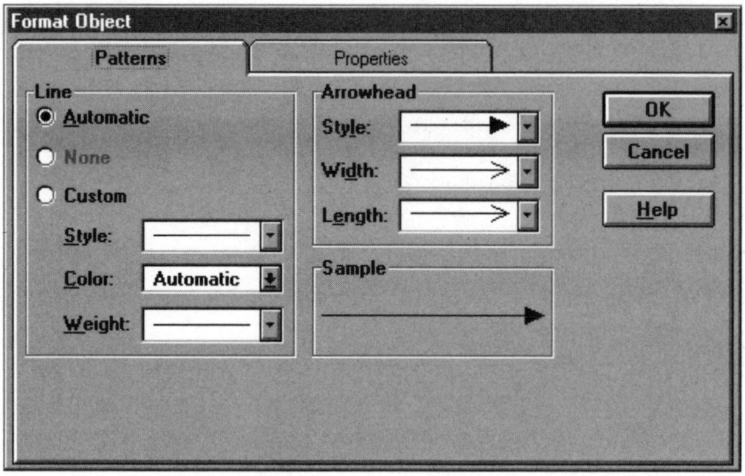

FIGURE 10-53
The Patterns tab of
the Format Object
dialog box.

Converting a Graph
to Graphic Objects

PowerPoint offers a wealth of choices that allow you to change the appearance of a graph, but for the ultimate in flexibility, you can convert the graph to a collection of graphic objects, each of which can be modified individually. You can convert the columns of a column graph to a collection of rectangles, for example, and then revise them with PowerPoint's comprehensive drawing and editing commands.

When you convert a graph to a set of graphic objects, it loses its identification as a graph object that represents an underlying set of data. You can no longer use Graph's commands and controls, and the datasheet is no longer available. The result of the conversion is a picture of what was once a graph. And the conversion process is a one-way street; you cannot convert the collection of graphic objects back to a graph.

Before you convert a graph to a set of graphic objects, you might want to copy the graph to another presentation slide. Then you can convert the copy of the graph to graphic objects, knowing that you can always return to the original, unchanged graph. You can even hide the slide containing the original graph so that you can access it even though it does not appear when you display the presentation.

To convert a graph to a collection of graphic objects, follow these steps:

1. Click the graph once to select it without activating it.

2. Choose the Ungroup command from PowerPoint's Draw menu. PowerPoint warns you that proceeding will permanently discard any embedded data, and asks *Convert to PowerPoint objects?*

3. Click OK to convert the graph. After a moment, the graph reappears as a collection of graphic objects, each of which is selected.

4. Click outside any of the objects to deselect all of them.

Now you can select the objects one by one and make any necessary modifications.

See Also For more information about editing graphic objects, see "Editing Objects," page 344.

In this chapter, you learned how to modify the appearance of the graphs in your presentation. In the next chapter, you'll learn how to use Slide Sorter view to make broad changes to the presentation's design.

Chapter 11

Using Slide Sorter View

By displaying the slides of a presentation as miniatures arranged side by side on the screen, Slide Sorter view, the third of PowerPoint's views, gives you a working view of the presentation as a whole. But Slide Sorter view allows you to do more than just view the presentation. You can also do real work on the presentation before switching to another view.

Some of the tasks you can accomplish in Slide Sorter view are:

- Checking the overall presentation for flaws and design consistency

- Rearranging slides

- Changing the template, color scheme, and background of all slides or only selected slides

- Duplicating slides

- Moving and copying slides between two presentations

- Setting up and previewing the transition and build effects that will appear in Slide Show view

All of these tasks except the last one are covered in this chapter. Creating slide shows while in Slide Sorter view is the subject of Chapter 16, "Creating Slide Shows."

Switching to Slide Sorter View

Switching to Slide Sorter view is as easy as clicking the Slide Sorter View button in the lower left corner of the presentation window. You can also choose Slide Sorter from the View menu.

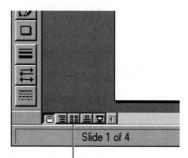

Slide Sorter View

When you switch to Slide Sorter view, the current presentation is displayed as a set of miniature slides, and the Slide Sorter toolbar appears below the Standard toolbar, replacing the Formatting toolbar. Figure 11-1 shows a presentation in Slide Sorter view.

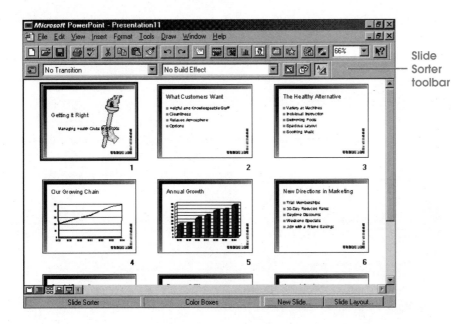

Slide Sorter toolbar

FIGURE 11-1

A presentation in Slide Sorter view.

To leave Slide Sorter view in order to look at a single slide in Slide view, double-click a slide. You can also use the arrow keys to move the highlighted border to a slide, and then press Enter.

Zooming In and Out

To zoom in and out on the slide miniatures in Slide Sorter view, use the Zoom Control box on the Standard toolbar or the Zoom command on the View menu. Zooming in allows you to inspect slides more closely to check for errors. Zooming out allows you to view more of the presentation as a whole so that you can check its design consistency. To change the zoom percentage, click the Zoom Control box, type a new zoom percentage, and press Enter. You can also click the arrow at the right end of the Zoom Control box, and select a zoom percentage from the drop-down list.

If you prefer to use menu commands, choose the Zoom command from the View menu. Then, when the Zoom dialog box appears, select one of the preset zoom percentages or enter a new percentage in the Percent edit box.

Changing the Content in Slide Sorter View

In Slide Sorter view, as in most other views, you can change both the content of the presentation and the appearance. You can rearrange slides, add and delete slides, duplicate existing slides, and move and copy slides between presentations. You cannot change the content of individual slides, however; creating and editing individual slides is a task that you must perform in Slide view or Outline view.

TIP   By clicking the Show Formatting button on the Slide Sorter toolbar, you can temporarily display only the slide titles. Then, as you work with the slides, you don't have to wait for them to redraw. To redisplay the slide contents, click the Show Formatting button again.

Rearranging Slides

The most common use of Slide Sorter view is to move slides to new positions in the presentation, the same way you'd sort 35-mm slides on a light table before placing them in a slide projector. The simplest way to move a slide is to use the good old drag-and-drop technique. However, you can also move a slide by using the Cut and Paste buttons on the Standard toolbar, the Cut and Paste commands on the Edit menu, or the Cut and Paste commands on the shortcut menu that appears when you select a slide and click the right mouse button.

To rearrange the order of slides using drag and drop, follow these steps:

1. Position the mouse pointer on the slide you want to move.

2. Hold down the left mouse button, and drag the vertical marker that appears to a position between two other slides. As shown on the facing page, the vertical marker indicates where the slide will drop when you release the mouse button.

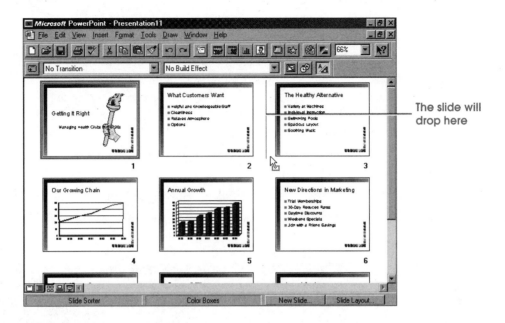

The slide will drop here

3. Release the mouse button to drop the slide into place.

    Here are the steps for moving a slide using Cut and Paste:

1. Click the slide you want to move.

2. Click the Cut button on the Standard toolbar or choose Cut from the Edit menu or the shortcut menu.

3. Click an insertion point to indicate the slide's new position (a vertical line appears), and click the Paste button or choose Paste from the Edit menu or the shortcut menu.

> **TIP** To copy a slide rather than move it, hold down the Ctrl key as you drag the slide, or click the Copy button instead of the Cut button on the Standard toolbar (or choose Copy from the Edit menu or the shortcut menu). The slide appears both at the destination and at the original location.

Rearranging a group of slides is just as easy as rearranging a single slide. After you select the group, you can use the same techniques described above for moving a single slide.

To select a group of slides, hold down the Shift key and click each slide. Each selected slide is surrounded by a highlighted border. You can use this method to select nonadjacent slides—that is, slides located in different parts of the presentation. When a group of nonadjacent slides is moved to a new location, the slides appear in the same relative order. A slide from the first part of the presentation appears first, followed by a slide from the next part of the presentation, and so on.

To select a group of adjacent slides, you can draw a selection box across the group, like this:

1. Position the mouse pointer just outside the first slide you want to select.

2. Hold down the left mouse button, and drag the selection box across the slides, as shown below.

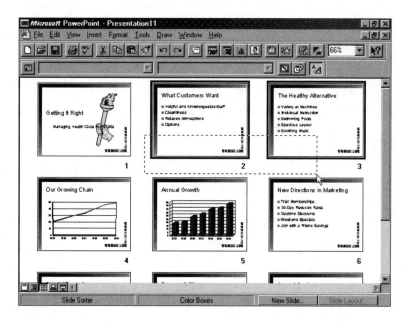

NOTE You don't need to enclose entire slides to select them. As long as any part of a slide is within the selection box, the slide will be selected.

After you select a group of slides, place the mouse pointer on one of the slides, and drag the group to its new location in the presentation. As with single slides, you can also use the Cut and Paste buttons on the Standard toolbar or the Cut and Paste commands on the Edit menu or the shortcut menu.

Adding and Deleting Slides

In addition to rearranging slides, you can also change the content of a presentation by adding and deleting slides. Slide Sorter view is a good place to be when you want to make these changes, because you can quickly see their effect on the entire presentation.

To add a slide, follow these steps:

1. In the presentation, click the slide that you want the new slide to follow.

2. Click the New Slide button at the bottom of the PowerPoint window, or click the Insert New Slide button on the Standard toolbar. (You can also choose New Slide from the Insert menu or press Ctrl+M.)

3. When the New Slide dialog box appears, select an autolayout and then click OK.

Deleting a slide is even easier than adding one. Just click the slide you want to delete, and press Delete. You can also delete a group of slides by using one of the methods described earlier for selecting a group, and then pressing Delete.

Duplicating Slides

Another handy use for Slide Sorter view is to duplicate slides that have some feature you want to reproduce. Let's say you need to create the same pie graph for each salon in a chain of six beauty salons. You can create the first graph on a slide, switch to Slide Sorter view, and duplicate the slide five times. Then you can switch back to Slide view and edit the data in each of the duplicate slides. The design of the first graph and any special formatting you've applied are carried over to the other slides, as in Figure 11-2 on the next page.

> **NOTE** If you often need to use the same graph design, you can save the formatting of the graph as an autoformat that you can apply to a new graph. For more information about autoformats, see "Saving Graph Formatting as an AutoFormat," page 297.

To duplicate a slide in Slide Sorter view, follow these steps:

1. Click the slide.

2. Choose Duplicate from the Edit menu or press Ctrl+D. The duplicate appears to the right of the original slide.

FIGURE 11-2

Duplicating a slide
lets you carry
special formatting
throughout a
presentation.

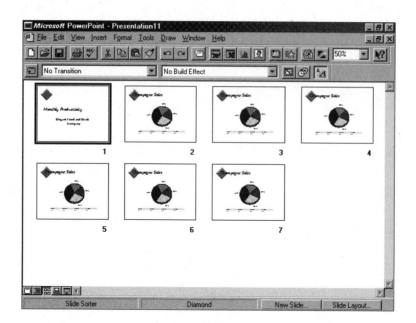

Moving and Copying Slides Between Presentations

Just as you can move and copy slides within a presentation, you can also move and copy slides between presentations. Moving and copying slides between presentations lets you transfer an existing slide to a new presentation rather than recreate its content.

Before you can actually move or copy slides between two presentations, you must arrange the presentations side by side in Slide Sorter view. Follow the steps below.

1. Open two presentations.

2. Switch to Slide Sorter view in each presentation.

3. Choose Arrange All from the Window menu to arrange the two presentations side by side, as shown on the facing page.

   NOTE You may want to use the same zoom percentage for both presentations. You can select a presentation by clicking it, and then change its zoom percentage independently. For more information about changing the zoom percentage, see "Zooming In and Out," page 307.

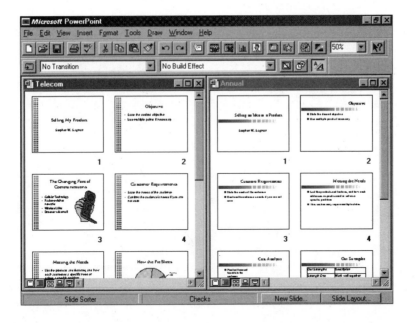

After the presentations are arranged side by side, you can move a slide from one presentation to another by clicking a slide in one presentation and dragging it to the other presentation. The moved slide takes on the design of the destination presentation's template. To copy a slide rather than move it, hold down the Ctrl key as you drag the slide to the destination presentation. In Figure 11-3 on the next page, the bottom slide has been copied from one presentation to the other. Note its appearance in each presentation.

You can also transfer slides between presentations by first selecting a slide in one presentation and using the Cut or Copy button on the Standard toolbar or by choosing the Cut or Copy command on the Edit menu or the shortcut menu. Then you can click an insertion point in the other presentation, and click the Paste button on the Standard toolbar or choose the Paste command from the Edit menu or the shortcut menu. Again, the slide takes on the template design of the destination presentation.

> **NOTE** You can move or copy a group of slides between presentations by selecting the group before you use the drag-and-drop technique, the toolbar buttons, or the menu commands. To select a group of slides, hold down the Shift key as you click each slide, or drag a selection box around the group. For more information about selecting a group of slides, see "Rearranging Slides," page 308.

FIGURE 11-3

A slide copied
to another
presentation takes
on the design
of the destination
presentation.

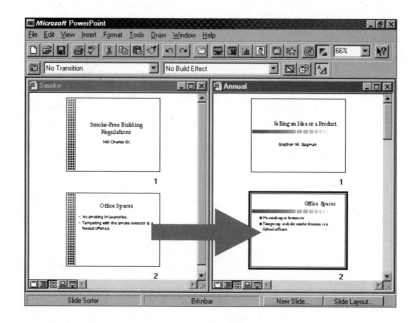

Changing the Design in Slide Sorter View

In Chapter 9, you learned about changing the template, color scheme, and background of a slide. Slide Sorter view is an ideal place to make these changes because you can see their effects ripple through the presentation.

Changing the Template and Color Scheme of the Presentation

In Slide Sorter view, you use the same techniques to change the template and color scheme of the presentation that you use in Slide view. For example, to change the presentation template, you click the Apply Design Template button on the Standard toolbar or choose the Apply Design Template command from the Format menu, and then select a different template in the Apply Design Template dialog box. As mentioned earlier, when you change the template and color scheme in Slide Sorter view, you can see the effect of the redesign on all the slides.

See Also For more information about changing a presentation's template and color scheme, see Chapter 9, "Making Overall Changes," page 213.

Changing the Color Scheme of Selected Slides

In Slide Sorter view, you can select specific slides and change their color scheme. For example, you can select all the slides that cover a general topic, and modify their color scheme. You can even give each segment of the presentation a different color scheme to differentiate it from the other segments.

To modify the color scheme for specific slides, first select the slides using one of the techniques described earlier. Then choose Slide Color Scheme from the Format menu, and make changes to the color scheme. Only the slides that you selected will display the revised color scheme.

> See
> Also   For more information about changing the color scheme, see "Changing the Color Scheme," page 219.

Copying Color Schemes Among Slides

After you change the color scheme for selected slides, you can copy the color scheme to other slides in the presentation. Copying the color scheme can be a real time-saver because you don't have to go through the process of choosing commands and selecting options. You simply select a slide that has already been formatted with the color scheme you want and copy the scheme to one or more other slides.

To copy a color scheme from one slide to another, first select the slide with the color scheme you want to copy, and then click the Format Painter button on the Standard toolbar. Next, click the slide to which you want to copy the color scheme. It's that simple!

To copy a color scheme from one slide to several other slides, select the slide with the color scheme you want to copy, and then choose the Pick Up Color Scheme command from the Format menu or the shortcut menu. Next, select one or more other slides, and choose the Apply Color Scheme command from the Format menu or the shortcut menu. After you apply a color scheme with this technique, the color scheme remains available in temporary storage so that you can use the Apply Color Scheme command again later to apply the same scheme to additional slides. The copied color scheme remains available until you use the Pick Up Color Scheme command to pick up a different color scheme.

TIP You can also use the Format Painter button and the Pick Up Color Scheme and Apply Color Scheme commands to copy a color scheme from a slide in one presentation to one or more slides in a different presentation.

Changing the Background

Just as you can change the color scheme of selected slides, you can also change the background color of selected slides by using the Custom Background command on the Format menu. The Custom Background command works as it does in Slide view. By changing only the background, you can change only the background color without affecting the other colors in the presentation. You can also change only the background shading of selected slides for a more subtle effect.

When you select slides in Slide Sorter view and then choose the Custom Background command, you can also click the Omit Background Graphics from Master option to turn the background design on or off on the selected slides. You might want to select slides and turn off their background graphics when you need a simple background on which to draw diagrams or create complicated foreground images. Figure 11-4 shows a presentation with two slides that have had their display of background graphics turned off.

FIGURE 11-4

The background graphics have been turned off on two slides in this presentation.

Slides with background graphics turned off

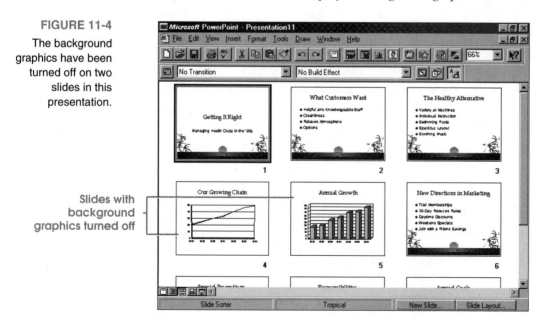

See Also For more information about changing the background scheme of a presentation, see "Altering the Custom Background," page 228.

In this chapter, you've learned how useful Slide Sorter view can be when you want to make overall changes to a presentation. In Part 4, you'll learn how to refine individual slides of the presentation by adding text annotations, drawings, clip art, and bitmapped images.

Part 4

Adding Annotations
and Graphics

Chapter 12

Working with Text Annotations and Speaker's Notes

During the presentation, you'll want to direct your energy and persuasive charm toward delivering your grand vision rather than detailing the minor technicalities in your graphs. Fortunately, you can leave the wherefores and the gotchas to helpful little notes that appear in text boxes alongside the other text and graphic objects on the slides. Figure 12-1 shows a typical, useful text annotation.

FIGURE 12-1

A text annotation can add important information to a slide.

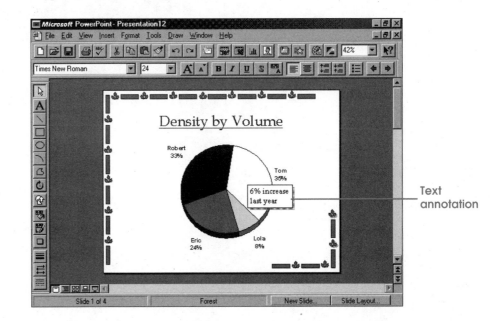

Text annotation

In this chapter, you'll learn how to add text annotations, as well as how to add speaker's notes to slides in Notes Pages view. While text annotations are designed to be seen by the audience, speaker's notes are seen only by the individual delivering the presentation. On the top half of a speaker's note page, the presenter sees a reduced version of the current slide. On the bottom half of the page, the presenter sees typed notes about the slide—points to make while the slide is on the screen and supporting information to bring up, if necessary.

Text annotations and speaker's notes are only two of the special additions you'll learn about in this part of the book. In Chapter 13, you'll learn how to add graphic objects that you can form into logos and diagrams, and in Chapter 14, you'll learn how to add clip art and bitmapped images to enhance your slides.

Adding a Text Annotation

The main difference between entering text in a text placeholder and adding text as a text annotation is in how you get started. To enter the main body text of a slide, such as bulleted text lines, you can simply click a *Click to add text* placeholder and begin typing. To create a text annotation, you must use the Text Tool button on the Drawing toolbar, which is shown below, and draw your own text box into which you type the annotation.

- Selection Tool
- Text Tool
- Line Tool
- Rectangle Tool
- Ellipse Tool
- Arc Tool
- Freeform Tool
- Free Rotate Tool
- AutoShapes
- Fill Color
- Line Color
- Shadow On/Off
- Line Style
- Arrowheads
- Dashed Lines

To comment on the contents of a slide, you can add as many text boxes as you see fit, and you can move and copy them just like any other objects. But you might want to limit your use of text boxes to one every few slides to avoid cluttering the presentation or giving the impression that the exceptions to the rule are the rule. Rather than use text boxes, you can group comments, restrictions, exemptions, exclusions, and other technicalities on a subsequent slide, so they won't seem ubiquitous. The subsequent slide can even be hidden so that you can display it only if necessary during a slide show.

To add a text box and enter a text annotation, follow these steps:

1. With Slide view active, move to the slide to which you want to add the text box.

2. Click the Text Tool button on the Drawing toolbar.

3. Position the mouse pointer where you want the text box to appear, hold down the left mouse button, and drag out a rectangle. If you plan to type a short one- or two-word label, you can simply click

the slide to add a small text box. The text box shown below was created by dragging.

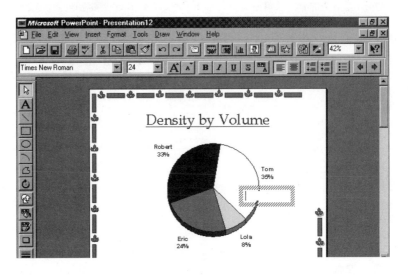

4. Type the text of the annotation. As shown below, the box grows vertically, if necessary, to accommodate the text you enter.

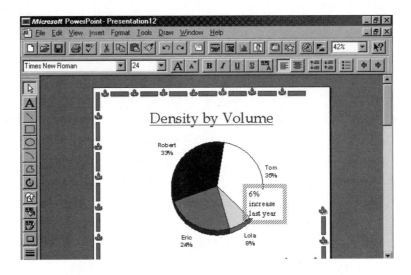

5. Click elsewhere on the slide to complete the text annotation or click the Text Tool button again to add another text box.

Formatting a Text Annotation

You can format a text annotation by adding formatting to the text box either before or after you actually enter the text. As with elsewhere in PowerPoint, you use the buttons on the Formatting toolbar or the commands on the Format or shortcut menu to format the text in a text box. As you know by now, before you can format existing text, you must select it. To select part of the text in a text box, drag across it with the mouse. To select the entire text box, click the border of the text box.

In addition to changing the appearance of the text in a text box, you can also change its position within the text box. To change the position of the text, choose Text Anchor from the Format menu, and select the appropriate options in the Text Anchor dialog box, shown in Figure 12-2. These options let you change the box margins, fit the boundaries of the text box to the text, and turn word wrap on or off.

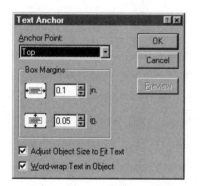

FIGURE 12-2
The Text Anchor dialog box.

See Also For more information about formatting text, see Chapter 5, "Working with Text in Slide View," page 91.

For more information about the Text Anchor dialog box options, see "Turning Word Wrap On or Off," page 118; "Changing the Box Margins," page 119; and "Fitting Text Objects to the Text," page 119.

Moving, Resizing, and Formatting a Text Box

PowerPoint is very flexible when it comes to moving, resizing, and formatting text boxes. For example, you can move a text box to any location on a slide, even if it obscures other text or objects on the slide. You can also increase or decrease the size of the text box to accommodate more or less text. And if you're interested in changing the text box's border or fill, PowerPoint offers a variety of options to choose from.

To move a text box, position the mouse pointer on the border of the text box between two handles, and drag the box to a new location on the slide. To resize a text box, simply drag one of its handles in the desired direction. (If word wrap is turned off, it is automatically turned back on so that the text rewraps within the resized text box.)

TIP   When you finish typing text in a text box, you can press Esc and then press the arrow keys to adjust the position of the text box incrementally.

Whether you create printed output or 35-mm slides or present an electronic slide show, by default only the text of a text box is displayed. The box itself does not appear because its fill and border are not formatted. To format the fill and border, you can select the text box, and then click the Fill Color button and the Line Color button on the Drawing toolbar. You can also click the Shadow On/Off button to add a shadow and give the box some depth. And you can use the Line Style and Dashed Lines buttons to change the style of the text box border.

The Colors and Lines command on the Format menu (and the shortcut menu) offers you the same options as the Fill Color and Line Color buttons, but the options are all located in one place. In the Colors and Lines dialog box, shown in Figure 12-3, use the Fill drop-down list to select a fill color, shading, pattern, and texture. Use the Color drop-down list to select a line color, and then use the Style and Dashed drop-down lists to select a line style. To format any new text boxes you create (in the current presentation) with the options you specify in the Colors and Lines dialog box, click the Default for new Objects check box.

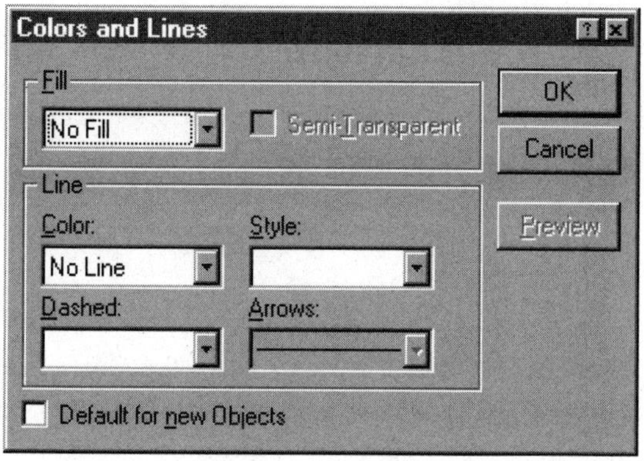

FIGURE 12-3
The Colors and
Lines dialog box.

TIP To create a text annotation with a more interesting shape, you can place an autoshape on a slide, and then enter text in the autoshape. (When you double-click the border of an autoshape, an insertion point appears inside the autoshape so that you can enter the text.) To get really fancy, you can also add a text annotation to a clip art selection. For more information about autoshapes, see "AutoShapes," page 341. For more information about using clip art, see Chapter 14, "Adding Clip Art Pictures and Bitmapped Images," page 361.

Duplicating a Text Box

Duplicating a text box creates a second text box with the same formatting as the original. First format both the original text box and its text, and then select the original text box and choose Duplicate from the Edit menu or press Ctrl+D. After the duplicate text box appears on top of the original text box, you can drag the duplicate to a new position, select the text inside by dragging across it, and type replacement text.

You can also use the Copy and Paste buttons on the Standard toolbar or the Copy and Paste commands on the Edit menu or the shortcut menu to duplicate text boxes in Slide view.

Adding Speaker's Notes

Every slide in the presentation can have a special type of output called speaker's notes or *notes pages*. On a notes page, which always has a portrait orientation even if the slide is landscape, you see two objects: the slide on the top half of the page and a text placeholder on the bottom half. The notes page for each slide is an integral part of the presentation, and is stored in the same file. To switch to Notes Pages view, click the Notes Pages View button in the lower left corner of the presentation window or choose Notes Pages from the View menu. As shown in Figure 12-4, when you switch to Notes Pages view, you see only the notes pages of the presentation.

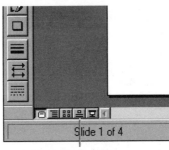

Notes Pages View

FIGURE 12-4
The current slide shown on a notes page in Notes Pages view.

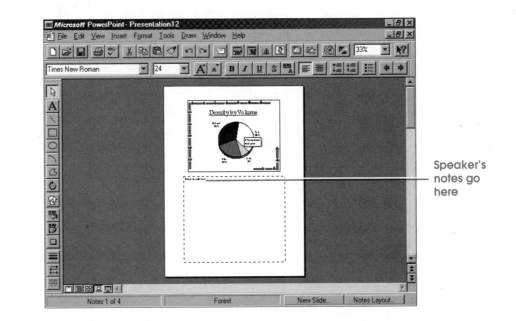

Speaker's notes go here

The notes page text, or any indication that notes page text exists, does not appear in any view other than Notes Pages view. But when you print the presentation, you can choose to print only the notes pages.

Your initial view of the notes page is reduced so that you can see the entire page, but you may want to zoom in to see the text you type in the text placeholder below the slide image. To zoom in, edit the zoom percentage in the Zoom Control box on the Standard toolbar or use the Zoom command on the View menu. A zoom percentage of 100 allows you to view the lower half of the notes page.

To enter a note, click the *Click to add text* placeholder below the slide image. Then begin typing in the placeholder as if you were typing text in a word processing program. The text will automatically wrap at the right edge of the text box. To start a new paragraph on the notes page, press Enter.

As with text annotations, you can use the buttons on the Formatting toolbar or the commands on the Format menu or the shortcut menu to format the notes page text before or after you type it. Again, if you want to format existing text, you must select the text first. You can also use the Line Spacing command on the Format menu to add line spacing within paragraphs or to add space before or after each paragraph. Figure 12-5 shows a completed notes page.

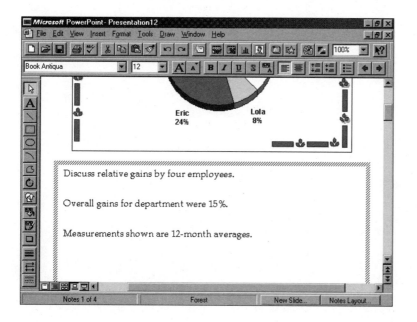

FIGURE 12-5

A completed notes page.

To enter speaker's notes for the next slide in the presentation, click the Next Slide button or press the PgDn key. To return to the previous slide, click the Previous Slide button or press the PgUp key.

After you enter text on the notes pages of a presentation, you should re-save the presentation to be sure the text is stored as part of the presentation file.

See Also For more information about printing notes pages, see Chapter 15, "Creating Printed Output and 35-mm Slides," page 379.

In this chapter, you learned how to add text that can enhance the slides of a presentation. In the following two chapters, you'll learn how to draw graphic shapes and add ready-made or scanned images to slides.

Chapter 13

Drawing Graphic Objects

You don't have to be an artist to create professional-looking graphics in PowerPoint. No matter what your artistic ability, you can use the program's drawing tools to add simple graphic shapes to slides. You can enclose an area within a rectangle, for example, or add a sunburst shape that contains a message like "Special!" or "New!" You can even combine individual shapes to create a more elaborate diagram or map. PowerPoint's commands for editing shapes are also easy to use. You can resize, rotate, and flip graphic objects, combine individual objects into a grouped object, and much more.

In this chapter, you'll learn how to use the drawing tools on the three drawing toolbars to add graphic objects to a slide, and you'll learn how to modify individual objects or groups of objects. In the next chapter, you'll learn how to add ready-made images to your presentation.

> **NOTE** If you're blessed with artistic skill, you'll naturally want to take PowerPoint's drawing capabilities even further. But the program's commands for adding and editing graphic shapes aren't sophisticated enough to please everyone. Professional-level artists might prefer to use a dedicated drawing application to create special graphics for a presentation and then transfer the graphics to a PowerPoint slide. For example, with Visio, a popular application that lets you create complex drawings by combining ready-made shapes, you can create an embedded drawing using Visio tools from within a PowerPoint presentation. For more information about using the tools of other applications from within PowerPoint, see Chapter 18, "Using PowerPoint with Other Applications," page 433.

Setting Up the Drawing Area

In Slide view, you can turn on two built-in PowerPoint features that help you position items with accuracy. PowerPoint's rulers, which run along the top and down the side of the presentation window, measure distances from the horizontal and vertical centers of the slide. Two movable guides—dashed lines that cross the slide horizontally and vertically—allow you to line up objects with great precision against measurements on the rulers or against each other. Figure 13-1 shows both the rulers and the guides.

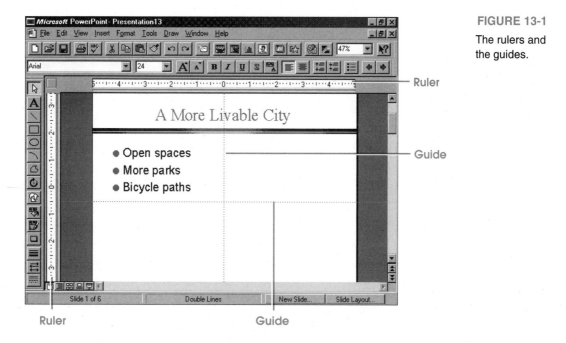

FIGURE 13-1

The rulers and
the guides.

To turn on the rulers, choose Ruler from the View menu. To turn on the guides, choose Guides from the View menu, too. You can also choose both Ruler and Guides from the shortcut menu that appears when you position the mouse pointer on the slide background and click the right mouse button.

Dashed markers on the rulers move when you move the mouse pointer to help you "eyeball" the position of the pointer as you draw and edit objects. The fixed, unchangeable zero point of the rulers is the exact center of the slide. To more accurately position objects on a slide, move the guides by dragging them. As you drag a guide, an indicator on the guide shows the guide's horizontal or vertical distance from the ruler's zero point. For example, to precisely place an object that must extend one inch to the left of the slide's center and two inches to the right, you can drag the vertical guide one inch to the left of the slide's center, as measured by the ruler. Next, you can draw the object from the guide to approximately two inches to the right of the slide's center, and then drag the guide to the exact two-inch mark. Finally, you can adjust the right edge of the object to align with the guide.

> **TIP** If two guides are not sufficient, you can replicate a guide by holding down the Ctrl key and dragging a copy of the guide off the original guide. You can then use the copy just as you would use the original.

The Drawing Toolbars

The basic set of drawing and editing tools is located on the Drawing toolbar that runs vertically near the left border of the PowerPoint window in Slide view. A second set of tools for editing objects is on the Drawing+ toolbar that you can turn on by choosing Toolbars from the View menu, selecting the Drawing+ option in the Toolbars dialog box, and then clicking OK or pressing Enter. A third set of drawing tools is located on the AutoShapes toolbar that you can display by clicking the AutoShapes button on the Drawing toolbar or by selecting the AutoShapes option in the Toolbars dialog box. Figure 13-2 identifies the three drawing toolbars.

FIGURE 13-2
The drawing toolbars.

Drawing+ toolbar —

Drawing toolbar —

AutoShapes toolbar —

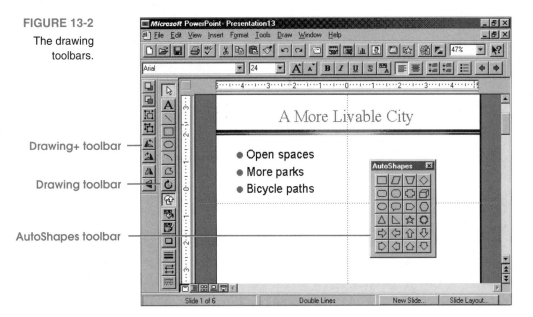

Drawing the Basic Shapes

On the Drawing toolbar, you'll find a button for each of the basic shapes you can add to a slide. Each shape becomes an *object* after it is drawn. Objects have an outline and an interior area whose default colors are determined by the current color scheme. The color scheme's Text & Lines color sets the outline color, and the Fills color governs the interior color. Because the color scheme controls these colors, any change to the color scheme also changes the colors in graphic objects you've drawn, unless you have directly formatted the color of an object by clicking the object and changing its line or fill color. Any object that has been directly formatted retains its own colors no matter what the color scheme dictates.

Lines and Arrows

A line or arrow is the easiest drawing you can create. A straight line simply connects two end points and becomes an arrow when you add an arrowhead.

To add a straight line or arrow to a slide, follow these steps:

1. Click the Line Tool button on the Drawing toolbar.

2. Position the mouse pointer at one end point for the line.

3. Hold down the Shift key if you want to constrain the line to exactly horizontal, vertical, or diagonal.

4. Hold down the left mouse button, and drag to the second end point.

5. Release the mouse button. A line appears between the first and second end points.

When you hold down the Ctrl key as you drag, the first end point becomes the center of the line, and the line grows in opposite directions from the first end point as you drag.

To change the appearance of the line and add an arrowhead, first select the line, and choose Colors and Lines from the Format menu or the shortcut menu. The Colors and Lines dialog box shown in Figure 13-3 on the next page appears. In the Colors and Lines dialog box, select a line color from the Color drop-down list and a line style from the Style drop-down list. When you open the Color drop-down list, you see the eight colors of the color scheme in small panels. If you don't like any of the eight colors, you can click the Other Color option in the list, and then select one of the colors on the Standard tab of the Colors dialog box, or click the Custom tab and create your own color.

FIGURE 13-3

The Colors and
Lines dialog box.

Colors and Lines

Fill

☐ Semi-Transparent

OK

Cancel

Line

Color:

Style:

Preview

Dashed:

Arrows:

☐ Default for new Objects

In the Style drop-down list, you can select from six preset line weights or four double- and triple-line combinations. In the Dashed drop-down list, you can leave the first option, a solid line, or select one of the dashed or dotted lines displayed. In the Arrows drop-down list, you can leave the first setting selected to produce a line without arrowheads, or you can select one of the other options to place an arrowhead at one or both ends of the line. After you select the changes, click OK to return to the slide.

If you want every line you create to look the same, click the Default for new Objects option at the bottom of the Colors and Lines dialog box after you make your selections.

You can also click the Line Color, Line Style, Arrowheads, and Dashed Lines buttons on the Drawing toolbar to change the corresponding attributes of a line.

TIP To copy the formatting of an existing object to a new object, click the object with the formatting you want to copy, click the Format Painter button on the Standard toolbar, and then click the new object.

See
Also
For information about creating custom colors, see "Creating a Custom Color Scheme," page 222.

Rectangles and Squares

You can use the Rectangle Tool button on the Drawing toolbar to draw a rectangle or a square in PowerPoint. As you'll see, drawing a rectangle is almost as easy as drawing a line.

To draw a rectangle or a square, follow these steps:

1. Click the Rectangle Tool button on the Drawing toolbar.
2. Position the mouse pointer at the location for one corner of the rectangle or square.
3. If you want to draw a perfect square rather than a rectangle, hold down the Shift key.
4. Hold down the left mouse button, and drag to the opposite corner of the rectangle or square.
5. Release the mouse button. A rectangle or square appears, displaying the line and fill colors of the current color scheme.

To have a rectangle grow outward from the first point you click, hold down the Ctrl key as you drag. To have a square grow outward from the first point you click, hold down both the Shift and Ctrl keys as you drag.

To change the colors and border style of the rectangle or square, select the rectangle or square, and choose the Colors and Lines command from the Format menu or the shortcut menu. In the Colors and Lines dialog box, select a fill and line color from the appropriate drop-down lists. Then select a line style, dashed line style, or both for the border of the rectangle or square. As with lines, you can also click the corresponding buttons on the Drawing toolbar to change these options individually.

To add a more interesting fill to the rectangle or square, you can select one of the special fills from the Fill drop-down list in the Colors and Lines dialog box. These special fills, which allow you to add shading, a pattern, a texture, or a background color, are covered in "Applying Special Fills to Objects," page 346.

TIP To draw a rectangle or square with rounded corners, use the Rounded Rectangle Tool button on the AutoShapes toolbar. You'll learn about autoshapes on page 341 of this chapter.

Ellipses and Circles

Like the Rectangle Tool button, which lets you draw rectangles or squares, the Ellipse Tool button on the Drawing toolbar lets you draw ellipses or circles.

To draw an ellipse or a circle, follow these steps:

1. Click the Ellipse Tool button on the Drawing toolbar.

2. Position the mouse pointer at the location of one corner of an imaginary rectangle that would enclose the ellipse or circle.

3. If you want to draw a perfect circle rather than an ellipse, hold down the Shift key.

4. Hold down the left mouse button, and drag to the opposite corner of the imaginary rectangle.

5. Release the mouse button. An ellipse or circle appears, displaying the line and fill colors of the current color scheme.

To have an ellipse grow outward from the first point you click, hold down the Ctrl key as you drag. To have a circle grow outward from the first point you click, hold down both the Shift and Ctrl keys as you drag.

To change the colors and border style of the ellipse or circle, select the ellipse or circle, and then choose Colors and Lines from the Format menu or the shortcut menu. In the Colors and Lines dialog box, select a fill and line color from the appropriate drop-down lists. Then select a line style, dashed line style, or both for the border of the ellipse or circle. You can also click the corresponding buttons on the Drawing toolbar to change these options individually.

Arcs

An arc is a segment between two points along the curve of an ellipse or circle. PowerPoint supplies the Arc Tool button so that you can easily add arcs to your slides.

To draw an arc, follow these steps:

1. Click the Arc Tool button on the Drawing toolbar.

2. Position the mouse pointer at the first point for the arc.

3. If you want to draw a segment of a circle rather than an ellipse, hold down the Shift key.

4. Hold down the left mouse button, drag to the second point for the arc, and release the mouse button. An arc appears, displaying the line color of the current color scheme.

To center an elliptical arc at the starting point, hold down the Ctrl key as you drag. To center a circular arc at the starting point, hold down the Shift and Ctrl keys as you drag.

You can change the color and style of an arc. To do so, select the arc, and then choose the Colors and Lines command from the Format menu or the shortcut menu, or use the Line Color, Line Style, and Dashed Lines buttons on the Drawing toolbar.

Free-Form Shapes

You might be relieved to discover that you're not confined to drawing only lines, rectangles, and circles in PowerPoint. The Freeform Tool button on the Drawing toolbar gives you the freedom to draw a combination of curved and straight line segments to create complex objects.

To draw a free-form shape, follow these steps:

1. Click the Freeform Tool button on the Drawing toolbar.

2. Position the mouse pointer at the beginning of the shape.

3. Hold down the left mouse button, and drag to draw a freehand shape, or click and move the mouse to draw a straight line segment.

4. Repeat step 3 until you have completed the entire shape.

5. Click once near the starting point of the shape to close the shape or double-click at any point to end the shape as it is and leave it open.

To constrain a straight line segment to exactly horizontal, vertical, or diagonal, hold down the Shift key as you drag.

Each point where two segments meet is called a *vertex*. (The free-form segments that look like curves are actually composed of many short, straight lines that connect vertexes.) While drawing a free-form shape in PowerPoint, you can remove the last vertex you created by pressing the Backspace key.

To modify the shape of an existing free-form figure, first double-click the figure. Every vertex in the shape is selected. (Notice that the status bar at the bottom of the PowerPoint window gives you advice about your options.) Then reshape the figure by dragging individual vertexes. If you want to add a new vertex, hold down the Ctrl key, and click between two existing vertexes. To remove a vertex, hold down Ctrl, and click the vertex you want to remove.

Note that when you add a vertex, the mouse pointer takes the shape of a cross hair, and when you remove a vertex, the pointer takes the shape of a large X.

To try drawing and reshaping a single figure, first click the Freeform Tool button on the Drawing toolbar, and then click three points in the shape of a V at the top of the current slide. Double-click the third point to end the shape. Next, select the shape, hold down the Ctrl key, and drag down to create a duplicate of the free-form shape. Then double-click the duplicate. Now place the mouse pointer on the vertex at the bottom of the duplicate V. When the mouse pointer becomes a small cross hair, hold down the left mouse button, and drag the vertex down an inch or so. Then release the mouse button. Figure 13-4 shows approximately how your screen should look.

FIGURE 13-4

Dragging a vertex to reshape a free-form figure.

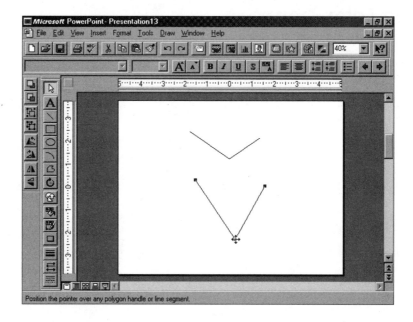

Finally, hold down the Ctrl key, and click anywhere along the duplicate V to add a vertex. Then, hold down Ctrl again, and click the vertex at the bottom of the V. When you remove a vertex, PowerPoint connects the two vertexes on either side with a straight line.

To change the colors and border style of a closed free-form shape, select the shape, and then choose Colors and Lines from the Format menu or the shortcut menu. In the Colors and Lines dialog box, select a fill and line color from the appropriate drop-down lists. Then select a line style, dashed line style, or both for the border of the shape. When the free-form shape is a straight line, the Fill options are unavailable, but you can select one of the arrowhead options. You can also click the buttons on the Drawing toolbar to change these elements individually.

AutoShapes

PowerPoint's autoshapes are familiar shapes that you are likely to use frequently, such as arrows and stars. They are generally more complex than those on the Drawing toolbar, and many of them have an *adjustment handle*, which allows you to adjust their most salient feature. For example, a cube autoshape has an adjustment handle that you can drag to adjust the depth of the cube. An arrow autoshape's adjustment handle changes the shape of the arrowhead.

To draw an autoshape, follow these steps:

1. If the AutoShapes toolbar is not already displayed on your screen, click the AutoShapes button on the Drawing toolbar; or choose Toolbars from the View menu, select the AutoShapes option, and click OK.

2. Click an autoshape on the AutoShapes toolbar.

3. On the slide, position the mouse pointer where you want the autoshape to begin, hold down the left mouse button, and then drag the autoshape into place.

4. If the autoshape has an adjustment handle, as shown below, drag the adjustment handle to adjust the autoshape.

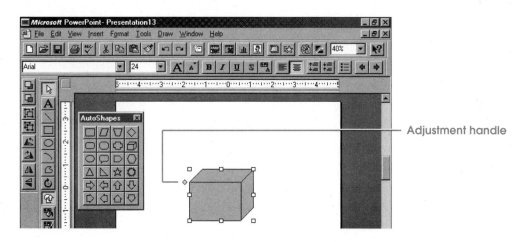

Adjustment handle

TIP If you want the AutoShapes toolbar to remain on your screen but out of the way, drag the toolbar to any edge of the PowerPoint window.

An autoshape can be filled and outlined, just like any other object you draw. You can also move, resize, copy and paste, and duplicate an autoshape.

Adding Text to an Object

By clicking any drawn object, except those created with the Freeform Tool button, and then typing, you can add text to the interior of the object. Because the text becomes an integral part of the object, when you move the object, the text moves too.

If you try to enter more than a few words, however, the text may overrun the borders of the object, as shown in Figure 13-5. To wrap the text within the object, choose Text Anchor from the Format menu, select the Word-wrap Text in Object option, and click OK. Be sure not to select the Adjust Object Size to Fit Text option, because the object will adjust to the text rather than the other way around. After you turn on word wrapping and click OK, you'll see the newly wrapped text, which fits within the left and right borders of the object, but may still overrun the top and bottom, as shown in Figure 13-6.

FIGURE 13-5

The text in this object has overrun the object's borders.

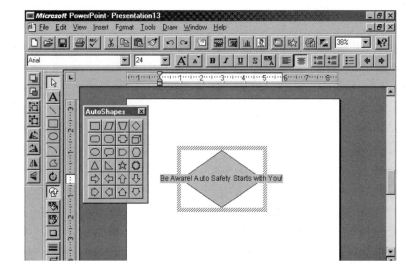

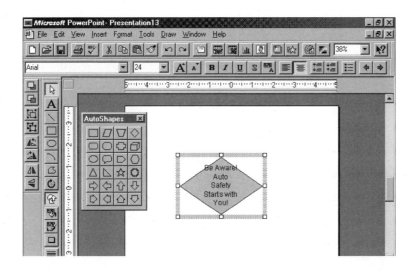

FIGURE 13-6
The text in this
object wraps
between the
object's left and
right borders.

To keep the text from overrunning the top and bottom borders of the object, you can either return to the Text Anchor dialog box and select the Adjust Object Size to Fit Text option or reduce the text size. To make minor adjustments to the size of the text in the object, select the text, and then click the Increase Font Size button or the Decrease Font Size button on the Formatting toolbar. You can also press Ctrl+Shift+> to increase the font size or Ctrl+Shift+< to decrease the font size. Figure 13-7 shows the final object.

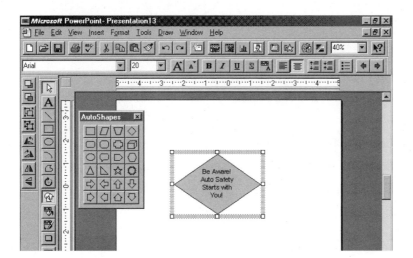

FIGURE 13-7
After final
adjustments, the
text fits neatly
inside the object.

Switching Shapes

A special command on the Draw menu, Change AutoShape, lets you replace a shape you've drawn with a different shape. You simply select the shape you want to replace, choose Change AutoShape from the Draw menu, and then select a new shape from the AutoShapes palette. Figure 13-8 shows the AutoShapes palette. You can convert a star to a sunburst, for example, or a thin arrow to a thick arrow.

FIGURE 13-8
The AutoShapes palette.

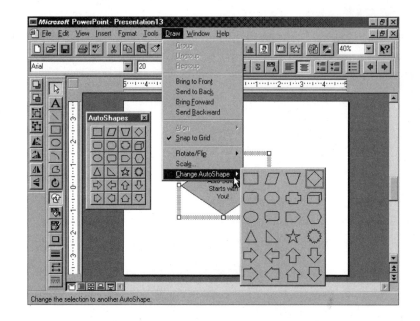

The new shape occupies the same size and positioning of the original shape and retains all of the original shape's formatting.

Editing Objects

Up to this point, you've learned how to change the fill and border color and the border style of objects. PowerPoint provides other editing options as well, such as adding a shadow or embossing an object. These are discussed in the following section. But first you must learn how to select single objects and multiple objects.

Selecting Objects

Before you can make changes to a graphic object in PowerPoint, you must select the object. If you want to make changes to more than one object, you can select multiple objects.

To select a single object, simply click the object. To select more than one object, do one of the following:

■ Hold down the Shift key as you click each object. (To deselect one of the selected objects, click the object again while holding down the Shift key.)

■ Click the Selection Tool button on the Drawing toolbar, and drag a selection box around the objects. Only objects that are completely enclosed by the selection box are selected. For example, Figure 13-9 shows a selection box that will select three of the four objects on a slide.

FIGURE 13-9

Three of the four objects on this slide will be selected.

To select all the objects on a slide, choose the Select All command from the Edit menu or press Ctrl+A. All objects, including titles, bulleted text, and graphs, are selected.

After you select multiple objects, any changes you make will affect all the objects in the selection.

Applying Special Fills to Objects

When you learned how to add basic shapes earlier in this chapter, you also learned how to use options in the Colors and Lines dialog box to change the fill and border colors and styles of a selected object. Special options in the dialog box also let you create objects filled with a color shading, objects filled with a pattern or texture, or objects filled with the slide background.

Filling an Object with Shading

Shadings in objects add richness and depth and can give the appearance that the objects have been illuminated from the side, top, or corner. Combined with shadows, shadings can create an impressive three-dimensional effect.

To add shading to an object, follow these steps:

1. Select the object.

2. Click the Fill Color button on the Drawing toolbar, or choose Colors and Lines from the Format menu or the shortcut menu and open the Fill drop-down list.

3. Select the Shaded option to display the Shaded Fill dialog box shown here:

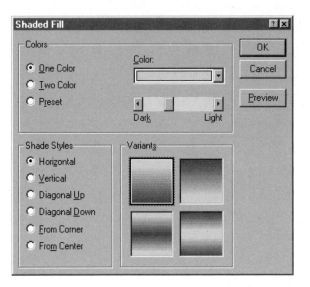

4. In the dialog box, select a shade style and one of the four variants, which depict how the shading progresses from light to dark, dark to light, and so on.

5. To change the color of the shading, select one of the color options at the top of the dialog box, and then fine-tune the color by selecting

options in the corresponding drop-down list(s). If you select the One Color option, you can also use the scroll bar in the Colors section to make the shading darker or lighter. To use one of PowerPoint's ready-made color schemes, click the Preset option, and then select a scheme from the Preset Colors drop-down list.

Filling an Object with a Pattern

Rather than fill an object with a solid or shaded color, you can fill it with a pattern made up of two colors. PowerPoint offers a number of patterns and a wide variety of foreground and background colors to choose from.

To fill an object with a pattern, follow the steps in the previous section, "Filling an Object with Shading," but select Patterned rather than Shaded from the Fill drop-down list in the Color and Lines dialog box. The Pattern Fill dialog box, shown in Figure 13-10, appears.

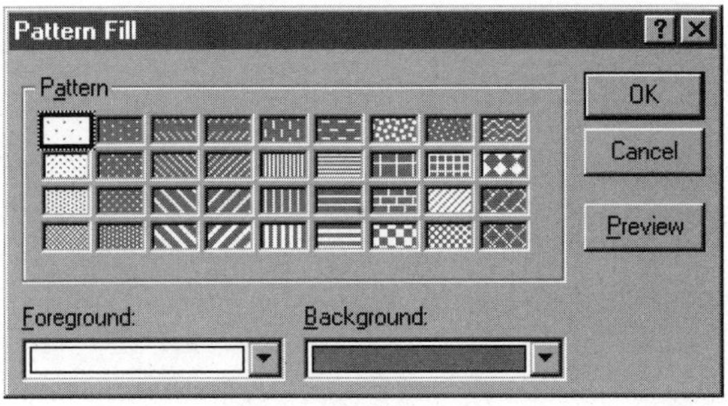

FIGURE 13-10
The Pattern Fill
dialog box.

In the Pattern Fill dialog box, the patterns shown are composed of the foreground and background colors displayed in the Foreground and Background boxes. You can select a different pattern and different foreground and background colors to create the combination you want.

Filling an Object with a Texture

Adding texture to an object can give the object a whole new feel. PowerPoint provides twelve different textures to choose from, including oak, green marble, cork, paper, and even sand.

To fill an object with a texture, follow these steps:

1. Select the object.

2. Click the Fill Color button on the Drawing toolbar, or choose Colors and Lines from the Format menu or the shortcut menu and open the Fill drop-down list.

3. Select the Textured option to display the Textured Fill dialog box
    shown here:

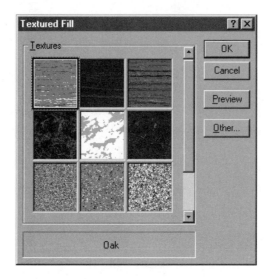

4. In the Textured Fill dialog box, select a texture and then click OK.

Displaying the Slide Background Within an Object

You can pile up as many objects as you want. But then if you add an object
to the top of the pile and fill it with the background, the background appears
within the top object, despite all the other objects beneath the top object. It's
like creating a hole in the shape of the top object that bores all the way down
to the background. Figure 13-11 demonstrates this effect.

FIGURE 13-11

A vertical rectangle
that is filled with
the background
overlays several
other objects.

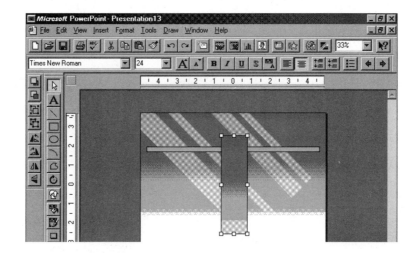

To fill an object with the background, follow these steps:

1. Select the object.

2. Click the Fill Color button on the Drawing toolbar, or choose Colors and Lines from the Format menu or the shortcut menu and open the Fill drop-down list.

3. Select the Background option.

Adding Shadows to Objects

PowerPoint lets you add a shadow behind objects and determine the shadow's color, direction, and size. You can add a shadow to any object you've drawn and to any text you've added to a slide.

To add a shadow, select the object, and click the Shadow On/Off button on the Drawing toolbar. A shadow appears with the shadow color specified by the current color scheme. To alter the color, direction, and size of the shadow, choose Shadow from the Format menu. Figure 13-12 shows the Shadow dialog box that appears.

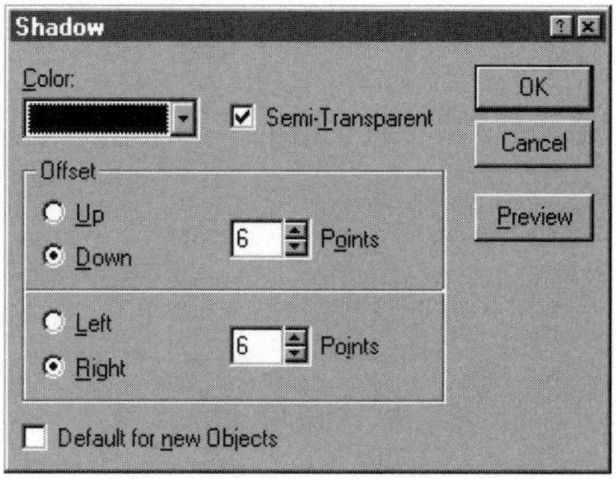

FIGURE 13-12

The Shadow dialog box.

In the Shadow dialog box, open the Color drop-down list to select a shadow color. One of the options on the list, No Shadow, removes any shadow that is already present. The Other Color option lets you select a color other than the eight colors of the color scheme. If you don't want the shadow to be opaque, be sure the Semi-Transparent option is selected. To vary the direction and degree to which the shadow extends behind an object, change the direction and Points settings in the Offset section of the dialog box. If you click the Default for new Objects option, any new shadows you add (to the current presentation) will have the formatting you specified in the dialog box.

TIP To create a slide that makes visual sense, apply the same shadow to every object on the slide, even the title of the slide.

Embossing Objects

In the Shadow dialog box, the Embossed option on the Color drop-down list gives objects a raised, three-dimensional look. It also fills the objects with the background color, so you can place them directly on the background for an impressive visual effect. Figure 13-13 shows a slide with an embossed text box.

FIGURE 13-13

The text box on this slide has been embossed.

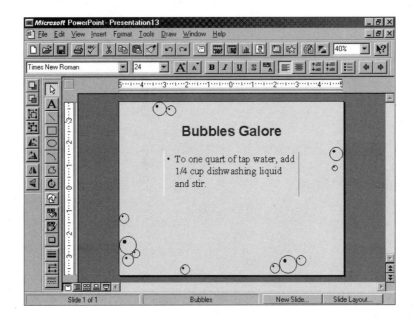

Transferring Object Styles

After you finish modifying the appearance of an object, you can transfer the object's style to another object by using the Format Painter button on the Standard toolbar. Simply select the object whose style you want to transfer, click the Format Painter button, and then select the object you want to transfer the style to. The Format Painter button only allows you to transfer an object's style to one other object.

If you want to transfer the style to more than one object, use the Pick Up Object Style and Apply Object Style commands on the Format menu or the shortcut menu. Select the object whose style you want to transfer, choose the Pick Up Object Style command from the Format menu or the shortcut menu, select another object, and choose the Apply Object Style command from the Format menu or the shortcut menu. You can use this procedure to format as many other objects as you want (that is, until you select a different style or begin a new PowerPoint session).

> **TIP**   Earlier versions of PowerPoint offered Pick Up Style and Apply Style buttons on the toolbar. Although the single Format Painter button has officially replaced the pair, these buttons are still available in PowerPoint 7, so you can install them on any toolbar, as you'll learn in Chapter 19, "Customizing PowerPoint," page 451.

Saving an Object's Style as the Default

After you spend time formatting an object with special attributes, you may want to save the object's style as a default. Then, when you draw new objects, they will automatically be formatted with the line weight, color, and other attributes of the default style.

To save an object's style as the default, follow these steps:

1. Select the formatted object.

2. Choose Pick Up Object Style from the Format menu.

3. Deselect the object by clicking away from it.

4. Choose Apply To Object Defaults from the Format menu or the shortcut menu.

The next time you draw an object (during the current PowerPoint session), the default style will be applied.

Arranging Objects

In addition to tools and commands that change the look of one or more objects, PowerPoint provides several features that allow you to arrange objects on slides.

Grouping Objects

If you frequently make changes to more than one object at a time, you might want to combine the objects in a group. The objects are then treated as a unit, and any changes you make affect the entire group. For example, you can select the group and then move all the objects as a unit or modify the fill color so that all the objects in the group change simultaneously.

To group objects, use either of the selection techniques described on page 345, and then click the Group Objects button on the Drawing+ toolbar. You can also choose the Group command from the Draw menu. When the objects are grouped, one set of handles surrounds the group, as shown in Figure 13-14.

FIGURE 13-14

A group of objects has one set of handles.

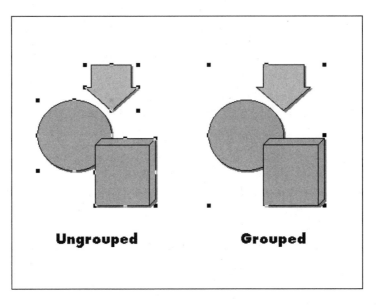

After you group objects, you can ungroup them by clicking the Ungroup Objects button on the Drawing+ toolbar or by choosing the Ungroup command from the Draw menu. The Regroup command, available on the Draw menu and the shortcut menu, regroups an ungrouped group, just as you'd think.

Cutting, Copying, and Duplicating Objects

You can cut, copy, and paste graphic objects as you would any object on a PowerPoint slide by using the Cut, Copy, and Paste buttons on the Standard toolbar; the Cut, Copy, and Paste commands on the Edit menu or the shortcut menu; or the keyboard equivalents (shown on the Edit menu). Not only can you cut and copy objects from one slide to another, but you can cut and copy objects from one presentation to another. By opening two presentations side by side in Slide view, you can cut or copy an object in one presentation and then paste it in another.

The fastest way to duplicate an object and simultaneously position the duplicate is to hold down the Ctrl key and drag a copy of the object into position. But you can also select the object, and choose Duplicate from the Edit menu or press Ctrl+D. Then drag the duplicate into position.

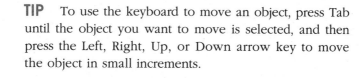

> **TIP**   Remember, you can undo most of the commands discussed in this chapter by clicking the Undo button on the Standard toolbar or by choosing Undo from the Edit menu.

Moving, Resizing, and Scaling Objects

To move an object, place the mouse pointer on the object, hold down the left mouse button, and then drag the object to a new location. To move an object horizontally or vertically, hold down the Shift key while you drag. To resize an object, drag one of the object's handles in the desired direction. If you want to maintain the proportions of the object, hold down the Shift key while you drag a corner handle. If you want the object to grow out from its center, hold down the Ctrl key while you drag a corner handle.

> **TIP**   To use the keyboard to move an object, press Tab until the object you want to move is selected, and then press the Left, Right, Up, or Down arrow key to move the object in small increments.

To help you position an object, you can choose Snap to Grid from the Draw menu. Then, as you drag the object, it will automatically jump to the nearest horizontal and vertical ruler marking. To temporarily turn off Snap to Grid and drag an object freely on a slide, hold down the Alt key as you drag. The object will move smoothly without little jerks as it jumps from ruler marking to ruler marking.

To resize an object to a precise degree, select the object and then choose Scale from the Draw menu. In the Scale dialog box, shown in Figure 13-15 on the next page, enter a percentage in the Scale To edit box or click the up or down arrow to increase or decrease the current percentage. For example, to double the size of an object, enter 200 as the Scale To percentage. Keep in mind that objects can be scaled no larger than the size of the slide.

FIGURE 13-15

The Scale
dialog box.

Scale

Scale To
100 ▲▼ %

☐ Relative to Original Picture Size
☐ Best Scale for Slide Show
Resolution:

OK
Cancel
Preview

**See
Also** For more information about the Scale dialog box, see Chapter 14,
"Adding Clip Art Pictures and Bitmapped Images," page 361.

Rotating and Flipping Objects

You can rotate a single object or a group of objects around its center, and you
can rotate multiple selected objects, each around its own center.

To rotate a single object or group of objects, follow these steps:

1. Select the object or group, as shown below.

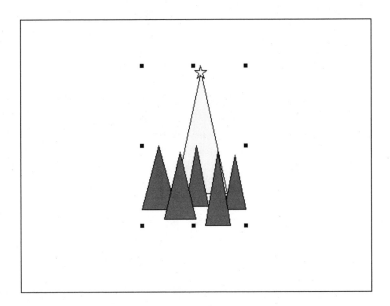

2. Click the Free Rotate Tool button on the Drawing toolbar, or choose
   Rotate/Flip from the Draw menu and then choose Free Rotate from
   the submenu.

3. Place the mouse pointer on a corner handle of the object or group, and then drag the handle left or right around the center of the object or group. The group of objects shown below is being rotated to the left.

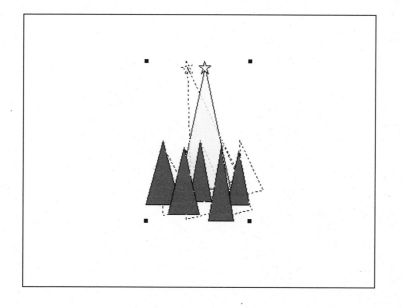

TIP For more precision while rotating, click a handle and drag the pointer away from the object before dragging in a circle around the object.

If you select multiple objects, each object rotates around its center when you rotate any one of the objects. In Figure 13-16 on the next page, the objects on the left were not grouped before being rotated, and each object has rotated around its own center. The group of objects on the right has rotated around its collective center.

On the Drawing toolbar, you'll find two buttons that rotate objects exactly 90 degrees to the left or right. You'll also find two commands on the Draw menu that accomplish the same task. To use these buttons or commands, follow these steps:

1. Select the object, objects, or group you want to rotate.

2. Click the Rotate Left button or the Rotate Right button on the Drawing+ toolbar, or choose Rotate/Flip from the Draw menu and then choose Rotate Left or Rotate Right from the submenu.

FIGURE 13-16

Rotating
ungrouped objects
(left) and grouped
objects (right).

To create a mirror image of one or more objects, use the Flip buttons or the Flip commands by following these steps:

1. Select the object or objects you want to flip, as shown here:

2. Click the Flip Horizontal button or the Flip Vertical button on the Drawing+ toolbar, or choose Rotate/Flip from the Draw menu and then choose Flip Horizontal or Flip Vertical from the submenu. The object shown below was flipped horizontally.

Stacking Objects

When objects overlap, you can change their order in the stack. You can move an object one level higher or lower in the stack or send an object to the top or bottom of the stack.

To move an object one level higher or lower in a stack, select the object, and then click the Bring Forward button or the Send Backward button on the Drawing+ toolbar. You can also choose the Bring Forward command or the Send Backward command from the Draw menu. If you want to move an object to the top or bottom of a stack, select the object, and choose Bring to Front or Send to Back from the Draw menu.

Figure 13-17 on the next page shows two versions of a simple scene. On the left, the pine tree is in the back. On the right, the pine tree has been moved forward one level using the Bring Forward command.

FIGURE 13-17

The pine tree on the right has been moved forward one level using the Bring Forward command.

Aligning Objects

To line up objects on a slide, select the objects and then choose Align from the Draw menu. The six commands on the Align submenu allow you to left-align, right-align, top-align, or bottom-align objects, as well as center objects vertically or horizontally. The objects align with the object that is farthest out. In other words, right-aligned objects align with the object that is farthest to the right. Figure 13-18 shows three objects before and after the Left Align command was chosen.

TIP   The six commands on the Align submenu are available as toolbar buttons that you can drag to any toolbar. For information about customizing a toolbar, see Chapter 19, "Customizing PowerPoint," page 451.

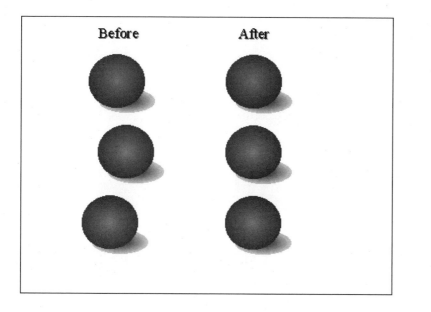

FIGURE 13-18
Three objects
before and after
being left-aligned.

Before   After

Saving a Drawing for Use in Another Presentation

One method you can use to save your most valuable drawings, such as logos, is to copy and paste the drawings into a special presentation. When you need a particular drawing, you can open the presentation, copy the drawing, and then paste it into a new presentation.

Another method is to add the drawing to PowerPoint's ClipArt Gallery. Unfortunately, the ClipArt Gallery doesn't offer an easy way to transfer graphic objects from a slide to the Gallery. Instead, you must copy and paste the objects into a drawing application such as CorelDRAW! so that you can export the objects into a file. Then, you can import the file into the ClipArt Gallery, where you'll always have access to the objects from within PowerPoint.

See
Also
For more information about importing files into the ClipArt Gallery, see Chapter 14, "Adding Clip Art Pictures and Bitmapped Images," page 361.

In this chapter, you learned how to create pictures by drawing them. In the next chapter, you'll learn how to import pictures that have already been created and stored in files or in PowerPoint's ClipArt Gallery.

Chapter 14

Adding Clip Art Pictures and Bitmapped Images

Your words and graphs can tickle the brain and invoke powerful mental images, but a picture settles deep in long-term memory, where it has an effect far into the future. But if you're not an artist, where do you get the pictures you need? You can let PowerPoint's AutoClipArt suggest an appropriate picture from PowerPoint's built-in ClipArt Gallery, or you can go directly to the ClipArt Gallery and select a picture from one of its many categories.

The ClipArt Gallery contains more than a thousand pictures drawn by professional artists. You can easily place any of the pictures on your presentation slides. If none of the clip art images is right, you can import an image from another program. Drawings and paintings from other Windows-based applications are especially easy to transfer over to a presentation. And if the image you need is a photo, you can insert a scanned picture into PowerPoint just as easily.

In this chapter, you'll learn how to use the AutoClipArt feature, how to browse and borrow images from the ClipArt Gallery, and how to import drawings, paintings, and scanned pictures into PowerPoint. You'll also learn how to work with the images, separating them into individual components, if it's possible, or cropping out portions that are unnecessary. You'll even learn how to transfer your favorite and most frequently used images to the ClipArt Gallery, so that you can pull them up for future presentations.

Using the ClipArt Gallery

The ClipArt Gallery is one of PowerPoint's optional components. If you installed the Gallery when you initially ran PowerPoint Setup, it is always available from within Slide view or Notes Pages view to dress up your pages with pictures. If, as you follow the instructions in this chapter, you find that the ClipArt Gallery was not installed, you can install it by running PowerPoint Setup and clicking the Add/Remove button. (The Gallery is shared with other Microsoft Office applications, so if you have an application such as Microsoft Word on your computer, you may already have access to the ClipArt Gallery.)

Adding Clip Art with AutoClipArt

If you used the AutoContent Wizard to create your presentation, or if your slide show is one of PowerPoint's presentations, PowerPoint can help you select an appropriate piece of art for your slides. AutoClipArt looks at some key words in your presentation and tries to find pictures to match.

In Slide View, choose AutoClipArt from the Tools menu. PowerPoint displays the AutoClipArt dialog box, shown in Figure 14-1.

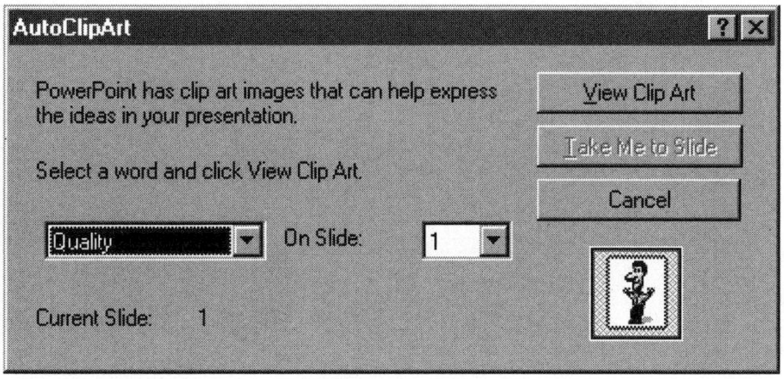

FIGURE 14-1
The AutoClipArt dialog box.

To go to a slide for which AutoClipArt suggests an image, select a word in the drop-down list, then select a slide from the On Slide(s) drop-down list and click Take Me to Slide.

After you've selected the slide to which you want to add art, click View Clip Art. The Microsoft ClipArt Gallery dialog box opens with the suggested picture selected. You can click Insert to add this picture to your slide, or select any other picture from the Gallery and click Insert.

Adding Clip Art Manually

You can manually add clip art to any existing slide while in Slide view, or you can select one of the two autolayouts that come with clip art placeholders when you start a new slide. Figure 14-2 on the next page shows the two autolayouts that have clip art placeholders. When you select an autolayout that has a clip art placeholder, you can double-click the placeholder to open the ClipArt Gallery.

> **NOTE** The first time you open the ClipArt Gallery, you may have to let the Gallery build its library of pictures by clicking Yes when you're asked if you want to add clip art now. If you don't see this prompt, the Gallery has already built its library and is ready for use.

FIGURE 14-2

The autolayouts with clip art placeholders.

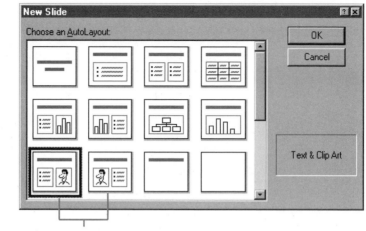

Clip art autolayouts

To manually add clip art to an existing slide that does not have a clip art placeholder, display the slide in Slide view and then do one of the following:

- Click the Insert Clip Art button on the Standard toolbar.

- Choose the Clip Art command from the Insert menu.

The Microsoft ClipArt Gallery dialog box appears, as shown in Figure 14-3.

FIGURE 14-3

The Microsoft ClipArt Gallery dialog box.

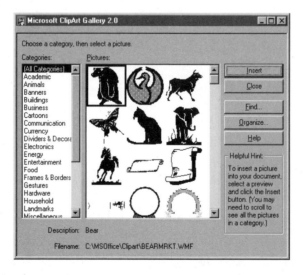

An alphabetized list of clip art categories appears on the left side of the dialog box, and clip art pictures from the currently selected category appear to the right of the list. By default, All Categories is selected in the category list so that you can scroll through all the pictures in the Gallery. If you want to see only the clip art in a specific category, click that category in the list and then scroll through the pictures.

Select the clip art image you want by clicking it. A dark border surrounds your clip art selection. To add the clip art selection to a slide, click Insert. (You can also double-click a clip art picture in the dialog box to add it to a slide.)

When you add a clip art image to a slide, the image appears in the placeholder you double-clicked to open the ClipArt Gallery, or it appears centered on a slide without a clip art placeholder.

After a clip art picture appears on a slide, you can drag the picture to move it. (Before you modify a picture, it's a good idea to create a copy of it so that you have a backup should you make a mistake. You can always delete the backup if it's not needed.) Figure 14-4 shows a clip art image that has been moved to the bottom of the slide. If you want to resize a clip art picture, drag a corner handle to maintain the clip art's proportions while you resize it, or hold down the Ctrl key and drag a corner handle to stretch or shrink the clip art picture without moving it. You can also hold down the Ctrl key and drag a copy of the clip art picture to a new location on the slide.

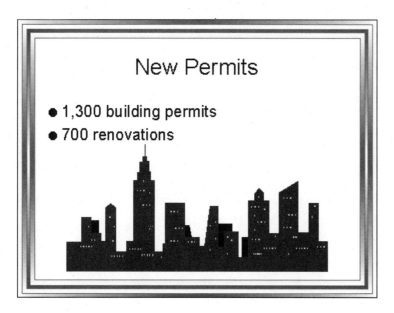

FIGURE 14-4
A clip art picture on a slide.

Adding Clip Art to the Background of a Presentation

To add a clip art picture to the background of every slide in a presentation, you can add the picture to the slide master background. First choose Master and then Slide Master from the View menu. Then open the ClipArt Gallery, select the image you want, and click Insert. After the clip art picture has been added to the background of the presentation, you can place the picture behind the text of the presentation by selecting the clip art and choosing Send to Back from the Draw menu.

Finding Clip Art with the Find ClipArt Dialog Box

Each picture in the ClipArt Gallery has a text description you can use to search for a particular image. To search for a picture, first click the Find button in the Microsoft ClipArt Gallery dialog box. The Find ClipArt dialog box appears, as shown in Figure 14-5.

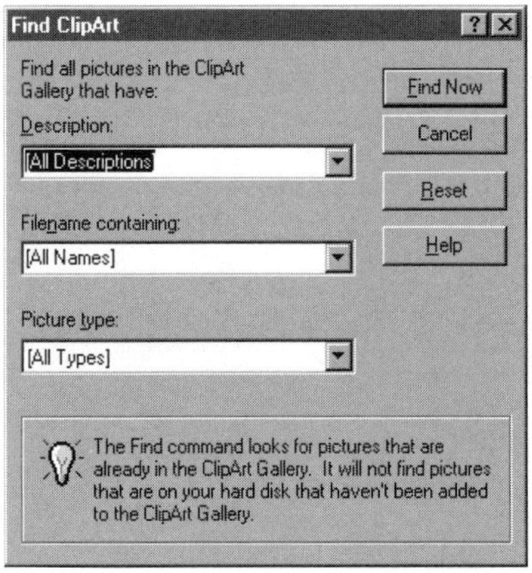

FIGURE 14-5

The Find ClipArt dialog box.

The Find ClipArt dialog box allows you to narrow down the list of images displayed in the ClipArt Gallery by selecting one of three search methods: by description, by filename, or by picture type.

To search for a keyword in the clip art picture's description, type the keyword in the Description edit box. To search for a picture filename that contains specific characters, type the characters in the Filename containing edit box. To search by picture type, select one of the picture types from the Picture type drop-down list.

For example, to find a clip art image that represents leadership, you can type *leadership* in the Description edit box and click Find Now to find all the images with the word *leadership* in their description. Figure 14-6 shows the results of the search in the ClipArt Gallery.

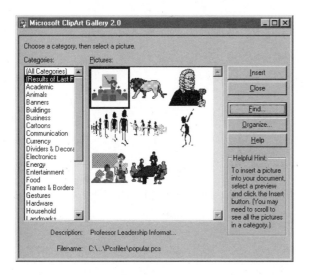

FIGURE 14-6

The Microsoft ClipArt Gallery dialog box after a search for descriptions containing the word *leadership*.

Replacing a Clip Art Selection on a Slide

After you add a picture from the ClipArt Gallery to a slide, you can replace the picture by first double-clicking it. (Or you can also select the picture, click the right mouse button, and choose Replace ClipArt Object from the shortcut menu.) Then, when the Microsoft ClipArt Gallery dialog box reopens, you can select a replacement picture.

Recoloring Clip Art to Match the Current Color Scheme

The clip art from the ClipArt Gallery has a preset combination of colors that may clash with the color scheme of your presentation. To recolor a clip art picture so that it displays colors from the current color scheme, select the clip art, and then choose Recolor from the Tools menu or the shortcut menu.

In the Recolor Picture dialog box, shown in Figure 14-7, find the original color that you want to change in the picture, and select a new color from the adjacent drop-down list of colors. To change only the background and fill colors in the picture without changing the colors of the lines, select the Fills option before you start changing colors.

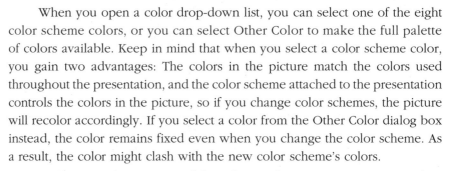

When you open a color drop-down list, you can select one of the eight color scheme colors, or you can select Other Color to make the full palette of colors available. Keep in mind that when you select a color scheme color, you gain two advantages: The colors in the picture match the colors used throughout the presentation, and the color scheme attached to the presentation controls the colors in the picture, so if you change color schemes, the picture will recolor accordingly. If you select a color from the Other Color dialog box instead, the color remains fixed even when you change the color scheme. As a result, the color might clash with the new color scheme's colors.

You can recolor as many of the colors in the picture as you want. Then click Preview to see the results. When the new colors of the picture are satisfactory, click OK.

Adding Clip Art to the Gallery

The ClipArt Gallery comes with a substantial number of images, but you may have additional clip art pictures on your system that were installed as part of other software or were purchased separately. Many word processing applications come with small libraries of clip art, for example. By adding the clip art that is already on your system to PowerPoint's ClipArt Gallery, you can view and gain access to all your clip art in one central place.

To add a clip art image to the Gallery, click Organize in the Microsoft ClipArt Gallery dialog box. Then, in the Organize ClipArt dialog box shown in Figure 14-8, click Add Pictures to add a picture to the Gallery. The Add Pictures to ClipArt Gallery dialog box opens, and you can use the Look in drop-down list to locate the clip art file you want to add. After you find and select it, click Open. PowerPoint automatically locates the correct graphics filter and imports the slide into the Gallery. You then see the Picture Properties dialog box, shown in Figure 14-9. Type a description for the picture, and then select which category you want it stored in. If you want to create a new category, click New Category and create the category. Once you've set all of the properties, click OK. The clip art is added to the Gallery in the category you specified.

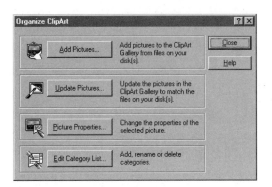

FIGURE 14-8
The Organize ClipArt dialog box.

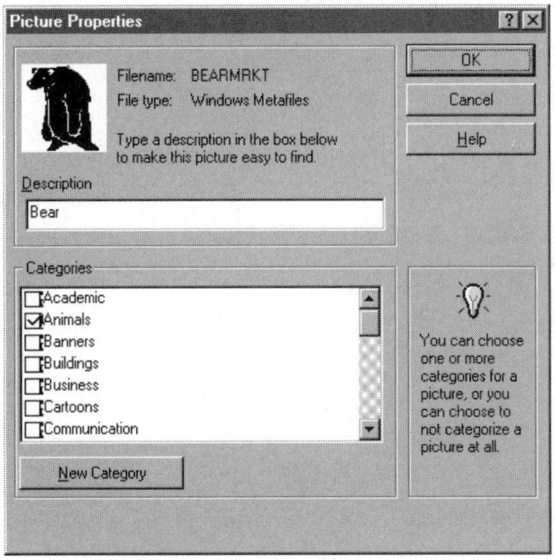

FIGURE 14-9
The Picture Properties dialog box.

The Update Pictures option in the Organize ClipArt dialog box allows you to refresh the Gallery, removing pictures whose files you have deleted, rereading pictures whose files you have changed, and adding new pictures that you have added to your system. The Picture Properties option and the Edit Category List option allow you to edit the description of a picture and create, delete, or rename a category of clip art, respectively.

> **TIP**   You can change the description of a picture, move it to another category in the ClipArt Gallery, or create a new category to put it in by pointing to the picture in the ClipArt Gallery and clicking the right mouse button. Choose Picture Properties from the shortcut menu to make changes, or choose Delete Picture to remove the picture from the ClipArt Gallery. You can delete, rename, or create a category by pointing to the category name in the Categories list, clicking the right mouse button, and choosing the appropriate command from the shortcut menu.

Importing a Picture from Another Application

You may want to add a particular graphic to a presentation but not maintain it in the ClipArt Gallery. Perhaps the graphic is customized for a special presentation and will never be used again. To directly import a graphic from a graphic file, choose Picture from the Insert menu while you are in Slide view. Then, in the Insert Picture dialog box, shown in Figure 14-10, use the Look in drop-down list to navigate to the appropriate folder. Select the graphic file you want, and then click OK to place the graphic on the current slide.

FIGURE 14-10

The Insert Picture dialog box.

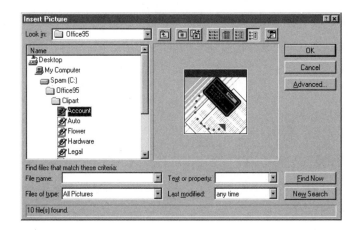

PowerPoint can import graphic files of two types: vector and bitmap. Vector files are produced by drawing and graphing programs, and contain an arrangement of individual objects—circles, rectangles, lines, filled areas, and text characters, for example. Bitmapped files contain a picture that is composed of a pattern of dots, much as newspaper photos are composed of tiny dots.

Because vector files contain objects, they can be easily edited. You can remove or resize an object to change the picture and leave other objects that are underneath untouched. Most clip art is provided in vector format so that it can be easily edited and resized to fit any need. Bitmapped files can be edited, too, but not as easily as vector files. To erase part of a bitmap, you must erase the dots, leaving a hole in the picture. Parts of objects that appeared to be behind the object you've erased are erased, too. But with their many dots, bitmaps can represent a photographic picture accurately, which is why software that you use with a scanner generates a bitmapped version of a photograph rather than a vector file. Therefore, if you intend to place a scanned image in a presentation—a photograph of a person or a scanned logo, for example—you must always import a bitmapped file.

Table 14-1 identifies the graphic file types you can import.

File Format	Type
Windows Bitmap (.BMP)	Bitmap
Windows Metafile (.WMF)	Vector
Computer Graphics Metafile (.CGM)	Vector
Encapsulated PostScript (.EPS)	Vector
Tagged Image File Format (.TIF)	Bitmap
PCX (.PCX)	Bitmap
Macintosh PICT (.PCT)	Bitmap
Micrografx Designer/Draw (.DRW)	Vector
CompuServe GIF (.GIF)	Bitmap
AutoCAD Format 2-D (.DXF)	Vector
CorelDRAW! 3.0 (.CDR)	Vector
DrawPerfect (.WPG)	Vector
Kodak Photo CD (.PCD)	Bitmap
Lotus 1-2-3 Graphics (.PIC)	Vector
True Vision Targa (.TGA)	Bitmap
Windows DIB (.DIB)	Bitmap
HP Graphics Language (.HGL)	Vector
JPEG	Bitmap

TABLE 14-1

The graphic file types you can import.

NOTE You can only import file types for which you've installed
a graphic filter. The Microsoft Office applications share the same
graphic filters, so if you installed a graphic filter when you installed
Word or Excel, for example, you can use the same graphic filter in
PowerPoint.

Adding a Bitmapped Image to a Slide

To add a bitmapped image to a slide, choose Picture from the Insert menu
while you are in Slide view. When the Insert Picture dialog box appears, as
shown earlier, select Windows Bitmap from the Files of type drop-down list.
Next, use the Look in drop-down list to navigate to the appropriate folder.
Then select the file you want, and click OK to import the file.

The imported bitmap appears on the current slide, ready to be moved
and resized to suit your needs. To move the bitmap, drag it to a new location
on the slide. To resize the bitmap, drag one of its handles in the desired direction. To maintain the bitmap's proportions, drag a corner handle. To stretch
the bitmap, drag a handle in the middle of one of the bitmap's sides.

NOTE If you added a bitmapped file to the ClipArt Gallery,
you can borrow the bitmap from the Gallery by following the
instructions in "Using the ClipArt Gallery," page 362.

After you stretch a bitmap out of shape, you can return the picture to its
original proportions by choosing Scale from the Draw menu, selecting the
Relative to Original Picture Size option in the Scale dialog box, and clicking
OK. Then you can resize the picture with its proper proportions by dragging
a corner handle or by entering a Scale To percentage in the Scale dialog box.
Select Best Scale for Slide Show to let PowerPoint scale the bitmap for you.

TIP Bitmaps take somewhat longer to draw than other
objects on a slide. Therefore, you might want to draw a
box on the slide to use as a temporary placeholder for a
bitmap while you create and format other elements of the
presentation. When the presentation is otherwise complete, you can import the bitmap.

Placing a Bitmap on the Background

By switching to the slide master before you insert a bitmap, you can place the bitmap on the background of every slide in a presentation except the title slide. First, choose Master and then Slide Master from the View menu. Then use the Insert Picture dialog box to place the bitmap on the slide master. If you want to place the bitmap behind the presentation text, select the bitmap, and choose Send to Back from the Draw menu. The figure below shows a bitmapped image on slides 2 through 8 of a presentation. To place a bitmap on the background of the title slide, choose Master and then Title Master from the View menu and follow the same procedure.

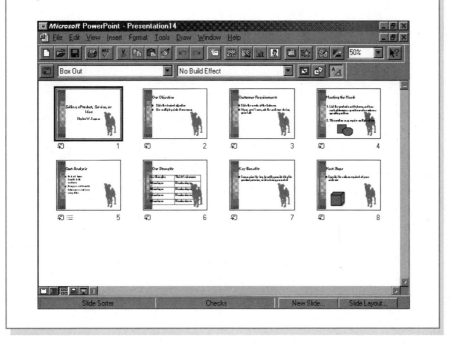

Cropping a Bitmap

To display only a rectangular portion of a bitmap, you can crop the bitmap, moving in the sides or corners to create a small window in which you see only the section of the picture you want displayed. Cropping a bitmap is like using a pair of scissors to cut away the parts of a photo you want to remove.

To crop a bitmap, first select the bitmap, and choose Crop Picture from the Tools menu or the shortcut menu. Then place the mouse pointer, which looks like the cropping icon shown in Figure 14-11, on one of the handles surrounding the bitmap, and drag the handle toward the center of the picture. To display only the left half of a picture, for example, drag the right side handle halfway across the bitmap to the left. You can drag other handles to close in on the part of the picture you want to display. When you're finished, click anywhere outside the bitmap.

FIGURE 14-11

Cropping a photo.

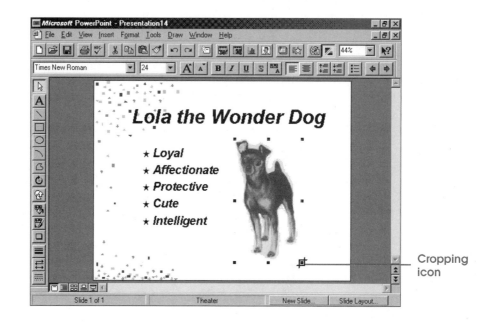

Cropping icon

You can restore parts of a bitmap that have been cropped, by choosing Crop Picture from the Tools menu or the shortcut menu and then dragging the handles back out to the edges of the bitmap with the cropping icon.

Recoloring a Bitmap

You can replace selected colors in a bitmap the same way you replace colors in a clip art picture, using the Recolor command on the Tools menu or the shortcut menu.

See Also   For more information about recoloring a picture, see "Recoloring Clip Art to Match the Current Color Scheme," page 367.

In this part of the book, you learned how to apply the finishing touches to a presentation by adding text, drawings, and pictures. In the next section, you'll learn how to turn your work into something tangible: a printed page, a 35-mm slide, or an electronic presentation called a slide show.

Part 5

SELECT EDITION

Performing
with PowerPoint

Chapter 15

Creating Printed Output and 35-mm Slides

Somehow, printing always seems to be the most difficult part of working with a computer. You work so hard to create a look on the screen, but when you print, the darks are too dark or the lights are too light. And once you print overhead transparencies in landscape orientation, you can't get audience handouts in portrait orientation without jumping through hoops and murmuring incantations over the system.

Well, PowerPoint solves these problems, as you knew it would. It takes care of all the portrait-to-landscape, overhead-to-slide, and screen-to-paper conversions behind the scenes so that you can concentrate on expressing yourself creatively.

In this chapter, you'll learn how to tell PowerPoint exactly what type of output you want to generate. You can print overheads from your slides, or you can print audience handouts with up to six slide miniatures on each page. You can also print the speaker's notes you created in Notes Pages view, or print the presentation to a PostScript file, which you can then take to a service bureau that converts the file to 35-mm slides.

Setting Up the Slides

The first step in creating printed output or 35-mm slides is to check the current slide setup. The slide setup determines the size and orientation of the slides you've created. You may be wondering why you don't have to change the slide setup before starting a presentation. The answer is that you can, but you don't have to. You can leave the default setting, which displays the presentation properly in a slide show and on landscape overheads printed on 8½-by-11-inch pages, and change the slide setup only if you need to print 35-mm slides or custom pages with odd heights and widths.

When you change the slide setup, PowerPoint does all the work to resize and reorient the material on your slides to fit the new page size and orientation. For example, you can create landscape slides, which have a horizontal orientation, and then switch to portrait slides if you need a vertical orientation. In most cases, PowerPoint adjusts everything on your slides so well that you'll think you've been creating portrait slides all along.

To check the slide setup, choose Slide Setup from the File menu. In the Slide Setup dialog box, shown in Figure 15-1, you see options for the slide width and height, the slide number, and the slide orientation.

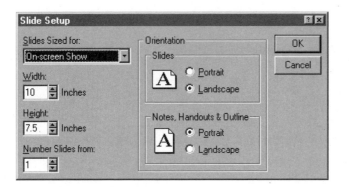

FIGURE 15-1

The Slide Setup
dialog box.

Slide Size

From the Slides Sized for drop-down list in the Slide Setup dialog box, select one of the five preset slide sizes (On-screen Show, Letter Paper, A4 Paper, 35mm Slides, or Overhead), or select Custom and then set a custom width and height in the Width and Height edit boxes.

> NOTE When you select the Custom option, the default settings for the Width and Height are set to the printable area of the page for the current printer.

Slide Numbering

In the Slide Setup dialog box, the number shown in the Number Slides from edit box sets the slide numbering that appears both on the slides and in the slide number indicator at the bottom of the PowerPoint window. Keep in mind that before the number is actually displayed on a slide, you must enter the page number symbol on the slide, by choosing the Slide Number command from the Insert menu.

You can start slide numbering at any number. For example, to number the first slide of the current presentation as 10, type *10* directly in the Number Slides from edit box or click the up arrow at the right end of the edit box to increase the setting to 10.

See Also For more information about numbering slides, see "Inserting the Slide Number, Date, or Time on Selected Slides," page 237.

Slide Orientation

You can set two different slide orientations: one for slides and one for notes, handouts, and outline pages. With these settings, you can print speaker's notes and audience handouts in portrait orientation even when you print slides in landscape orientation.

TIP Slides, outlines, handouts, and speaker's notes have masters that you can embellish with headers and footers, text, slide numbers, and graphics. To open one of the masters, hold down the Shift key as you click the corresponding view button. For example, to open the handout master, hold down the Shift key and click the Slide Sorter View button. To return to one of the standard views, click a view button without pressing the Shift key.

Printing Pages

To begin the printing process, make sure the presentation you want to print is displayed in the active presentation window in PowerPoint, and then choose Print from the File menu or press Ctrl+P. The Print dialog box opens, as shown in Figure 15-2.

FIGURE 15-2

The Print dialog box.

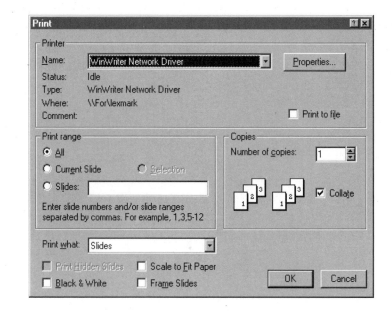

NOTE To bypass the Print dialog box, click the Print button on the Standard toolbar. PowerPoint prints the entire presentation.

The name of the currently selected printer is displayed at the top of the Print dialog box. To print the presentation on a different printer, select a printer from the Name drop-down list. If you want to transport a presentation file to another system for printing, select the Print to File option, which prints the presentation to an output file on disk.

NOTE To access additional options for the currently selected printer, click the Properties button at the top of the Print dialog box.

The Print range options let you print all or selected slides of the presentation. To print the entire presentation, click the All option. To print only the slide shown in Slide view, click the Current Slide option. To print selected slides, click the Slides option and enter the corresponding slide numbers in the Slides edit box. You can separate nonconsecutive slides with commas and separate the first and last number of a range of slides with a hyphen. You can even combine nonconsecutive slides and ranges of slides by using both commas and hyphens. For example, to print slide 3 and also slides 6 through 8, you can enter *3,6-8* in the Slides edit box.

You can increase the number in the Number of copies edit box to print multiple copies of the slides. If you print more than one copy, you can also select the Collate option to print multiple, properly sequenced sets of slides rather than multiple copies of the first page followed by multiple copies of the next page, and so on. Printing collated copies can take considerably longer, because the computer must resend each page to the printer several times rather than send the page once and have the printer churn out multiple copies.

The default setting for the Print what option is Slides, but you can also select Handouts, Notes Pages, or Outline View from the drop-down list.

Another way to select the slides you want to print is to switch to Slide Sorter view or Outline view, and hold down the Shift key as you click each slide or slide icon. Then, when you open the Print dialog box, click the Selection option in the Print range section to print only the selected slides.

NOTE If the presentation contains slides with builds, you can select either Slides (with Builds) or Slides (without Builds) from the Print what drop-down list. When you select Slides (without Builds), only the completely built version of each slide is printed. For more information about builds, see "Assigning Build Effects," page 394.

The Special Print Options

The options at the bottom of the Print dialog box let you make important changes to the way the presentation prints, although the defaults work well in most cases. Each of these special options is described in the following list:

- The Print Hidden Slides option prints slides that you have hidden using the Hide Slide command on the Tools menu.

- The Black & White option prints color slides properly on a black and white printer, such as a black and white laser printer. Black & White replaces fills in objects with white, and it replaces color patterns with patterns of black and white. This option also adds a thin black outline to objects that do not otherwise have borders, except text objects. If you select the Black & White option to print your presentation, some objects may not appear the way you'd like them to. For example, a dark object may no longer be visible against a dark background. You can adjust the color of an individual object by selecting the object and using the Colors and Lines command on the Format or shortcut menu. (If you want to change the color of a text selection, use the Font command on the Format menu.)

- The Scale to Fit Paper option properly scales the slides to fit the printed page even if the slides have been set up for a different page size. For example, to print a slide that you sized for 35-mm slides (in the Slide Setup dialog box) on an 8½-by-11-inch page, you can use the Scale to Fit Paper option.

- The Frame Slides option prints a narrow frame around each slide. This option is useful if you want to display your slides as overheads.

Figure 15-3 shows versions of a color slide printed on a black and white laser printer. The left page was printed with the default print options, and the right page was printed with the Black & White option.

Printing Handouts and Speaker's Notes

To print audience handouts, choose Print from the File menu or press Ctrl+P, and then select one of the three Handouts options from the Print what drop-down list in the Print dialog box. These options allow you to print two, three, or six slides per page. The orientation of the handouts is determined by

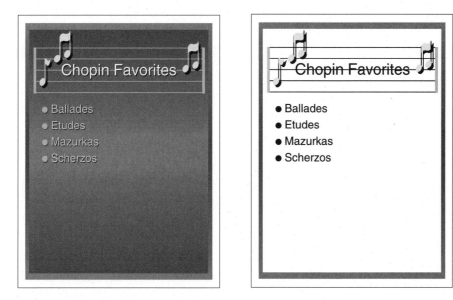

FIGURE 15-3
A page printed with two different print options: default (left) and Black & White (right).

the Orientation setting in the Slide Setup dialog box shown earlier. Figure 15-4 on the next page shows a handout page with three slides per page, which leaves audience members plenty of room to jot down notes about each slide.

To print speaker's notes, select Notes Pages from the Print what drop-down list. As with handouts, the orientation of the notes pages is determined by the Orientation setting in the Slide Setup dialog box.

Printing the Outline

To print the presentation outline just as it appears in Outline view, select Outline View from the Print what drop-down list box in the Print dialog box. The outline prints with as much detail as is currently displayed in Outline view. Collapsed entries do not print.

The size of the text on the printed page is affected by the zoom percentage in Outline view. If the zoom percentage is at 50%, for example, text formatted to appear as 40-point in Outline view prints as 20-point text on the page.

FIGURE 15-4

A handout page
with three slides
on the page.

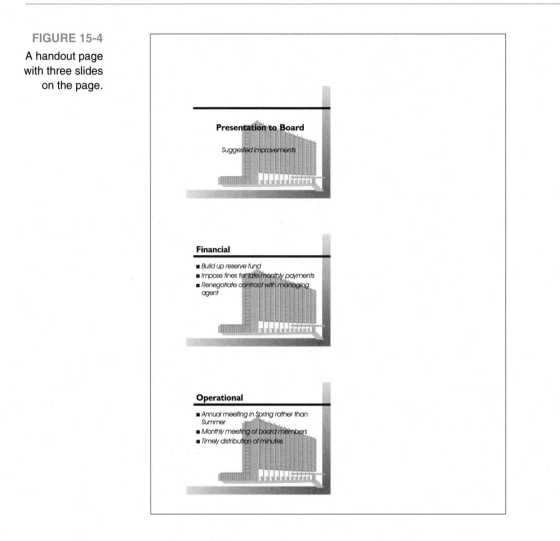

Creating 35-mm Slides

If you're lucky enough to have a film recorder attached to your system and the Windows printer driver for the film recorder, you can select the film recorder as your printer and then print to the film recorder as if you were printing to any other printer. The film recorder creates an image of each slide on 35-mm slide film. You can then develop the film to produce 35-mm slides. You may need to refer to the documentation for the device for special instructions on using it with a Windows-based application such as PowerPoint.

Most people do not have large and expensive film recorders at their disposal, however. Instead, they rely on a service bureau that takes a PostScript file generated from PowerPoint and feeds it into a film recorder. Many service bureaus provide overnight service, returning the developed 35-mm slides by next-day delivery. A local service bureau may even provide same-day service.

PowerPoint comes with software that makes it especially easy to use the Genigraphics Service Center as your service bureau. When you install Power-Point, you can also install the Genigraphics Wizard, which automatically creates a PostScript file that Genigraphics can accept. When you install the Geni-graphics Wizard, a communications program called GraphicsLink is also installed so that you can transmit the PostScript file to the Genigraphics Service Center by modem.

To create a PostScript file to send to Genigraphics, choose the Send to Genigraphics command from the File menu to activate the Genigraphics Wizard. The Genigraphics Wizard prompts you for the type of products or electronic services you need in addition to your mailing and billing information. You can use the wizard to send your request electronically or save it to a file to send later either by disk or modem.

If you have a modem, you can launch the GraphicsLink software to send any files saved earlier by the Genigraphics Wizard to Genigraphics over the telephone line.

In the following chapter, you'll learn about an alternative method of presenting with PowerPoint that avoids printing: the electronic presentation, which displays your work in a slide show on the computer screen. However, even if you display a slide show, you may still want to print audience handouts so that your viewers can take home pages for future reference.

Chapter 16

Creating Slide Shows

The payoff for all your hard work in PowerPoint comes at presentation time, when your slides go on display. Traditionally, 35-mm slides have been the medium with the most professional look, but a newer presentation method, the electronic slide show, is rapidly overtaking slides.

Electronic presentations—PowerPoint calls them slide shows—display your images right on the computer screen. If your monitor is large enough, you can use it in a conference room, but for a sizable gathering, you can use a computer projector or LCD projection panel to display a PowerPoint slide show on a large screen. The most obvious advantage of a slide show is the fancy transitions you can include between slides. Fades, wipes, dissolves, and other effects give your show the "wow" power of a Hollywood production. But slide shows also offer many other, less obvious advantages.

Bulleted text slides can incorporate automatic builds, also called *progressive disclosures*, that gradually reveal each bulleted item as the speaker refers to it. Slides can also include video, sound, animation, and music. By embedding information from another application, you can integrate a drill-down document in a slide—perhaps a Microsoft Word letter or a Microsoft Excel spreadsheet—that you can open to reveal supporting information, such as the figures behind a confident projection. And with PowerPoint's special mark-up mode, you can mark up slides during a show, sportscaster-style.

In this chapter, you'll learn how to add transition and build effects to the slides of a presentation and how to run a slide show in Slide Show view. You'll also learn about advanced slide show techniques, such as adding multimedia objects and creating interactive shows that can branch off at the presenter's discretion.

Developing a Slide Show

Just by creating a basic sequence of slides, you've already created a simple slide show in PowerPoint. To see the slide show, move to the first slide, and then switch to Slide Show view by clicking the Slide Show button at the bottom of the presentation window or by choosing Slide Show from the View menu. The first slide fills the entire screen and remains there until you click the left mouse button or press the Right arrow key, which advances the show to the next slide. Initially, each slide simply replaces the previous slide, like an actual slide show with 35-mm slides and a projector. But as you'll find out in this section, you can add transition, build, and animation effects and even hide particular slides to create a presentation that will really wake up your audience.

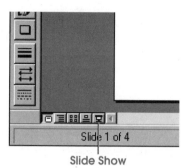

Slide Show

Assigning Transitions

Transitions are special effects that you can include between slides. During a presentation, as you progress from one slide to another, a transition "draws" the next slide on the screen using one of a variety of techniques. You can also assign a sound to be played when you change slides.

The best place to assign a transition effect is in Slide Sorter view, where you can see a number of slides at once and preview the transition effects. To switch to Slide Sorter view, click the Slide Sorter View button or select Slide Sorter from the View menu. You can then use the buttons and list boxes on the Slide Sorter toolbar to specify a transition effect for any or all slides.

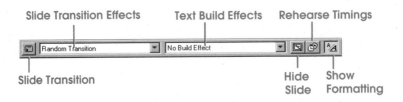

To assign a basic transition effect to a slide, click the slide and then select a transition effect from the Slide Transition Effects drop-down list. Watch the slide carefully in Slide Sorter view, and you'll see that it previews the transition. If you want to see the preview again, click the small transition effect icon that has appeared just below the slide. Figure 16-1 shows these icons.

FIGURE 16-1

Click a transition effect icon to preview the transition effect applied to the slide.

Transition effect icon

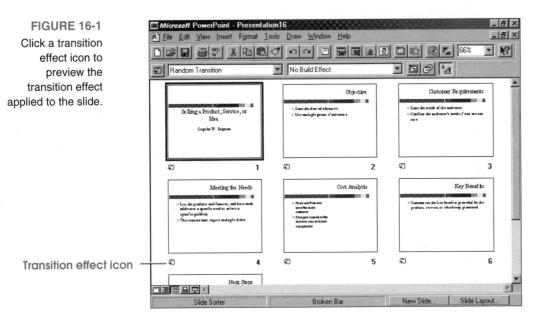

To apply the same transition effect to slides in a sequence, select the slides and then select an effect from the Slide Transition Effects drop-down list. Remember, you can select multiple slides by holding down the Shift key as you click each slide or by drawing a selection box around a group of slides using the mouse pointer. To apply a single effect to all the slides, choose Select All from the Edit menu or press Ctrl+A, and then select an effect.

TIP If you select the same transition effect for all the slides in a slide show, you might consider using a different effect for the title slides of each segment of your presentation. Simply select the title slides, and then select a different effect from the Slide Transition Effects drop-down list.

By clicking the Slide Transition button to the left of the Slide Transition Effects box on the Slide Sorter toolbar, you can open the Slide Transition dialog box shown in Figure 16-2. (Another way to access this dialog box is to select one or more slides and choose Slide Transition from the Tools menu, or click the right mouse button and choose Slide Transition from the shortcut menu.) In the Slide Transition dialog box, you can select not only a transition effect, but also a speed for the effect and the amount of time you want the slide to remain on the screen. The default Advance option, Only on mouse click, requires you to click the left mouse button or press the keys listed in Table 16-1 on page 401 during the slide show to advance to the next slide. If you have a Windows 95–compatible sound card installed, you can also add sound transitions to your slide show by selecting sounds from the Sound drop-down list. If you want the sound(s) to run continuously during a slide show, select the Loop until next sound option.

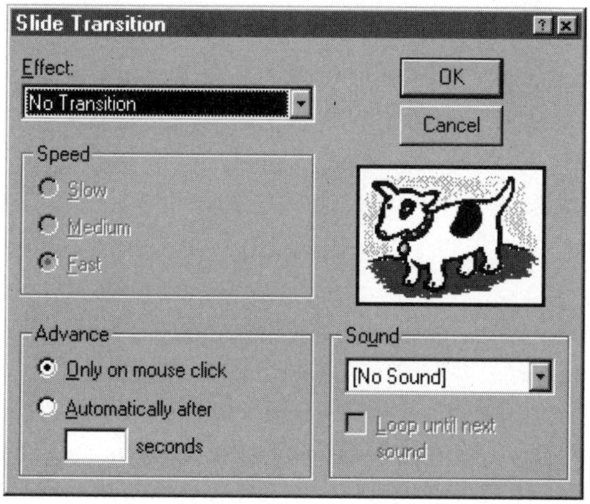

FIGURE 16-2
The Slide Transition dialog box.

TIP Transition effects are undoubtedly snazzy, but don't let them detract from the content of your presentation by using too many different effects during a slide show or by setting them all to Slow to heighten the drama. Instead, use Fast for the transition speed whenever possible, and use one effect repeatedly, changing effects only for new presentation segments.

Assigning Build Effects

The bulleted text items on text slides can appear either all at once or sequentially during a slide show. To have the bulleted text "build" on a slide, you must assign a build effect by selecting one or more text slides with bulleted items and then choosing an effect from the Text Build Effects drop-down list on the Slide Sorter toolbar or from the Animation Settings dialog box shown in Figure 16-3.

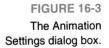

FIGURE 16-3

The Animation Settings dialog box.

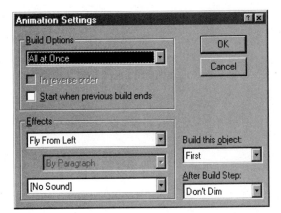

To open the Animation Settings dialog box in Slide Sorter view, select one or more slides, and choose Build Slide Text and then Other from the Tools menu or the shortcut menu. If you happen to be in Slide view, you can access the Animation Settings dialog box by selecting an object on a slide and choosing Animation Settings from the Tools menu, or by clicking the Animation Effects button on the Standard toolbar to display the Animation Effects toolbar and then clicking the Animation Settings button.

In the Build Options section of the Animation Settings dialog box, you can select whether the bulleted items are built all at once or by paragraph level. You can also specify that bulleted items appear in reverse order, and that one build automatically starts when the previous build ends. (If you don't select the Start when previous build ends option, you must manually display each bulleted item by clicking the left mouse button.)

In the Effects section of the Animation Settings dialog box, you can select a build effect to draw each new bulleted item. (The build effects drop-down list in the dialog box provides the same options as the Text Build Effects drop-down list on the Slide Sorter toolbar.) You can also specify whether bulleted items are built letter by letter, word by word, and so on; and you can select a sound effect like those available in the Slide Transitions dialog box shown earlier on page 393.

Use the After Build Step drop-down list in the lower right corner of the Animation Settings dialog box to select a color with which to dim the bulleted items once they have been revealed and discussed. (The dimmed items remain readable on the screen.) Each newly revealed bulleted item then appears in the bright text color. You can also hide the bulleted items rather than dim them.

In Slide view, if you select a text object on a slide, such as a title or bulleted text object, and then open the Animation Settings dialog box, you can use the Build this object drop-down list to specify the order in which you want the selected object to appear on the slide during a slide show.

After you apply a build effect, an animation settings icon appears in Slide Sorter view next to any transition effect icon. Although you can click the transition effect icon to preview a slide's transition effect, you cannot preview a slide's build effect before you run the show. The animation settings icon simply denotes slides with builds.

Using the Animation Effects Toolbar

As mentioned earlier, you can display the Animation Effects toolbar shown in Figure 16-4 by clicking the Animation Effects button on the Standard toolbar. (Or choose Toolbars from the View menu, and select the Animation Effects option.) You can then use the toolbar buttons to include additional effects in your slide show. Keep in mind, however, that in order to use most of the buttons on the Animation Effects toolbar, you must be in Slide view and you must first select an object on the current slide, such as a title or bulleted text. When you have time, explore these buttons further. You'll have a blast sending bullets flying and dropping in titles out of thin air.

FIGURE 16-4

The Animation
Effects toolbar.

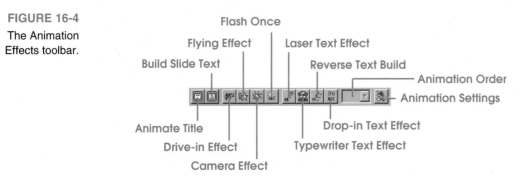

Hiding Slides

To hide one or more slides during a slide show, select the slides, and click the Hide Slide button on the Slide Sorter toolbar or choose Hide Slide from the Tools menu or the shortcut menu. A slash appears through the slide number in Slide Sorter view to indicate that the slide is hidden. Although the hidden slide continues to display in Slide Sorter view, it does not appear in a slide show. To show a hidden slide, move the mouse pointer over the current slide, and when the button shown in Figure 16-5 appears in the lower left corner of the slide, click the button to display the pop-up menu also shown in Figure 16-5. Next choose Go To from the pop-up menu. If a hidden slide follows the current slide, the Hidden Slide command becomes available on the Go To submenu. Choose this command to show the hidden slide. To display a hidden slide without opening the pop-up menu, press the H key.

FIGURE 16-5

The slide show
pop-up menu
and button.

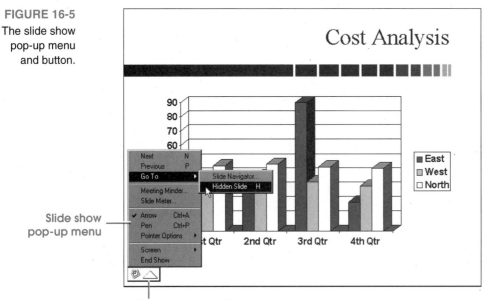

To unhide a hidden slide, select the slide and click the Hide Slide button again or choose Hide Slide again from the Tools menu or the shortcut menu.

> **NOTE** You can assign transitions, apply builds and effects, and hide slides in Slide view by moving to a slide and then choosing Slide Transition, Hide Slide, or Build Slide Text from the Tools menu. But you cannot preview transition effects in Slide view, so you might prefer to create the show in Slide Sorter view.

See Also For more information about the slide show pop-up menu, see "Controlling the Slide Show with the Mouse," page 400.

Making a Slide Show Interactive

What could be better than a slide show with fancy transitions and animation effects? A slide show that lets viewers control what they see and when they see it! PowerPoint's new Interactive Settings command lets you add buttons or hotspots to your slides so that when the button or hotspot is clicked, the viewer can jump to any slide in the slide show, play a video, play a sound, or even start another software application. Of course, you can use the Interactive Settings command to control the slide show when you are the presenter, but the command's real power lies in its ability to let your viewers move through a slide show at their own pace and in their own order.

You can make any image you import or graphic object you draw interactive. Simply select the image or graphic object in Slide view, and choose the Interactive Settings command from the Tools menu. The Interactive Settings dialog box appears, as shown in Figure 16-6.

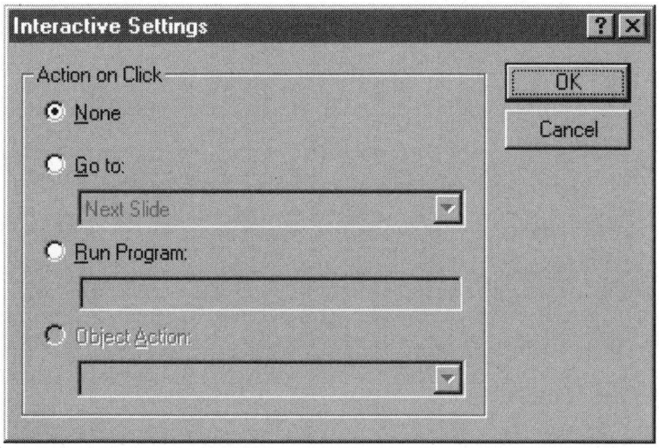

FIGURE 16-6

The Interactive Settings dialog box.

Next, select one of the interactivity options: Go to, which allows viewers to move to a specific slide when they click the interactive object; Play Sound, which allows viewers to play a sound when they click the interactive object; Run Program, which allows viewers to open a different application when they click the interactive object; and Object Action, which allows viewers to play, edit, or open a media clip or underlying application when they click the interactive object.

When you select the Go to option, you must also specify the slide you want viewers to move to by selecting one of the slide options from the Go to drop-down list. (If you select the Slide option at the bottom of the list, the Go To Slide dialog box appears. You can then select a specific slide, even if it's hidden.) When you select the Play Sound option, you must also select a sound to be played from the drop-down list. When you select the Run Program option, you must enter the full pathname for the application you want viewers to open. (For example, enter the pathname for a Word document that you want viewers to read or print.) When you select the Object Action option, you must also select one of the actions in the Object Action drop-down list. (For example, select Edit to allow viewers to edit the underlying data for an Excel chart.)

TIP You can supply your viewers with additional information that they only see if they want to by creating a slide with the information, hiding the slide, and then making the slide the target of an interactive object on another slide.

Running a Slide Show in Slide Show View

As you know, when you develop a slide show in Slide Sorter view, you can preview the transition effects for individual slides. But to see the transitions full-screen and to see the builds in bulleted text slides, you must switch to Slide Show view, where the show takes place.

Starting the Slide Show

Before you actually start a slide show, you can designate the slide at which you want the show to begin, even if the slide is hidden. Simply select the slide in Slide Sorter view or turn to the slide in Slide view. Then, when you click the Slide Show button at the bottom of the presentation window, the slide show starts at the currently selected slide. To advance to the next slide, click the left mouse button or press N. To return to the previous slide, press P or the Backspace key. To discontinue the slide show and return to the previous view, press Esc, Ctrl+Break, or the minus key on the numeric keypad.

To run the entire show, select the first slide, and then click the Slide Show button or choose the Slide Show command from the View menu. When you choose the Slide Show command, the Slide Show dialog box shown in Figure 16-7 appears. You can then select All and click Show to run the entire show, or you can enter a starting and ending slide in the From and To edit boxes and click Show to view a segment of the slide show.

FIGURE 16-7
The Slide Show dialog box.

> **TIP** To run a slide show as an unattended demonstration (in a store window or building lobby, for example), click Loop Continuously Until 'Esc' in the Slide Show dialog box. The show will run as an ever-repeating loop that can only be interrupted when someone presses the Esc key. To make the Esc key unavailable, you can remove the keyboard and the mouse after you start the show and leave only the monitor and system unit.

Controlling the Slide Show with the Mouse

We all like to control the show, but it's usually not as easy as PowerPoint makes it. During a slide show, you can use the button and pop-up menu, shown in Figure 16-5 on page 396, to control various aspects of the show. As mentioned earlier, the button appears in the lower left corner of the current slide as soon as you move the mouse pointer. You can then click the button to display the slide show pop-up menu.

TIP To hide the pop-up menu button during a slide show, choose Options from the Tools menu, and deselect the Show Popup Menu Button option on the View tab of the Options dialog box. You can still access the pop-up menu by clicking the right mouse button during a slide show (unless you also deselect the Popup Menu on Right Mouse Click option in the Options dialog box).

The Next and Previous commands on the pop-up menu let you move forward or backward through the slides in your slide show. To move to a specific slide, choose Go To and then Slide Navigator from the menu, and when the Slide Navigator dialog box appears, select a slide and click Go To. As discussed on page 396, you can use the Hidden Slide command on the Go To submenu to move to any hidden slides in your slide show. To stop a slide show at any time during your presentation, simply choose End Show from the pop-up menu.

The remaining commands on the slide show pop-up menu let you access the Meeting Minder for note taking, turn on the Slide Meter to gauge your progress during a slide show, and change the arrow pointer to a pen so that you can mark up slides (you can even change the color of the pen's "ink"). You can also pause an automatic slide show or replace the current slide with a black screen (say, during an interruption in the proceedings). With the exception of Meeting Minder, you'll learn more about these commands in the following sections.

See Also For more information about the Meeting Minder command, see Chapter 17, "Giving Your Presentation at Home or On the Road," page 413.

Controlling the Slide Show with the Keyboard

In addition to the slide show pop-up menu, you can use the keys listed in Table 16-1 to control various aspects of the show.

Press or Enter This	To Perform This Action
Spacebar, Right arrow, Down arrow, PgDn, or N	Advance to next slide
Backspace, Left arrow, Up arrow, PgUp, or P	Return to previous slide
Slide number+Enter	Go to slide number
B or period	Black screen/resume
W or comma	White screen/resume
Ctrl+A	Show mouse pointer as arrow
Ctrl+P	Show mouse pointer as pen
S or + (numeric keypad)	Pause/resume automatic show
H	Show/hide hidden slide
Ctrl+H	Hide pointer now
Ctrl+L	Hide pointer always
Esc	End show

TABLE 16-1

The Slide Show keyboard controls.

Rehearsing Automatic Slide Show Timings

To create a slide show that proceeds on its own from slide to slide while you speak, you can simply enter the amount of time you want each slide to remain on the screen in the Slide Transition dialog box. A better method, however, is to practice giving the presentation first and have PowerPoint record the length of time you keep each slide on the screen. You can then use PowerPoint's findings to determine the amount of time to display each slide. You can also ascertain the overall length of the show.

To enter the display time manually for each slide, first select the slide in Slide Sorter view and click the Slide Transition button on the Slide Sorter toolbar, or move to the slide in Slide view and choose Slide Transition from the Tools menu or the shortcut menu. In the Slide Transition dialog box, enter the number of seconds in the Advance section's Automatically after edit box.

To record the slide durations during a rehearsal of the slide show, click the Rehearse Timings button on the Slide Sorter toolbar; or choose Slide Show from the View menu, select Rehearse New Timings in the Slide Show dialog box, and then click Show. When the slide show begins, the Rehearsal dialog box shown in Figure 16-8 is displayed in the lower right corner of the slide.

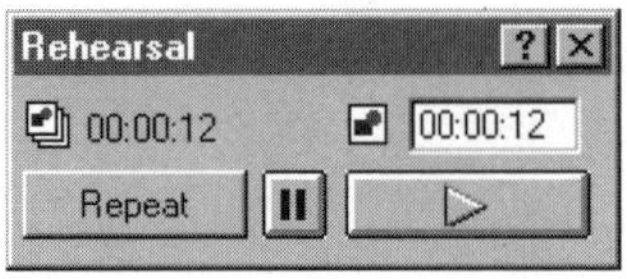

FIGURE 16-8

The Rehearsal
dialog box.

Practice giving the presentation, advancing the slides manually when needed. As you speak, the elapsed time for the slide show is displayed on the left in the Rehearsal dialog box, and the elapsed time for the current slide is displayed on the right. To advance to the next slide, click the left mouse button as you normally would, press P, or click the arrow button in the Rehearsal dialog box. You can also pause the slide show by clicking the button with the double vertical line, or you can click Repeat to repeat the current slide if you want to re-record the time for that slide.

After you complete the last slide, a dialog box shows the total length of the show and gives you the option to place the new timings in Slide Sorter view. If you click Yes, the timing for each slide appears under the slide in Slide Sorter view. To run the show with the timings, choose Slide Show from the View menu, select the Use Slide Timings option in the Slide Show dialog box, and then click Show to activate the timer.

To remove slide timings, select one or more slides in Slide Sorter view, click the Slide Transition button on the Slide Sorter toolbar, and then select Only on mouse click in the Advance section of the Slide Transition dialog box.

Using Slide Meter

If you want to manually run a slide show that has rehearsed timings (to allow for interruptions, questions, ad-libbing, and so forth), you can use Power-Point's Slide Meter to gauge your progress against the rehearsed times. To display Slide Meter during a show, choose the Slide Meter command from the slide show pop-up menu. The dialog box shown in Figure 16-9 appears.

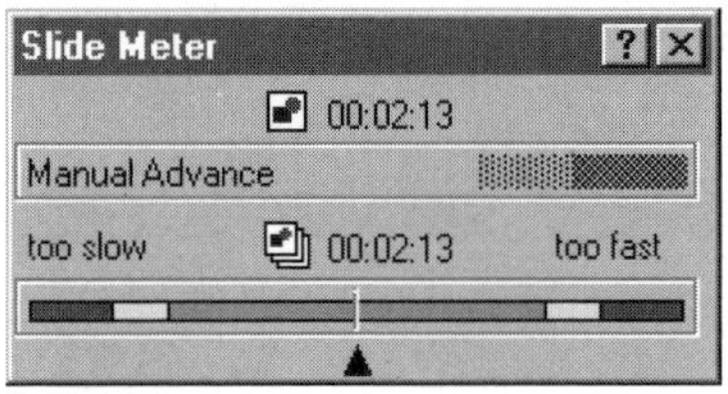

FIGURE 16-9

The Slide Meter
dialog box.

The clock at the top of the Slide Meter dialog box records your time for the current slide, and the clock at the bottom of the dialog box records your cumulative time for the slide show. In addition, the progress bar in the middle of the dialog box measures how you are doing against the original rehearsed time. If you are within the time, the progress bar displays green boxes. As you get closer to the end of the rehearsed time, yellow boxes appear. And when you exceed the time, red boxes are displayed. At the bottom of the Slide Meter dialog box, a second bar indicates, on the basis of the rehearsed timings, whether you are going too slow or too fast.

Marking Up Slides

To call special attention to a slide, or if you just don't know what to do with your hands during a slide show, you can use the mouse pointer to draw directly on slides. You can circle items, draw arrows, or add written comments, much as sportscasters do when drawing football plays on TV during a game.

To draw on a slide, click the pop-up menu button and choose Pen from the slide show pop-up menu or press Ctrl+P to activate the pen pointer. Next press the left mouse button while moving the pointer on the slide to express yourself dramatically with scribblings. To clear everything you've drawn on a slide, choose Screen and then Erase Pen from the pop-up menu or press the E key (for erase). Figure 16-10 shows annotations drawn during a slide show.

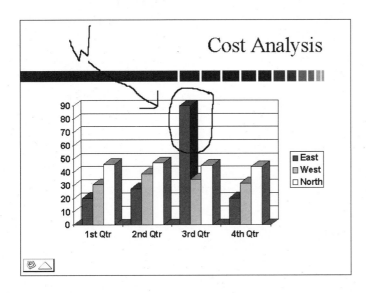

FIGURE 16-10

Annotations drawn on a slide.

403

You can also change the color of the pen pointer's "ink" by choosing Pointer Options and then Pen Color from the slide show pop-up menu. When you're finished marking up your slides, choose Arrow from the pop-up menu or press Ctrl+A to return to the normal mouse pointer.

TIP If you want to hide the mouse pointer, whether it's an arrow or a pen, choose Hide Now (Ctrl+H) or Hide Always (Ctrl+L) from the Pointer Options submenu on the slide show pop-up menu. To make the pointer reappear, press Ctrl+A.

Special Slide Show Features

Special slide show features let you create basic multimedia presentations, add backup documents, and create interactive shows that can branch to other presentations. You can even instruct PowerPoint to run a series of slide shows, one right after another.

Adding Video, Sound, and Music

Nothing brings a presentation to life like adding multimedia objects—video, sound, and music—to a slide show. As long as you have the objects available on your system and you have a Windows 95–compatible sound card installed, adding multimedia objects to a presentation is straightforward, and the effect is truly dramatic.

On any slide, you can embed one or more objects—perhaps a short music clip as the slide fades into view, followed by a video quote from someone involved with the project. These clips can play automatically when the slide appears, or after a set interval. A presenter can also double-click on a slide's video, sound, or music icon to start playing a particular object.

When you add a slide to a presentation, you can select any one of the Text and Media Clip autolayouts that has a *Double click to add media clip* placeholder. Double-clicking this placeholder leads to the Media Player window shown in Figure 16-11.

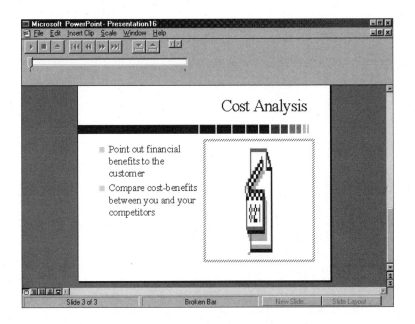

FIGURE 16-11
The Media Player
window.

TIP   You can also add a multimedia object to a slide by
moving to the slide in Slide view, choosing the Object
command from the Insert menu, and selecting the object
type in the Insert Object dialog box.

With the Media Player window open on your screen, choose one of the
commands at the top of the Insert Clip menu to add a media clip to the current
slide. After you choose a command, the Open dialog box appears so that you
can select the file containing the video or sound clip you want. The three most
popular multimedia file types are AVI (Video for Windows files), MID (MIDI
music files), and WAV (sound files).

After you select a file, an icon representing the media clip appears on
the slide. You can then use the Media Player control bar shown in Figure 16-12
on the next page to play the clip.

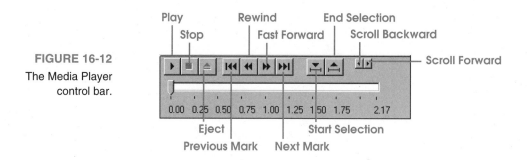

FIGURE 16-12

The Media Player
control bar.

Most of the buttons on the control bar are self-explanatory. For example, to play a media clip, click the Play button on the control bar. To rewind a clip, click the Rewind button. To navigate through a media clip, use the Scroll Backward and Scroll Forward buttons. You can also use the Start Selection and End Selection buttons to mark specific sections of the media clip, and then use the Previous Mark and Next Mark buttons to move quickly to those sections. (If you don't mark any sections, the Previous Mark and End Mark buttons take you to the beginning and end of your clip, respectively.)

The Options Command

In addition to the Media Player control bar, you can use the Options command on the Media Player's Edit menu to control how a media clip is played. When you choose the Options command, the dialog box shown in Figure 16-13 appears.

FIGURE 16-13

This dialog box
appears when you
choose Options
from the Media
Player's Edit
menu.

The following list describes each option in the Options dialog box:

- Auto Rewind automatically returns you to the beginning of the clip after it has finished playing.

- Auto Repeat plays the clip continuously until you click the Stop button on the Media Player control bar.

- Control Bar On Playback displays the Media Player control bar when the clip plays.

- Caption lets you add a caption to the clip's icon on the slide. Simply type the caption in the Caption edit box.

- Border around object adds a narrow black border to the clip's icon on the slide.

- Play in client document plays the clip without opening the Media Player window.

If the clip you've selected is a video clip, you can also set the resolution of the colors in the clip to VGA so that the colors are displayed more clearly on a VGA monitor.

The Properties Command

The Properties command on the Media Player's Insert Clip menu changes, depending on the type of media clip you've selected. For a video clip, the Properties command controls the size of the screen on which the clip is played. For a sound clip, the Properties command determines the amount of memory reserved to play or record a particular sound. Because PowerPoint intuits whether you've selected a video or sound clip, you can set a property by simply choosing Properties from the Insert Clip menu.

The Scale Menu Commands

The scale bar located just below the buttons on the Media Player control bar lets you keep track of your location in a media clip. You can use the commands on the Media Player's Scale menu to specify the type of scale you want to display based on the type of media clip you are playing. For example, if you want to play a sound clip, choose the Time command from the Scale menu; and if you want to play a video clip, choose the Frames command.

 TIP   If you have a CD-ROM drive and you want to track a CD you're playing, choose the Tracks command from the Media Player's Scale menu.

Finishing Up a Multimedia Presentation

When you have set all of the initial options and properties, you can move along to another slide, or close the Media Player window and continue working with the current slide. You can always reset options or properties by selecting the clip icon and clicking the right mouse button to display the shortcut menu. Choose Open Media Clip Object to return to the Media Player controls or Edit Media Clip Object to replace the current media clip with a new one. Play Media Object plays your clip with all of the options and properties you've selected.

> **TIP** You can use the Crop Picture and Recolor options on the shortcut menu to change the appearance of the media clip's icon on the slide.

With the media clip's options set, you are ready to specify how the clip will play for your audience. A media clip has animation settings, just like any other object. Select the clip icon, and choose Animation Settings from the Tools menu or the shortcut menu to display the Animation Settings dialog box shown in Figure 16-14.

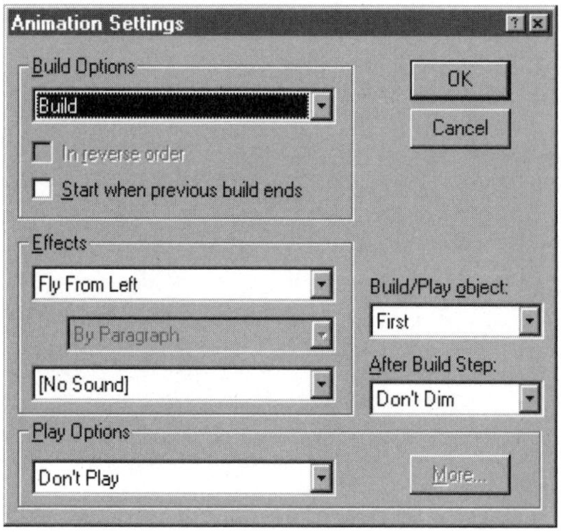

FIGURE 16-14

The Animation Settings dialog box for a media clip.

Animation Settings	? X

Build Options

Build ▼

☐ In reverse order
☐ Start when previous build ends

[OK]
[Cancel]

Effects

Fly From Left ▼

By Paragraph ▼

[No Sound] ▼

Build/Play object:
First ▼

After Build Step:
Don't Dim ▼

Play Options

Don't Play ▼   [More...]

Using the options in the dialog box, you can set a media clip to build or not build, to build with an effect, to have a sound associated with it when it builds, to play in a particular order, and to dim when the build is completed. But because it is a media clip, you can also select Play options. Select Play from the Play Options drop-down list, and then click More to open the dialog box shown in Figure 16-15.

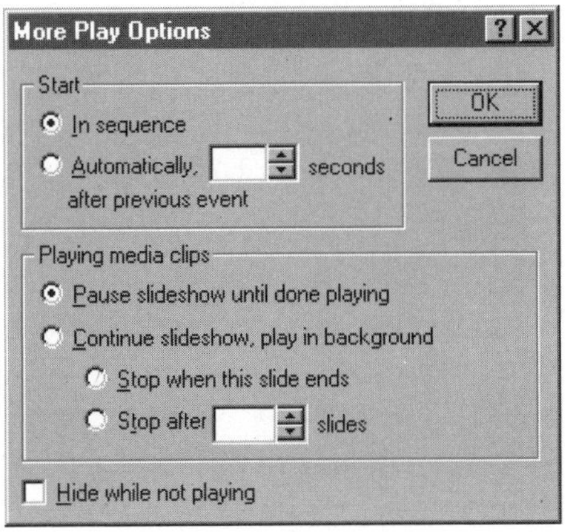

FIGURE 16-15

The More Play Options dialog box.

The options in the More Play Options dialog box let you determine the following for a media clip: when the clip starts, what happens to your slide show while the clip is playing, and whether your audience can see the clip before and after it plays. Select In sequence to have the clip play after other effects in the slide or after a left mouse click. If you want a clip to play automatically after a specified number of seconds, select Automatically and then enter a number in the seconds after previous event edit box.

If your slide show is running by itself, you might want to select the Pause slideshow until done playing option to pause the slide show while your clip runs. This option is particularly useful for playing a video clip. (With sound, you can choose to keep the slide show running while the music or narration continues.) If you select Continue slideshow, play in background, you can designate whether the clip should stop at the end of the current slide or after a specified number of slides have been shown.

To prevent the clip's icon from displaying on screen during a slide show, click Hide while not playing. The clip or its icon still appears in Slide view, but is not visible during the actual slide show.

Adding Drill-Down Documents

If you have data in another Windows 95–based application that can support an assertion you've made in a presentation or provide additional information, you can embed the data as an object on a slide so that it appears as an icon. During the slide show, you can then double-click the icon to "drill down" to the information and display the data in its original form. For example, you can embed a Microsoft Word document or a Microsoft Excel spreadsheet as a drill-down document. In fact, you can embed any file created by a Windows 95–based application that can act as an OLE server or an OLE object application. Most Windows 95–based applications can provide OLE objects for use in PowerPoint.

To embed an existing object, first choose Object from the Insert menu, and when the Insert Object dialog box appears, select Create from File and click the Browse button. In the Browse dialog box, select the file you want and then click OK. When you return to the Insert Object dialog box, select the Display As Icon option and click OK. The object appears on the current slide as an icon that you can double-click to open and work with the original object. Figure 16-16 shows an embedded Excel object on a slide.

FIGURE 16-16

An embedded Excel object represented by an Excel icon.

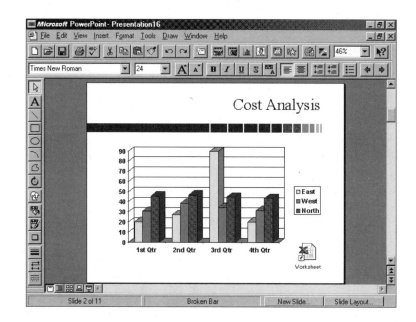

When you double-click the object, the application opens in its own window. Certain applications let you drag and drop files from the Windows Explorer to a PowerPoint slide. You'll have to test your application to see if it supports this feature.

Creating a Slide Show with Branching

By embedding a PowerPoint presentation as a drill-down object, you can branch to that presentation from within another slide show. The embedded presentation can provide detailed information on a topic covered by the main presentation. To embed a PowerPoint presentation, follow the procedure described in "Adding Drill-Down Documents" on the previous page, but select a PowerPoint presentation as the object you want to embed.

By adding embedded PowerPoint presentations, you can create an interactive training or informational presentation in which the viewer can select particular topics to review. Figure 16-17 shows a menu of topics within a presentation that you can present to a viewer. Double-clicking each topic's icon starts a different PowerPoint slide show.

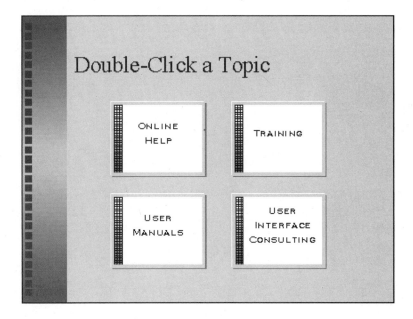

FIGURE 16-17

A menu that a viewer can use to branch to other presentations.

Playing a Series of Slide Shows

To play a series of slide shows automatically, you can create a batch file with a command line that contains the following: the command to start PowerPoint, the /s switch to activate Slide Show view, and the full pathname for each presentation you want to show.

For example, using a text editor like Microsoft Word or WordPad, you can create a batch file called Nextyear.bat to run the sales and project presentations stored in the slideshow folder on your system. In this case, your batch file would consist of the following command line:

```
start PowerPnt /s c:\slideshow\sales.ppt c:\slideshow\project.ppt
```

When you run this batch file, the slide show for each presentation plays in the order in which the presentations appear in the command line.

Displaying slide shows can be the ultimate thrill in using PowerPoint, but you'll also appreciate some of the advanced topics covered next, in the final section of this book.

Chapter 17

Giving Your Presentation at Home or On the Road

PowerPoint 7 for Windows 95 includes several new features designed to make giving an electronic slide show more efficient and foolproof. For example, do you really need to find a conference room, schedule it, set up a computer, projector, and screen, and make sure the coffee pot is full before you can present a slide show to your coworkers and superiors? Not anymore! With Presentation Conferencing, you can use your computer network to give your presentation to as many people as you want, and they don't have to leave their offices! Presentation Conferencing allows you to schedule a time for a "virtual" meeting, designate which computers on the network will receive the presentation, and then orchestrate the slide show from your desktop while you use the telephone to talk with the "meeting" attendees.

Have you ever left a meeting without a list of the tasks everyone agreed to perform, and then had a hard time following up to see that things got done? Whether you are on the road, in a conference room down the hall, or at your desktop, you can ensure more productive meetings by using Meeting Minder to make notes to yourself, create a list of action items, and take meeting minutes. When the meeting is done, clicking a button sends the minutes and action list to Microsoft Word, where you can check spelling, and then sends them to meeting attendees via electronic mail, using Microsoft Exchange.

No matter how professional your slide show, if you show up at a meeting without the Microsoft Excel spreadsheet you embedded in slide 15, the meeting will not go well. Before you take a presentation on the road, you can use PowerPoint's Pack and Go Wizard to assemble all of the files you need to run your slide show and put them on a floppy disk or anywhere else you designate. No more mad scrambles to air express a missing file before tomorrow's meeting! And, as with the earlier version of PowerPoint, if you know you won't be changing your presentation after you leave the office, you can pop the PowerPoint Viewer on your laptop so that you can give your slide show without taking up a lot of hard disk space with the complete PowerPoint program.

Giving a Slide Show Across the Network

When you need to make a presentation to people within your own company but don't need everyone to be physically present in a conference room, you can host a presentation conference. As the host, you prepare for the conference by scheduling a time for the conference, selecting the Stage Manager tools you want to use during the conference, and telling PowerPoint which computers on the network will participate in the conference.

Setting Up a Presentation Conference

The first step in setting up a presentation conference is gathering the names of the computers that will participate in the conference. If you don't know the name of your own computer, choose Settings and then Control Panel from the Start menu on the desktop, and double-click the Network icon. Click the Identification tab, and make a note of your computer's name, which is in the Computer name edit box. Have the people you are inviting to the presentation conference let you know their computer's name, and then make a list (you'll need it in a minute).

TIP If you frequently invite the same group to your presentation conferences, make a Conference Address List file and save yourself from having to reenter the same list of computer names over and over. A Conference Address List file is a text file listing the computer names, with one name on each line. You can create the list in Notepad, WordPad, or Microsoft Word. If you use Word or WordPad, be sure to save the file as text only.

With the list of names in hand, open the presentation you want to show. Then choose Presentation Conference from the Tools menu. The wizard's first dialog box appears, as shown in Figure 17-1. Select Presenter, and then click Next to get going.

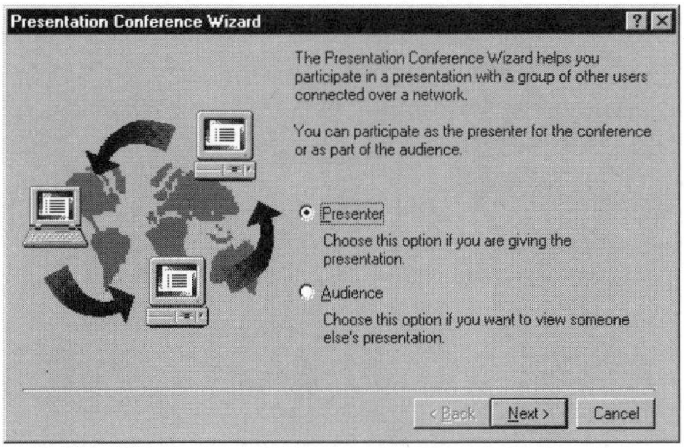

FIGURE 17-1

The Presentation Conference Wizard's first dialog box.

In the second dialog box, shown in Figure 17-2, you have a chance to select which Stage Manager tools you want to use during your presentation.

FIGURE 17-2

The Presentation
Conference
Wizard's second
dialog box.

Your choices are:

- Meeting Minder, for keeping notes, a list of action items, and taking minutes

- Slide Navigator, for seeing which slide is coming up and branching to another one

- Slide Meter, for checking how you are doing against your rehearsal time

Check the boxes of the tools you want, and then choose Next to display the third dialog box, shown in Figure 17-3.

FIGURE 17-3

The Presentation
Conference
Wizard's third
dialog box.

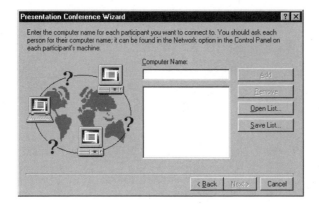

In the Computer Name edit box, type the name of one of the computers participating in the conference, and then click Add. The name is added to the list box underneath. Keep adding names until all the computers are listed. If you add a name by mistake or later need to remove the computer name of someone who cannot "attend" the conference, select the name in the list in this dialog box, and click Remove. If this particular list of computer names is one you will use again, you can click Save List and assign a filename to create a Conference Address List file. If you have already created a Conference Address List file, you can open it rather than typing each computer name, by clicking the Open List button and selecting the file in the Open Conference Address List dialog box.

When the list of computer names is complete, click Next to display the fourth Presentation Conference Wizard dialog box, shown in Figure 17-4. As soon as all attendees have used the Presentation Conference Wizard to join the conference, click Finish to start the conference.

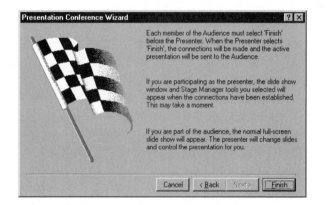

FIGURE 17-4

The Presentation Conference Wizard's fourth dialog box.

The invited computers must join the conference and be waiting for you to use the Presentation Wizard to host the conference. Your computer will then connect to the computers you've invited to the conference. This might take a couple of minutes. PowerPoint must find the computers, download a copy of your presentation to each computer, and create a temporary copy of the presentation on the host computer.

If a computer is missing, you will see a message that says the computer is not available or cannot be found. When you click OK to close this message box, you return to the wizard's third dialog box to check the spelling of the computer's name and reenter it if necessary, or to remove it from the list.

At least one computer must be connected to the conference for it to proceed.

Joining a Conference

A minute or so before a presentation conference is scheduled to start, each attendee must start PowerPoint and join the conference. To join a conference, choose Presentation Conference from the Tools menu, and in the Presentation Conference Wizard's first dialog box, select Audience, click Next, and then click Finish. If your computer's name is on the conference list, a message lets you know that you have successfully joined the conference. When the conference host starts the presentation, you see the first slide on your computer screen.

Conducting a Conference

When you host a presentation conference, you have several tools to help ensure that the meeting is productive. When you attend a presentation conference, you can participate, but your role is more limited.

When a conference begins—with one host and at least one attendee connected—all the attendees see a full-screen slide show on their computer screens. The host computer's screen displays the slide show as the attendees see it, it displays Stage Manager for controlling the slide show, and it displays any other tools you selected when starting the conference.

For example, if you selected Meeting Minder in the second Presentation Conference Wizard dialog box, your screen might look like the one in Figure 17-5. Only the host can see Meeting Minder, so it's a great place to keep your notes to yourself.

 TIP During a presentation conference, it's a good idea to minimize PowerPoint so that your screen is less cluttered, as shown in Figure 17-5.

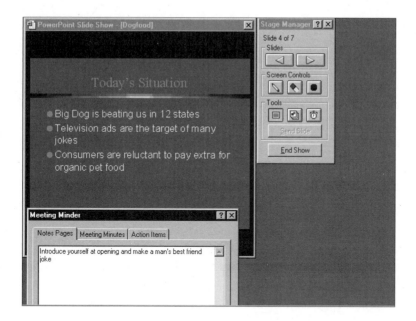

FIGURE 17-5

The host computer's screen, showing a slide, Stage Manager, and Meeting Minder.

Controlling the Slide Show with Stage Manager

When you host a presentation conference, you use Stage Manager, as shown below, to control your presentation. If you close Stage Manager, your conference ends.

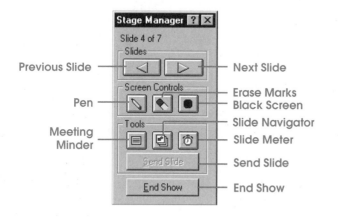

You can use the Previous Slide and Next Slide buttons to move from slide to slide; or you can click the slide window to move to the next slide.

The Screen Controls section allows you to change the mouse pointer to a pen. You use the pen to mark up slides—for example, you can underline an important word to emphasize a point. Audience members see any marks you make on a slide.

TIP Using the mouse to move the pen on a slide isn't easy! Practice before you do it for a crowd, especially if you want to write words rather than making marks such as underlines and circles.

You can black out the slide show screen for intermission using the Black Screen button in the Screen Controls section. The Erase Marks tool in this same section lets you clear all the marks from the screen so that the slide is shown in its original state.

If you need to use a conferencing tool that you did not select when you started the conference, you can activate the tool during the conference by clicking the appropriate button in the Tools section of Stage Manager. You can also close a conferencing tool you no longer need by clicking the appropriate Tools button.

If the ideas are flowing fast and furious and you want to make sure everyone gets a copy of a slide they might need later, you can click Send Slide to copy the currently displayed slide, complete with any marks you've added, to the hard disk of each attendee. Clicking Stage Manager's Close button or the End Show button ends the presentation conference.

Switching Slides with Slide Navigator

Suppose the reaction of your audience to your presentation indicates that you can skip some details and move on to a new point. Or suppose the conference is running long and you want to speed things up by not showing some of the slides. Slide Navigator lets you select any slide in your slide show, preview its contents, and then either show it to your audience or skip it. When Slide Navigator is loaded with the slide show, the host computer looks as shown in Figure 17-6.

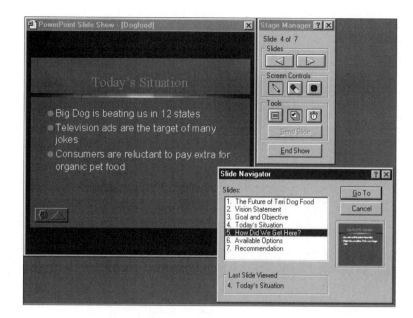

FIGURE 17-6

The host computer's screen, showing a slide, Stage Manager, and Slide Navigator.

The Last Slide Viewed box at the bottom of the Slide Navigator dialog box displays the title and number of the slide you are currently showing your audience. If you want to skip over slides, you can scroll through the list of slides in the Slides box to find the one you want. Selecting a slide displays a preview in the box on the right. To display this slide to conference attendees, click Go To.

Keeping Track of the Time with Slide Meter

Slide Meter keeps track of the elapsed time of your presentation, and if you rehearsed your slide show before presenting it, Slide Meter lets you know if you are going slower or faster than you planned. Figure 17-7 on the next page shows how the host computer's screen looks when Slide Meter is loaded with the slide show.

See Also For details on rehearsing a slide show and using Slide Meter, see "Using Slide Meter," page 402.

FIGURE 17-7

The host computer's screen, showing a slide, Stage Manager, and Slide Meter.

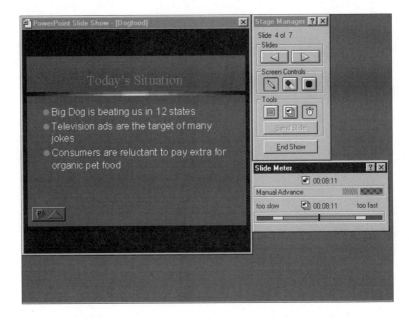

Participating in a Conference

You may be running the show when you host a presentation conference, but don't expect your audience to sit on their thumbs and watch. As participants, they can comment on your ideas or correct your facts and figures by picking up the pen and marking the current slide. (The pen is activated when the conference starts.) Pressing Ctrl+P deactivates the pen; so does choosing the Pen command from the slide show shortcut menu. When an attendee marks up a slide, everyone else sees the marks. Careful, though: Too many marks from too many opinion-holders can make a slide unreadable.

Conference attendees cannot control the flow of the slide show; only the host can switch the slide on everyone's screen. Attendees can control the pen color they use to mark up slides. (You can assign a different pen color to each attendee at the beginning of a conference to differentiate the many marks that may accumulate on a slide.)

To leave the conference, attendees can choose End Show from the shortcut menu. When a conference is over, the presentation's slides remain in each attendee's computer memory as a new presentation. The presentation can be saved for future use, or when each attendee exits, he or she can click No to discard the presentation.

See Also For more information about using the pen, see "Marking Up Slides," page 403.

Managing the Meeting

Meetings are more productive when someone keeps accurate minutes of what is decided and who is assigned to which follow-up tasks. You can use Power-Point's Meeting Minder during a meeting or presentation to jot down these minutes or to refer to notes you made before the meeting.

To open Meeting Minder, which is shown in Figure 17-8, choose it from the slide show shortcut menu while running a slide show, or click the Meeting Minder button in the Tools section of Stage Manager while hosting a presentation conference.

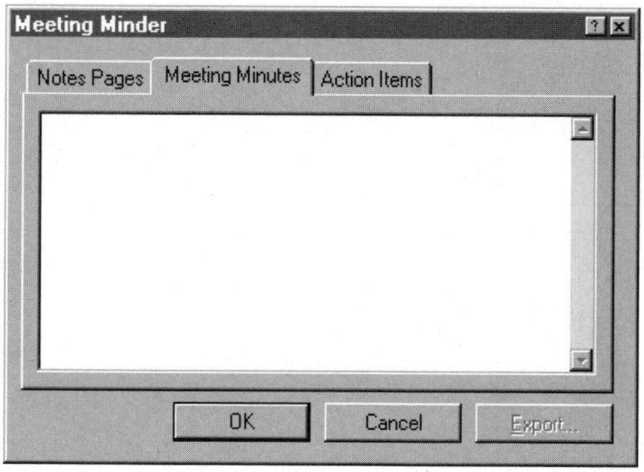

FIGURE 17-8

The Meeting Minder dialog box.

> **TIP**   If you are running a slide show from your computer and projecting it on a screen or a large monitor, your audience sees Meeting Minder when you open it. You can probably interrupt the slide show to record minutes and action items without distracting your audience too much, but this method doesn't work very well as a way of consulting notes to yourself. You are better off creating your notes in Notes Pages View and printing them out. If you are giving a presentation conference, only you can see Meeting Minder when you open it, so you can check your notes without distracting other conference participants.

After you have opened Meeting Minder, click the appropriate tab and type your notes in the edit box. Click OK to save your notes. You can close Meeting Minder and continue the presentation, and then open it again as necessary to record notes, minutes, and action items for other slides.

Any notes you enter on the Notes Pages tab become part of the slide that was active when you made the notes. Later, when you choose Notes Pages from the View menu, PowerPoint displays the notes you made while using Meeting Minder for the current slide. Any notes you enter on the Meeting Minutes and Action Items tabs also become part of the active slide, but the easiest way to view these notes again is to open Meeting Minder and click the appropriate tab.

Another way to view minutes and action items is to export them to Microsoft Word. Exporting the minutes and action items gives you a chance to polish them before distributing them to the meeting's attendees. To export them, click the Export button in the Meeting Minder dialog box when the meeting is over. A second Meeting Minder dialog box appears, as shown in Figure 17-9, offering you two export options. If you select the Send Meeting Minutes and Action Items to Microsoft Word option, PowerPoint exports your notes to a Word document and opens Word so you can edit your notes. If you select the Add Meeting Minutes to Notes Pages option, PowerPoint adds the text you entered on the Meeting Minutes tab of each slide to that slide's Notes Pages tab. Simply select the export option you want, and then click the Export Now button.

FIGURE 17-9

The Meeting
Minder export
dialog box.

If you enter any tasks on the Action Items tab during the meeting, PowerPoint displays a list of all the task assignments as the last slide in your slide show or presentation conference. You can then check the list's accuracy and remind everyone of their individual tasks before they leave the meeting. Later, after you've had a chance to refine the list of action items in Word, you can send it to everyone as electronic mail or as a fax.

Packing Up Your Slide Show

Suppose you are going to deliver your presentation to clients in their offices on their equipment, or you need to send a presentation on disk to a colleague who is not on your computer network. Or suppose you have designed a sales presentation that will be offered to prospective customers at a trade show or will be mailed to people responding to an advertisement. In all of these situations, it is critical that you include all of the pieces required to show the presentation on the disk. The Pack and Go Wizard is designed to ensure that you do exactly that.

To use the Pack and Go Wizard, first open the presentation you want to pack, and then choose Pack And Go from the File menu to display the first Pack and Go Wizard dialog box, which introduces you to the wizard. Click Next to move to the second dialog box, shown in Figure 17-10.

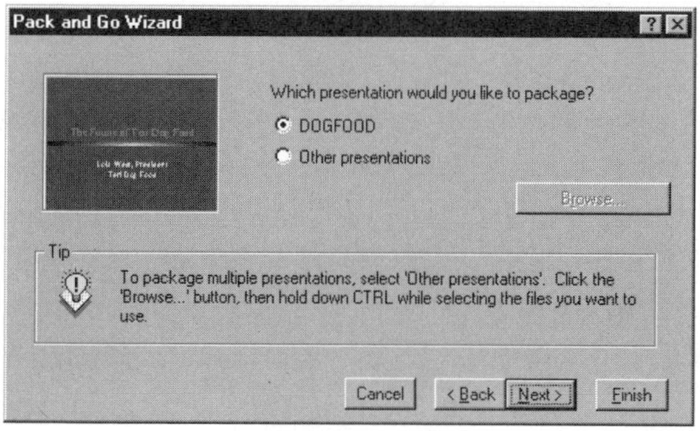

FIGURE 17-10

The second Pack
and Go Wizard
dialog box.

In this dialog box, the wizard asks which presentation you want to pack and selects the current presentation by default. To select a presentation other than the current one, select the Other presentations option, click the Browse button, and select the presentation you want in the Select a presentation to package dialog box. When you have answered the wizard's question, click Next to display the third dialog box, shown in Figure 17-11.

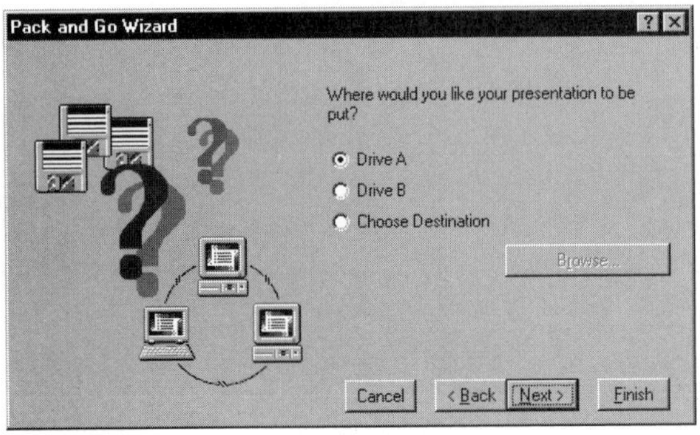

FIGURE 17-11

The third Pack and Go Wizard dialog box.

You now need to tell the wizard where to put the packed presentation. The wizard selects a default drive, usually drive A. To specify a different drive, select the Choose Destination option, click the Browse button, and select a destination in the Specify directory dialog box. Then click Next to display the fourth dialog box, shown in Figure 17-12.

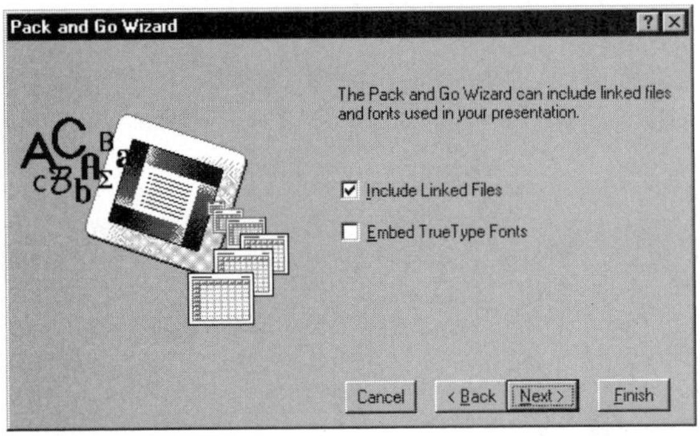

FIGURE 17-12

The fourth Pack and Go Wizard dialog box.

If your presentation includes linked files, be sure to select the Include Linked Files option. If you want the Pack and Go Wizard to pack the fonts you have used in the presentation, select the Embed TrueType Fonts option. (You need to use this option if your presentation includes any fonts that might not be installed on the computer that will run the presentation.)

When you click Next, the dialog box shown in Figure 17-13 asks whether you want to include the PowerPoint Viewer on the disk. If you are not sure whether PowerPoint will be installed on the computer that will run the presentation, be sure to include the Viewer. Otherwise, click the check box to deselect it.

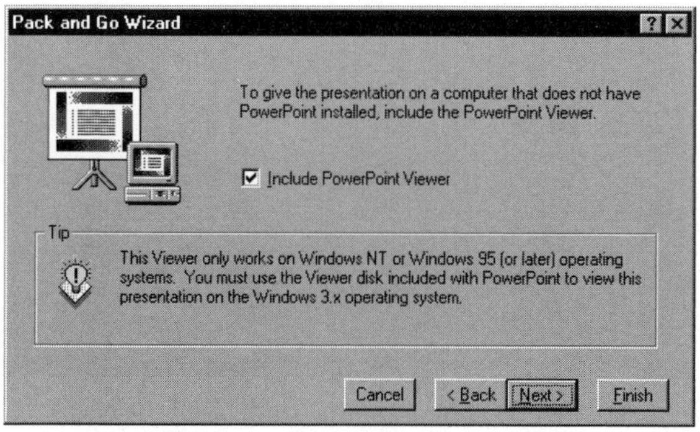

FIGURE 17-13

The fifth Pack and Go Wizard dialog box.

Clicking Next displays the last dialog box, which summarizes the options you selected with the wizard and reminds you to run the Pack and Go Wizard again if you make any changes to the presentation. After verifying the options, click Finish. The Pack and Go Wizard then swings into action, packing up everything you need to run the presentation.

Using the PowerPoint Viewer

You don't need to have the entire PowerPoint program installed on a system to run a slide show. You can install only the PowerPoint Viewer, which displays your presentations just as if you were running the slide show in Slide Show view. The PowerPoint Viewer allows you to display PowerPoint slide shows on a portable computer where hard-disk space is too limited to install the entire PowerPoint application. It can also display slide shows created in PowerPoint for the Macintosh. In addition, you can copy a slide show to floppy disk and then send the show, along with the PowerPoint Viewer, to another location for viewing. (When you copy a slide show, you must also copy the viewer application, and the recipient of the disks must install the PowerPoint Viewer and the presentation on his or her system, because a presentation cannot be read and displayed fast enough from floppy disk.)

Before you can use the PowerPoint Viewer to display a slide show, you must add the transition effects, builds, and timings you want for the show; make sure the Use Slide Timings option is selected in the Slide Show dialog box; and save the presentation in a file. Then double-click the PowerPoint Viewer icon to start the PowerPoint Viewer application. The Microsoft Power-Point Viewer dialog box appears, as shown in Figure 17-14.

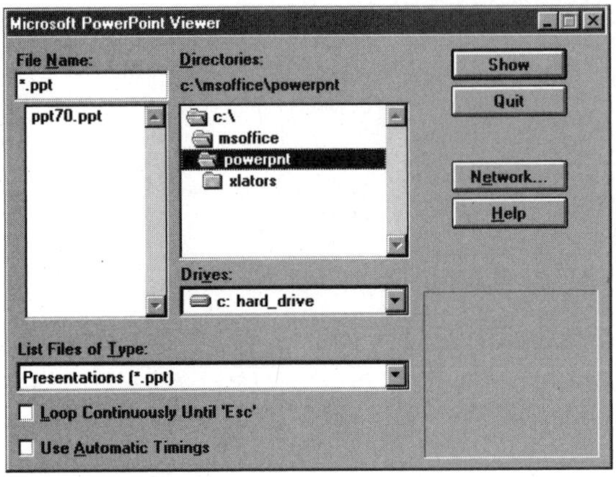

FIGURE 17-14
The Microsoft
PowerPoint Viewer
dialog box.

In the Microsoft PowerPoint Viewer dialog box, select the presentation file you want to display, and click Show or press Enter to run the slide show. You can also select the Loop Continuously Until 'Esc' option to display the slide show indefinitely, and you can select the Use Automatic Timings option to use the slide timings you recorded during a rehearsal. As the show progresses, you have all the mouse and keyboard control capabilities that you have in PowerPoint's Slide Show view. After the show, click Quit to exit the PowerPoint Viewer.

To prepare a slide show that can be viewed on a system not equipped with PowerPoint, first copy the floppy disk containing the PowerPoint Viewer (keep the original, of course), and then copy the presentation file to a floppy disk. Make sure the person giving the slide show knows that the Pngsetup application on the floppy disk must be run from within Windows in order to install the PowerPoint Viewer on a local system. The presentation file must also be copied from the floppy disk to a directory on a local hard disk. You can copy and send the PowerPoint Viewer to as many recipients as you want, unlike the main PowerPoint application.

NOTE You cannot drill down to embedded documents while using the PowerPoint Viewer to run a slide show. Nor can you branch to other presentations. For more information about drilling down to embedded documents, see "Adding Drill-Down Documents," page 410. For more information about branching to other presentations, see "Creating a Slide Show with Branching," page 411.

The Presentation Conference Wizard, Meeting Minder, the Pack and Go Wizard, and the PowerPoint Viewer are designed to help you present your slide shows efficiently. As you've seen in this chapter, using them can take a lot of the hassle out of setting up, delivering, and following up on your electronic presentations.

Part 6

SELECT EDITION

Advanced
PowerPoint

431

SELECT EDITION

Chapter 18

Using PowerPoint with Other Applications

Version 7 of PowerPoint contains many improvements over previous versions of the software, not the least of which is that it is designed to take full advantage of Windows 95, with its new, easier-to-use design on the desktop and in dialog boxes, and its long filenames, true multitasking, and increased printing speed. And while PowerPoint still stands on its own just fine, it becomes even more powerful when combined with its partners in Microsoft Office 95: Microsoft Word and Microsoft Excel. Word 7 is the word processor of the Office 95 group, and Excel 7 is the number cruncher. Power-Point 7 is the public voice of Office 95, telling the world your story with professionally and consistently designed images. And with Microsoft Exchange, one of the new communications features of Windows 95, that world is not limited to your local computer network or a particular online information service. If one of those services is The Microsoft Network, you can register PowerPoint electronically, visit forums where you can discuss PowerPoint, get technical support, find free multimedia files to enhance your slide shows, and access the whole Internet.

Although the Office applications are available separately, they share many features and reveal new powers when you use the applications together. You first notice the common menus, dialog boxes, toolbars, and procedures that make switching from one application to another easy. The applications also share things like spelling dictionaries, AutoCorrect word lists, and the ClipArt Gallery. And using the Office Binder, you can bundle all of the pieces of a project together for even easier access.

Below the surface of Office is a powerful technology called OLE that lets you share information among applications as a natural extension of the way you work in a single application. For example, not only can you move objects, such as passages of text or ranges of numbers, from place to place within a document, but you can also move them from application to application with the same ease. And when you move an object to a second application, an OLE feature called *in-place editing* gives you access from within the second application to all the menus, dialog boxes, toolbars, and procedures that you used to create the object. You can move a worksheet from Excel to PowerPoint, for example, and then gain access to Excel's menus and toolbars from within PowerPoint to edit the object. When you select the worksheet for editing, Excel's menus and toolbars appear temporarily within the PowerPoint window; when you finish editing the object, PowerPoint's menus and toolbars reclaim the PowerPoint window. OLE is also at work when you open Media Player to insert a video clip or use WordArt to create fancy effects with fonts.

The drag-and-drop method is the key to embedding information in an Office application. You can almost always select an item in one application and drag it to another application's window. When you have an entire document or presentation to embed, you can drag it from a folder or the desktop into an open application. And if you want a copy of the information to remain in the original application, all you have to do is hold down the Ctrl key as you drag. In this chapter, you'll learn how to select objects and drag them between applications. You'll also learn about a few considerations to keep in mind as you exchange information between the Office applications, and you'll learn about menu alternatives that you can use with other Windows-based applications that do not support the drag-and-drop procedure.

Using PowerPoint with Microsoft Word

In Chapter 4, you learned how to exchange outlines between Microsoft Word and PowerPoint, and in Chapter 17, you learned how to export meeting minutes and action item lists from PowerPoint to Word. But you can also exchange one paragraph or one picture with similar ease. Best of all, you can embed an entire PowerPoint slide show in a Word document, transforming a drab report into a lively, stimulating presentation complete with special effects, sound, music, and perhaps even video.

Of course, you can embed individual multimedia elements in a Word document without using PowerPoint, but embedding them in a PowerPoint presentation and then embedding the presentation in Word allows the multimedia objects and the presentation to be played together in a slide show.

Dragging Text from Word to PowerPoint

You'll appreciate dragging and dropping when you need to enter text in PowerPoint that you've already typed in Word. Rather than retype the text, you can simply drag it from Word to PowerPoint as easily as you drag it from place to place within a Word document.

To drag text from Word to PowerPoint, start by opening the Word and PowerPoint windows, and then arrange them so they share the screen, even if one window overlaps the other. Make sure the slide in which you want to embed the Word text is displayed in the PowerPoint window and that Slide view is active. Figure 18-1 shows how you might arrange the windows. Then, select the text in Word—a word, a paragraph, or anything else you've created in Word, including a Word table. Place the mouse pointer on the selection, and drag the selection to the current PowerPoint slide. To copy the text to PowerPoint rather than move it, hold down the Ctrl key as you drag it.

It's important to note that when the text arrives in PowerPoint, it appears as a picture of the text, with all of its Word formatting intact. When you stretch or compress the picture by dragging its handles, the text becomes distorted. By contrast, text that you've entered in a PowerPoint text box (using the Text Tool button on the Drawing toolbar) maintains its size and shape when you stretch or compress its text box, but the word wrapping changes. Figure 18-2 illustrates the difference between text that has been dragged from Word and text that has been entered in a PowerPoint text box.

FIGURE 18-1

The PowerPoint window over-lapping a Word document.

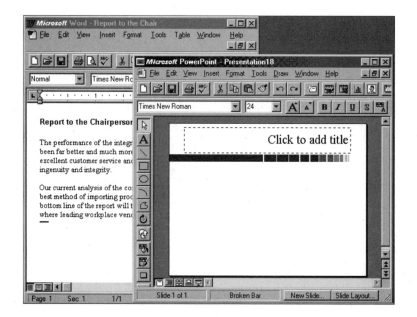

The only way to get rid of a temptation is to yield to it. —Oscar Wilde — Original text

The only way to get rid of a temptation is to yield to it. —Oscar Wilde ——— Embedded text from Word

The only way to get rid of a temptation is to yield to it. —Oscar Wilde ——— PowerPoint text

Another important point is that because the object is a picture of the text from Word, you cannot edit the text with PowerPoint's text editing tools. Instead, you must return to Word by double-clicking the text picture. Word's menus and toolbars replace those of PowerPoint, and a frame that represents a small Word editing window, complete with its own rulers, appears around the text. Without leaving PowerPoint, you can work within this frame and use all of Word's commands and controls as if you were actually in Word. When you finish editing the text, click the PowerPoint slide outside the frame. The frame disappears, but the revised text picture remains, and all of PowerPoint's menus and toolbars reappear within the PowerPoint window.

You can also edit the text using Word's menus and toolbars by clicking it with the right mouse button and choosing Edit Document Object from the shortcut menu. When you have finished your edits, simply click outside the text picture to save your edits and return to the PowerPoint slide.

If you would be more comfortable editing the text in a separate Word window, you can use the right mouse button to click the Word text picture within PowerPoint, and then choose Open Document Object from the shortcut menu. After you edit the text, you must choose Update from Word's File menu, and then choose Close and Return to *Presentation* from the File menu.

The alternative to using drag and drop is to select the text in Word, copy the text using the Copy command on the Edit menu (or using one of the shortcuts for copying items, such as clicking the Copy button on the Standard toolbar), switch to PowerPoint, and then choose Paste from the Edit menu (or use one of the shortcuts for pasting items, such as clicking the Paste button on the Standard toolbar). This procedure always copies selected text from another application to PowerPoint, but it does not always embed the text in PowerPoint. Therefore, when you double-click the text, you might not return to the application from which the text originated. To embed the Word text in PowerPoint, choose Paste Special rather than Paste from PowerPoint's Edit menu, make sure the Paste option (not Paste Link) is selected in the Paste Special dialog box, and then select the description of the text that includes the word "object," in this case Microsoft Word Document Object, from the list in the dialog box. Only when the text is embedded as an object can you double-click the object to return to the original application and revise the text.

TIP To place a Word icon that represents embedded text in a PowerPoint presentation, select the Display as Icon option in the Paste Special dialog box.

See Also For more information about the Paste Special dialog box, see "Linking a PowerPoint Presentation to Word," page 441.

Embedding a Slide in a Word Document

By using the Insert Object command in Word, you can access the Microsoft Graph module as easily as you can from within PowerPoint, so you don't need PowerPoint to create a graph for a Word document. WordArt is also available in Word, so you can have fancy headings in memos as well as in a slide show. In addition, PowerPoint gets its tables from Word, so you don't need PowerPoint's help there. But by dragging a PowerPoint slide to Word, you can place an image of the slide in a document, complete with a background design and a combination of foreground and background text and graphical objects. You can also copy and paste individual objects from a PowerPoint slide into a Word document using the Copy and Paste commands.

To drag a slide from PowerPoint to Word, arrange the PowerPoint and Word windows on the screen, and make sure the slide you want to drag is visible in PowerPoint's Slide Sorter view. Then drag the slide from PowerPoint to Word, holding down the Ctrl key if you want to copy the slide rather than move it.

After the slide appears in Word, you can drag and drop it within the Word window as you would a block of text. You can also drag a corner handle to resize the slide proportionally. By clicking the slide with the right mouse button, you can bring up a Word shortcut menu with commands that apply to the slide. For example, you can add a border, shading, and caption to the slide, or frame the slide so that you can wrap text around it and use other techniques that apply only to framed elements. Figure 18-3 shows the shortcut menu that appears in Word.

Also on the shortcut menu, you'll see a command called Edit Slide. When you choose this command or double-click the slide, the menus and toolbars change to those for PowerPoint, even though the Microsoft Word title bar remains. Edit your slide just as you would if you had opened PowerPoint yourself. After you finish, move the insertion point to anywhere in your Word document; the menus and toolbars change back to Word's, and you can continue editing the rest of your Word document.

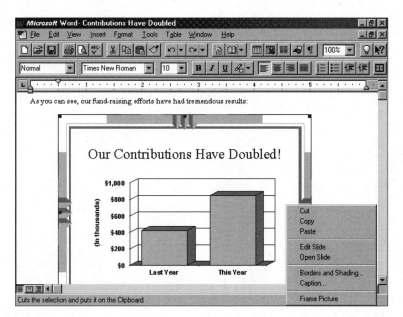

FIGURE 18-3

The shortcut menu for a slide dragged to a Word document.

TIP   To open one Office application from within another, display the Microsoft toolbar, and then click the second application's button. If the Microsoft toolbar is not present, click any toolbar with the right mouse button, and choose Microsoft from the shortcut menu.

You can try dragging and dropping a slide into any other Windows-based application in the same way, but if it won't budge, you must use the Cut or Copy command in PowerPoint's Slide Sorter view, switch to the other application's window, and then use the Paste command.

Transferring a Graphic to Word

To transfer a graphic from a PowerPoint slide to a Word document, position Word and PowerPoint side-by-side as you would to transfer text, and then drag the graphic from one to the other. You can then edit the graphic directly in Word by double-clicking it to display Word's drawing tools, which work just like PowerPoint's drawing tools. Since Word and PowerPoint share the same ClipArt Gallery, you can also open the Gallery to get a duplicate of a picture you used in PowerPoint.

TIP   To copy the entire text of your presentation to Word (but no graphics), click the Report It button on Power-Point's Standard toolbar. PowerPoint copies the text to Word, creating a new document.

Embedding a PowerPoint Presentation in Word

To embed an entire PowerPoint presentation in a Word document, you can drag the document icon from a folder or the desktop into Word, or you can open the presentation and then select the entire presentation in Slide Sorter view by choosing Select All from the Edit menu or by pressing Ctrl+A. Drag any one of the selected slides to Word while holding down the Ctrl key. The first slide of the presentation appears in Word, and when you double-click the slide, the presentation displays as a full-screen slide show. To edit the presentation, click the slide displayed in Word once with the right mouse button, and choose Edit Presentation from the shortcut menu. After you make changes to the presentation, click anywhere else in the Word document to leave the presentation. Remember that the changes you make in Word exist only in Word. The original presentation is not changed.

You can also create a brand-new slide show for your Word document without ever leaving Word.

To create a new PowerPoint presentation or a single slide from within Word, follow these steps:

1. From the Word Insert menu, choose Object to open the Object dialog box.

2. In the Object Type list, select Microsoft PowerPoint Presentation or Microsoft PowerPoint Slide. If you want to display only the PowerPoint icon in the Word document and not a slide, select Display as Icon.

3. Click OK.

The object is inserted in your Word document, and the Word toolbar and commands are changed to the PowerPoint toolbar and commands. If you selected Display as Icon, Word will open PowerPoint for you to create your slide. When you have finished creating your slide, first choose Update from the File menu, and then Close and Return to *Document*. You can then edit your slide or presentation just as if you had opened PowerPoint without being in Word. However, you will not be able to open this slide show from within PowerPoint; an embedded slide show exists only within the document in which it is embedded.

Linking a PowerPoint Presentation to Word

If you want to show a slide show from within Word but also make sure that it resides in PowerPoint and reflects any changes you make to it in PowerPoint, you can link it to Word. The presentation's data is stored in PowerPoint rather than in Word, and only a representation of the first slide of the presentation is displayed in Word. When you double-click the representation in Word, the presentation is displayed as a slide show, just as if you had embedded it.

Because you have linked the presentation, any changes you make to it in PowerPoint are reflected in the representation in Word. The advantage is that you don't have to update the presentation twice—once in PowerPoint and again in Word. The disadvantage is that you can't move the Word document to another computer without also moving the PowerPoint file. If you move the Word document without moving the PowerPoint file to the same destination,

Word cannot access the PowerPoint data at the destination. Only when you drag and drop a presentation or use Paste Special to paste the presentation in Word as an embedded object can you transport the document and simultaneously transport the data.

You can link an existing PowerPoint presentation to a Word document in one of two ways: by using the Insert Object command or by using the Paste Special command.

To link a PowerPoint presentation using the Object command:

1. From Word's Insert menu, choose Object.

2. Click the Create from File tab of the Object dialog box.

3. In the File Name edit box, type the name of the presentation you want to link, or click the Browse button to locate it.

4. Select the Link to File option, and then click OK.

The Paste Special command allows you to link individual slides of a presentation to a Word document. To link a slide from a PowerPoint presentation using Paste Special:

1. Open the presentation containing the slide you want to link.

2. Select the slide you want to link and choose Copy from the Edit menu.

3. Switch to Word and place an insertion point where you want the slide to appear.

4. Choose Paste Special from Word's Edit menu.

5. In the Paste Special dialog box, shown in Figure 18-4, select the Paste Link option, and then click OK.

FIGURE 18-4

The Paste Special dialog box in Word.

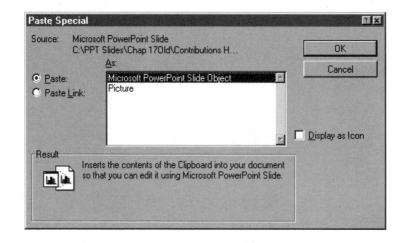

To run a linked presentation, double-click its "representative" slide in Word. To edit the presentation, click the slide once with the right mouse button and choose Edit Presentation Link from the shortcut menu; or select the slide, choose Linked Presentation Object from Word's Edit menu, and then choose Edit from the submenu. After you make changes to the presentation in the PowerPoint window, save the presentation again. As soon as you save the file, the linked copy of the presentation in Word is updated with the same changes.

Modifying the Link

When you save a PowerPoint presentation in a file, link it to Word, and then modify it in PowerPoint, the changes flow through to Word as soon as you save the modifications in the PowerPoint file. If Word is closed, the changes appear the next time you open the Word document that contains the linked presentation.

To prevent changes to a linked presentation from flowing through to Word, select the presentation's representative slide in Word, and choose Links from the Edit menu. In the Links dialog box, shown in Figure 18-5, select Manual rather than Automatic as the Update option. The linked presentation will be updated only when you click Update Now in the Links dialog box, or when you select the representative slide and then choose either Update Link from the shortcut menu or press F9. To prevent the presentation from being updated even when you use the Update Now command, select the Locked option in the Links dialog box.

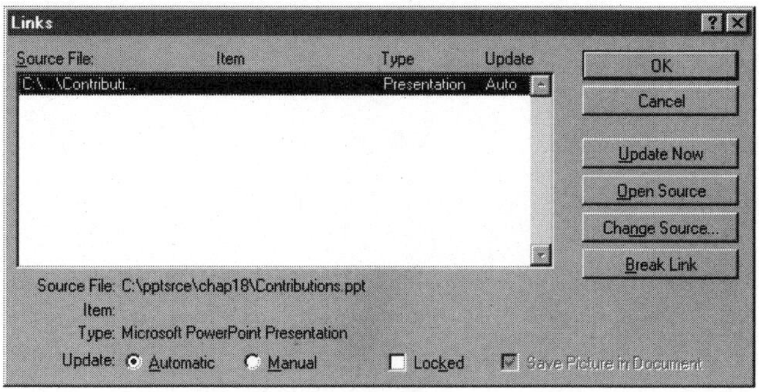

FIGURE 18-5

The Links dialog box in Word.

Other options in the Links dialog box are: Open Source, which opens the presentation in PowerPoint for editing; Change Source, which allows you to link a different object from another application; and Break Link, which severs the link and leaves a static presentation in Word that cannot be edited or updated in PowerPoint.

Using Word to Format and Print Notes Pages and Handouts

PowerPoint lets you print handouts that have blank lines for audience notes, but it does not let you print handout sheets based on your notes pages, and it does not let you print notes pages with blank lines. It also provides no easy way to include the handouts for a slide show in a report or training manual that contains other material written in Word. At times like these, choose the Write Up command on the PowerPoint Tools menu to move your slides and notes to Word.

Choose one of the four layout options in the Write-Up dialog box, shown in Figure 18-6—you can always change the formatting and layout once you have the information in Word. You can also choose whether to link the slides and notes to Word, so that any changes you make in the original slide show are also made in the Word document. Click OK to begin the write-up.

FIGURE 18-6

The Write-Up dialog box.

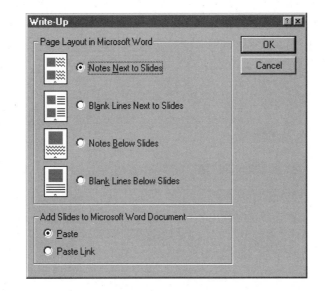

If you select one of the side-by-side layouts, Word creates a table, as shown in Figure 18-7. In the first column is the slide number, in the second column is the slide, and in the third column are the notes or blank lines.

For the other layouts, Word inserts the slide number in the first paragraph of the page, the slide in the second paragraph, and the notes or blank lines in the third paragraph. Each slide is on its own page.

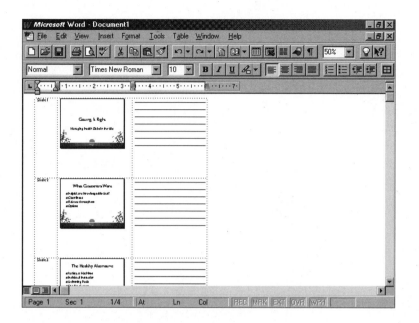

FIGURE 18-7

The layout for these handouts is a table with three columns.

Using PowerPoint with Microsoft Excel

The vast majority of presentations relate information using words rather than numbers, but if you have numeric data, you are likely to accumulate it, calculate it, and analyze it in a spreadsheet program such as Microsoft Excel. You'll be glad to know that you can communicate between PowerPoint and Excel as easily as you can between PowerPoint and Word. In fact, you can create an Excel worksheet from within PowerPoint, drag a worksheet from Excel to PowerPoint, or drag a PowerPoint slide or presentation to an Excel worksheet using the same techniques you use with Word.

Embedding an Excel Worksheet in PowerPoint

By clicking the Insert Excel Worksheet button on PowerPoint's Standard toolbar, you can embed a new Excel worksheet on a PowerPoint slide. This has the same effect as choosing Object from the Insert menu and then selecting Excel Worksheet as the object type. While you are creating the worksheet, Excel's menus and toolbars appear in PowerPoint, and a framed worksheet window overlaps the PowerPoint slide. When you finish the worksheet and click outside of it, PowerPoint's menus and toolbars reappear, and a picture of the Excel worksheet is displayed on the slide.

NOTE It's best to format the worksheet while Excel's menus and toolbars are available so that the worksheet's picture looks just right when it appears in PowerPoint.

When you first click the Insert Excel Worksheet button, a grid of empty cells appears. Drag across as many as 11 columns and up to 6 rows of cells, and then release the mouse button. A worksheet frame opens on the current slide, displaying the number of columns and rows you specified. Using the Excel menus, toolbars, and procedures, create the worksheet within the worksheet frame. When the worksheet is complete, be sure all the cells that you want included in it are visible in the worksheet frame, and then click outside the frame to place a picture of the worksheet on the PowerPoint slide. You can move and stretch the picture by dragging its handles.

As in Word, you can embed an entire Excel worksheet in PowerPoint by dragging the worksheet icon from a folder or the desktop onto a slide. A picture of the worksheet will appear on the current PowerPoint slide. You can also drag any part of an existing worksheet to a slide. Arrange the Excel and PowerPoint windows on the screen (and be sure Slide view is active), and then select the worksheet range that you want to move or copy. Drag the border of the range to move the worksheet from Excel to the current PowerPoint slide. If you want to copy rather than move the worksheet, hold down the Ctrl key as you drag. Figure 18-8 shows a range of numbers in Excel and the same range copied to PowerPoint using drag and drop.

FIGURE 18-8

An Excel worksheet that has been copied to PowerPoint using drag and drop.

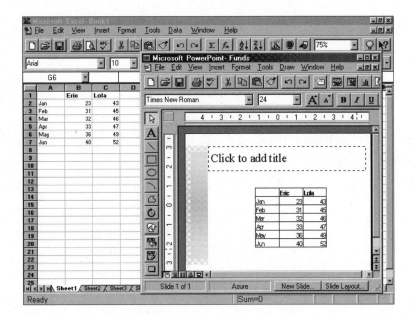

Once again, because the Excel worksheet appears in PowerPoint as a picture, you can move and stretch the worksheet by dragging its handles.

> **TIP** If you want to accentuate a worksheet on a slide, use the Shadow command on PowerPoint's Format menu. Adding a shadow gives the worksheet a slightly raised look.

Modifying an Embedded Worksheet

To edit the worksheet, double-click it, or click it with the right mouse button and select Edit Worksheet Object from the shortcut menu. Excel's menus and toolbars appear in place of PowerPoint's, and the worksheet is surrounded by a frame. After you finish editing the worksheet, click outside the frame. To reopen the worksheet in a separate Excel window, select the worksheet, click the right mouse button, and choose Open Worksheet Object. When you finish editing from within Excel, choose Update from Excel's File menu, and then choose Exit and Return to *Presentation* from the File menu.

> **TIP** You can crop a worksheet that has been placed on a PowerPoint slide by clicking the worksheet's picture with the right mouse button, choosing Crop Picture from the shortcut menu, and placing the cropping icon on one of the worksheet picture's side handles. Then drag the handle inward to reduce the width or height of the picture.

Linking an Excel Worksheet to PowerPoint

You use either the Object command on the Insert menu or Paste Special to link an Excel worksheet to Powerpoint.

To link an Excel worksheet using the Object command:

1. From the PowerPoint Insert menu, choose Object.

2. Select the Create from File option.

3. In the File edit box, type the name of the Excel worksheet you want to link, or click the Browse button to locate it.

4. Select the Link option, and then click OK.

To link an Excel worksheet using Paste Special:

1. Open the worksheet, select the data you want in the slide, and copy it using the Copy command on Excel's Edit menu (or use one of the shortcuts for copying items, such as clicking the Copy button on the Standard toolbar).

2. Switch to PowerPoint's Slide view, and choose Paste Special from the Edit menu.

3. Select the Paste Link option in the Paste Special dialog box, and then click OK.

The worksheet appears in PowerPoint. If you make subsequent editing changes to the worksheet in Excel, the changes will flow through to the linked PowerPoint presentation when you resave the Excel file. If you make changes to the Excel file when the linked presentation is closed, the changes will appear the next time you open the presentation.

Remember, when you link an Excel worksheet to a PowerPoint presentation and you move the presentation to another system, you must also move the Excel worksheet.

Displaying a PowerPoint Slide or Slide Show in Excel

To display a PowerPoint slide or slide show in an Excel worksheet, follow the same procedures you use to display a slide or slide show in Word. Simply drag a single slide from PowerPoint's Slide Sorter view to Excel, select all the slides in PowerPoint's Slide Sorter view and then drag the entire presentation to Excel, or drag a presentation icon from a folder or the desktop to the worksheet.

TIP After you drag a slide to Excel, you can resize the slide's width and height proportionally by dragging one of its corner handles.

If you've dragged a single slide to Excel, double-click the slide to place it in the PowerPoint window for editing. If you've dragged an entire presentation to Excel, double-click its representative slide to start the slide show. You can control the slide show as if you were displaying it in PowerPoint's Slide Show view. To edit an entire presentation, select its representative slide in Excel, click the right mouse button, and choose Presentation Object and then Edit from the submenu.

Mailing a Presentation with Microsoft Mail

If Microsoft Mail is installed on your system, the Send command appears on PowerPoint's File menu. After you complete and save a presentation, you can choose the Send command, fill out the Mail dialog boxes to identify the recipient of the presentation, and click the Send button. The presentation is sent to another Mail user as an attachment to a Mail note.

Posting a Presentation to Microsoft Exchange

If Microsoft Exchange is installed on your computer, you can use it to send or receive a presentation as electronic mail or as a fax message, or you can post it to a public folder that is accessible to everyone on your network, by choosing the Post To Exchange Folder command from the File menu. Exchange allows you to set up multiple "profiles" for different kinds of electronic communication services, including Microsoft Mail and The Microsoft Network. When you choose the command, you see a dialog box that allows you to select which profile, or service, you want to post the presentation to.

Chapter 19

Customizing PowerPoint

A s PowerPoint guides you through the presentation-making process, you must follow the steps the software expects you to follow. But fortunately, you have plenty of control over how PowerPoint works. You can customize the way PowerPoint looks, change the default choices it makes, and even circumvent some of the steps that it would otherwise have you follow in its quest to guide you through the process unharmed.

In this chapter, you'll learn how to customize PowerPoint from top to bottom, changing the defaults for everything from the blank presentation to the composition of the toolbars. Only when you've demonstrated your total domination over the program can you truly be considered a PowerPoint master.

Creating a Default Presentation

When you select Blank Presentation from the PowerPoint dialog box or on the General tab of the New Presentation dialog box, PowerPoint loads a default presentation. You can replace the default presentation with a customized presentation so that the customized presentation appears when you select Blank Presentation.

You might want to change the default presentation when you've taken the time to customize a presentation with your corporate colors, a corporate standard background design, your corporate logo, and special text. You can then start each new presentation with your customized look already in place.

To change the default presentation, start a new presentation or open an existing presentation, and then change any or all of the following elements:

- The template attached to the presentation
- Any graphic objects on the slide background, such as logos
- Special text on the slide background, such as the date, time, and slide number
- The color scheme
- The formatting of the slide master
- The Slide Setup dialog box options

NOTE You only need to format the slide master of the presentation. Special formatting that you apply to particular slide layouts is not applied to the default presentation.

When you have finished customizing the presentation, save it as a PowerPoint Presentation Template with the name Blank Presentation in the folder that holds the other PowerPoint templates (the TEMPLATES subfolder of the MSOffice folder—unless you specified a different folder when you installed PowerPoint).

> **WARNING** Instead of overwriting the default presentation that comes with PowerPoint, you should rename the Blank Presentation file—to Old Blank, for example—before creating a new Blank Presentation file. Then, you can always retrieve the original blank default presentation.

When you next select Blank Presentation on the General tab of the New Presentation dialog box, all the formatting of the sample presentation appears in the new presentation.

Changing the Start-Up Defaults

You can set up PowerPoint to skip the PowerPoint dialog box that appears whenever you start the program. When you opt to skip this dialog box, PowerPoint loads the default presentation and displays the New Slide dialog box, where you can select an autolayout whose placeholders you'll fill with text, charts, and graphics. You lose the opportunity to use the AutoContent Wizard to start a presentation, and you get whatever formatting is applied to the default presentation. But you can always use the AutoContent Wizard later by selecting it on the Presentations tab of the New Presentation dialog box. You can also select a template by clicking the Apply Design Template button or by choosing Apply Design Template from the Format menu.

You can also skip the New Slide dialog box and display the Title Slide autolayout. The title slide is displayed with all the attributes of the default presentation, including the presentation's template, its background design and color scheme, the formatting of its slide master, and its Slide Setup dialog box settings (which determine the shape and size of the presentation pages). With the title slide on your screen, you can jump right in and enter the presentation's text and charts.

You might find it handy to skip the PowerPoint dialog box if you almost always use the same presentation design or when you have the presentation's content worked out, such as when you use PowerPoint to prepare presentations that vary only slightly. To set PowerPoint to skip the first dialog box, choose Options from the Tools menu. In the Options dialog box, shown in Figure 19-1 on the next page, deselect the Show Startup Dialog option on the General tab.

FIGURE 19-1

The Options
dialog box.

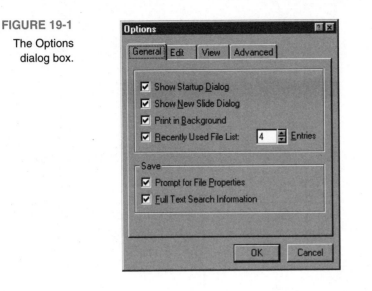

By also deselecting the Show New Slide Dialog option on the General tab, you can have a new PowerPoint presentation proceed directly to the Title Slide autolayout without stopping at the New Slide dialog box. Then, each time you click the New Slide button, the Bulleted List autolayout appears. To select a different layout, you can always click the Slide Layout button at the bottom of the PowerPoint window, or hold down the Shift key as you click the New Slide button. This might be the ideal setup if you frequently create presentations that consist of series of text slides. The first slide of the presentation is a title slide, and successive slides are bulleted list slides, unless you choose otherwise when you add each slide.

If the Print in Background option on the General tab is selected, you can continue to work on a presentation while another presentation is printing. Otherwise, the Print Status dialog box appears each time you print, tying up your computer until the printer has finished.

The Recently Used File List option lets you determine how many recently used presentations are listed at the bottom of the File menu. Choosing one of these presentations loads the presentation's file.

If you deselect the Prompt for File Properties option in the Save section of the General tab, the Properties dialog box does not appear when you save a presentation. If you deselect the Full Text Search Information option, PowerPoint won't create the index used when you select Full Text Search from the File Open dialog box.

Setting Other Defaults

The three other tabs in the Options dialog box provide options you can use to change the PowerPoint defaults. The options on the Edit tab let you change how text is handled, as follows:

- Replace Straight Quotes with Smart Quotes enters typographically correct quotation marks (opening and closing) when you type a passage of text enclosed in quotation marks.

- Automatic Word Selection selects the entire first and last words of a text passage even if you don't drag the mouse pointer across the beginning of the first word and the end of the last word.

- Use Smart Cut and Paste tries to ensure that spaces are adjusted when you cut and paste text so that only one space appears before and after the text.

- Drag-and-Drop Text Editing lets you use your mouse to select text and then move and copy text by dragging it to a new location.

- Always Suggest in the Spelling section determines whether the spelling checker suggests alternatives to a misspelled word. If you select this option, the spelling checker functions more slowly than if it simply has to point out spelling errors.

The following options on the View tab let you change what you see in the PowerPoint window:

- Status Bar controls whether the status bar appears at the bottom of the PowerPoint window. If you deselect this option, the presentation window occupies a little more space on the screen, but you lose important information about your slides, such as the slide number. You also lose access to the New Slide and Slide Layout buttons. You must click the Insert New Slide button on the Standard toolbar, choose New Slide from the Insert menu, or choose Slide Layout from the Format menu to accomplish the same tasks.

- Vertical Ruler determines whether the vertical ruler appears along the left side of the presentation window. Deselecting the Vertical Ruler option lets you see more of the presentation window. If you've selected the Vertical Ruler option but still do not see the ruler, choose Ruler from the View menu.

The options in the Slide Show section of the View tab let you change how Slide Show view behaves, as described on the next page.

■ Popup Menu on Right Mouse Click tells PowerPoint whether you want the pop-up menu to appear when you click the right mouse button in Slide Show view.

■ Show Popup Menu Button determines whether you can click the pop-up menu button in Slide Show view to display the pop-up menu.

■ End with Black Slide adds a black slide to the end of each slide show so that you know when you have displayed the last slide, providing a cleaner ending for your presentations. When this option is turned off, you return to the application from which you started the slide show immediately after you display the last slide.

Finally, the Advanced tab provides three specialized options:

■ Maximum Number of Undos determines how many actions you can reverse. Clicking the Undo button on the Standard toolbar reverses your most recent action. (You can also choose Undo from the Edit menu or press Ctrl+Z.) To undo the action before that one, you can click the Undo button again, and so on. When you have clicked the Undo button the maximum number of times, PowerPoint will not reverse any more actions.

■ Render 24-bit Bitmaps at Highest Quality controls the print quality of bitmapped graphics.

■ Export Pictures determines whether pictures are rendered to look their best when they are printed or when they are viewed on screen.

■ Default File Location allows you to specify where new files are stored by default when you save them. (You can override this default by specifying a different location in the File Save dialog box.)

Customizing the Datasheet Settings and Default Graph

When you start a graph, the Microsoft Graph module always displays a default set of data for you to modify in the datasheet. It also displays a default graph based on the data. You can modify the default data and graph so that a graph design more suited to your needs appears whenever you start Graph.

To modify the default data and graph, follow these steps:

1. Load Graph by clicking the Insert Graph button on the Standard toolbar, choosing Microsoft Graph from the Insert menu, or by double-clicking a *Double click to add graph* placeholder.

2. Modify the data in the default datasheet and/or change the graph type and formatting of the default graph.

3. Choose Options from Graph's Tools menu.

4. On the Chart tab of the Graph Options dialog box, click the Use the Current Chart button in the Default Chart Format section. A new option called Custom Default appears in the Default Chart Format box, as shown here:

5. Click OK.

The next time you start a graph, the revised default graph will appear. To return to the original graph, select (Built-in) as the Default Chart Format option in the Graph Options dialog box.

On the Chart tab of the dialog box, you can also specify whether empty cells of the datasheet should be omitted from the graph or plotted as zero. When empty cells are omitted, gaps may occur in the graph.

The Datasheet Options tab of the Graph Options dialog box provides two options that you can use to control the datasheet. The first option, Move Selection after Enter, determines whether the cell pointer moves to the next cell of the datasheet after you press Enter or whether it remains in the current cell. The second option, Cell Drag and Drop, turns drag and drop on or off within the datasheet window.

NOTE The Color tab of the Graph Options dialog box displays the colors used to fill the markers (Chart Fills) and the colors used for the lines and outlines (Chart Lines) of the graph. These colors are set by the current color scheme of the presentation. You can override the colors of a graph by formatting its markers and lines directly, so you should not need to modify the colors on the Color tab.

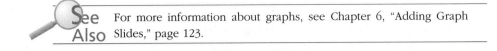

See
Also   For more information about graphs, see Chapter 6, "Adding Graph
Slides," page 123.

Setting the Drawing Defaults

To change the default fill color, line style, and text style of objects you draw using PowerPoint's drawing tools, follow this procedure:

1. Draw an object and apply settings for the fill color, line style, text style, and other attributes.

2. Select the object.

3. Choose the Pick Up Object Style command from the Format menu or the shortcut menu.

4. Click somewhere else on the slide to deselect the object.

5. Choose Apply To Object Defaults from the Format menu.

   Now when you draw any object, the new default settings are applied.

See
Also   For more information about drawing objects, see Chapter 13, "Drawing
Graphic Objects," page 331.

Customizing Toolbars

As you've seen, PowerPoint's toolbars give you easy access to the most popular menu commands. But you may not find a toolbar button for every command you use frequently. Fortunately, you can customize the toolbars. You can add and remove buttons, move buttons from one toolbar to another, and create a custom toolbar with your favorite buttons.

Displaying a Toolbar

The easiest way to display a toolbar is to click any visible toolbar with the right mouse button. On the shortcut menu that appears, the toolbars accompanied by check marks are already displayed. To bring any other toolbar to the screen, click its name on the shortcut menu. Figure 19-2 shows the shortcut menu for toolbars.

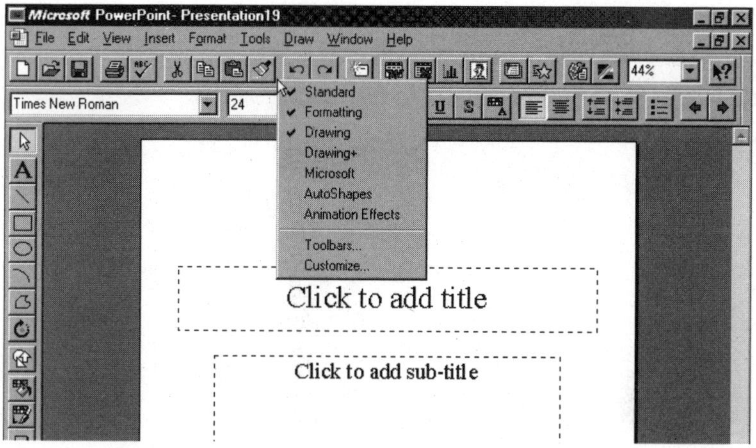

FIGURE 19-2

The shortcut menu for toolbars.

You can also choose Toolbars from the View menu to open the Toolbars dialog box shown in Figure 19-3. In the dialog box, select the check boxes for the combination of toolbars you want displayed, and then click OK.

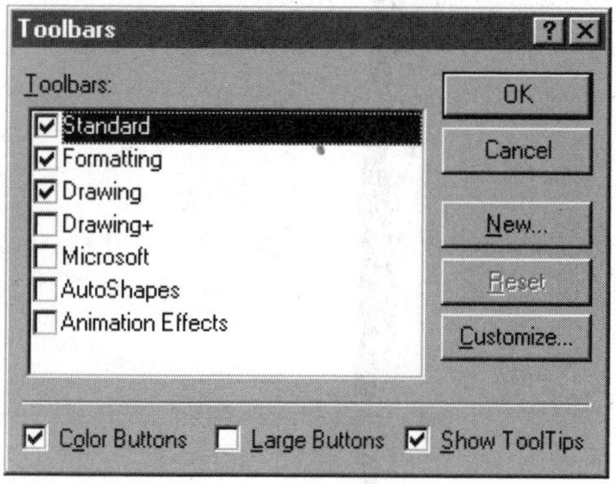

FIGURE 19-3

The Toolbars dialog box.

Adding and Removing Buttons

To add a button to a toolbar, make sure the toolbar you want to customize is visible, and then click it with the right mouse button. From the shortcut menu, choose Customize. You can also choose Toolbars from the View menu, and click Customize in the Toolbars dialog box. Either way, the Customize Toolbars dialog box appears, as shown in Figure 19-4 on the next page.

FIGURE 19-4

The Customize
Toolbars dialog box.

Customize Toolbars

Categories:

File
Edit
View
Insert
Format
Tools

Buttons

Close

Select a category, then click a button to see its description.
Drag the button to any toolbar.

Description

In the Customize Toolbars dialog box, you see a list of categories that corresponds to the PowerPoint menus, and a set of buttons that represents the commands in the selected category. Simply follow the instructions in the dialog box by selecting a category, clicking a button to see its description, and then dragging the button you want to any toolbar. You can drag as many buttons from as many categories as you want, and you can drop the buttons in exact positions on the toolbars. When you're finished adding buttons, click Close to close the dialog box.

Removing a toolbar button is even easier. With the Customize Toolbars dialog box open, simply drag the button off its toolbar. The button is always available in the Customize Toolbars dialog box if you need it again.

TIP You don't have to open the Customize Toolbar dialog box to remove a button from a toolbar. Simply hold down the Alt key, and drag the button off its toolbar.

Moving Buttons
Within and Between Toolbars

If you don't like the order of buttons on a toolbar or if you want to move a button to another toolbar, you can drag buttons within toolbars and between toolbars. You can drag a button up two positions in a vertical toolbar, for example, or drag a button from one toolbar to another. You can even choose to display the Custom toolbar, which starts with no buttons, and then drag your favorite buttons to it.

To move a button from one toolbar to another, hold down the Alt key and drag the button. To copy a button from one toolbar to another, hold down both the Alt key and the Ctrl key as you drag the button. As always, a small plus sign appears next to the mouse pointer to indicate that you are copying rather than moving an object.

Creating a New Toolbar

To create a custom toolbar, first choose Toolbars from the toolbar's shortcut menu or choose Toolbars from the View menu, and then click New. When the New Toolbar dialog box appears, type a name in the Toolbar Name edit box, and click OK. A small, empty toolbar appears floating on your screen, as shown in Figure 19-5.

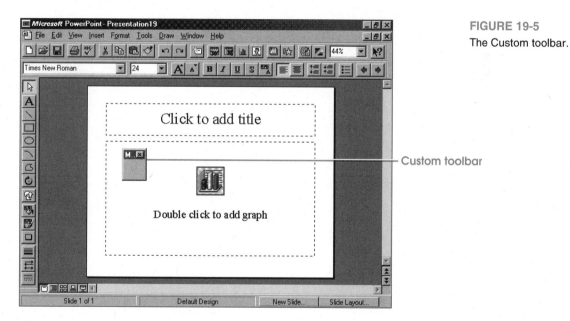

FIGURE 19-5
The Custom toolbar.

— Custom toolbar

Now all you have to do is drag copies of your favorite buttons from the toolbars displayed on your screen or from the Customize Toolbars dialog box to the custom toolbar. Then you can reposition the toolbar by dragging it to one side of the PowerPoint window.

With that final bit of customization, you've done it. You've achieved the coveted status of PowerPoint guru. You're now ready to go out and present to the world!

Index

B

H

M

T

W

X

Z

The manuscript for this book was prepared and submitted to Microsoft Press in electronic form. Text files were prepared using Microsoft Word 6 for Windows. Pages were composed by Online Press using Ventura Publisher 4.2, with text in Garamond and display type in Avant Garde Bold. Composed pages were delivered to the printer as electronic postscript files.

Cover Designer
Rebecca Geisler

Cover Illustrator
designlab

Interior Graphic Designers
Kim Eggleston
Amy Peppler Adams (designlab)

Interior Graphic Artist
Michael Victor

Page Layout
Bill Teel

Proofreaders
Christina Dudley
Ken Sanchez

Indexer
Shane-Armstrong Information Services

Making Presentations Interactive

Want to get the viewers of your presentation involved in the action? Try using the Media Clip slide layout to add video or sound.

PowerPoint opens the Media Clip Editor so that you can adjust the file's settings, including whether you want to play all or just a portion of the file.

When your viewers click the clip, the file plays—as often as they want, whenever they want, interactively!

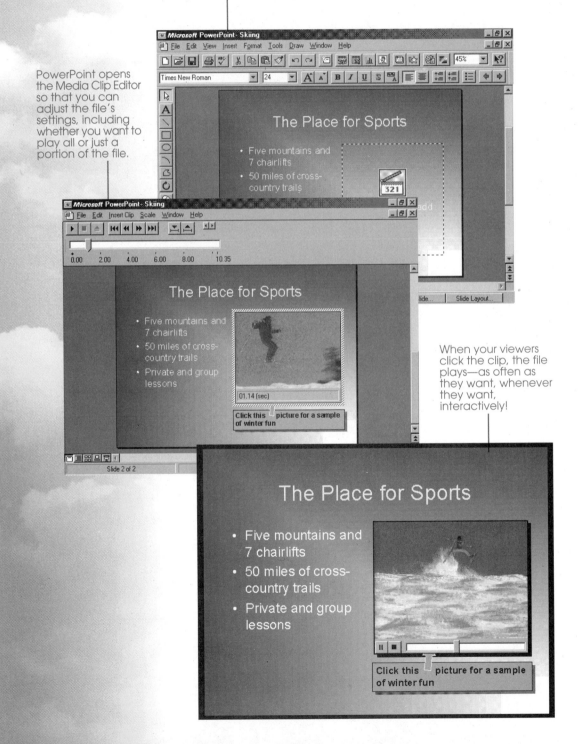

Quick Procedures

To Do These Common Things	Do This
Open a new presentation	Click 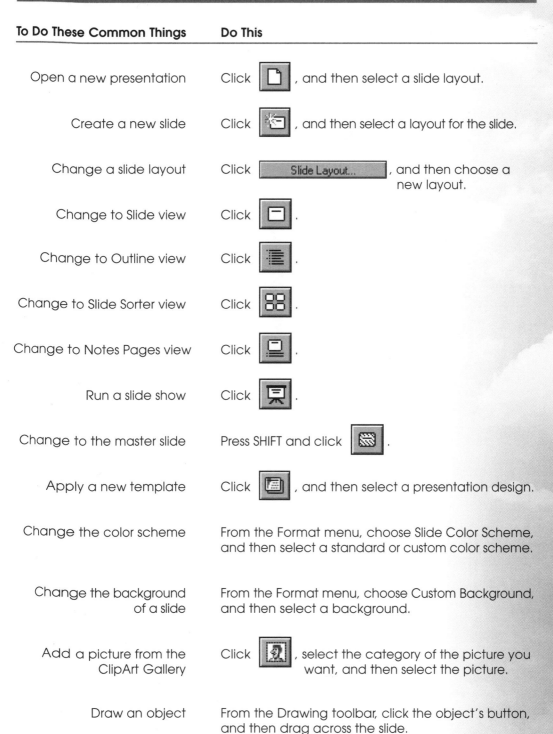, and then select a slide layout.
Create a new slide	Click , and then select a layout for the slide.
Change a slide layout	Click Slide Layout... , and then choose a new layout.
Change to Slide view	Click .
Change to Outline view	Click .
Change to Slide Sorter view	Click .
Change to Notes Pages view	Click .
Run a slide show	Click .
Change to the master slide	Press SHIFT and click .
Apply a new template	Click , and then select a presentation design.
Change the color scheme	From the Format menu, choose Slide Color Scheme, and then select a standard or custom color scheme.
Change the background of a slide	From the Format menu, choose Custom Background, and then select a background.
Add a picture from the ClipArt Gallery	Click , select the category of the picture you want, and then select the picture.
Draw an object	From the Drawing toolbar, click the object's button, and then drag across the slide.

Common Toolbar Tools

Standard Toolbar

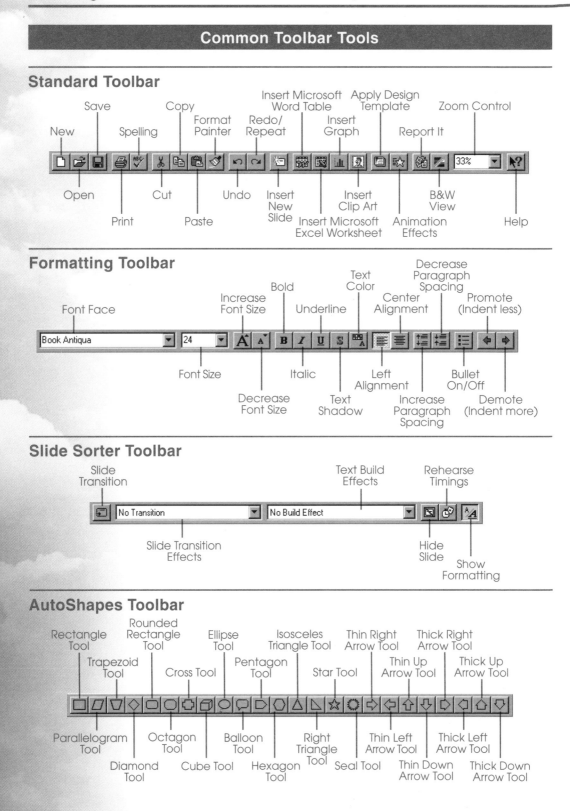

Formatting Toolbar

Slide Sorter Toolbar

AutoShapes Toolbar

Graph's Standard Toolbar

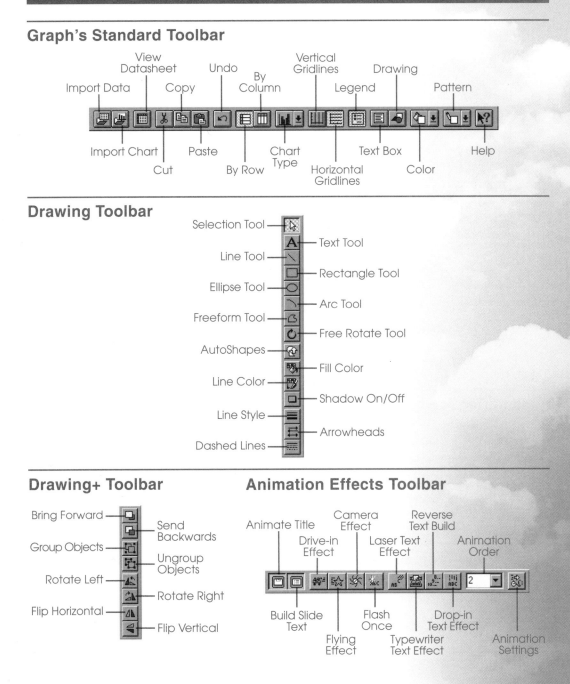

Drawing Toolbar

Drawing+ Toolbar

Animation Effects Toolbar

Running PowerPoint for Windows 95 quick reference card

Using Keyboard Shortcuts

To Create and Edit Presentations

CTRL+N	Open a new presentation
CTRL+O	Open an existing presentation
CTRL+W or CTRL+F4	Close a presentation
CTRL+S or SHIFT+F12	Save a presentation
CTRL+P or CTRL+SHIFT+F12	Print a presentation
CTRL+F	Find a word or a phrase
CTRL+M	Create a new slide
F7	Check spelling
F1	Display help topics
CTRL+Q or ALT+F4	Exit/Quit

To Move Around

LEFT ARROW	One character left
RIGHT ARROW	One character right
UP ARROW	One line up
DOWN ARROW	One line down
END	End of line
HOME	Beginning of line
CTRL+SHIFT+F6	To previous presentation window
CTRL+F6 or CTRL+TAB	To next presentation window

To Select Text and Objects

Double-click the word	Select a word
Triple-click within the paragraph	Select a paragraph
CTRL+A	Select all

To Delete and Copy

CTRL+X	Cut
CTRL+C	Copy
CTRL+V	Paste
CTRL+select and drag	Drag and drop a copy
CTRL+Z	Undo
BACKSPACE	Delete character to the left
DELETE	Delete character to the right

To Work in an Outline

ALT+SHIFT+ LEFT ARROW	Promote paragraph
ALT+SHIFT+ RIGHT ARROW	Demote paragraph
ALT+SHIFT+ UP ARROW	Move selected paragraphs up
ALT+SHIFT+ DOWN ARROW	Move selected paragraphs down
ALT+SHIFT+PLUS	Expand text under a heading
ALT+SHIFT+MINUS	Collapse text under a heading
ALT+SHIFT+A	Show all text and headings

To Manage a Slide Show

<Number>+ENTER	Go to slide <number>
A	Show/hide pointer
S	Stop/restart automatic show
ESC	End show
H	Advance to hidden slide
Mouse click	Advance to next slide
BACKSPACE	Return to previous slide